JUSTICE DENIED

An Historical Sojourn

Dr. Joe Wendel

ARCHWAY
PUBLISHING

Archway Publishing books may be ordered through booksellers or by contacting:

Archway Publishing
1663 Liberty Drive
Bloomington, IN 47403
www.archwaypublishing.com
1 (888) 242-5904

ISBN: 978-1-4808-5277-8 (sc)
ISBN: 978-1-4808-5279-2 (hc)
ISBN: 978-1-4808-5278-5 (e)

Library of Congress Control Number: 2017915296

Printed in the United States of America.

Archway Publishing rev. date: 11/14/2017

Justice Denied is dedicated in memoriam to the victims of the American and South American internment program; to the millions of Germans killed in the fire-bombings of all German cities, including the Dresden Holocaust; to the millions of Germans driven out of their homes and homeland at the end of and following World War II; to the German POWs in Ike's Rhine death camps; and to the millions of Germans shipped as slave labor in cattle cars to Siberia as a gift to Joe Stalin, most of whom never returned.

Contents

PREFACE

Water embodies the minerals and all the distinct characteristics of the earth it traverses. We too embody our unique characteristics, traits, features, and entire heritage that have been passed down to us by our parents and ancestors. We arrive in our cradle with all our unique physical features and on our journey through life, acquire our own qualities and personal identity.

I am a product of all my unique experiences. I lived the war years and the years following the war as a child in Austria. The summer before the end of the war, my kindergarten classmates and I were walking home, crossing an open meadow, when a twin propeller plane appeared on the horizon. As it approached, it began firing at us children. The plane flew so close to the ground that I could see the whites in the pilot's eyes. He was a young man in his early twenties, perhaps fifteen years older than we were. As if guided by an invisible hand, we all fell to the ground. After the plane passed over our heads, I rose to see if any of my friends were hit. Fortunately, all of us stood up to see another day.

Within the vicinity of our village was a POW camp. It housed about a hundred English soldiers. The camp was enclosed with a regular ten-foot fence. The POWs appeared well fed, perhaps better than the civilians. We never heard of any soldiers escaping. On many evenings and on Sunday afternoons, they would play soccer. We children would stand at the fence and watch them. On many occasions, they would play against their German guards.

On a sunny Sunday afternoon, two weeks after the war, my brother, my cousin, and I were playing in the nearby woods when we stumbled upon a foxhole filled with hundreds of grenades. Unaware of the danger, we climbed into the foxhole, and each of us put two grenades into our pockets. We then proceeded to throw them around, like tennis balls, until one of them exploded. There were English soldiers stationed not far away and occupied our region; they caught up with us and rushed us to the nearest hospital, about five kilometers away. My brother suffered two minor lacerations on his knee, and I had a minor cut on my left thumb. But our cousin Ferdinand was seriously injured and was fighting for his life. He had to stay in the hospital for about ten weeks, undergoing several surgeries. He never fully recovered from this tragedy.

My great-uncle Peter immigrated to the States in 1890. He settled down in Dayton, Ohio. His future wife, Julia, came a couple of years later. Before the war, German social and cultural clubs were vibrant, with many activities and much entertainment, which Peter and Julia Grosch would frequent. Their oldest son, Franz, was born in Dayton. After World War I, in 1918, they decided to return to Europe. They bought a farm in a place called Schutzberg. Their second child, Eva, was born there. Then came World War II with all its destruction and suffering. On many occasions, after the war, when we socialized on weekends, Peter and Julia talked about their years in the States and encouraged us to emigrate, if the opportunity arose. We applied and in the beginning of June 1952, we took in the breathtaking view of the Statue of Liberty, just after the sun rose in the east.

Life in America proved to be a bigger challenge than I imagined, especially as a youth. Housing was in very short supply. The first two weeks, we lived in the basement of kind friends and members of our church. Then we lived in two rooms with kitchen privileges until our parents saved enough money for a down payment on our own home. Five years after we arrived, our parents built their dream home in a beautiful development in a suburb.

The war ripped apart not only many countries but also millions of families. Gradually, the healing began and many are still healing from the ravages of war. The homesickness that we experienced at first was replaced with a love and devotion to our new adopted country. As an educator, I was often invited to view documentaries about what the Germans did, but I was never invited to see a documentary about what was done to the Germans or the German Americans in our internment camps. Some textbooks even falsified the facts that German Americans and others were placed into American internment camps. I myself was not aware of the internment program until I interviewed dozens of survivors and listened to their personal stories. There still exists a significant resistance to openly and honestly discussing that part of our history. The public deserves balance to the history of the last century, especially since the war has been over for generations.

What I began to realize is that most Americans do not know that German Americans were accosted and incarcerated in American internment camps during both world wars. What was missing are the many positive images of German Americans. Germans have just reason to be proud of their accomplishments. John Jacob Astor organized the first monopoly on the North American continent. By 1835, he was the richest man in North America. The first books in America were published in German by Christoph Sauer, including Martin Luther's translation of the Bible. Frank Luke was the first US airman to receive the Congressional Medal of Honor. John Roebling built the first railroad bridge, as well as many suspension bridges, including the Brooklyn landmark bridge in Manhattan. Dr. Werner von Braun and his German Space Research Team took us to the moon and beyond. By the nineteenth century, immigration by Germans surpassed every other ethnic group, reaching its summit in 1854, when every other immigrant was a German.

Even though far more than a third of Americans are proud of their German roots and they have done so much to build our great nation, they were persecuted and forced to become the silent majority. Tragically, German Americans themselves may be partially to blame for this predicament. While they have excelled in every endeavor, they have not involved themselves in politics, following the motto "Nur keine Politik," which has served them rather poorly. Throughout our history, German Americans did not show much interest in politics and even less interest in holding public office. Had the German Americans been politically more engaged and spoken with one voice, American and German history would have been very different. What the German Americans need to internalize and learn to appreciate is the basic fact that a disagreement does not equate to disloyalty or disrespect. Germany's religious schism has proven to be a curse, as it hindered a sense of national unity and identity. For centuries, Germany has influenced and deeply affected every one of her neighbors.

Justice Denied familiarizes the reader with historical facts that have, all too often, been ignored or killed with deafening silence. It is hoped that this book will motivate others to conduct additional research concerning all the mistreatments, the terror, the mass murder, the starvation, the expulsions, and the raping of millions of German girls and women. This book covers more than four hundred years of German-American history and contributions.

I am indebted to many individuals who influenced me generously in so many ways. They motivated, inspired, guided, and helped me become who I am. First and foremost, my gratitude goes to my family, especially my mother and my maternal grandfather, who provided a solid and caring support network; bestowed me with unconditional love, care, and encouragement; and gave me direction, purpose, and a solid foundation. My dearest friend and companion, Sharon, has been a constant source of gentle inspiration and motivation. Professor William Konnert was my co-advisor during both phases of my doctoral program. Without writing the dissertation, I doubt I would have ventured upon writing *Justice Denied*. Dr. Konnert made many valuable suggestions. George Voinovich, a lifelong friend with an impressive political career, served as mayor of Cleveland and as governor and senator from Ohio. I am indebted to Senator Voinovich for his feedback to this book. Paul Hentemann, attorney at law, made many valuable suggestions. Professor Frank Engelmann made many detailed and specific recommendations.

The initial spark for *Justice Denied* came from the personal stories of the many survivors of the American internment camps who were my guests on my radio shows on the Cleveland NPR station, WCPN-FM. It was the pain reflected in their voices as they shared their recollections on the air. There were also many individuals who refused to talk about their experiences because they did not want to be reminded of their suffering during the expulsions and deportations. They broke down sobbing while listening to the horror others were subjected to. Before internees were released, these unfortunate German Americans and others were forced to sign an oath never to speak or write about their experiences. This governmental gag order added further insult to injury. Far too many internees took their oaths very seriously and their secrets to their graves. None of them was ever charged with any wartime crime; they were detained "for their own safety." After many years of silence, many survivors did speak and write about these massive human rights violations. Most Americans are familiar with the internment of Japanese Americans, but few know anything about the incarcerations and human rights violations of tens of thousands of German Americans during both world wars. We are indebted to so many outstanding Americans, such as Eberhard Fuhr, Professor Arthur Jacobs, attorney Caron Ebel, and so many others, who have been so instrumental in bringing this dark period of our history to light.

I chose to write *Justice Denied*, hoping to provide more light on and greater understanding of the American internment program and to remove that cloud of deafening silence regarding this part of our history. It covers the twentieth century and more. There are various reasons, including guilt and shame, that Congress has been reluctant to pass the Wartime Treatment Study Act. Once the public is informed of all the facts, it will demand action. It is hoped that Congress will be morally motivated to finally pass the long overdue Wartime Treatment Study Act. This action will greatly contribute not only to the healing process for so many American families who suffered unnecessarily but also will enable the nation to come to terms with its own past. These human rights violations turned the largest ethnic group into the silent majority. I am reminded that our most painful experiences, individually and nationally, can become a most powerful driving force for positive change. May justice postponed not become *Justice Denied*!

Sincerely,
Joe Wendel

INTRODUCTION

The pages of *Justice Denied* are gradually unfolding as the painful experiences of millions of people have been collected and recorded. We learn how tens of thousands of German Americans were incarcerated and millions of German women, from eight to eighty, were brutally raped by the occupying forces in Europe and many were then left to die. Millions of ethnic Germans were ruthlessly terrorized, and many were brutally killed. This book covers human rights violations to millions of Germans, German Americans, Latin-German Americans, some six million German POWs in Ike's Rhine death camps, and ethnic Germans in Eastern as well as Central Europe and elsewhere. These are stories that thus far have been killed by the media and the textbook industry with deafening silence.

Most Americans are aware that our entire Japanese population on the West Coast was uprooted and placed into ten relocation camps in America's interior. What most Americans seem not to be informed about is that these contemptible, cruel injustices were perpetrated also against thousands of German Americans, as well as Italians, Hungarians, Bulgarians, Latin-American Germans, German Jews, and Jehovah's Witnesses. Not even one solitary person interned was ever charged with or found guilty of any war-related crime. They were incarcerated to silence their opposition to the war and for their own "personal" safety.

What is amazing is that all these human rights violations have not been reported on the evening news or mentioned as a footnote in any of our history textbooks. Prior to being released, the internees and their guards were forced to sign an oath never to speak or write about their experiences in these internment camps, with threats of being reincarcerated. This constituted a massive governmental gag order that so many seem to be fearful or ashamed to talk about. Far too many internees have taken their secrets to their graves.

The Wartime Treatment Study Act has been introduced nine times in Congress but failed each time. Passage of this act will provide light and understanding on all the related issues. We must understand the causes of these human rights violations, so that we can prevent them from ever happening again against any group of people. The Study Act will provide an accurate diagnosis, which is always essential for an effective remedy.

Justice Denied comprises twelve chapters. The first chapter gives us a historical overview of the largest ethnic group in America. It covers their monumental contributions in building our great nation from 1607 at Jamestown to the present, from the agricultural, industrial, and commercial growth to the space program. German immigrants and their descendants founded many businesses that improved our lifestyle. More than a third of Americans proudly trace their roots to Germany. In 1851, 64 percent of our population was foreign-born, and of that, nearly two-thirds were born in Germany. In 1854, every second immigrant was German. They became the brew masters in their new homeland. German immigrants were very interested in education and classical music. The American school system has been modeled after the German system from kindergarten to the university, namely a strong mind in a strong body. Most of our symphony orchestras are an outgrowth of the German concert orchestras.

German Americans have participated in greater numbers than their percentage in our population in all our wars. No war that America has won was more important than the revolution itself. It crystalized us as a new nation. General Friedrich Wilhelm von Steuben was recruited by Benjamin Franklin for the American cause. Von Steuben trained our starving, undisciplined, and unpaid Colonial Army at Valley Forge. German settlers and farmers kept the army from starving by getting the needed food supplies to the soldiers. Each fall, New York City, Philadelphia, and Chicago honor the contributions of German Americans in the annual Steuben parades, attended by millions of patriots.

Throughout our history, German Americans have played a significant and central role in our history from Jamestown in 1607 to the present. In 1760, German Americans issued the very first protest against the institution of slavery and supported vigorously the antislavery movement. The Conestoga wagons carried the pioneers across this beautiful continent. Dr. Werner von Braun and his German Space Team created our American space program and took us to the moon and beyond. The way Americans celebrate Christmas, New Year's, and the Fourth of July were shaped by German settlers. They brought the Christmas tree and other traditions to make Christmas the celebration it is today.

Germany helped us gain our independence, and yet we entered the European theater of war twice on England's side, fighting against Germany. Most Americans saw getting involved in the European war as a huge mistake; German Americans were saddened. Special interests dragged us into the wars and turned them into world wars. We put German Americans into internment camps to silence them. The entire twentieth century was one big holocaust. A historical overview in this book is essential for a better understanding of the current events and challenges facing Europeans and Americans.

The research that culminated in *Justice Denied* began in earnest after the author aired a program on Cleveland Public Radio, WCPN-FM, about the internment of German Americans during both world wars. It was based on an article in the "*New Yorker Staatszeitung,*" about the American internment program during World War II. A colleague at the station challenged the validity of such camps ever existing in the United States. He told the author that they were a reality in Nazi Germany and the Soviet Union but never in the United States. This lack of knowledge by a radio personality clearly demonstrated the extent of the influence of the media and the textbook industry in killing this part of our history with deafening silence. Rather than debate the issue, the author chose to interview more than two dozen survivors of these internment camps, which FDR called nothing more than concentration camps. The author is still interviewing the children born in American internment camps.

The author was faced with the question of covering the internment program only or also including the relevant and pertinent issues related to our internment program. To provide a voice to all who no longer have a voice, the choice was rather simple, and the big picture emerged. Included are the contributing causes of both world wars, the Berlin-Baghdad Railroad, the Versailles Peace Treaties, Judea declaring war on Germany, other losses, and millions of Germans sent to Siberia as slaves. Especially heart-wrenching are the many personal accounts of the survivors from the internment program, the Dresden holocaust, the ethnic cleansing, and the expulsions and the deportations of millions of displaced ethnic Germans, driven from their ancestral homeland. It is part of Churchill's and the victorious Allied leaders' redrawing of German and European border lines.

Justice Denied is the story that has been patiently waiting to unfold. The millions of dead deserve nothing less than that their compelling accounts of starvation, rape, and the unspeakable brutality of torture and mass murder be told. "The truth shall set us free" are not merely idle words; they are a solemn promise from God. The author talks about how the largest ethnic group became the silent majority and how Germany is still suffering because of FDR's demands of "unconditional surrender."

Our great nation was built on the premise that all men are created equal and all are equal under the law. The challenges to our sacred liberties come from outside forces as well as from within, in the form of corruption, false patriots, disappointed ambitions, and inordinate hunger for power and greed. It is our responsibility to preserve the principles contained in our Constitution, if this republic shall long endure. We must display the courage to ensure that such atrocities be never again inflicted on fellow Americans of any ethnic group. May justice delayed not become *Justice Denied*!

This beautiful Lady of Freedom, the Statue of Liberty, stands on Liberty Island. Since 1886, immigrants and visitors were welcomed by this impressive monument of freedom as their ships entered the New York Harbor with the sun, which is the beauty and glory of the day, rising in the east.

CHAPTER 1

German and German-American History

History, real history, is the stuff of mystery, intrigue, murder, greed, seduction, arrogance and deception, romance and tragedy, cowardice and courage, good and evil, cruelty, corruption, hate and love, and all our divergent human bearings. *Justice Denied* provides insight and understanding relevant to the internment of German Americans during World War I and again during World War II, as well as the anti-German hysteria that was generated during that period. There is a fundamental need to promote historical truth and provide balanced reporting. There are always two sides to every story. It is written "The truth shall set you free." The image we have within us of God the Creator is reflected in our love of truth and justice. Balanced and accurate reporting is essential to a truthful and just portrayal of our current events as well as our history. Transparency of both remains essential to peace.

Most Americans have heard about the lamentable tragedy the US government caused by using military force to uproot our entire Japanese population living on the West Coast. More than one hundred thousand Japanese Americans were incarcerated in ten relocation camps in America's interior during World War II.

Regrettably, what most Americans appear to be uninformed about, largely because our mass media and American history textbooks, intentionally or otherwise, overlooked, ignored, or just simply killed it with deafening silence, is that these contemptible, cruel injustices were perpetrated also against many thousands of German Americans, as well as Italians, Hungarians, Bulgarians, Latin-American Germans, German Jews, and Jehovah's Witnesses. Truth is an absolute and should never be compromised by any establishment.

Thousands of innocent German Americans were dragged out of their homes, usually during the darkness of night, without any provocation or cause from the standpoint of our national security. In just one day, the day following Pearl Harbor, more than sixty thousand Americans of German descent were rounded up, as if German Americans were responsible for Pearl Harbor. Our government ordered the arrest and internment of thousands of German Americans in federal prison camps during World War I and again during World War II, creating fear and anxiety while engaging in terror against the largest ethnic group in America. These actions caused huge turmoil and a mammoth amount of unprecedented anti-German hysteria.

It is imperative to emphasize that not even one solitary person arrested, imprisoned, and terrorized was ever charged with or found guilty of any war-related crime in these massive roundups. Hundreds of German Americans remained incarcerated as late as 1948, three full years after World War II was officially over. Tragically, all were merely pawns in an ugly political chess game. We must never mistake prejudice for truth, passion for reason, sensationalism for patriotism, or conjecture for documentation. Both life and history can best be understood looking backward, but it must continue to be lived forward.

One basic question demands a truthful answer: Why were Americans of German descent and others so brutally terrorized and subjected to such cruelties and their human rights violated by their own government? Furthermore, why has this dark side of our history been hushed up—not yet taught in our schools, not reported or mentioned in the media, and not even included as a footnote in our textbooks?

Passage of the Wartime Treatment Study Act will provide some light on these and related questions and begin a long overdue healing process. The Wartime Treatment Study Act would create two independent, bipartisan fact-finding commissions. One commission would review the US governmental policies directed against Germans, Italians, other Europeans, and Latin German Americans. The other commission would review the government's denial of asylum to European refugees in the United States facing persecution in Europe.

As the oldest democracy in the world, we claim to be committed to promoting freedom, protecting individual liberty, and pursuing peace. To be of any substance, these noble principles must be practiced first and foremost on the home front; otherwise, they are just so much empty rhetoric. Our actions must always reflect our oratory. What were the hidden purposes and possible objectives of our government's policies of engaging in massive human rights violations? The result of these actions destroyed every ounce of human dignity in many thousands of victims. They lost their earthly possessions in their chosen land, which had promised them unlimited opportunities and freedom. Their constitutionally protected personal liberties were violated.

To intensify the suffering of the internees, the US Treasury Department froze all the assets of all internees on March 23, 1943. Hence, the internees lost all their belongings, including their businesses, homes, cars, and bank accounts. They were left destitute and incarcerated. These were upright and law-abiding American citizens. This was a travesty of justice of historic proportions. Yet only very few people in America even know about it.

What remains are emotional, psychological, and physical wounds and scars that have not healed. They will not totally heal without a proper remedy—at least an apology. These injustices perpetrated against fellow Americans of German and other descents will unfortunately remain a dark stain on our proud heritage and history. The media needs to display the same resolve in reporting these atrocities as they have in reporting political corruption and human rights violations in other countries.

Senators Russ Feingold, a Democrat from Wisconsin, and Chuck Grassley, a Republican from Iowa, have repeatedly introduced the Wartime Treatment Study Act in the Senate; Robert Wexler, a Democrat from Florida, has been the lead sponsor of the House resolution. Thus far, the bill has been introduced nine times, the first in August 2001. Each time, it has been cleared for adoption by unanimous consent on the Democratic side in the Senate but has not cleared the Republican side. It must be remembered that this is a national issue and not just one political party's agenda. It is perplexing that most German Americans are registered Republicans, and yet the Republican side of the aisle caused it to fail.

Passing this bill is urgent, as more and more victims are dying. Passage would fulfill a covenant to the dead and the living, a re-ratification that the principles of our Constitution are still alive and well. The victims and their families continue to be filled with hope; there is no incentive greater and more powerful than hope. Millions of immigrants have been told, upon arriving at our ports, "Du bist jetzt im Land der Gerechtigkeit" (You have arrived in the land of justice).

I will discuss at length the many injustices committed against thousands of German Americans and others in chapter 2. But now let us go down the memory lane of German-American history and these people's monumental contributions to our great country. Far more than a third of Americans proudly trace their roots to Germany, just as our American language has its roots in the Germanic language of centuries past.

Ever since the first Europeans set foot on this continent, Germans have played a vital and integral part in our history. They landed with Captain John Smith on May 14, 1607, and established Jamestown, which was nothing more than a wooden fort on a swampy island. That was some thirteen and a half years before the Pilgrims landed on Plymouth Rock in Massachusetts.

Smith brought along several English gentlemen and a good number of Germans on three small vessels. Among them was Dr. Johannes Fleischer Jr., the first physician and first trained botanist as well as the first Lutheran to set foot on this continent. He came in search of new healing plants. Due to the extremely unhealthy conditions on this swampy island, he, like most of his fellow travelers, died within a year. But he did send back to Europe a report in Latin about the plants and vegetation he found in the New World.

The next group of Germans arrived on the *Mary and Margaret* in October 1608. Among them were five unnamed glassmakers and three carpenters, Adam, Franz, and Samuel. The records show that the Germans were the only skilled craftsmen in the colony. In time, they established the first glassworks, the first sawmill, and the first tobacco plantation. They also introduced viticulture (grape horticulture) and viniculture (winemaking) and became the brew masters in the New World.

Europeans were needed to settle these vast territories. Profit-seeking promoters, including William Penn, seized the opportunity to persuade Germans to come to the new colonies.

Penn himself made several trips to Germany. He spoke German fluently since his mother was a German Quaker.

The first organized group that accepted Penn's invitation arrived in Philadelphia on October 6, 1683, aboard the *Concord*, which was considered the German *Mayflower*. Hence, October 6 is celebrated as German American Day. Under the leadership of Franz Daniel Pastorius, thirteen Quaker and Mennonite families from Krefeld and Kriegsheim ventured to take the journey. They settled six miles north of Philadelphia and established *Deutschstadt*—Germantown. Today, it is a suburb of the city of brotherly love. The descendants of all who arrived on the *Concord* are just as proud to be brave Americans as those whose ancestors came aboard the *Mayflower* or on any other boat. The conditions in Europe, especially in Germany, explain why so many undertook the journey into an unknown world. Hopes and aspirations for something better filled the hearts of all who braved the journey.

Centuries before the Germans ventured across the Atlantic to the New World, thousands accepted the invitations by various rulers to settle in their respective lands, which might be called the "wild east." The "Drang nach dem Osten" began already under the great German emperor Karl dem Grossen (Charlemagne), obeying a papal charge to carry Catholicism eastward and convert the heathen Slavs. The cradle of Western Civilization had always been Western Europe. With the Germans having been converted to Catholicism themselves and spreading Catholicism eastward and farther, the papacy became a very powerful earthly force. For centuries, Germans spread not only Catholicism but also their advanced skills to Eastern and Central Europe. They left their imprint on the entire region from the Baltic to the Balkans. They bestowed their influence and skills to Estonians, Latvians, Lithuanians, Poles, Czechs, Slovaks, Hungarians, Romanians, Slovenes, Croats, and others. They willingly and freely shared their legacy.

The German settlers maintained their language and culture for centuries virtually unchanged. It was considered a sign of cultural refinement to be able to speak German. Language, like religion, is a unifying force and the pinnacle of culture. Until World War I, when nationalism raised its ugly head, the majority of the inhabitants of Prague and Budapest spoke German, rather than Czech or Hungarian. The first German university was founded in Prague, which at the time was the seat of the Imperial German government. Most of the mayors of Buda, Hungary's capital before it merged and became Budapest, were German. For many centuries, the Germans and their native neighbors lived harmoniously together, until the brutal ethnic cleansing of the twentieth century ended their peaceful coexistence.

Since Charlemagne, who was crowned emperor of the Holy Roman Empire of the German Nation on Christmas Day in AD 800, the Germans have played a central role in the dissemination and perpetuation of Christianity and Western civilization. Drang nach dem Osten was not a military conquest of the East. The respective rulers used special rights and privileges as incentives to persuade Germans to settle in their land. It was a peaceful and mutually beneficial arrangement. They came as cultivators of the land and builders of urban centers and farming towns.

Katherine the Great, a German princess who became a great Russian empress, invited Germans to settle the lower Volga region. The German settlers developed the land into a major grain-producing area. Thus, Russia became the largest supplier of grain for Western Europe and remained so for two centuries. German settlers were granted rights and privileges, allowing them to maintain and preserve their heritage. Centuries later, after these rights were revoked, many families immigrated to the New World, where they continued their well-developed method of grain production. One of them was the family of the famous and very successful American band leader Lawrence Welk.

Bohemia, including Silesia, was part of the Czech kingdom, which was part of the German Holy Roman Empire. Its rulers were powerful members of the Seven Electors of the German emperor.

Empress Maria Theresia of Austria Hungary resettled the devastated regions of southern Hungary with people from the Rhine region. These lands had been devastated by Turkish conquest and liberated from the Ottoman Turkish rule. Theirs was a very challenging task, rebuilding the region. Much of it was covered by swamps and wilderness. It took the settlers three generations to fully reclaim the land and turn it into fertile fields. It was a very difficult task, which was reflected in the motto: "Dem ersten der Tod, dem zweiten die Not und dem dritten erst das Brot."

The empress established towns and farming villages as purely Catholic or Protestant communities, adding further mistrust and discrimination among her subjects and maintaining the religious schism. The German settlers who settled and rebuilt this region are known as Donauschwaben, because they traveled to their new destination on and many settled along the Danube River. However, most of them did not originate from the Schwabenland but merely started their voyage on flat-bottom boats at Ulm. They came primarily from Alsace, Lorraine, the Black Forest, the Palatinate, Switzerland, Bavaria, and Austria. When they arrived at their destination, they used the wood from the boats to build their homes, churches, and businesses.

The Serbs petitioned the emperor and received permission to settle in this region. The empress continued to settle Serbs in this region. The Serbian presence became a serious political issue during the twentieth century. The Allies justified their actions to amputate these regions from Hungary following the world wars because of their presence. It became part of the newly formed and short-lived state of Yugoslavia. Until then, these regions were part of the Austro-Hungarian monarchy. At the end of the war, the ethnic Germans, the Donauschwaben, were driven from their homesteads, robbed of all their belongings, and forced to flee. Women were raped. More than 240,000 were brutally murdered by Tito and his willing and inebriated executioners, and many thousands ended up in Siberia as slave laborers.

In 1330, the duchy of Gottschee was established as part of the new settlements in the lower Krain region, which was part of the Austrian Empire. The Gottschee encompassed an area of some 860 square kilometers of devastated, desolate, and uninhabited land. The first settlers came from South and East Tyrol and other parts of Austria and from present-day Switzerland and parts of Germany. Their task was to cultivate the area.

They toiled the land and practiced their craft. Over many generations, they founded 176 communities, including their capital, Gottschee, which was elevated to city status in 1471. From 1469 until 1584, the Turks invaded and devastated the entire region ten times, and in the beginning of the nineteenth century, the French occupied the region. In 1515, the farmers and craftsmen of the Gottschee participated in the peasant revolt, which also spread to Kaernten (Corinthia) and Steiermark (Styre) in Austria proper.

The Gottscheers are religious, hard-working, honest, family-oriented, generous, and very proud of their beautiful heritage, which they cheerfully perpetuated. The elder generation still speaks and communicates in their unique dialect, which they maintained for centuries virtually unchanged. German settlers, outside of Germany proper, vigorously preserved their language and heritage, resisting change, following the motto "Nur der ist seiner Ahnen wert, der ihre Sitten wohl verehrt."

At the end of World War I, life for the Gottscheers became increasingly problematic. German was eliminated as an official language. German schools and learning institutions were converted into Slovenian institutions. German social and cultural organizations were closed and German property confiscated, as were the German orphanage and the German hospital. German officials and teachers were dismissed. Thirty teachers found employment in Kaernten, Austria. The capital city Gottschee received a Slovenian mayor. They lost their legal rights, and no longer were allowed to purchase real estate. They were now treated as unwanted foreigners. The Gottscheer German heritage was being eradicated.

Because of a secret agreement between Hitler and Mussolini, the Gottschee, like the inhabitants of South Tyrol, were torn away from Austria. At the end of World War II, they were driven from their homes and land and were forced to leave all their belongings behind. They fled, and many were murdered by Tito and his partisans. Many of their homes and barns were burned to the ground. Like autumn leaves, they scattered all over the world. Some settled in America and Canada. They all fled first to and many stayed then in Austria.

The German settlers in Eastern Europe were given land on which they built their walled cities and farming communities. Royal charters guaranteed rights and privileges, including the right to preserve and promote their language, music, and culture. They elected their own internal leaders, exercised and perpetuated their craft, held fairs and festivals, engaged in commercial trade, maintained control over the land that had been granted to them, and willingly shared their skills with the natives. They enjoyed good neighborly relations until anti-German hostilities were fueled with huge sums of money leading to World War I.

In return for these rights, the German settlers agreed to

support the rulers monetarily and militarily with soldiers in time of war, develop the agricultural output, and contribute to its commercial and industrial base. Germans encouraged literacy and learning and introduced the Protestant work ethic, which contributed to attaining higher cultural and production levels. In 1725, Peter the Great of Russia established the Russian Academy at the urging of Gottfried Wilhelm Leibnitz. Most of its faculty members were German.

The German farming villages and their surrounding fields were laid out in a manner that made farming more efficient and more productive. The German cities are easily recognizable in their architecture and the way they were laid out as an urban community. In contrast, the cities of the locals had the appearance of an overgrown village, lacking urban characteristics. Some of these German urban centers included such cities as Riga, Koenigsberg (Kaliningrad), Praha (Prague), Pressburg (Bratislava), Ofen (Buda, Budapest), Hermannstadt, and Kronstadt.

We can learn some important lessons from the beginning of recorded German history. Let us go back some two thousand years to Arminius or Hermann; the year is AD 9. Hermann united the various German tribes into one unified force, soundly defeating the far superior and much larger Roman legions, basically ending Roman incursions into German territory. This victory stands out as a splendid example of what German unity can accomplish. The question could be raised, why talk about Arminius? The answer would be the same as talking about George Washington when discussing American history.

At the time, Arminius was twenty-seven years old. Never has there been a victory more decisive or the freeing of an oppressed people more spontaneous and more complete. They succeeded in liberating their homeland and securing the survival of the German people. Unfortunately, throughout the centuries, the Germans diluted their own strength with endless internal petty quarrels and feuds and fighting each other because of the curse of their religious schism.

This part of German history has many parallels to contemporary German challenges. Just as the victorious Allies ravaged Germany after each world war, the Romans also ravaged and reeducated the German youth with Roman ideology at the expense of their own beautiful and colorful heritage. Some Germans believed it fashionable to even romanize their names. Arminius was acutely aware that his homeland was being exploited with ever new taxes and duties. He studied the organization, the manner of fighting, and the resources of his people's oppressors. He was educated in Rome, after the Romans took him hostage.

The former Roman governor of Syria Rublius Quinctilius Varus was a typical corrupt politician who was entrusted with ruling the Germans. Prior to exploiting the Germans, he entered and ruled wealthy Syria as a poor man, and as a wealthy man, he left it impoverished. He was convinced that he could govern the Germans as he dealt with the Syrians, easily being enslaved. He considered the German tribes to be cowards and stupid. He permitted abductions into slavery, molestation and rape of German women, and public whipping to punish disobedience. Arminius's loyalty to Rome was described in the following way: "He is a simple, harmless German. There is more fraud and deceit in a little wether that grazes by the Tiger … than the whole nation he belongs to." Nevertheless, the flame of freedom and independence, ever so small, erupted and was maintained and kept alive. Arminius and his fellow patriots were victorious. The Germans throughout history have all too often not followed Arminius's example of unity. Leider ist Einbildung zu oft der grosse Elephant im Saal.

This was the first of several victories over the powerful Roman forces. This victory accomplished several things. The

Germans became cognizant of their unified strength, which fueled pride and patriotism. They passed on their courage and energy to their descendants, who, four centuries after the Teutoburger Forest battle, subdued the Roman Empire and took possession of Europe, which they developed into a modern civilization with Germanic, Judeo-Christian ideals of fairness and honor. It has been claimed that this victory gave the Anglo-Saxons the Bill of Rights and Common Law, based upon the republican institutional forms of Old Saxony. It gave the presumption of innocence until found guilty, as well as a speedy trial.

Furthermore, it became the foundation that formed a cohesive society bound by language, culture, affinity, and a willing acceptance of one's duties. Lately, the Germans are again slowly regaining their justified pride in their colorful and beautiful heritage and their many achievements. However, tribal pride is still reflected in the way Germans describe and think of themselves. First and foremost, they will refer to themselves as belonging to a tribe, such as Franks, Bavarians, Schwabs, Pomeranians, and so on. There is an element of pride in this tribal association. What appears missing is national pride and affinity. This regional feeling of belonging also holds true after they have immigrated to another country. German Americans will all too often refer to the tribe or region their ancestors came from rather than the whole of Germany.

Arminius was the first Germanic chieftain who succeeded in unifying the numerous tribes of his countrymen into a common cause to free themselves from corrupt oppressors. Hermann or Irmin, as he was known to his own people, was the leader of the Cheruski tribe. This young man in his twenties dared to oppose a seemingly unstoppable world power, the Roman Empire at its height under Octavian Augustus Caesar. In comparison, this would be the same as if some young military leader in a third-world country would attempt to bring the powerful United States to its knees.

Irritated at the cunning ways of those who enslaved his people, Arminius was enraged over the kidnapping of his wife, Thusnelda, who was with child. His wife and his unborn son were betrayed by her bootlicking father to the Romans. Arminius succeeded in uniting a relatively small army of citizen soldiers from various tribes, who were determined to stop the Roman oppression. They yearned to live free from oppression and as free men.

Knowing the Roman ways and weaknesses, Arminius lured them into the Teutoburger Forest near Detmold. There, the Germans destroyed three Roman legions under General Publius Quinctilius Varus. Arminius stopped forever the Roman advance and the Roman might. Hermann's decisive victory preserved and perpetuated the colorful German culture and the Germans as a unique race and people.

Unfortunately, throughout Germany's history, they have more often been at odds with each other than standing united against a common enemy, such as Catholic Germans fighting Protestant Germans and Prussia at odds with Vienna. Bavaria even fought with Napoleon against Protestant Prussia. This national disunity caused them to be easily exploited by their neighbors and by Rome. For many Germans, it appeared to be more important to be a Bavarian, a Prussian, a Schwab, or ein "echter" Wiener and attach great importance to their religious affiliation, rather than to be proud and stand up united for their common German national unity. This has made them easy targets of exploitation.

The Reformation and Counter-Reformation

The corruption of morals in the church prevailed to such a degree as to call for sweeping reforms; the laxity of discipline invaded even the inner sanctum, the inner sanctuary. Reform within the church was resisted at every level. The Reformation was cradled in the new printing press. The Counter-Reformation became a military offensive in defense of the status quo. Thus, the church unwittingly contributed to the destruction of its own Christian Western cultural heritage.

For some 120 years following the Reformation and Counter-Reformation, Germany was devastated by religious wars, ending with what is historically referred to as the Thirty Years' War (1618–1648). The Catholic Hapsburg Monarchy in Vienna, honoring a papal request, activated its military under General Wallenstein to force all Germans back into the Roman Catholic fold. Rome needed money. "Wenn der Thaler im Teller klingt, eine Seele aus dem Fegefeuer springt." Salvation was on sale; it no longer required good works. This religious conflict turned into a massive and brutal bloodbath. Almost half of the population of Germany, about eight million people, perished defending their religious convictions; many also died because of the plague. Religious freedom was not yet a protected right or an individual option. The church displayed its worldly power.

These military conflicts were further fueled by cunning French monarchs, profiteering by promoting continuous war supported by intrigues and bribes. The French were selling weapons to both sides, even switching sides whenever one side appeared to be winning to keep the conflict going. Ever since, Germany has been plagued by its religious schism, reflected in diminished mutual trust between Catholics and Protestants. German national pride and a sense for national unity suffered. Germans identified more readily with individual states and their religious affiliation than their nation. That attitude of local identity and religious schism, rather than national unity, has plagued Germany ever since the religious wars, like a cancer.

The intrigues and religious wars finally ended with the Treaty of Westphalia. And then, by the grace of France, Germany was divided into three hundred different, "independent" small states. Each minor monarch was granted considerable power, including the power to determine the religion of his subjects. The Treaty of Westphalia constituted for Germany the same as if the American Civil War had left the country divided into three hundred different independent states by the grace of France or England. That would have made a total mockery of any meaningful concept of a union or a nation. That is, tragically, what the Treaty of Westphalia forced onto the German people. Partially, the Germans need to blame themselves and their own religious fanaticism for this condition.

It was at the conclusion of the Thirty Years' War that the French burned down the Heidelberg Castle and the city of Mannheim. Furthermore, Switzerland, Alsace-Lorraine, and Holland were taken and torn away from Germany. It was merely another attempt at reducing Germany in size. The intent of Germany's adversaries has been to keep Germany divided, powerless, and as small as possible. Der Deutsche blieb der deutsche Michel; leider sah und sieht er seine eigene Dummheit nicht.

For two centuries, Europe was involved in military conflicts over religious dogma. It was an attempt to deliver the opposing side from the chains of the Antichrist; each believed to have the true God on its side. Unfortunately, the battles were fought on German soil. Christians butchered each other over differing Christian convictions. This was an example of being blinded by extreme religious fanaticism and the allurement of earthly power. There was no religious tolerance or brotherly love.

Germans still do not enjoy a separation of church and state, and they still pay taxes to the church.

Without a strong central government, a fragmented Germany was easier to control and much easier to manipulate by foreign interests. It was the desire for national unity that the poet Hoffmann von Fallersleben had in mind when he wrote the lyrics for the German national anthem, "Deutschland, Deutschland ueber alles." He was appealing to German unity within Germany and not conquering the world, especially with France and England ever vigilant in keeping Germany from uniting and small and powerless. During both world wars, the Allies twisted these lyrics for purposes of anti-German propaganda.

German thinkers and national heroes, such as Johann Wolfgang von Goethe, Friedrich Schiller, and others propounded the concept of a united German nation rather than a collection of some three hundred independent, small states. In the spring of 1813, Ernst Moritz Arndt raised the question "Was ist des Deutschen Vaterland?" What is the German's Fatherland? National pride and a rising German national consciousness permeated the climate; they aspired to a united, greater Germany that could less easily be exploited by its neighbors. It was a battle cry for German national unity and national pride, a realistic and sound German patriotism, the same way Americans and others rightfully enjoy their national patriotism. This is no different than the patriotism displayed by other nations.

Was ist des Deutschen Vaterland?
So weit die deutsche Zunge klingt
Und Gott im Himmel Lieder singt;
Das soll es sein! Das soll es sein!
Das, wackerer Deutscher, nenne dein!

These men ushered in a transformation of the German Holy Roman Empire into a body of some thirty states called der Deutsche Bund, the German Confederation. The final resolution of the Imperial Delegation was passed by the Imperial Diet on February 25, 1803, which decreed the dissolution of most of the ecclesiastical states and the imperial cities in the empire, diminishing church and monarchical influence.

Due to the absence of a strong central government and Germany's lack of unification, Germany was unable to maintain a huge navy like England, Spain, Portugal, and France and use it to acquire colonies. England maintained the largest navy, which was generally ten to twenty percent bigger than the navies of the two nearest rivals combined.

The Voyage

It is the intention of this short historical overview to provide insight and understanding to the causes of why so many Germans could so easily be persuaded to leave religious, economic, and political struggles and intrigues behind. America appeared on the horizon and promised many opportunities for a better life and a new beginning. However, many who were willing to immigrate were too poor to pay for their own voyage; thus, they agreed to sell themselves into indentured servitude. Indentured servants could not leave the vessel until their new owners paid for their voyage. Frequently, their children were separated from them to work in entirely different homes and workshops. Many children became orphans; one of them was Johann Peter Zenger. He later became famous for his fight for the freedom of the press. For the ship companies, these huge migrations translated into big business and huge profits. It was all about money.

The voyage itself was extremely dangerous. Many vessels

were described as mere swimming coffins. By 1710, some seventeen thousand immigrants out of a total of about thirty thousand died either in England waiting or during the six- to eight-week voyage crossing the Atlantic. That constituted more than 50 percent casualties. And yet, no one seemed to care, and it did not slow down the migration business. The conditions in Germany must have been very bad. Christian principles did not prevail. German writer Friedrich Kapp wrote, "If there were gravestones and crosses on the ocean waves, the route of the immigration ships would seem like one long cemetery."

Some eight million German immigrants have arrived on our shores, in spite of all the difficulty. Many more began the journey but died en route or in England. Silesians, from what was, prior to World War II, eastern Germany, and Salzburg Protestants from Austria arrived in 1734. They were unceremoniously expelled from their homes by their Catholic Hapsburg monarch. The Hapsburg monarchy could have been a blessing for all Germans but chose to promote Catholicism at the expense of German national interests.

The German Protestants lost everything except what they could carry on their backs. Many traveled to Savannah and other parts of Georgia. They were horrified at the slavery they found in Georgia and the mental attitude of the British, which they observed as being that "money is everything." Nevertheless, they considered what they found as being much better than living under the rule of one of the three hundred tyrannical, oppressive minor German monarchs. Sadly, throughout the centuries, religious intolerance has all too often raised its ugly head, contradicting all the religious rhetoric. Greed and money trumped human compassion and empathy.

German Settlers

For more than four hundred years, German Americans have had a profound and lasting impact on the growth and development of our nation and on the formation of many of our deepest-held values. Their many contributions have enriched every aspect of our society, as for example, they displayed their compassion for the underprivileged. In 1760, German Americans issued the very first protest against the institution of slavery and supported vigorously the antislavery movement. It has been stated so accurately that the problem of slavery is not the problem of the Negro. It is the eternal conflict between a small privileged class and the great nonprivileged class, the eternal struggle between the elite aristocracy and democracy. Furthermore, had the German-American attitude prevailed, the Native Americans would have never been the victims of all the brutal massacres that mark our pioneer history.

It would be impossible to list all the German-American contributions, influences, and achievements, especially since so much of the German culture and heritage has disseminated into and became an integral, core part of the American way of life. So much of what we consider to be American is actually German American. They had a decisive influence on American industry, labor, the arts, music, agriculture, education, and politics. Outstanding athletes of German descent displayed their talents, including such greats as Babe Ruth and Lou Gehrig. The Kentucky rifle was produced by German-American gunsmiths in Lancaster County, Pennsylvania. Walter Percy Chrysler founded the Chrysler Corporation in 1925. Years later, Dr. Werner von Braun and his German space team created the American space program and took us to the moon and beyond. In 1851, 64 percent of the population was foreign born, and of that, nearly two-thirds was born in Germany. In 1900, about one-third of Texas was of German descent. In spite of all the adversities, there are still over eight million Americans who speak German in their homes and their social gatherings, and many churches still hold services in German.

Legend has it that Turker, the foster father of Leif Erikson, was the first German to land on American soil in AD 1000. The mapmaker Martin Waldseemueller gave us our name *America*, after examining accounts of the voyages of the Italian explorer Amerigo Vespucci. Amerigo is Emmerich in German, hence, the name Ammericha (Amerika).

The first Bible printed in America was not in English but in German. It was published by Christopher Sauer in 1743. He issued the first almanac in German in 1739. He also published the first newspaper, written entirely in German, as well as hymnals and catechisms for most of the German sects. Prior to 1754, over two hundred different publications were issued from the various German presses, and William Rittenhausen erected the first paper mill in Pennsylvania.

German cooks added much to our culinary choices. Many items kept their original German names, such as wieners, frankfurters, hamburgers, sauerkraut, wiener schnitzel, braunschweiger, leberwurst, lebkuchen, German coffee cake, cottage cheese pie, coleslaw, potato salad, noodles, dill pickles, rye bread with caraway seeds, pumpernickel, German pancakes, and what would a party be without pretzels and a stein of beer, perhaps in a Rathskeller. As a result of the extreme anti-German hysteria, Westfalian ham was changed to Canadian bacon in World War I.

The German Americans are certainly a group large enough to be noticed. Now, each autumn, there are over two thousand major Oktoberfests from coast to coast, in Canada and around the world. The biggest Oktoberfest in the United States is in Cincinnati, Ohio, attracting over half a million people on the third weekend each September. The Joe Wendel Orchestra has been a featured attraction for over thirty years. Many organizations and churches have put on Oktoberfests as a means of raising money for their clubs and organizations. This is just one of the many ways that our German American heritage has become an American tradition, people enjoying German music, food, dance, and libation, while meeting old friends and making new ones.

German immigrants and their descendants founded many businesses that improved our lifestyles. These firms have affected us in our daily lives in chemistry, pharmaceuticals, industry, engineering, clothing, military leadership, and the production and distribution of the food we eat.

Let us mention some of the German-American giants in industry. Among them are such names as Kroger, with about 2,500 supermarkets and pharmacies nationwide, based in Cincinnati, Ohio. Others include Eddie Bauer in sports clothing, Bausch and Lamb in telescopes, Bayer aspirin, Boeing aerospace, Black and Decker tools, Diebold bank vaults and ATM machines, Doppler weather instruments, Eckerd drugstores, Engelhard chemicals, Fender electric guitars, Gerber baby foods, Hershey (Hirsche) chocolates, Hertz car rentals, Hilton (Hilten) hotels, Hoover (Huber) vacuum cleaners, Kaiser aluminum, Keebler (Kiebler) cookies, Koehler faucets and bathroom fixtures, Kraft foods, Heinz ketchup, Lays potato chips, Mack trucks, Maytag appliances, Meineke mufflers and auto service, Merck pharmaceuticals, Oscar Meyer meats, Orville Redenbacker popcorn, Schering pharmaceuticals, Schick razors, Schlage locks, Schweppes soft drinks, Charles Schwab investments, Schwinn bicycles, Smucker jams, Steinway pianos, Stouffer foods and hotels, Trump premium real estate, Walgreen's drugstores, Weber grills, Westinghouse appliances and lighting, Weyerhaeuser paper, Ziebart car enhancements, and so, so many more. This list of German-American industrial giants merely scratches the surface, as does their many contributions to our great country. The first US millionaire was John Jacob Astor.

One of the many German industrial giants was the inventor George Westinghouse. Numerous patents are accredited to him, and his inventions made travel by train much safer. He found solutions to seemingly insurmountable difficulties. Another giant among German inventors was Charles Steinmetz, who was born in Breslau, Germany, in 1865. His brilliant mind in electrical engineering was unparalleled. He was known as the "Wizard of Schenectady." He is accredited with more than two hundred inventions. By 1902, Steinmetz was the recognized authority in the electrical field. Harvard University bestowed him with an honorary degree as "the foremost electrical engineer in the world."

In 1854, every second immigrant was German. Wherever they settled down, the disciplined and detail-oriented Germans have thrived and prospered. If the Germans would have been able to apply their industrial skills to their political aptitude, they would have been a blessing to all mankind and history would have been different. Warren Bechtel founded the Bechtel Corporation, and it is still owned by the Bechtel family four generations later. The Bechtel Company participated in the building of the Hoover Dam in the 1930s and later in the construction of the English Channel Tunnel, the Hong Kong International Airport, and in many other major projects.

Captain Eddy Rickenbacher is recognized as the greatest American fighter pilot in World War I and was the recipient of the Medal of Honor. He founded the Eastern Air Lines. The airport in Columbus, Ohio, has been named after him. Chuck Yeager (Jaeger) was an ace fighter pilot in World War II; the Charlotte, West Virginia, airport bears his name.

Almost every major beer brand in America is of German

origin. They include such names as Coors, Anheuser-Busch, Michelob, Miller, Pabst, Schaefer, Schlitz, Schmidt's, Stroh's, Rheingold, Yuengling, and many more. Mexico's Corona and Dos Equis beers and China's Tsing Tao beers were founded by German immigrants in those countries. The German-American beer industry was an integral part of the colorful German-American heritage and its social and cultural life. They supported financially the German press and other community endeavors.

German immigrants were very interested in education, as they continue to be to this day. Before the Civil War, many German private schools were established. Many were parochial schools connected primarily with Lutheran churches. They would organize a "Schulverein" and hire a teacher to instruct their children. They promoted and established vocational schools, training and graduating excellent craftsmen.

The contributions of the German settlers to the life of colonial America are best reflected in the history of the Pennsylvania Germans, or the "Pennsylvania Dutch," as they are known to this day. Dutch is a mispronunciation of "Deutsch," meaning German. One of their many contributions is the Conestoga wagon. The Conestoga wagon originated in the Conestoga region of Pennsylvania and was designed and built by German Mennonites in that region. It had a unique design, incorporating many practical features. The bottom of the wagon was not flat but lower in the middle to prevent freight from shifting and rolling off the wagon when traveling up or down hills. The covering was also curved, with the rear and front protruding like a bonnet to keep the rain and sun out. The Conestoga was not only easy to identify by its shape but also by its colors. The wagon was usually painted light blue, the covering was white canvas, the wheels were red, and anything made of iron was painted black. The Conestoga came in different sizes. The larger wagons measured about twenty-five feet in length and weighed 1.5 tons empty. They could carry up to eight tons in freight. In most cases, the wagon was drawn by six horses. The Conestoga wagon carried the pioneers westward all the way to California.

Another version of the Conestoga wagon was the prairie schooner. It was lighter and needed at most four horses, even two. Oxen were often used instead of horses. The prairie schooner was fitted with a top, drawn in at both ends, with only an oval opening to allow air and light into the interior, where children and women usually rode and slept. In crossing the Great Plains, larger groups of schooners traveled together for mutual assistance and protection. The Conestoga wagon reminds us of a simpler, slower, more romantic time in our past.

At the time of the American Revolution, the total American population was a little more than three million. By 1830, the population increased to about ten million. In 1851, 64 percent of the population was foreign-born, and of that nearly two-thirds were born in Germany. In 1766, Benjamin Franklin reported that the Germans made up about one-third of the entire population of Pennsylvania. The two major religious faiths of the German settlers were Lutheranism and Calvinism. The great patriarch of the German Lutherans was Heinrich Melchior Muehlenberg. The various forms of German Protestantism were primarily responsible for the preservation and perpetuation of our proud and beautiful German-American heritage.

German settlers courageously stood up for personal freedom and against the oppressive demands of the British colonial governor. Johann Peter Zenger championed the rights of citizens to criticize public officials in the press. Zenger published articles critical of the royal British governor. On Sunday, November 17, 1734, Zenger was arrested and charged with seditious libel. Understandably, Zenger protested, arguing that all his criticisms were nothing less than the absolute truth and for a commonsense German that was really the only important issue that mattered.

Governor William Cosby, on the other hand, claimed that any truth is libelous that damaged the government and "the respect for authority." Zenger was superbly defended by attorney Andrew Hamilton, who successfully argued that the truth is and it can never be libelous. The jury nullified Cosby's claim as unjust, because, according to the court, exposing "Public Wickedness is a duty which every Man owes to the Truth and his Country." Zenger's victory over the colonial royal British governor was one of the most important cases during our colonial period because it directly led to the demands for a First Amendment and a Bill of Rights.

German Americans fought for and many paid the ultimate price in our struggle for America's independence from the controls and exploitations of the British Empire. A German-language newspaper, the *Pennsylvania Staatsbote*, was the first that published the Declaration of Independence on July 5, 1776—not in English but in German.

Prior to 1754, over two hundred different publications were issued from various German presses. With ever more German immigrants arriving, the number of German language presses increased. The work of another German American, Joseph Pulitzer, further advanced the American legacy of freedom of the press, as it also greatly advanced the field of journalism.

German Americans overwhelmingly supported the efforts of our Revolution, our struggle for independence from British oppression. An entirely German Provost Corps, under the command of Major Bartholomew von Heer, served as General Washington's personal bodyguards to the end of the war and escorted him to his home. Since none of them spoke English, it is assumed that Washington spoke some German. Some British Americans wanted to kidnap General Washington and turn him over to the British crown. That would have significantly weakened our resolve to fight for our independence and our freedom. Also, Benjamin Franklin learned German and published his own German newspaper, *Die Philadelphia Zeitung*.

The impact of the German settlers upon our unique American heritage is not only statistically significant, but it has also influenced our American society and our nation in every aspect conceivable. Many generations have marveled at Emmanuel Gottlieb Leutze's 1851 painting, *Washington Crossing the Delaware River*. It is a well-recognized and cherished symbol of American and German-American courage and resolve.

In the middle of the nineteenth century, Gettysburg was an insignificant trading post. The German settlers called it Goetzburg, probably in honor of Goetz von Berlichingen, a German hero of the oppressed. The name was subsequently anglicized like many other German names. Goetzburg gained historical significance because the bloodiest battle of the Civil War took place there and the now famous Gettysburg Address was delivered there by President Lincoln. Abraham Lincoln is claimed to be of German ancestry. His grandfather's name appears on a land office treasury warrant as Abraham Linkhorn. Daniel Boone spoke Pennsylvania Dutch (Deutsch); his family name was Bohne.

Less known is the fact that of the twenty-four Union regiments, twelve were composed primarily of German Americans and under the command of German-American officers. The entire Eleventh Potomac Army Corps was under the command of General Carl Schurz. General Adolph von Steinwehr, a former officer of the Prussian Army, was in command of the Second Division. It was General Steinwehr's decision to take position on the Cemetery Hill that proved to be the decisive factor in the victory for the Union Army. The ground in Gettysburg is soaked with German-American blood. Many who died there were indentured servants.

General Carl Schurz immigrated from the Rhineland and subsequently became a US Senator and secretary of the interior. His wife, Margarethe Schurz, established the first kindergarten in America. In 1733, Johann Roggenfelder arrived, also from the Rhineland. His descendants became oil billionaires and politicians under the name of Rockefeller. President Donald Trump's paternal grandparents came from Germany.

Another immigrant from the Rhineland was Thomas Nast, who was America's greatest cartoonist. Through his artistic abilities, Nast established himself as a political voice for the underprivileged and a champion of equal rights for all citizens. It was Thomas Nast who gave us the political symbols for the Republican and Democratic Parties—the elephant and the donkey. But our American version of Santa Claus was indisputably his greatest German-American contribution. It was not an invention of Coca-Cola, as commonly believed.

General Von Steuben

By far, the greatest service to America gaining its freedom and independence from Britain's bloody domination and taxation was rendered by General Friedrich Wilhelm von Steuben. Benjamin Franklin recruited him in Paris for the American cause. Steuben was General Washington's true right-hand man, from Valley Forge to the final victory in the Revolution at Yorktown, where he commanded the right wing and Lafayette the left.

Von Steuben trained our starving, undisciplined, and unpaid Colonial Army at Valley Forge and turned them into a decisive fighting force. German settlers and farmers kept the army from starving by getting the needed food supplies to the soldiers. Now each autumn, parades in New York, Chicago, and Philadelphia honor this great German American for his service to our country, our independence, and our freedom. The Steuben Parades are attended by thousands and thousands of patriots.

Von Steuben's key contributions were classical Prussian military strategy—discipline, morale, and endless training to the point of perfection. He was a great source of inspiration to our American volunteers, encouraging them to keep confidence in themselves and maintain faith in their cause. He wrote a military manual, called the *Blue Book*; an updated version is still in use. After three years of war, our American freedom fighters had the discipline and military skills to boot the British forces back across the shining sea to bloody old England.

We need to remind ourselves, not everyone was in favor of severing our ties with dear old England. There were also intensely pro-British English Americans interested in keeping a bond to the mother country rather than a clean break after our victory. As a direct result of America's victory, many British Tories returned to dear old England. Tragically, that British bond was reignited during the brutal and bloody twentieth century.

No war that America has won was more important than the Revolution itself. It crystallized us as a new nation. Baron von Steuben is honored with a magnificent thirty-foot statue that stands in Lafayette Park across from the north side of the White House. And a bust of the baron graces the entrance of the Citadel.

Perhaps our bloodiest battle was the ambush at Oriskany Creek on August 6, 1777. General Nickolas Herkimer's (Herchheimer) grandparents came from Heidelberg. Like so many Germans from the Palatinate, they worked as indentured servants along the Hudson until they were freed to settle in the Mohawk Valley as a buffer zone to secure the frontier. Almost at the outset of the battle, General Herkimer was seriously wounded just below his knee, but he continued to command his eight-hundred-man militia. For six hours, the injured Herkimer directed his men sitting on a saddle propped up against a tree while smoking his pipe to demonstrate his confidence in the outcome. The tactical strategy was to put two men behind each tree. They were victorious. However, a quarter of the German settlers died in the battle. General Herkimer died ten days later because of a botched leg amputation.

It has been stated, and let it be proclaimed, without the unselfish dedication and commitment of the German settlers, the war would not have ended so victoriously and we might still be British subjects and a British colony, paying taxes to and taking orders from bloody old England.

The German Lutheran and Reformed churches of Philadelphia vigorously supported the fight against English oppression and despotism. To persuade others, they sent a pamphlet to the Germans of New York and North Carolina, encouraging them to form militia companies and corps of sharpshooters, as they had done themselves. Muehlenberg and Schlatter, the patriarchs of the two denominations, enthusiastically supported the cause of freedom.

Heinrich Muehlenberg became pastor of the Lutheran church at Woodstock, Virginia, in 1772. Patrick Henry recommended Muehlenberg be made commander of the Eighth Virginia Regiment. In 1776, he delivered his last sermon in the little church at Woodstock. He ended his sermon by proclaiming, "There is a time for preaching and praying, but also a time for battle, and that time has now arrived." He took off his clerical robe and descended from the pulpit in the uniform of a Continental colonel. To the roll of drums, he marched to the open front door. The people, both inside and outside, cheered.

That Sunday morning, more than three hundred young men joined; another hundred joined the next day.

Muehlenberg proved to be not only an outstanding preacher but also a brave soldier. He gained the reputation of being that "Devil's Pete." On February 21, 1777, he was raised to the rank of brigadier-general and placed in charge of the First, Fifth, Ninth, and Thirteenth Virginia Regiments. His troops encountered the British at Charleston, Brandywine, Germantown, Monmouth, Stoney Point, and Yorktown. Following his distinguished military career, he became a prominent member in the political circles. He represented Pennsylvania three times in Congress 1789–1791, 1793–1795, and 1799–1801. It was Mr. Muehlenberg who was credited for the tradition of addressing the president of the United States as "Mr. President."

In every one of our wars, German Americans have served with distinction and in far greater numbers than their percentage in our population. Even during World War II, fighting against Germany, one-third of the eleven million soldiers and over seven hundred officers in our armed forces were German Americans. General Dwight D. Eisenhower (Eisenhauer), supreme commander of the Allied Forces in Europe; General Carl Spaatz of the US Air Force; Admiral Chester W. Nimitz of the Pacific Fleet; and Generals Eichelberger and Krueger commanding two armies under General MacArthur in the Pacific were all proud Americans of German descent. Tragically, while German Americans served so heroically and many paid the ultimate price, thousands of their relatives were relentlessly persecuted and forced into federal internment camps at home.

The way America celebrates Christmas, New Year's, and the Fourth of July was shaped by German Americans. They brought the Christmas tree and other traditions to make Christmas the celebration it is today. The New England Puritans did not celebrate Christmas. In many parts of the country, as late as the Civil War, this day was celebrated with mischief and rowdiness—a kind of Halloween party. The German immigrants popularized Christmas as a religious holiday, attending church services and family gatherings. Today, a decorated Christmas tree is an international symbol of the holiday and "Silent Night" is a seasonal anthem.

Our educational system was modeled after the German system, from kindergarten to the university. Engineers, such as Johann August Roebling, originally from Thuringia, and his son Washington Roebling, built many suspension bridges and gave New York its landmark, the Brooklyn Bridge.

Martin Luther declared that every man is his own minister and accountable for his own actions. However, in order to know what one was accountable for, one had to be able to read the Bible. Thus, Luther became the father of public education. Germans were instrumental in developing our educational system. Horace Mann was sent to Germany to study the German school system and returned with specific recommendations. Many of his suggestions were implemented. We copied much of Germany's system from kindergarten through the university. The first German university was the University of Prague, founded in 1348. Prague, at the time, was the seat of the German imperial government. Czechs migrated into this region from Russia during the Middle Ages; most of them assimilated well but not all.

Universities in America sprang up, such as Harvard in 1636, William and Mary in 1693, Yale in 1701, Princeton in 1746, and Brown in 1764. These were all teaching universities, educating and preparing future clergymen in their respective denominations. The concept that a university could be more than a preparatory institution for the clergy but also engage in original research emerged in Germany. The University of Berlin became the leading research institution. German research universities excelled in new discoveries. Many American luminaries attended these new research universities in Germany. Many American scholars returned very inspired by their experiences and brought the concept of research universities to America. Cornell University was founded in 1865, as the first American research university, modeled after the German research university, where research became part of the curriculum. Soon other American research universities followed, such as Johns Hopkins and Stanford Universities. Now most major American universities are research institutions.

The presence of a symphony orchestra in many cities, including New York, Cincinnati, and Cleveland, is a direct development of the German concert orchestras and the importance that music played in their lives. Theodore Thomas founded the Chicago Symphony Orchestra in 1891. Of the ninety-four musicians in the New York Philharmonic Society in 1890, eighty-nine were German. The Turners (athletic fitness clubs) left a profound influence on physical education in our schools, stressing the classical concept of a strong mind in a strong body.

Perhaps Carl Schurz expressed German patriotism most eloquently when he stated that German immigrants "could render no greater honor to their former fatherland than by becoming conscientious and faithful citizens of their new country." Time and time again, they demonstrated their love for America by being law-abiding, productive, loyal citizens. So much of what is typically considered to be American is German American. German Americans have just cause to be proud of their legacy in our great country.

Germans contributed their fair share and gave willingly their skills, common sense, sturdiness, love of life, love of music and the arts, talents, and utmost loyalty and devotion, and many, many gave their lives. German Americans have demonstrated their unconditional patriotism and their love of God and country time and time again.

The World Wars

The wars against Germany and the sufferings of the German Americans during the last century are tragically also a part of our proud history, as well as the internment camps where so many of our fellow Americans suffered and were subjected to such undue cruelties and brutality. It is significant that none of them were ever charged with or found guilty of any war-related crime. These injustices need to be rectified. We need to provide truth in discussing that part of our history with a pure heart.

Americans have recently experienced a rebirth in our roots and our heritage. Several authoritative books have been written about our history and German-American contributions, such as *The German American Experience* by Dr. Don Heinrich Tolzmann. As suggested reading in our high school and college history courses, these books would provide a greater amount of insight and understanding of our heritage, making our history courses far more interesting and relevant.

We as a nation and as individuals go to great length in professing our total commitment to human rights issues. Like charity, human rights and respect begin at home. For a democracy such as ours, it is imperative to be totally truthful and transparent. Transparency is essential for gaining and maintaining peace on earth. Let us join hands and rise to the challenge; equal rights for all without distinction of race, nationality, or religion. We cannot honestly try to help others without helping ourselves first. Let us join hands and become a positive force for the good of all. We can gradually change through honest communication and realistic inner reflection.

Our democracy will long endure, if "We the people" remain vigilant.

The sole purpose of this historical overview, which merely scratches the surface of the abundant contributions and the many positive influences of German Americans, is to promote a better understanding of our past. German and German-American contributions to the development of Western civilization have been massive. Their peaceful ways are reflected in the fact that during the past one hundred years, Germany has waged far fewer wars than England, France, Russia, or the United States.

Nothing is more important than improving the state of all Americans and the world for the present and future generations, without discrimination. George Orwell tells us that he who controls the past also controls the future. If our past is not understood, or misunderstood, it will have an adverse effect on our future. Let us build bridges based on truth, mutual trust, and understanding. There is no greater blessing than knowledge and understanding. Let us demonstrate by our actions that we hate the ruthless hand of ignorance and the devastation of war as much as sin and death. Bungling in politics and intrigues leads to misery and the ruination of millions of people.

Let our fervent prayer be the words of our seventh president, Andrew Jackson, "May He who holds in His hands the destinies of nations make you worthy of the favors He has bestowed and enable you, with pure hearts and pure hands and sleepless vigilance, to guard and defend to the end of time the great charge He has committed to your keeping." So may it ever be!

If German Americans had spoken and acted politically with one voice and been more united, stood politically closer together, and been politically more engaged and better informed, our and world history would have been considerably different. Brotherly love, relief, and truth are virtues that beckon to be emulated. Let our aspirations be directed toward a purity of life and rectitude of conduct, a never-ending argument for nobler deeds, for higher thoughts, and for greater achievement.

President Abraham Lincoln's paternal grandfather was Abraham Linkhorn (May 1738 to May 1786), buried in Springfield, Illinois.

CHAPTER 2

American Internment Camps

World War I

The twentieth century may well be the bloodiest and deadliest century in the history of mankind. Both world wars are really two acts of the same deadly tragedy. They have been referred to as the Thirty Years' War of the twentieth century. It has been stated many times before, if profit and greed were taken out of the equation, there would be no reason for war and therefore, no war. War has been referred to as murder in uniform. War will disappear, like the dinosaur, when changes in world conditions have destroyed its survival value. As President John F. Kennedy stated, "If man does not put an end to war, war will put an end to man."

We are a mosaic of the world, a nation of nations. We are the United States of America and man's best hope for human rights, peace, and freedom. We have an inherent obligation to uphold the principles of the US Constitution, else our democracy may be gradually degraded to hypocrisy, where big money, greed, and profit dictate our internal and external affairs. Our Constitution guarantees that "no person shall be deprived of life, liberty, or property without due process of law." The Fourteenth Amendment guarantees every person equal protection of the law; however, thousands of Americans were denied these basic guarantees of due process during both world wars, i.e., the opportunity of telling their side of the story and to cross-examine their accusers. The system was forced to fail by denying due process guarantees. Tragically, during the last century, the world has witnessed the propagation of a totally irrational and intense hatred of Germans and German Americans.

Americans of German descent were terrorized and their personal liberties were violated by our own government and by some of their neighbors. Our government, of, for, and by the people, is obligated to protect all the people equally and not discriminate against any group, but it did. This did not happen in the Bolshevik Soviet Union, Nazi Germany, North Korea, or Communist China; this happened in the United States of America, where we pride ourselves on having constitutionally protected personal rights. Unfortunately, no one either dared or cared to raise his or her voice in support of his or her terrorized neighbors.

Passage of the Wartime Treatment Study Act will provide some of the answers to these and related questions. Passage of the bill has been long overdue, as more and more internees are dying. Therefore, let us now raise our voices, so that those who can no longer speak will not have suffered in vain. We must act so that this brutality and these human rights violations will never be repeated against anyone else again. Sadly, there are groups who feel very uncomfortable with this part of our history and would like nothing better than to have it swept under the carpet forever. That cannot and will not happen. Truth and justice must prevail.

In the previous chapter, we presented a historical overview so that the multitude of German-American contributions and sacrifices would be remembered. It is only proper to demonstrate our gratitude for their monumental tasks and contributions and their many personal sacrifices. In this chapter, we will illuminate the many injustices and cruelties they were subjected to. The importance of this dialogue cannot be overstated, particularly since our history textbooks and our media, thus far, have woefully been totally silent about this part of our history. Freedom of speech cannot survive in a climate of denial and silence.

Tragically, Germans and German Americans were the victims of many cruelties, injustices, and hate crimes that cannot and may not be forgotten and brushed under the carpet. Some of our textbooks, if the topic is mentioned at all, have even claimed that German Americans were not forcibly placed into internment camps at all, solely because they were white, in contrast to the Japanese Americans. This is a rude inference of racial discrimination. The overriding question remains: Why is this part of our history still being falsified or totally denied? Is it our susceptibility to a feeling and admission of guilt? Are our actions, de facto, an admission of guilt?

A walk down our historical memory lane is not only enlightening but imperative to our understanding and greater appreciation of our past. Throughout our history, German Americans have made every effort to faithfully preserve their history and traditions and promote their beautiful and colorful heritage. They have passed down their strong work ethic from generation to generation. Germans have been a solid pillar in their communities, turned millions of acres into fertile land, helped build our nation, and died protecting our freedom and independence. Their generous contributions have shaped the United States into the great and prosperous land of the free and the brave, but German-American contributions and loyalty suddenly no longer mattered under President Woodrow Wilson's administration. It became a crime for German Americans to pray or sing in German and to preserve and promote their language, their music, their culture, and their heritage. Why were they discriminated against so viciously?

The years leading up to about 1900, especially the nineteenth century, are generally regarded as the Golden Age of American-German relations. For over a century, from Frederick the Great to Bismarck, there endured a genuine and mutually beneficial and cordial relationship between the two nations. Many aspiring American scholars went to Germany to secure inspiration for their life's work. Among them were such future luminaries as Washington Irving, Henry W. Longfellow, James F. Cooper, Edvard Everett, Joseph Cogswell, James F. Baucroft, and George Tichnor, to mention but very few. Following the war, Germany has again emerged as a beacon of learning and research and humane mercy.

Various factors contributed to this positive image of Germany in both the United States and England. First, prior to Bismarck's unification, Germany was militarily and politically weak. France ravished Germany continuously, thus Bismarck's unification of Germany was greeted as desirable and positive by the United States and England alike. At that time, England did not yet feel threatened by Germany industrially and commercially.

Furthermore, Germans were producing truly monumental achievements in every sphere of cultural, intellectual, and scientific endeavor. The world spoke of Germany as a nation of Dichter and Denker. This image was sparked by the many literary contributions of Johann Wolfgang von Goethe, Friedrich von Schiller, and the Grimm brothers; the historical works of Niebuhr and Ranke; the philosophical studies of W. F. Hegel, Immanuel Kant, F. Nietzsche, Arthur Schopenhauer, Marx and Engels; the achievements in science and mathematics by Max Plank, R. W. Bunsen, Robert Koch, William von Leibnitz, R. Roentgen, Alexander von Humboldt, and K. F.

Gauss; and the magnificent musical compositions of J. S. Bach, F. J. Haydn, Beethoven, Mozart, the Strausses, von Webber, Felix Mendelssohn, Friedrich Haendel, Franz Schubert, and Richard Wagner, as well as Hermann Hesse, Carl Zeiss, Max Weber, Werner von Siemens, Wilhelm von Humboldt, Carl von Clausewitz, Carl Friedrich Benz, Mayer Amschel Rothschild, and so, so many more.

While Germany was militarily and politically weak, its intellectual achievements and accomplishments blossomed. Claudia Schiffer, Germany's supermodel, stated, during the World Soccer Cup in 2006, that for the last hundred years or so, six out of ten new inventions came from Germany. Included among them are the motor car, aviation technology, aspirin, x-rays, space travel and exploration tools, Doppler radar to predict our ever-changing weather, women's bras, and so many other inventions that make our lives ever more comfortable.

Roentgen discovered the x-rays in 1885, which opened the door to the human body. Rudolf Virchov, a pathologist and advocate for underground city sewage systems, performed the first successful heart operation in Berlin. Street and oil lights were replaced by electric lights. The world's first airline was established on January 13, 1917, with service between Berlin and Weimar, Hamburg, and Amsterdam. In 1926, *die Deutsche Luft Reederei* merged with *Junkers* Airline and became the still flying *Lufthansa*. Germany built the first helicopter, which was flown by Hannah Reitsch. Television and video are German inventions. And the list goes on and on.

Most Americans welcomed Germany's achievements as a triumph for progress, liberty, and civilization. Germans were regarded as models of progress, and their work ethic was truly respected worldwide. On the twenty-fifth anniversary of Wilhelm II's ascension to the throne, distinguished Americans, such as William Howard Taft and Theodore Roosevelt, showered praises on the German monarch. Even the *New York Times* chimed in with praise. On June 8, 1913, President Taft called Kaiser Wilhelm II the world's greatest single force for peace.

America was first settled by Europeans who wanted to exchange the hatred, the persecutions, the intrigues, and the religious, political, and economic struggles for the promise of individual liberty and unlimited opportunities. They were willing to pay the ultimate price so that we could enjoy our freedom and independence. The final resting place for many German American heroes is Arlington Cemetery. We won our independence from England while she was at war with France. German Americans overwhelmingly supported our fight for independence, unlike the English Tories. The same nationalities that were fighting each other in Europe found the path to living peacefully and harmoniously together. They respected each other's colorful heritage, married each other, and formed a new nation, founded upon human dignity, tolerance, and liberties.

For good reason, our founding fathers warned us against becoming involved in perpetually changing European alliances and intrigues. We established the Monroe Doctrine. For over a hundred years, we maintained neutrality. We did not get involved in other nations fighting among themselves. Then, in 1917, America became restless and entered the European theater of war on England's side. Why England's and not Germany's side? The kaiser was hailed as a pillar of peace, and during his entire reign as emperor, until 1914, was not involved in even a single war, while England and France were engaged in numerous wars. In the United States, there were more Americans of German than of English descent. Why go to war at all, unless our national security is being challenged, which it was not?

As the twentieth century approached, ominous dark clouds of war began to gather again on the European horizon. The sounds of war drums and with them the media propaganda became increasingly louder, like an approaching hurricane. That friendly and cooperative climate that had existed thus far was about to change catastrophically. Within a year, Kaiser Wilhelm II was accused of being "the beast of Berlin." The combined collaboration of historians and journalists were about to produce the first great triumph of the art of modern war propaganda, unlike the world has ever seen. Even the devious Lord Bryce of England eagerly lent his name to the veracity of British anti-German propaganda and lies. He spent days and nights fabricating vicious lies about Germany and the kaiser.

Nations do not start wars. Wars are initiated by individuals. How and why did America, a shining beacon of hope and peace, allow itself to be dragged into the European theater of war, especially since the majority of Americans were strongly opposed to us fighting in a European war? To what extent was the ruling elite in America willing, even eager, to participate in the war, and why did President Wilson push the United States into a world war?

There are two motivators for human action, the mercenary and the spiritual, the greed for material gain and the hope for heavenly blessings. Without the spoils of war, war would not be profitable. The driving and primary causes for the Anglo-German estrangement was Germany's astonishing industrial and commercial growth, becoming a serious industrial and economic competitor to England's coal and steel supremacy prior to World War I. In addition, Kaiser Wilhelm II had the audacity of starting the construction of a railroad from Berlin to Istanbul. Wilhelm II suffered from a severe case of an inferiority complex. England sent its navy to that part of the world, under the command of Winston Churchill, to stop the construction and to teach the Germans a lesson, engaging in such an enterprise without Great Britain's permission and blessing. The English navy was soundly defeated. The economic consequence of Germany's growth became England's obsession to stop it, and her only solution was war. England began to weave together a network of alliances, as she has done for centuries. Wars are not acts of God, but a total absence of human wisdom and human compassion.

Kaiser Wilhelm II was the eldest grandson of Queen Victoria. He was ever so proud of his British relatives and cognizant that British royalty was German. Queen Victoria passed away in his arms, and he walked proudly behind her casket dressed in his royal British uniform and not as Germany's monarch. He was mistakenly determined to avoid war with England at all cost. Tragically, Churchill did not share his sentiments. Winston Churchill was determined to leave an indelible mark upon history, and so he did. Kaiser Wilhelm II was not and did not prepare for war. He did everything to avoid war especially against his English relatives. The German government made great efforts to maintain peace with its neighbors, while London was procuring secret agreements for war with France, Russia, and the United States.

The kaiser's unwillingness or inability to accurately diagnose the political climate surrounding Germany and take the possibility of war with England more seriously was Germany's tragic loss. The kaiser could have done much to prevent England from encircling Germany. Obviously, Churchill and his Allies did not share the kaiser's amicable, naïve sentiments. Churchill was determined to go to war and leave his mark upon history. Germany was not and did not prepare for war. Kaiser Wilhelm II did everything he could to avoid war, especially against his English relatives. Germany was industrially and commercially very successful; war would only disrupt Germany's success and prosperity. Tragically, that is precisely what Churchill and the English elite wanted to accomplish.

German bankers, merchants, and manufacturers did not want war. They were commercially very successful and knew that a war would only spoil their success. Churchill's strategy was to interfere in Germany's success. He did everything he could to start a war and interfere in Germany's prosperity. For England, World War I was not a war of necessity but of choice. Britain resented the rise of Germany and feared her preeminence in Europe and a possible eclipse of Britain as an economic world power. England wanted to eliminate Germany as a competitor in the global marketplace. Winston Churchill demonstrated a strange affinity and attraction to war; he visualized himself as a driving force in "this glorious delicious war" and as some kind of a Greek god of war.

At the beginning of the twentieth century, Europe was at the peak of her power. Europe ruled the world. Tragically, Britain, France, Germany, Portugal, Russia, Spain, and the other countries could not get along for any length of time. Their big national egos got in the way. They were constantly in competition with each other, engaged in empire building and accumulating wealth and power rather than being engaged in any meaningful tolerance and cooperation that would have been mutually beneficial in the long run. When egos get in the way, as they too often do, all meaningful cooperation flies out the window.

The British media, ever supersensitive to the wishes of its government, quickly adjusted to this new state of affairs. What is remarkable is that this reversal was suddenly also reflected in the American media, as if we were still an English colony and taking orders from bloody old England. On August 5, 1914, the British navy engaged in an act of war and dredged up and cut the German cables, stopping all news and information from Berlin and Vienna. This gave England complete control to spoon-feed the American news media. That gave England an uninhibited domain to generate an effective and powerful propaganda operation with virtually no opposition and high levels of British-government control in our internal affairs.

The media is all too often not neutral, especially in times of war. It displays a tendency to cater to the wishes of the major advertising money sources. With only very few exceptions, most, not all, of the newspapers were pro-war and pro–Anglo-Saxon. Most were significantly influenced by English propaganda, and many were heavily subsidized by Allied money. As always, follow the money trail to get to the source of the problem, England supplied all American newspapers with sensational "war news" material that was always favorable to England's point of view. England has always been better at generating gruesome propaganda than Germany. For the Germans, the means does not justify the end; the Germans always have to check the validity and accuracy of their sources. Lord Northcliffe observed that Americans proved more gullible than any other people. He referred to Americans as "a bunch of sheep."

Britain attacked Germany for three reasons: 1) to down her navy before it got any larger, 2) to capture her trade, and 3) to take her colonies. These were mere economic reasons. However, not all English were in favor of another war; there were many resisters. There were demonstrators in England, telling the working people to unite with their German counterparts and not have workers fighting and killing workers. These demonstrations were forcefully put down, and many demonstrators were jailed. Seventy-five hundred conscientious objectors were jailed in America, and others were imprisoned for merely speaking out against the war. Eugene V. Debs spent over two years behind bars in dear old England for urging men to resist the draft. At the Green Corn Rebellion in 1917, three were killed and five hundred were arrested. That was just so much for the British version of "freedom of expression."

The best organized resistance movement was in the United Kingdom because many Englishmen felt that their country should mind its own business. Keir Hardie addressed a crowd in London, frustrated that working men were fighting one another rather than fighting for their rights. Needless to say, there are no monuments in London or anywhere else honoring opponents to either war, nor does the media sing their praises. The Seventh Commandment still states, "Thou shall not kill," and in civilized societies, murder is still a crime. Does a uniform provide immunity?

In order to comprehend the various forces pushing for war, it is critical to understand how propaganda works, fueled by big money and special interests. Will Rogers stated that we have the best government that money can buy.

Propaganda is like a sales promotion or the promotion to vote for a certain political candidate or party, the central and critical driving force in manipulating the masses, while filling them with noble emotions of patriotism and heroism and also getting them to take "ownership" of the cause. The media removed all questions of any special financial interests being involved behind the scene and gave the public the impression that the honor of the nation or the empire was identical with the interests of the average steel or factory worker. The media has performed well in brainwashing the masses as it allowed itself to be manipulated by big money. Therefore, whoever controls the media can control the democratic will of the masses. It needs to be pointed out that none of the emperors wanted war but were powerless in the face of a huge and well-funded bureaucracy and a media blitz pushing for war.

A massive amount of historical revisionism was produced during World War I and even more during World War II. Our histories were completely revised, claiming that Germany had always been America's enemy and that Germany started the war in 1914; it even started the Franco-Prussian War in 1870. The revisionists even went so far as to claim that in our Revolutionary War (War of Independence from Britain) we were not fighting the British but the Hessians. These are bold-faced lies. British propaganda knew no limits. The historical truth is that until 1914, the German army never fought a war against England or the United States. Britain, on the other hand, was engaged militarily against America repeatedly. America's Civil War was fueled financially by London and Paris. During the preceding one hundred years, Germany was engaged in far fewer military conflicts than either England or France. During that period, Britain was involved in ten wars, Russia in seven, France in five, Austria-Hungary in three, and Germany in three. Since the end of World War II, the United States has been involved in some hundred smaller and larger military conflicts.

There are two ways to have the biggest and tallest building in the community. One way is to build it yourself the old-fashioned way, and the other is to destroy everything around and level it to the ground. England has historically chosen the latter; the end justified the means. For the kaiser and for the German people, the means was as important as the end. England has consistently been prepared and ready to maintain her empire and her world power at all cost.

England wanted to eliminate Germany as an industrial and commercial rival and prevent any possibility of becoming a world power in the future ever again. England's jealousy of Germany's industrial and commercial success gave rise to her provocative attitude toward Germany. She was determined to break up the economic Axis alliance on the continent and thereby increase her own influence and power on the continent and beyond. In 1912, Churchill stated that "it has been England's policy for four hundred years to oppose the strongest power in Europe by weaving together a combination of other countries strong enough to face the bully." For centuries, England cleverly played all powers against each other to her advantage, thus remaining the first and foremost power.

Until 1914, the world politics was orchestrated by the five power states. England was leading the way by controlling 22 percent of the globe, followed by France, Germany, Russia, and Austria-Hungary. Those five countries controlled 80 percent of the world and 60 percent of the world population. Britain, France, Russia, and Austria were not nation states but empires of long standing. An empire's primary mission is to expand its domain and power and increase its wealth and influence.

Britain's big world chess game involved having Germany fight against Russia. England would eliminate her two strongest advancing competitors. Russia and England had very little in common and were vehement enemies for most of their history. To persuade Russia to England's side, Russia was infiltrated with false Russian patriots. Germany fighting Russia would solve two problems simultaneously. The British strategy was to do away with the czar and annex Russia's resources before Germany could. Germany and Russia were natural allies. Germany's and Russia's economic growth during the preceding two decades was about 10 percent annually. From England's point of view, a victory of both Germany and Russia was totally unacceptable, so she did everything in her power to prevent that. For centuries, British policy was to divide, conquer, and rule, and whenever possible, persuade others to do her fighting.

One of England's strongest weapons was her superior ability to create massive amounts of propaganda, horrendous monster stories, fueling hatred toward Germans. For Churchill and for England, the end always appeared to justify the means. The Nobel Peace Prize laureate and great humanitarian Dr. Albert Schweitzer warned that the escalating climate of hostility of some of the European nations, especially England and France, would lead to a catastrophe. He begged the nations to change course and avoid war. His request was arrogantly ignored, and the hostilities toward Germany increased. The French incarcerated him as a German spy, which, of course, he was not. Schweitzer was a theologian, the greatest authority on J. S. Bach, a physician, and a humanitarian, but he was not a politician.

Most of these same seductive propaganda strategies were again employed very effectively during World War II. Revising intellectual history and fabricating lies proved to be a gold mine for propaganda purposes. Arthur Ponsonby, a member of the British Parliament, privileged to British classified information, wrote an authoritative book Falsehood in *Wartime—Propaganda Lies of the First World War*. It was first published in 1928 in London. Kommt der Krieg ins Land, gibt es Luegen wie Sand. The first casualty of war was and always has been truth. Transparency remains a very vital ingredient to peace, as it will also motivate toward negotiations rather than war. Success in war, like charity in religion, covers a multitude of sins. Thus far, no authoritative document like Arthur Ponsonby's, discussing war propaganda, has thus far appeared after World War II.

Ponsonby presents a devastating indictment of the way British and Allied politicians and journalists deceived and fraudulently lied to incite the public to war and saturated them with hate, enough hate to commit murder. In war, every country uses propaganda deliberately to deceive its own people and mislead the enemy. The public, unable or unwilling to establish the truth, is usually unaware that it is being misled and manipulated. Such deceptions should not be regarded lightly, especially in a democratic and civilized society such as ours.

Prior to 1914, Germany had not gone to war in forty-three years. Kaiser Wilhelm II had never gone to war and the German army had never fought the English or the Americans, and yet Churchill did his utmost to save the world from Prussian militarism. That was the same Prussia that supported our young nation in our struggle for independence from bloody old England's oppression and exploitation. Churchill called the kaiser a "continental tyrant" whose goal was nothing less than "the domination of the world." Churchill intentionally confused England's role and ambitions in the world with those of Germany. Political candidates are not the only ones who use falsehoods to attack and discredit their opponents. The fact remains the kaiser did not want war with England or anyone else.

The kaiser was a coward and not a military monster; he avoided war every way possible. The fact remains Kaiser Wilhelm II and the German elite did not want war with England or anyone else. War was skillfully forced upon them. The French historian Philippe Simonet wrote, "Germany did not want war and it did not start the war." He said, "Nein, Deutschland war nicht schuldig."

It is a significant and far-reaching fact that if Britain had not declared war on Germany in 1914, there would have been no Versailles Treaties, no Lenin, no Stalin, no Mussolini, no Hitler and no World War II. The world would be different, and England might still be an empire. Often, wars are not what they appear to be; often, they are a sideshow to something else. Millions of lives would not have been sacrificed on the altar of war, profit, and greed. The world would be a better place if America would have stayed strictly neutral and never turned the European conflict into a world war. Wilson, however, could be blackmailed, and he was also obligated to the banks who bankrolled his election. As an obligation to the banks, he reestablished the Federal Reserve Bank.

World War I destroyed the German, Austro-Hungarian, and Russian Empires and ultimately the British. Why did

Britain declare war on Germany twice? The root cause of all the catastrophic destruction of the twentieth century ultimately leads back to Churchill and World War I. Churchill had a tragic anti-German obsession. In his memoirs, Randall Churchill explains how his father, Winston Churchill, was going to win the war by dragging the United States into the war, not once, but twice.

What is rather remarkable is that the British negative and sinister portrayal of Germans was also strongly reflected in the American media as well. Any semblance of balance in our news reporting suddenly disappeared. The poisonous venom dispersed like an epidemic. There were only negative portrayals of Germans, positive images no longer existed. There was no balance in the media. Now Germans were represented as mindless, burr-headed, heel-clicking, mono-clad robots, possessing no human qualities whatsoever. They suddenly became militaristic, aggressive, and authoritarian, bent on conquering the world. World War I bond posters depicted German faces as monsters, far worse and sinister than present-day caricatures of Arab faces. According to the media, Germans have been that way since the beginning of time, and furthermore, they started every war since time immemorial. Unfortunately, all this propaganda did have an extreme negative effect on the way many Americans now looked at and saw their German-American neighbors.

Monster stories were created to build hatred against the Germans. Unfortunately, Americans proved all too susceptible to sinister British propaganda. It is now common knowledge that the sinking of the *Lusitania* was a calculated risk by Winston Churchill to drag the United States into the European war. Contrary to the law for passenger ships, the ship was armed and carried a cargo of US war supplies of four thousand cases of bullets and explosives. Divers found the *Lusitania* and its military cargo on the ocean floor. Pro-English and

Allied propaganda has been vigorously denying and unwilling to accept the obvious truth. The ship's list of its cargo has been sanitized: artillery shells became "castings," aircraft engines became "machine components," and ammunition became "metallic packages."

The British cover-up and deception has persisted. In light of overwhelming evidence to the contrary, successive English governments have stood firm that there was no contraband on board the *Lusitania*. The fact that different research teams have found its cargo consisting of ammunition and other high explosives in the wreck may ultimately become not only a huge embarrassment but also literally blow up in their faces. The customs collector for the Port of New York entered in the ledger: "Practically all her cargo was contraband of some kind." That is likely why President Wilson refused to send the collector's report to Britain as evidence in the court of inquiry; he was not about to incriminate himself.

Furthermore, US Senator Robert La Follette reported, "Four days before the Lusitania sailed, President Wilson was warned in person by Secretary of State Bryan that the Lusitania had 6 million rounds of ammunition on board, besides explosives." Tragically, Wilson was not giving but receiving orders; he was being blackmailed.

A warning appeared in the *New York Times* on May 1, 1915, signed by the "Imperial German Embassy, Washington, D.C." directly beneath the Cunard Line's notice announcing the sailing of the British-flagged ship *Lusitania*.

> Travelers intending to embark on the Atlantic voyage are reminded that a state of war exists between Germany and Great Britain and her allies; that the zone of war includes the waters adjacent to the British Isles; that, in accordance

with the formal notice given by the Imperial
German government, vessels flying the flag of
Great Britain, or any of its allies, are liable to
destruction in these waters and the travelers
sailing in the war zone on ships of Great Britain
or her allies do so at their own risk.

It should be remembered that the U.S. was still not
"officially" at war.

William Jennings Bryan resigned shortly thereafter. He
later wrote, "A ship carrying contraband should not rely on
passengers to protect her from attack. It would be like putting
women and children in front of the army." Tragically, Wilson
failed to warn Americans of the dangers of traveling on the
Lusitania. That would have spoiled Churchill's plan to trick the
United States into the war. A copy of her secret cargo was found
years later in FDR's private papers. FDR's son Elliott stated
that his father was deeply committed to getting the United
States involved in World War I. At the time, FDR was assistant
secretary of the navy.

The question has been raised: Was there a cover-up by the
British and American governments to suppress the facts in this
treacherous and treasonous act? The records show that the
Lusitania was modified in 1913 to specifications mandated
by the Royal Navy so it could be functional as a navy warship.
Its twelve-inch guns were hidden in recessed areas of the deck
from which they could be elevated for military action. The
secret cargo manifest for the *Lusitania*'s last voyage lists fifty-
one tons of artillery shells, over four million rifle cartridges,
and six hundred tons of a type of gun-cotton that was prone to
detonate spontaneously when it came in contact with seawater.
Reports have described a heavy detonation followed by a strong
explosion cloud that came from within the ship.

Despite the warnings not to travel on British vessels, 123 Americans sailed on the *Lusitania*. In New York, a new captain, William Thomas Turner, was placed in charge of the return trip. Noteworthy is the fact that after his rescue, Captain Turner was met by Churchill and taken directly to king George V and knighted for his service on the return trip of the *Lusitania*. Churchill calculated that the destruction of a British ship with American passengers aboard would inflame American passions against Germany and help create a political climate for coming into the war. History proved him to be right; this fraudulent deception worked. It took two more years before Wilson could persuade Congress to declare war on Germany. The Allied media failed to provide actual and balanced reporting concerning these events.

Lord Mersey was put in charge of an official inquiry into the sinking of the *Lusitania*. It was not an investigation but a cover-up. He was instructed by Churchill, who was first lord of the admiralty, to place the entire blame on Captain Turner. Lord Mersey obeyed his orders but refused payment for his services. He also declined to accept further judicial assignments. In later years, he said the affair "was a damn dirty business."

The sinking of the *Lusitania* in 1915 was cunningly packaged and became exceedingly effective propaganda. British and American media condemned those German "Hun barbarians" for such sinister acts and used it to demonstrate for the Americans that Germans had an innate contempt for the most elementary principle of decency and humanity. Our media paid no attention to the charges that Winston Churchill used it as bait to bring America into the war. With the sinking of the *Lusitania*, the American media, fueled with British sources, demanded that the United States declare war on Germany at once.

The sunken *Lusitania* has been searched and explored several times. In the 1950s, it was explored by American scuba divers. In 1982, underwater photographs were taken, and in 1993, a submersible research vessel examined the wreck of the *Lusitania*. They all confirmed a massive explosion originating inside the ship. There is conclusive evidence that the second massive explosion was not caused by a German torpedo. When will London admit to its deceptions and its guilt?

What is rather disturbing is the appearance that the passengers on the *Lusitania* were the sacrificial lambs in hopes that the deaths of American passengers would stampede Americans into the war against Germany. These victims demand and deserve nothing less than an in-depth international investigation. The least that these victims deserve is that justice be served.

Edvard Mandel House was the man who secured Woodrow Wilson's nomination for president and who, thereafter, became the hidden power at the White House. He negotiated a secret agreement to draw the United States into the war, while, at the same time, Wilson was campaigning on the promise to keep America out of the war. "Who keeps us out of war?" was one of Wilson's campaign slogans in 1916. For that reason, German Americans, misguided, voted overwhelmingly for Wilson. Wilson was again elected president on the false promise of no war. On April 2, 1917, Wilson asked Congress to declare war on Germany. A few days later, Congress passed the Draft Act. German Americans were betrayed by President Wilson; he spoke with a forked tongue.

While in England, Edvard M. House was asked, "Colonel, what will America do if the Germans sink the *Lusitania*?"

He responded, "I believe that flame of indignation would sweep the United States, and by itself would be sufficient to carry us into the war."

Allegations of monstrous stories saturated every venue in Hollywood and the entire media. It was reported as fact that the most scandalous, monstrous, and outrageous acts were committed by this new breed of Germans. What was not mentioned is the fact that Britain was waging unrestricted submarine warfare, sinking unarmed Swedish, Norwegian, and German merchant ships.

Woodrow Wilson professed to be neutral, but his actions were anything but neutral. Our secret shipments of munitions to England were increasing, and he also ordered the sinking of German ships, long before we officially declared war on Germany. Secretary of State Bryan was so outraged that he resigned from his office because Wilson did not maintain neutrality, as he promised while campaigning and totally ignored all requests to stay out of the war. There were powerful special interests lobbying for war, such as the banks and the war-production industry. Was Wilson being blackmailed and pressured to go to war? Decades later, President Dwight D. Eisenhower warned us of the dangers of such powerful special interest groups.

On May 17, 1915, the *Lusitania* was entering the most dangerous part of her voyage. German U-boats had been effectively targeting Allied shipping in the North Atlantic. Captain William Turner, who was assigned the responsibility of the return trip, instead of speeding up, slowed the *Lusitania* down considerably, making her an even easier target. Captain Walter Schwiger of the German submarine U-20 saw a huge four-stacked ship in his periscope. He fired his last torpedo. It struck *Lusitania* at midship. Because of the huge amount of contraband on ship, there was a second and larger explosion. The *Lusitania* sank in eighteen minutes. Of the 1,959 passengers, 1,195 went with her to the bottom of the sea, including 123 Americans. Captain Turner miraculously was one of the survivors. In this case, the captain did not go down with his ship.

Coincidentally, on May 11 and 12, 1915, the week following the sinking of the *Lusitania*, the notorious Bryce Report on alleged German atrocities was front and center in our media. This was sensationalized front-page news. This fabricated report would have been totally unnecessary if Wilson had no intentions of going to war. The report fueled American indignation at Germany and German Americans. In addition, both British and American scholars displayed an astute willingness to write vicious propaganda. Germany was depicted as an incurable militaristic villain and Britain as an antimilitaristic virtual saint. Nothing could have been further from the truth. That is the nature and power of propaganda. Its perpetuation will make wartime propaganda permanent history, at least for a while.

Perhaps the most damaging wartime propaganda was that of Henry Morgenthau claiming that the kaiser, along with his top bankers, diplomats, military leaders, and German industrialists decided to go to war at a secret crown conference held at Potsdam on July 5, 1914. However, there was one major problem with this deceptive and fake news, which was not verified for its accuracy. Most of the individuals that supposedly were at this conference were later proven to be somewhere else. Such a crown conference never happened. Yet, this outrageous fabrication became sole justification for Article 231 of the Versailles Peace Treaty, the notorious sole German "war guilt clause." Sadly, the truth was denied and might was turned into right.

The English people did not know until August 3, 1914, in case of war with Germany, that England was under a military and naval secret agreement with France, dating to 1906. The Franco-Russian military alliance carried with it a contingent liability. If Russia went to war with Germany, France was committed and, therefore, England was committed as well. The statements of English politicians for public consumption were one thing, and the reality established by these secret agreements was something altogether different. Americans were mostly kept in the dark about European international relations; what we knew was mostly fueled by propaganda. Americans were persuaded to come to the aid of a defenseless Europe.

Politicians never lie just for the fun of it; their margin of truth is always so narrow that they keep within it when they can. Lloyd George stated on March 3, 1921, in the House of Commons, "For the Allies, German responsibility for the war is fundamental. It is the basis upon which the structure of the treaty of Versailles has been erected, and if that acknowledgement is repudiated or abandoned, the treaty is destroyed … German responsibility for the war must be treated by the Allies as a chose jugee."

The Versailles Treaty is based upon the unique and erroneous theory of a single guilty nation, which is contrary to all the known facts. Furthermore, if that theory were true, there would be no difficulty in establishing what the war was fought over. The theory claims a German plot against the peace of the world; that is a preposterous claim.

On February 18, 1905, the Belgian minister said in Berlin,

> The real cause of the English hatred of Germany is the jealousy aroused by the astonishing development of Germany's merchant navy and of her commerce and manufacturers. This hatred will last until the English have thoroughly learned to understand that the world's trade is not by right an exclusively English monopoly.

England found the means to her end when she drew France into her alliance. She would bring about a war that would annihilate Germany's navy, her merchant fleet, and her foreign commerce.

Russia communicated with London, requesting, "The English Government could render us a substantial service if it would agree to send a sufficient number of boats to our Baltic ports to compensate for our lack of means of transport, before the beginning of the war operations."

This statement is very damaging to the claim of an "unprepared and unsuspecting Europe" and the "sole guilt" of one nation. Those English boats were there, prompt to the minute, empty, ready, and waiting. Furthermore, the Russian staff in London was instructed to exercise great caution in talking about the landing in Pomerania or about the dispatch of English boats to the Russian Baltic ports before the outbreak of the war. This was two weeks before the assassinations in Sarajevo.

Historically, we have trusted our media to report nothing but the whole truth, thereby providing us with a balanced report, reporting both sides of the story honestly and objectively. Sadly, that did not happen. The media told us about German soldiers amusing themselves by cutting off the hands of Belgian babies and amputating the breasts of Belgian women out of sheer viciousness. Several teams from the United States went to investigate the validity of these stories and found none of these monster stories to be true. They found no nuns that had been raped, children whose hands were cut off, women whose breasts were cut off, or any German soldiers parading with Belgian children on their bayonets. These reports were to inform the American people that these monster stories were pure fabrications and had no validity, but no one was willing to listen, especially President Woodrow Wilson and the media.

These repulsive fabrications had their desired effect. Atrocity propaganda became an exact science. In addition, Wilson prohibited all antiwar demonstrations, fueling much of the anti-German sentiment. He claimed that all Americans supported his war efforts and even outlawed praying for peace, stating, "Woe to the man or group of men that stand in our way." Wilson made it known to the nation that anyone publicly talking peace or even praying that the war with Germany would end soon, other than with the Reich's surrender, was a traitor to our nation and our cause. Philippe Simonnet stated that Wilson saw himself as one of the great saviors of Western civilization, comparing himself to Charlemagne, Joan of Orleans, and even Jesus of Nazareth.

The *Manchester Guardian* reported that Wilson and his second wife, Edith Galt, had always been sympathetic to the Anglo-Saxons and wanted to force America into the war on England's side as soon as circumstances would permit. His personal view was completely Anglo-Saxon, with little or no knowledge or appreciation of German culture and institutions or of German-American contributions and heritage.

Wilson broke American neutrality and ultimately forced us into the European military conflict, against the expressed wishes of the great majority of the American people, some 90 percent. He turned a European conflict into a world war. Furthermore, Wilson enforced a different set of policies toward England and the Allies than toward Germany. England violated American neutrality rights far more fragrantly between 1914 and 1917 than she did even before the War of 1812, when she acted as if we were still one of her many colonies, even flying the American flag on her ships. Wilson demonstratively condoned and encouraged England's defiant, confrontational actions.

Thomas W. Gregory shared a rebuke that Wilson administered to cabinet members who protested over the flagrant English violations, stating "that the ordinary rules of conduct had no application to the situation; that the Allies were standing with their backs to the wall, fighting wild beasts; that he would permit nothing to be done to hinder or embarrass them in the prosecution of the war … and that this policy must be understood as settled." That was the sum total of Wilson's neutrality.

Secretary of State William Jennings Bryan, a true man of peace and a patriot, protested against Wilson's unfair, void of any neutrality, and discriminatory policies. He resigned in protest and total disgust. Lansing, who replaced him, admitted in his memoirs that they made absolutely no attempt to hold England accountable for her many international infractions. He wrote that in 1917 we had better reasons and legal grounds for fighting England than Germany. Wilson's skewed policies greatly contributed to and perpetuated the brutal English starvation blockade. As a direct consequence of the blockade, more than one and a half million people in Germany, Austria, and Hungary were starved to death. Wilson could have voiced some objections, but he chose to remain totally silent.

In April 1916, Wilson called a meeting to sound out Speaker Champ Clark of the House of Representatives and congressional leaders Claude Kitchen and H. D. Floyd and see if they would support him in a plan to bring America into the war. This meeting is referred to as the "Sunrise Conference." These honorable men sharply disagreed and refused to have any part of Wilson's devious, deceptive, and fraudulent plan, bordering on being treasonous. Wilson could ill afford to split the Democratic Party over entering the war, after he was elected on the platform of staying out of the war. Wilson had to settle on getting the country into the war after the election.

A year prior to the Democratic Convention, Wilson sent Colonel House to dear old England requesting, "The United States would like Great Britain to do whatever would help the United States to aid the Allies." House reported from England that "whenever England consents, France and Russia will close in on Germany." He also stressed that the kaiser did not want war; he wanted peace. McMeekin described the situation thus: "The Germans went into it kicking and screaming as the Austria noose snapped shut around their necks." House further observed that George V of England was "the most pugnacious monarch loose in these parts."

Wilson was astutely aware that the sentiments of the country were overwhelming for peace and America staying out of the war. Thus, he and Colonel House, who was the hidden power behind Wilson, sent Governor Martin Glynn of New York and Senator Ollie James of Kentucky to the Democratic Convention at St. Louis in June 1916 with explicit instructions to emphasize in all the keynote speeches Wilson's heroic effort to keep us out of war, coining the slogan, "He kept us out of war." This fraudulent deception secured Wilson's reelection. Wilson cunningly never promised that he would keep us out of war. He deceptively ran a platform of peace but was a man of war. We were not at war until Wilson deceptively forced us into a war and turned it into a world war.

The election of 1916 was a referendum on war; the American people voted overwhelming against war. Wilson, however, had an obligation to the bankers who bankrolled his election, and they were pushing for war. Tragically, the referendum and the democratic will of the people did not keep us out of the war. Wilson had an obligation to the bankers who bankrolled his election; they visualized big profits and pushed for war. In 1916, the feuding countries in Europe were tired and exhausted and ready to stop fighting, but then Wilson sent more money and fresh new troops to the European battle field. He sent enough money for armaments and fresh soldiers for the bloody war to grind on for another two years and many more young men and women to die needlessly. American soldiers were brainwashed and saturated with propaganda of going to war "to make the world safe for democracy," while ignoring the contradiction that bloody old England and France were denying the people in all their colonies in Asia and Africa the right to vote and self-determination.

England's situation in 1916 was desperate. German troops occupied much of France and Belgium, Italy was suffering under the Austro-Hungarian military assault, the Russian giant was crumbling, and the French army was rioting. During the first two years, the fortunes of war were against England and her allies. In 1916, the English War Cabinet began discussing accepting the German offer for a negotiated peace on the basis of the "status quo ante," returning to the status that existed before the war. No one would gain or lose territory nor any economic or political rights. All that happened before Wilson's American blood transfusion in the form of money, men, and military hardware. The armistice in discussion did not happen; it is always important to follow the money trail to find the reason.

Wilson promoted financial credits to England and the Allies for the sole purpose of purchasing American military armament and munitions on a huge scale. Wilson and House bear the primary responsibility for the continuation of the bloodshed in Europe. The bankers were pulling in huge profits. The influence of the bankers in Wilson's presidency has been discussed in Ray Stannard Baker's book *Life and Letters of Woodrow Wilson* and in Professor C. C. Tansill's book *America Goes to War.*

Wilson spoke with a forked tongue; his rhetoric and his actions contradicted each other. He spoke of peace and deceptively forced America into war. He reasoned that Americans could be sold on the deception that he did his very best to "keep us out of war." He calculated that one way or another he would have a united country behind him ready to go to war, in spite of the referendum and the expressed wishes of the American people. He somehow rationalized his stand for war on a moral purpose, based on fabrications and deceptive propaganda, which were totally void of substance. The media served his purposes well. And he surrounded himself with cabinet members who were intensely pro-English like himself. It served Wilson's purposes to publicly accept Bryce's deceptive fabricated lies and propaganda as truth. It has been stated that all is fair in love and war; Wilson took it to extremes.

Cecilia Odorfer remembered a painful experience during a Christmas Mass in a church in Queens, New York. During the religious service in 1917, the pastor invited the congregation to pray for peace on earth and goodwill to all men, as it has been customary for centuries, when suddenly no less than fifty churchgoers jumped from their seats and attacked the elderly priest. They obviously went to church for all the right reasons. Fortunately, an equal number of parishioners restrained them from harming the priest and they also were able to reestablish peace and order in the church. In a short time, several hundred protesters gathered in front of the church shouting anti-German slogans and threatening the priest. It took the mounted police to break up this angry mob. On many other occasions, the police were not present to restrain the mob, and the hysteria took its ugly course. By definition, a mob is a group of many individuals without intellect.

The media kept portraying Germans as antidemocratic and anti-Western. Furthermore, they spoke a "guttural language," conveniently ignoring the fact that English is a Germanic language. Even German breeds of dogs were not safe from this acute case of German phobia. Imagine the hysteria that was fermented in Columbus, Ohio, when mobs invaded private homes and stole hundreds of Dachshunds, German shepherds, Schnauzers, and other German breeds from their loving owners. After killing the dogs, these offenders buried them in Schiller Park. After this criminal behavior, the name of the park was changed to Freedom Park. Today, the park is again known as Schiller Park and part of German Village. No one was ever held accountable for these and other criminal acts.

It is not difficult to see why Americans were easily sold on the propaganda that Germany, and Germany alone, had provoked the war and was the only one guilty of all war crimes. After the United States declared war against Germany on April 2, 1917, anti-German hysteria swept through our entire country like a wildfire. Just like England, Australia, and Canada, the United States swiftly developed a serious case of German-phobia. This hysteria reached such intensity that many states passed legislation banning German in schools and public gatherings. Throughout America, German language newspapers were closed and music by German masters banned. Even church services in German were verboten, and telephone conversations were monitored. Their personal liberties were severely violated. Lady Liberty totally turned her back on Americans of German descent. They were no longer allowed to pray to God in German, as if God no longer accepted His children speaking to Him in German. Honoring their German language and heritage made them extremely suspect and justified incarceration. The minister at the Immanuel Lutheran Church in Cleveland, Ohio, was put in jail for continuing the religious services in German and defying presidential orders not to sing German hymns, such as "A Mighty Fortress Is Our God" and "Stille Nacht (Silent Night)." This constituted criminal persecution against the largest ethnic group in America.

The British succeeded in dragging the United States into the war. They also succeeded in unleashing an acute hysteria against all things German. In some segments of our media and cyberspace, there are still fragments of this poisonous venom that needs to be eradicated from our civilized society forever. There should be serious concern about our freedom and liberties; if these human rights violations happened to the largest ethnic group in America, they can happen to any group.

The bloodiest battle of the war, which was a series of battles, occurred after the United States entered the war. It is generally referred to as the Hundred Days Offensive and occurred at the end of the war. The Allies launched a series of attacks on the western front from August 8 to November 11, 1918. It began with the battle of Amiens, a surprise attack consisting of a large fleet of tanks. During the slaughter, the Central Powers lost 785,733 killed or wounded and many taken prisoners, for a total of 1,172,075. France lost 531,000, England 411,636, and the United States 127,000, for a total of 1,070,000 human beings. The media referred to them, rather impersonally, as casualties.

Could anything have been more senseless than World War I? There was no real compelling cause or reason; to "make the world safe for democracy" sounds so shallow and empty, especially for the millions who lost a loved one. To claim that the assassination in Sarajevo caused the war is total nonsense. Germany tried to keep the conflict localized, which the Allies used as an excuse. Countries that had the most in common ended up fighting each other. The best of European manhood ended up either dead or maimed. These great Europeans even had the great "Christmas Truce," in 1914, where good men on both sides laid down their weapons to celebrate the real meaning of Christmas.

Wilson's indiscretions and the love affair with Mrs. Mary Hulbert Peck were kept off the radar during his tenure as governor and then as president. Mrs. Peck went to a New York lawyer, Samuel Untermeyer, to intervene on her behalf, demanding $30,000 in return for Wilson's many love letters. Untermeyer contacted Wilson and told him that Mrs. Peck demanded $250,000 for his incriminating letters. A week later, Wilson told Untermeyer he could only raise $100,000. Untermeyer told Wilson that if in addition to the $100,000 Untermeyer could select the next Supreme Court Justice to fill the next vacancy, the case would be settled. Wilson got his many incriminating love letters back, Louis Brandeis was appointed to the Supreme Court, Mrs. Peck received $30,000, and Untermeyer got the rest. This is what intrigue looks like in high places. Wilson ran as a candidate of virtue, both in private and public life, but a virtuous man would have resigned. Wilson lacked virtue and allowed himself and the nation to be blackmailed.

The great majority of Americans were strongly opposed to us entering the war in Europe. The people demanded a congressional investigation to determine the extent that war profiteering played. In 1934, the Nye Committee, named after Senator Gerald Nye, was established. After a year of investigating, the committee reported that the arms industry garnered huge amounts of profit. Furthermore, it found that bankers pressured President Wilson into the war to protect their loans abroad, primarily to England. It further determined that the arms industry engaged in unlawful price fixing. These special interests exercised undue influence on American foreign policy leading up to and during the war. The committee further concluded that the United States entered the war for profit, because it was in America's commercial and financial interest for England not to lose. Under public pressure and not to repeat the slaughter again, Congress passed the Neutrality Acts in 1935, 1936, 1937, and 1939.

The persecution of German Americans was severe, the mockery, insults, and abuse unrelenting. On many occasions, mobs beat up people of German descent. The anti-German hysteria led to mob violence and several murders. A well-known case of lynching of a German American took place on April 5, 1918, in Collinsville, Illinois. Robert Prager was hanged just for being a German American. He was a martyr to his fidelity. By any definition, that was premeditated, yet no one was ever held accountable for this murder. Now, each April 5, Collinsville commemorates Robert Prager Day. President Wilson's immediate total silence and lack of condemnation concerning this and other crimes against German Americans only fueled more violence and more hate crimes.

The intentional and malicious acts were so intense that scores of Germans anglicized their names. Zimmermann became Carpenter, Schmidt became Smith, and Mueller became Miller. Imagine, for a moment, the level of hysteria that existed for good people to feel compelled to change their family name. Even names of cities and streets became anglicized. Hamburg Avenue became Wilson Avenue, New Berlin became North Canton, and New Dresden became East Canton. Typical German food was renamed. Hamburgers became Salisbury steaks, and sauerkraut became victory or liberty cabbage. The politically correct thing became bashing and smashing everything German, ignoring the mammoth amount of German-American contributions and sacrifices. It was open season on all things German. German Americans were humiliated, horse-whipped, and flogged by vigilantes just for having a German surname. No one raised a voice on behalf of these terrorized German-American victims, least of all President Wilson. World War I forced the obliteration of the German-American society and community as we knew it and as it had been thus far preserved.

More than 7,500 German Americans were put into internment camps for the duration of World War I. Some of the politicians in Washington called them nothing more than concentration camps. There was no justifiable reason to incarcerate law-abiding German Americans, except to intimidate and silence German-American opposition to the war. Freedom of speech and antiwar demonstrations were suddenly no longer a constitutionally protected right. This affront against all things German became an orchestrated attempt to destroy the

German-American heritage. There was open season on German Americans; they were forced into becoming the silent majority, which they remained for over a century. They are now slowly freeing themselves from these shackles.

Communities and even entire states had "Security" or "Citizens Patriotic Leagues," or volunteer vigilante groups that attacked anything and everything that was German. Some of these mobs smeared the homes of German Americans with yellow paint, smashed their store windows, and forced them to kiss the American flag on their knees to prove their loyalty and patriotism. Many were subjected to severe public and private ridicule. These mob atrocities left emotional, psychological, and physical scars upon thousands of innocent German-American victims. No one was ever held accountable.

These persecutions committed against German Americans throughout our country were mostly perpetrated without official government sanctions. However, in Texas, House Bill 15 "made it a felony punishable by jail terms of two to five years for making all criticism, even a remark made in casual conversation, of America's entry into the war and its continuation in the war." Freedom of speech, one of our basic constitutionally protected rights, was denied and no longer protected. It appears Wilson was not very certain that the country was behind him in his war efforts, so he took drastic measures against German Americans.

The First Amendment's guarantees of free speech, free press, and peaceful assembly are at the core of all other freedoms guaranteed by the Bill of Rights. Without the First Amendment, the rest of our rights are in constant peril. Both Wilson and FDR chose to ignore these rights because it served their political expediency. Both created internment camps for German Americans and others and they terrorized them.

Still today, Germans and German Americans are struggling to rebuild their destroyed and lost culture and heritage. Lies and deceptions were part of Wilson's game. The purpose of the hysteria was in getting the German Americans to become invisible and also remain the backbone of the nation. Kurt Vonnegut related the experiences of his family. He stated that "the anti-Germanism of this country during World War One so shamed, dismayed and frightened my parents that they resolved to raise me without acquainting me with language or the literature or the music or the oral family histories which my ancestors had loved. They made me ignorant and rootless as part of their patriotism." Vonnegut was captured during the Battle of the Bulge and was one of twenty-six thousand American POWs in Dresden. He survived the Dresden fire-bombings on February 13 and 14, 1945. That was on Ash Wednesday. He describes the inferno of Dresden in his antiwar novel *Slaughterhouse Five*.

The American Armed Forces fighting Germany included a large percentage of German Americans, including a soldier by the name of D. W. Eisenhower and was led by a German American, General John Pershing. Unfortunately, all that meant absolutely nothing to the Wilson administration as it violated our Constitution in its persecution of German Americans, engaging in human rights violations. World War I was the war that did not end all wars. More than eight million lives were lost at a cost of $337 billion. The Versailles Peace Treaty was rightfully voted down by the US Senate. It failed to keep peace because it was so extremely unjust and reckless. It may have ended the war, but it did not end the hate that got us into the war. Hatred continued to run high. Hollywood and the media glorified the war. For the men on the front lines, however, there was misery, muddy trenches, dodging shells, fighting off tank charges, and staying alive. That was their reality, so unlike the media hype and propaganda.

At the end of the war in 1918, joyous crowds celebrated

on the streets, similar to crowds celebrating and cheering at sporting events, but in the huge cemeteries in which millions of young men lay buried, there was a terrible and painful silence. Some soldiers who came home could not find jobs that paid enough to live on, despite a boom in business. For them, the war solved nothing; it created only burdens. Thousands became homeless and ended up living on the streets. The reality remained that the brutality of the battlefield had very little to do with the glorified media images and hype of war.

After the war, Americans blamed "the Merchants of Death," the war profiteers and the British propagandists who lied about raped Belgian nuns and babies being tossed around on Prussian bayonets. World War I came out of a great failure of man, out of fear, failure of wisdom, a lust for power, greed, injustice, intrigues, and misery left unresolved. Most Americans saw getting into war as a big mistake. The war to make the world safe for democracy failed to do so abroad and at home. What we got is permanent war for permanent peace, a total contradiction.

The challenges to our liberties and freedom came from outside forces as well as from within, in the form of corruption, disappointed ambitions, inordinate hunger for power, and grand theft. We have been paying for the war in many ways, including inflation. Inflation has proven to be the most destructive of all the consequences of war. If we value our Constitution and all it stands for, we must remain vigilant in preserving that precious document and all it stands for. We must maintain inner fortitude to prevent human rights violations and remain determined to defend our precious Constitution.

Patrick J. Buchanan wrote a scholarly and well researched book, *Churchill, Hitler, and the Unnecessary War*, covering the entire twentieth century. The work explains how Britain lost its empire and the West lost the world. We must educate ourselves and provide light and understanding to our children, because learning is like a light that shows the way to a new beginning. The greatest and most sublime blessing is knowledge and understanding.

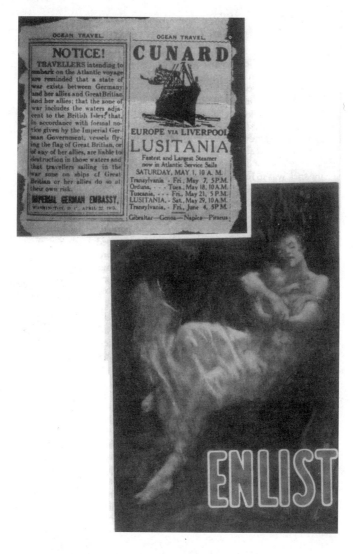

The German embassy attempted to place ads in fifty newspapers warning potential passengers that the *Lusitania* was a target of war because of its military cargo, but the US government interfered with them being printed except this ad, which was run in the *Des Moines Register*. When the ship was sunk off the coast of Ireland with 195 Americans aboard, it became the focus of a national campaign to generate emotional support for Americans to enter the war. The poster shows a mother with her baby sinking to the bottom of the ocean, telling Americans to *enlist*.

GERMAN-AMERICAN KULTURABEND

"The Unknown Internment of Europeans in the USA during World War II "

Friday April 19, 2013   7:00 p.m.—9:00 p.m.
Sandstone 3 in the Strosacker College Union at 120 E. Grand St.
Berea, OH 44017

Come hear **Mr. Eberhard Fuhr** tell his personal story of life in wartime internment camps on American soil from March 1943-September 1947. His family had brought him to America at the age of 3, where he went to school in Ohio and even attempted to enlist in the US Army. However, during WWII, their German birth certificates earned them the official designation as "Alien Enemies" and they were removed from their home.
German Wallace College, one of the founding institutions of the present Baldwin Wallace University, taught all classes in German until the merger with Baldwin University in 1913. With that tradition in mind, the Department of Foreign Languages and Literatures would like to extend a special invitation to attend this German-American presentation.

For more information, contact
Prof. Stephen Hollender 440 826 2248
or email shollend@bw.edu

Since his retirement from a career in business, Eberhard Fuhr has lectured about internment at The Art Institute of Chicago, St. Paul Traces Museum, and Concordia College, as well as in schools and libraries throughout the Midwest and South. He has also appeared in newspaper and radio interviews with Cleveland Public Radio and BBC London and in a German television documentary .

CHAPTER 3

Ellis Island Remembered

With the sun, which is the beauty and glory of the day, slowly rising in the east over a beautiful New York skyline, some fifty internment camp survivors took the ferry back to Ellis Island. It was a journey back into their history, a very painful personal history.

For millions of immigrants, this was a port of entry to the Promised Land, the biblical land of milk and honey, but for thousands of German Americans and others, it was a place of inhumane, cruel treatment and suffering. It was an island of tears, of untold human rights violations. It is a tragic reflection on our national moral consciousness that this part of our recent history remains one of our best-kept secrets.

The relocation and internment of German, Italian, and Japanese Americans and others during World War II might not have occurred and most definitely would not have been as brutal and cruel without the precedents established as part of the hysteria generated against all things German during World War I. Another acute case of German-phobia and anti-German hysteria was again forced upon German Americans during World War II.

Tragically, German Americans had nowhere to turn for help.

Let us be reminded that World War I, the war that did not end all wars, was barely over when various interest groups were already scheming about the next war. The war was very profitable to the few. How swiftly the masses forget the propaganda that led them into war. Unable to have his Fourteen Points accepted at the Versailles Conference, President Woodrow Wilson verbalized concern on his return trip from Europe, claiming that he had just signed a declaration for the next war. The terms were so unjust and outrageous that Congress rightfully never ratified the Versailles Peace Treaty.

It is a sad part of our history that the world wars, the Cold War, and every other war gave us nothing remotely resembling peace. Economic advantages and the benefits and the spoils of war have been and continue to be the driving force; patriotism and imminent threat to our national security have been skillfully employed to justify the human cost. Wilson was a man with many contradictions, so was FDR twenty years later.

One of Wilson's main points was national self-determination for all people, except the Germans. Furthermore, Wilson's points were vehemently derailed by England and France. They appeared to be more concerned about exploiting and eliminating Germany indefinitely as an economic, industrial, and commercial competitor than ensuring conditions for sustainable peace. They professed, erroneously, that they wanted to "leave the world a better place than they found it." That was pure propaganda and deceptive rhetoric. England was determined, at all cost, to maintain its empire on which the sun would never set, but the sun did ultimately set.

The Versailles Peace Treaty stripped from Germany one-tenth of its people and one-eighth of its territory. Europe's borders were redrawn at the expense of Germany and Austro-Hungary. The Allies selfishly confiscated every German colony as well as all the private property of the Germans who had lived in those colonies. The latter is unprecedented in modern history. These were part of the spoils of the war. Huge war reparations, primarily to England and France, were placed upon Germany. They were forced to sign the Versailles Treaty, literally at gunpoint, agreeing to the fallacy that they alone were to blame for the war, the so-called "sole German guilt clause." The power of the propaganda was well demonstrated; there was not even an ounce of fairness in the "peace treaties."

Among the more conspicuous points of this two-hundred-page, seventy-five-thousand-word "Peace Treaty" were that Germany must accept full responsibility for the war, referred to as the Sole Guilt Clause, which was without justification. Wilhelm II and eight hundred other so-called war criminals were to be handed over to the victorious Allies for a show trial. Wilhelm II was granted asylum in Holland and was not handed over. Germany was ordered to surrender more than 700,000 square kilometers of its territory. This was in total contradiction to the International Peace Treaties of 1899 and 1907 in The Hague, which stipulated that no goods or land were to be taken from the vanquished. However, tragically might became right and justice was denied.

During and after the world wars, the US military-industrial complex expanded exponentially. President Dwight D. Eisenhower warned us that this would create a lopsided economy favoring military and corporate growth more than grassroots prosperity. This military industrial imbalance still exists. Large corporations, such as Bechtel and Halliburton, service the military now in Iraq, Afghanistan, and elsewhere, as key elements of the military-industrial complex.

The conclusion of each war gave way to another renewed and continued conflict. We embarked upon "preventive wars," thus engaging and justifying an open-ended war on terror. According to the American historian William Blum, the United

States has been involved in more than seventy military conflicts since World War II. Otto von Bismarck told us preventive war is "like committing suicide due to fear of death." The greatest paradox just might be civilized warfare. Since when is killing, even in uniform, civilized?

Three different US governmental programs authorized the terror inflicted upon US-born citizens, naturalized citizens, and legal resident aliens, justifying the ransacking of German American homes, the round-ups, arrests, imprisonment, and repatriation. The War Relocation Authority had unrestricted authority to relocate and intern all German, Japanese, and Italian "enemy aliens" or anybody they deemed as an enemy alien. The loyalty of patriotic German Americans was seriously being called into question as tens of thousands of German Americans simultaneously served in our armed forces.

As part of this program, the victims were denied fundamental due process rights and legal representation. They were stripped of all their constitutional rights as part of FDR's presidential proclamation #9066. Over one million US residents were labeled "enemy aliens." Another program was the Alien Enemy Control Unit, based on the Aliens Enemies Act of 1798. It was passed at that time to address the issue of British sympathizers. The third program was run by the State Department, which was responsible for blacklisting and abducting more than 8,500 German Latin Americans and other Axis residents in Latin American countries. Their earthly belongings were forcefully taken from them; it was simply stolen. Grand theft was legalized.

Why is there so little, virtually nothing, known about this part of our recent history? One possible reason might be the fact that prior to being released from internment, both the internees and guards were forced to sign an oath never to speak or write about their experiences in the camps. This was a virtual federal gag order. Fortunately, after decades of silently suffering, many survivors began sharing their horrifying experiences with the rest of the world. The time is long past due; we must stop procrastinating and honestly face our own past, the sublime as well as the ugly by critically reviewing all facets of the internment program. We need to look at ourselves without blinders or through rose-colored glasses.

Forcing prisoners to sign an oath and denying them constitutional due process protection and legal representation far outreached constitutionality. In order that our Constitution may remain strong and a solid pillar of our democracy and our freedom, it is imperative that every reasonable course of action be explored to prevent future erosion of our treasured civil liberties and rights. This will honor all who paid the ultimate price for our liberties.

Let us try to fathom some sympathy and understanding for the victims who were innocently locked up by their own government as "dangerous alien enemies." This was and remained the country that they loved and defended with their lives. It must be emphasized that not even one person that was interned was ever charged with or found guilty of the accusations that allegedly led to their internment. They were just being detained "for their own safety." That was a deceptive legal mirage and total fraudulent trickery. Civil liberties were ignored purposely. It is difficult to imagine the level of hysteria that was generated by governmental policy and the power of the media, making a mockery of any truthful and balanced reporting.

A chronological overview of policies and events leading up to World War II provides much needed clarity. Already in the 1920s, many years prior to World War II and Pearl Harbor, J. Edgar Hoover and his FBI, armed with only FDR's verbal authorization, began very secretly to work on a five-year plan, compiling a list of enemy aliens and citizens who ever so remotely might pose a potential security risk in the future. This program was kept "top secret" because the minutest leak of this governmental covert activity would rightfully have caused a constitutional outcry. This action would have been totally superfluous had FDR himself not been planning and scheming for a war.

On August 27, 1940, Congress passed the Alien Registration Act, which mandated all noncitizens register at their local post offices, where they were also fingerprinted. Continuing the flurry of war preparations, FBI and Justice Department agents crisscrossed the nation registering any and all aliens they could possibly find and some they didn't find. It is important to be reminded that America was at peace and not at war. However, the Justice Department was ordered to "arrest and detain those persons deemed dangerous in the event of war." As a result, there were many prewar arrests, allegedly just as a precaution, making a mockery of our constitutional guarantees. It was open season on German Americans and Latin German Americans. The public was kept ignorant about FDR's intentions.

The FBI procured an army of voluntary and paid informers. The reliability of the information from these anonymous informers was never questioned nor their accuracy treated with any measure of importance. A self-perpetuating hysteria was intentionally being created. What made this even more preposterous is the fact that once someone ended up on J. Edgar Hoover's infamous list, he or she was considered guilty and it became nearly impossible to prove otherwise. No due process, cross-examinations, or legal representations were granted; they were verboten. Our entire constitutional legal system was hijacked. There were no heroes protecting our Constitution and what it stands for; they could not be found anywhere.

Imagine being asked, "When did you stop beating your wife?" You never abused your wife, physically or otherwise. She was your best friend, and you loved and protected her. Now if you answered that you never stopped, you obviously must be still abusing her. And if you claim that you stopped, that must mean that you must have abused her in the past. Either way, you were sent to an internment camp because you were allegedly guilty but never charged nor proven guilty.

No one who was German, Japanese, Italian, Hungarian, Bulgarian, Romanian, Jehovah's Witness, or homosexual was immune from being placed on the *list*, arrested, and interned. Everyone knew that the *list* existed, even though it was kept "top secret." What were the government's intentions? Membership lists from every German-American organization were confiscated. Lists from cultural and social clubs, singing societies, and German-language honor societies; church membership rosters; and even guest books from German-American restaurants were taken. No warrants were ever presented. It was open season on everything German. The wild chase was on, and no one was there to stop it. Informants collected license plate numbers of cars parked at German-American cultural and social functions and at German religious services. Praying in German and singing German songs made one suspect. It was worse than the wildest Wild West, the government engaging in what some called criminal activities.

The critical and crucial issue is the fact that these covert crimes were committed during peacetime. This was an obvious abuse of power and a blatant violation of human rights. Six months prior to the United States declaring war, members of the Justice and War Departments were discussing the internment program. In a memo by J. Edgar Hoover to FDR, Hoover stated, "The majority of those to be arrested were American citizens rather than German enemy aliens." The internment program was initiated and implemented under obvious deceptive and false pretenses. Perhaps this is one reason our government has been so reluctant to address these incriminating and shameful human rights violations initiated at the highest governmental level. The news from that era would be today's history, but this never made the evening news.

Hollywood and our influential and powerful media were being effectively utilized in shaping public opinion, reigniting a barrage of anti-German propaganda material, and brainwashing the public. Movies were being produced about wicked, abominable, monstrous Nazi agents masquerading as American citizens. Movies, newsreels, and caricatures were effective tools of propaganda, fueling hate and dissension against Germany and Germans. The media greatly intensified German-phobia, thriving on sensationalism and negativism. We are willing to accept that the media in other countries may be influenced by their governments but not in America. The sole purpose of this mendacious propaganda during both world wars was to create a favorable climate in support of the banks and the war industry, which were poised to profit from the wars.

The first overt propaganda movie against Hitler's Germany was the 1939 blockbuster *Confessions of a Nazi Spy*. It was a story about a group of fanatic Nazi spies in America planning to destroy our Constitution and our Bill of Rights. Our first lady, Eleanor Roosevelt, speaking at a Fight for Freedom rally, demanded a declaration of war against Germany—*at once*. The British intelligence agency, working in America, would seek out people with useful, pro-British views, like our former first lady and then support and guide them in attacking Britain's enemies. The media produced spies and saboteurs on every street corner, a virtual media blitzkrieg, and all of this during peacetime. These were blatant attacks and abuses of our Constitution. So far nothing has been done to rectify this nepotism. The guilty still have not been held accountable.

FDR himself encouraged the production of anti-German propaganda movies and Hollywood complied. FDR, like

Woodrow Wilson, had a hidden agenda. Some of the movies featured Charlie Chaplin and the Three Stooges. It turned into an all-out cultural war. Even after World War II was over, the TV series *Hogan's Heroes* presented Germans exceedingly uncomplimentarily and as acutely naive. FDR himself contributed to the deceptive and utterly dishonest propaganda, fueling fear and hate. On October 27, 1941, he told the American people that he had come across a secret German map revealing a Nazi design to conquer South America and that Hitler had intentions to abolish all existing religions. In his address, he told the nation, "I have in my possession a secret map, made in Germany by Hitler's government—by the planers of the New World Order—it is a map of South America as Hitler proposes to reorganize it. The geographical experts of Berlin, however, have obliterated all the existing boundary lines. Bringing the whole continent under their dominion ... This map makes clear the Nazi design not only against South America but against the United States as well."

FDR claimed he had another secret document, "made in Germany by Hitler's government ... it is a plan to abolish all existing religions—Protestant, Catholic, Mohammedan, Hindu, Buddhists and Jewish alike ... In the place of the churches of our civilization, there is to be set up an international Nazi Church ..." The media sensationalized these fabrications.

These documents were never produced by FDR or any of his advisors or any historian, because they were British fake news and lies. Had they really existed, they would have been used as evidence at the Nuremberg Trials to support the claim and the verdict of "sole German guilt." It should be mentioned that Father Charles Coughlin of national radio fame called FDR the "great liar and betrayer." FDR said further that any individual who attempted to be both German and American simultaneously was not an American but a traitor. He ignored the fact that Winston Churchill was not the only one who possessed dual citizenship. Remarkably, there were absolutely no antiwar demonstrations. The demonstrators would have been arrested and chastised by the media. How free was our media and how balanced the reporting?

Lately, we have heard much about fake news. Patrick J. Buchanan warns us,

> Americans should be on guard against 'fake news' and foreign meddling in US elections. Yet it is often our own allies, like the Brits, and our own leaders who mislead and lie to us leading us into unnecessary wars ... History suggests that it is our own War Party that bears watching ... who mislead, deceived, and lied about Saddam's weapons of mass destruction, the 'fake news' that sucked us into one of our country's greatest strategic blunders?" (*New York Staatszeitung*, No. 50, Dec. 10, 2016, pg. 10)

Buchanan referred to Churchill as the grandmaster of fake news and war party lies. Churchill knew that FDR was itching to drag the United States into the war. Their twenty thousand telephone conversations are sealed for all posterity for good reason. Wars are not started by nations but by individuals motivated by greed and power.

The populist Roman Catholic radio priest Father Charles Coughlin first took to the airwaves in 1926, broadcasting weekly sermons. In the early 1930s, the focus of his broadcasts shifted from theology to economics and politics, as the nation was more occupied with these issues during the Great Depression. At first, he was a Roosevelt supporter but then turned disappointed against FDR and became one of his harshest critics. Coughlin's social justice was an extreme challenge to the unbridled capitalism and to many of the political institutions of the day.

Social tranquility can be maintained if the work of the men and women who built this great nation is respected by them enjoying income equality; inequality creates social unrest. Reward everyone with the opportunity to achieve the American dream of prosperity and justice, leaving no one behind.

At the conclusion of the war Coughlin witnessed the unjust Versailles Peace Treaty, the birth of Bolshevism and universal poverty. The priest voiced his concerns over the intentional destruction of our moral ideals and the miscarriage of justice as it has never been so blatantly displayed, shrouded in the Godlessness of wealth and power. Instead of making the world "safe for democracy," the church bells rang its requiem, as civilians were burdened by regimented forces of greed, selfishness, arrogant ignorance, and opinions rather than facts. He claimed that the war was fought to make the world safe for Wall Street and for the international bankers.

In 1914, England's financial and commercial supremacy were in serious jeopardy because of Germany's rapid advance industrially and commercially. During the first two years of the war, the American industrialists and bankers poured billions of credit dollars into England's war chest. The United States was pushed into the war to protect the bankers' investments in dear old England. It was more sacred to protect the capitalistic dollar than to preserve the life of a mother's son. Coughlin asserted that the chief concerns of government shall be for the poor, because the rich have ample means of their own to care for themselves. Father Coughlin promoted "the abolition of the privately owned Federal Reserve banking system and the establishment of a government owned central bank." Furthermore, he believed in rescuing from the hands of private owners the right to coin and regulate the value of money, which he wanted to be restored to Congress. Father Coughlin preached that there must be a conscription of wealth as well as a conscription of men. The Constitution assigns the responsibility "To coin Money, (and) regulate the value thereof ..." to Congress.

Films became an instrument of propaganda without equal. FDR was personally responsible for the film *Battle Cry of Peace*. Germans were always portrayed most unfavorably. Isolationists didn't fare much better; they were presented as total fools and as Nazis. Hate propaganda was used to eradicate everything of German origin in America. Speaking German was considered evidence of a conspiracy. German books were thrown out of libraries as trash or burned in the public square with patriotic ceremonies. The government produced lists banning German books. The Boy Scouts from Chardon, Ohio, participated in a book-burning ceremony at the Cleveland Public Library. And, of course, the works of German composers disappeared from symphony programs. German Americans were humiliated and insulted, intimidated, harassed, and treated violently.

Our founding fathers, in their profound foresight and wisdom, warned against enterprising individuals wanting to increase their own influence by increasing governmental powers. Such activities lead to ever greater transgressions against constitutional boundaries, leading to ever more mischievous acts and usurpation of power.

The British Invasion

As if our own agencies needed help, the British government conducted a massive top-secret covert campaign in the United States in the years just preceding and during World War II, just as they did in other parts of the world. Their objective was focused on procuring financial and military support and to get the United States involved in the war on England's side.

To accomplish that mission, they had to wear down the isolationist forces wanting to stay out of another European war and terrorize the German Americans and others. Without FDR and the Americans, the British could not have won the war and there probably would not have been another world war. With FDR's support, the British secret intelligence operation succeeded in bringing the United States into the war and unleash a second wave of hysteria against all things German. Sadly, remnants of that poison still linger in the media and elsewhere.

In the summer of 1940, more than two thousand British intelligence agents came to New York. Of course, without FDR's support and invitation, that would have never become a reality. As may be expected, this British invasion was not reported on the evening news. The British ran a well-funded covert intelligence operation from the Rockefeller Center virtually rent free, namely a penny a year. The Rockefeller family proved very helpful to the English. Many other expenses were covered by them as well. The English were able, with Anglophile elite help, to wield excessive influence.

The British secret intelligence organizations, MI5 and MI6, are the organizations that America modeled its FBI and CIA agencies after. Like the American FBI, MI5 is responsible for the British domestic security service. MI6 was the World War II designation of the British Secret Intelligence Service (SIS). Releasing the secret British archives revealed that they even secured the services of Benito Mussolini during World War I. He served Her Majesty as an MI5 agent, for which he received one hundred British pounds per week. Money has always proven to be a great seducer in the political and private arena.

A very cunning and able spy, William Stephenson, a

Canadian millionaire with the code name "Intrepid," directed the British SIS operations. He proved worthy of his code name, being resolute and fearless. SIS members were not afraid of any kind of subversive activities. Forgery, fraud, lies, deception, seduction, and murder were part of their job descriptions. They often went far beyond international law and the ethical and moral limits of propriety. The end always justified their means. FDR's speechwriter was Robert Sherwood, who was a British intelligence collaborator. The American FBI and CIA learned the intelligence game and all the dirty tricks from the British, copying their methods and style and even surpassing them in many areas.

The British government mounted a massive secret political campaign to destroy American isolationists in Congress and weaken America's reluctance to enter the war. It is important to remind ourselves that the British secret service could not and would not have operated in the United States without FDR's approval and support. Since when did our government allow foreign secret agencies to operate freely in our country? The British covert operation enjoyed FDR's blessings because they served his objectives, but they were bitterly resented by J. Edgar Hoover, who strongly objected to a foreign secret agency operating in his territory.

The British agents went to great lengths to keep their identities, their covert operations, and all their involvements under cover and completely secret. It was very difficult to trace them because they all were hiding behind code names. They were the ultimate experts on deception. Always paying special attention to all the details, they left absolutely nothing to chance. They stayed completely hidden behind the scene as if they did not even exist. That made them more affective and more dangerous.

Sir William Samuel Stephenson's (agent Intrepid) mandate

was to bring the United States into the war on England's side and to do whatever needed to be done to accomplish that mission. The British agents stayed hidden, and they did everything to ensure their covert activities in America and elsewhere stayed undetected, hopefully forever. To accomplish their objectives, they created patriotic-sounding front organizations, such as America First, American Irish Defense Association, American Labor to Aid British Labor, Fight for Freedom, Friends of Democracy, League of Human Rights, Non-Sectarian Anti-Nazi League, and others. All of them were deceptive British intelligence creations as covers for their covert, deceptive activities.

Nine out of ten Americans were isolationists. Charles Lindbergh, an isolationist, warned us, "If we enter the fight for democracy abroad, we may end by losing it at home." Lindbergh was a major figure in the campaign to keep America neutral and out of the war. He warned us that "we must keep foreign propaganda from pushing our country blindly into another war." The British SIS destroyed this American hero; he became another American victim of British intrigue.

Because of the great loss of human lives and suffering and having felt deceived by war profiteers, Americans came home from World War I to stay home, never to participate in another European war. They became isolationists and Americans first. To make their position binding and meaningful, they passed the Neutrality Act. The British SIS did their utmost and succeeded in having Congress repeal the Neutrality Act, which shifted the flow of goods and arms to England and France. Americans were being deceived on a massive scale. England displayed its ability to deceive on a massive scale.

The Supreme Court Decision

Our political system adapted quickly. Antitrust laws have not been enforced for decades. The Supreme Court has just decided in a five to four ruling that big and powerful corporations and monopolies have free speech rights to spend as much money as they need to destroy their opponents and enemies. They have proven the claim that America has the best government that money can buy. During the 2008 campaign, a nonprofit corporation called Citizens United, was demonstrating their free-speech rights with massive amounts of money available to persuade the electorate that Hillary Clinton was evil. It appears that even slander is protected by free speech. It has been stated before that what destroys a great system, such as the United States, are its excesses. One pill will help and cure; the entire bottle may kill or subdue the patient.

Big corporations won't have to bankroll elections anymore. They won't need to buy fifty-one Senators and a majority in the House to get what they want, as they did thus far. They can get the same results as the British secret service agents did decades ago by eliminating one candidate at a time. This way, they will put the fear of God into elected officials and frighten enough of them to vote in big corporations' and special interests' favors. Members of Congress fully recognize that the five justices have just put poison into the House and Senate cookie jar.

British Secret Service

FDR was very sensitive to public opinion. He read several newspapers each morning to gain a pulse of the American public opinion. The British SIS would rig public opinion polls and distribute their scientific-sounding results and thus manipulate the newspapers. One such opinion poll asserted that 94 percent of the delegates at a FFF (Fight for Freedom) rally in Detroit thought that defeating Hitler was more important than for the United States to stay out of the war. Another poll claimed that 90 percent of eighteen- to twenty-four-year-old males in America were eager to go to war and fight for freedom. There are only two things that men in that age group will agree on and that is women and beer, not going to war and getting killed. British fabrications of propaganda remained unrelenting and ever more sensational.

The British intelligence arsenal also included beautiful and sexy female MI6 agents, who would single out important men of influence and seduce them, thereby persuading them to the British agenda. Cynthia, the code name of the beautiful wife of British diplomat Arthur Pack, jumped into bed with isolationist senator Arthur Vandenberg. She was able to change his mind in support of the British agenda after he set himself up for possible blackmail.

The British secret service's dirty tricks operation left nothing to chance. Ernest Cuneo, whose code name was "Crusader," was a lawyer, journalist, author, and British intelligence officer. He was the attorney for columnist Drew Pearson and Walter Winchell, and he wrote much of Winchell's material. The Crusader turned out tons of anti-German propaganda material. What made him so effective is the fact that he was privileged to be a Roosevelt administration insider. It is interesting to note with whom FDR surrounded himself.

Another example of British dirty tricks was coordinated by Lt. Commander Sanford Griffith. He was a BSC (British Security Coordination) intelligence agent with SOE (Special Operation Executive) who hid behind his cover code G112. He ran several BSC patriotic-sounding front organizations, such as France Forever and American Irish Defense Association, with conspicuously few Irish in the organization. Griffith orchestrated a campaign to drive out isolationist Hamilton Fish from Congress. Agent Griffith engaged in many deceptive British covert and overt operations against American isolationists, effectively defeating all opposition. We must remind ourselves that all these foreign secret activities would not and could not have occurred without FDR's personal involvement and support.

The British intelligence operation succeeded in changing American opinion and policy. Imagine the orchestrated effort it took the British to be able to repeal the Neutrality Act, produce rigged opinion polls favoring the draft to prepare the American military for war, approve the destroyer deal, and drive Hamilton Fish and Arthur Vandenberg from public office. This was done with FDR's blessings. These were impressive accomplishments. British propaganda was relentless in getting America to accept its role as a world power guided by the wiser, more mature, self-assured, and arrogant British political elite.

Thomas E. Mahl wrote a very scholarly and well-researched book about British covert activities in America *Desperate Deception*. Dr. Mahl painstakingly gives the history of the Anglo-American alliance and America's entry into the war. *Desperate Deception* reads better than any detective story, because it is a masterpiece of true historical detective work.

The British Starvation Blockade

Another example of British inhumane and cruel practices was the starvation blockade of Germany and other European countries after the war was over. The blockade was a very ruthless British display of power. The savage British blockade caused the starvation of millions of men, women, and children after Germany laid down its arms and weapons and surrendered her warships. After the armistice, Winston Churchill stated, "We are enforcing the blockade with rigor, and Germany is very near starvation." People like that go to church not to pray for divine guidance but to be seen and all the other wrong reasons. It appears that for Churchill and the British elite, the end always justified the means.

Churchill denied Berlin's request for permission to purchase 2.5 million tons of food for its starving people. Pope Benedict XV's plea to end the starvation blockade was arrogantly ignored by the British ruling elite. An Episcopal Bishop, Henry W. Hobson, a FFF member, not only excused but blessed Britain's starvation blockade, claiming the Germans were being starved for their own good, namely to save their sinful souls. Bishop Hobson claimed to be a man of God. Such was the pompous, misguided arrogance of a British religious leader. President Herbert Hoover initiated a grand humanitarian action, feeding the starving civilians of Europe and thereby saving millions of lives by breaking the British starvation blockade.

One of the greatest humanitarians in recent history is President Herbert Hoover. Hoover saved millions of lives from starvation. He displayed typical German virtues, such as thrift, honesty, decency, hard work, efficiency, and genuine human compassion. James Bacque dedicated his book *Crimes and Mercies: The Fate of German Civilians under Allied Occupation* to his memory. In the spirit of true Christian charity, Hoover led worldwide food relief efforts after both world wars. Bacque claims that after World War II, Hoover probably saved as many as eighty million European lives. Hoover organized shipments of food to starving millions of people in Germany, Austria, and Hungary and elsewhere.

There are other examples of British starvation tactics. One such example occurred during the Boer's war at the turn of the last century. Starvation was an effective method the British used to force their opponents into accepting British rule. Rather than fighting the soldiers in the field, they cowardly terrorized and starved the civilians.

The British were extremely motivated, because this region has the largest concentration of the world's resources of platinum, chromium, vanadium and titanium. This region experienced the world's greatest diamond rush beginning in 1871, as well as huge amounts of gold. It is always imperative to look behind the scene for the real culprits and their devious behavior.

The British produced mountains of fake news, lies and special pressure groups supporting their underhanded maneuverings that ultimately resulted in the Anglo-Boer wars. They fabricated a trail of lies justifying the war, including "atrocity" propaganda, allegations of Boer barbarity and corruption among the Boers and fake news about a Boer's armament build up, which they claimed to be a serious "Boer's threat". The British claimed this to be sufficient justification for a British takeover of the region and its mineral wealth.

During the first Boer war (1880-81), the British were soundly defeated. The Boers were Dutch settlers. During the second war, the British deployed more than 347,000 soldiers. The Boer republics were not able to field more than 35,000 men. The combined population of both Boer republics was less than 280,000 men, women and children. The British implemented their "scorched earth" policy and first introduced the world to concentration camps.

Emily Hobhouse (1860-1926), a British welfare campaigner, exposed the deplorable and utter inhumane brutality during the Boer wars, the British concentration camps and the way the Boer women, children and men were mistreated, displaying that the British are not the finest and most honorable people on planet earth.

The British destroyed all their farming equipment, their crops, bales of wool, vegetable gardens and flower beds. Their orchards were chopped down, sacks of grain were set on fire, churches were destroyed, and homes were burned to the ground. Sheep and cattle were herded into corrals and dynamited. Sheep were rounded up into grassy areas and set ablaze. They even forced the women and children to witness this display of animal cruelty. The British destroyed their food supply. Then they were shipped into a new British invention – concentration camps. 20,000 of the Boer fighting men were deported to various POW camps throughout the British Empire as far away as India.

It is indicative that from 1948 until 1994, these embarrassing atrocities of the British Anglo-Boer wars and the British concentration camps were omitted from British history textbooks.

FDR'S Erroneous Promise

In 1940, FDR won reelection on a false pledge and deceptive promise. He stated, "While I am talking to you mothers and fathers, I give you one more assurance. I have said this before and I shall say it again and again and again. Your boys are not going to be sent into any foreign wars." Of course, if we are attacked, we are going to defend ourselves. If FDR did not plan on going to war, all his preparations would have been a totally mood point. Deception worked for Wilson, why not for FDR?

Understanding the political landscape is imperative in comprehending the fury that was unleashed against German, Japanese, and Italian Americans to silence their opposition to the war and to create negative feelings toward them, just like Wilson did two decades earlier.

FDR went to great lengths to appear to be neutral, but his actions were anything but neutral. A little-known incident that nearly derailed the Roosevelt presidency was his clandestine message to Winston Churchill regarding America's entrance into World War II. It was intercepted by Tyler Kent, working at the American embassy in London. He was about to release it to FDR's isolationist opponents in the United States when British agents arrested him and confiscated the communication. The document would have shown that Roosevelt was deceiving our nation about his promise and pledge to stay out of the war. Only one in ten books on FDR even mentions this incident. In 1939–40, 90 percent of Americans were strongly opposed to entering another European war. They were steadfast, resolute isolationists and patriotic Americans and wanted nothing to do with another European war.

Several months prior to FDR and the United States officially entering the war, the United States took German seamen hostage and kept them incarcerated for the duration of the war; this was an act of unprovoked aggression. Furthermore, FDR gave orders to sink German merchant ships. The only plausible explanation for such actions might be his intention to entice Hitler and Germany to retaliate and thus provide FDR a reason to justify going to war. However, Germany did not retaliate.

The sailors kidnapped by the United States served on some of the finest and best-known German luxury lines. At the time, we were not at war, and these seamen were not part of the German military navy. For what purpose were they arrested and detained? For the answer to this question, we need to research the tons of classified documents and the thousands of FDR's telephone conversations with Churchill.

President Herbert Hoover stated in his book *Freedom Betrayed: Secret History of the Second World War,* that his disgust and contempt for FDR increased considerably as he got to know the man better over the years. Hoover considered Americans to have been deceived by FDR's propaganda, scare-tactics, demonstrations of Hitler and Germany and the distortions of the truth and lies to the American people. FDR forced the issue of war by replacing his "day of infamy" with his "infamous" ultimatum ten days before the "official" outbreak of the war. All attempts by Japan to negotiate and concede to FDR's demands were brushed aside. Hoover does not forgive FDR that he, in 1943, lured and forced Japan to attack Pearl Harbor. He stated that FDR made the world safe for Joe Stalin and helped win the war for Communism, as he took a major step towards world domination, replacing the British Empire.

Senator Fish was more critical, he stated, "If any American leader deserved to be impeached for their deliberate cover-up, trickery, deceit and lying to the American people between Nov. 26 and Dec. 7, 1941, it is FDR and his war cabinet."

Latin American Involvement

Since the discovery of the New World, Germans settled in both North and South America. They brought with them their ethics of honesty and hard work and their cultural heritage. Their diligence brought them success and prosperity. In Latin America, they owned large plantations, factories, and businesses. The British Special Operations, in cooperation with the FBI, extended their combined operation to include not only the United States and Canada but also South America.

Just as England wanted to eliminate Germany permanently as a business competitor in Europe, the United States' industrial elite considered the German Latin Americans as serious business competitors who needed to be gotten rid of. The aim of US policy was to eliminate all competition from our southern backyard.

Nelson Rockefeller maintained an office in Latin America. Its primary mission was the elimination of all German businesses. The removal of German Latin American companies created a void, which US industries were eager to fill. We accomplished our mission by bribing Latin American politicians to cooperate in our deceptive activities. While we preached free market enterprise, we practiced protectionism.

The United States sought to extend its authority over Latin America before and during World War II, to solidify its business interests. To begin with, German Latin Americans and their businesses were blacklisted. Nelson Rockefeller's office asked more than 1,700 American businesses to terminate their business transactions with German Latin American businesses and to fire all their German employees. It proved to be an effective way to eliminate competition.

In Latin America, blacklists were circulated first by the British and then by the American agencies and published in local and national newspapers. Anonymous informants could list anybody and send in names with a coupon in the newspapers. The claim was that buying from blacklisted people and businesses was tantamount to supporting the enemy of democracy and claiming that German Latin Americans were the enemies of democracy. In addition, FDR's proclamation 2497, on July 17, 1941, emphasized that anyone doing business with a blacklisted person or company would be placed on that list him- or herself and become an enemy of democracy. Could there still be any doubt about FDR's true intentions? It appears that Churchill and FDR were two birds of a feather.

What followed was another significant British and US surreptitious operation, in total violation of international law, namely the abductions of thousands of German Latin Americans. The men were arrested and taken to prisons built by the United States. For weeks, families would not be informed as to the men's location, which increased their anxiety, frustration, fear, and panic level considerably. Weeks and often months later, the rest of the family would be arrested and taken to join the men in prison. The State Department classified them as "prisoners of war" and stigmatized them as "dangerous enemy aliens." None of the victims understood why they suddenly became dangerous enemies. Due process was totally ignored and any legal defense eliminated and not permitted. Kangaroo legal methods were applied.

A State Department memo in November 1942 explains its mission and makes its objective quite clear, stating, "We could hold them in escrow for bargaining purposes ... It is particularly desirable that the repatriation of inherently harmless Axis nationals may be used to the greatest possible extent," namely to exchange them for American and Allied citizens. These citizens and legal residents of a foreign sovereign nation were abducted, mistreated, and used as an exchange commodity. Except for Argentina, Brazil, and Chile, most Latin American countries succumbed to US pressure and bribes. German Latin American victims, like those of the United States, lost all their earthly possessions.

Far more than 8,500 German Latin Americans were kidnapped, abducted, in violation of international law. Who was going to enforce international law? Thousands were repatriated against their will and sent back directly to Germany. More than 4,000 were transported in dark boat holds, in deplorable conditions, to US shores, forced to cross our borders at gunpoint, and then charged with illegally entering the United States. Among the German Latin Americans were eighty-one German Jews. The last German Jews were released from internment in 1946.

Texas native Jan Jarboe Russel details how the US government secretly exchanged some 4,500 legal German American residents and their American-born children for POWs in Europe in her book *The Train to Crystal City*. While most people know about the Japanese internment camps, few know about the more than 75,000 German Americans who were interned in some sixty-nine camps, including Crystal City. The internment camp at Crystal City, Texas, was used as a very secret prisoner exchange program. The families could reunite in exchange for agreeing to repatriate to Germany.

Our media have flourished and still flourish with sensationalism, exaggerations, and alleged fabrications. The truth and nothing but the truth was put on a back burner. Newspapers across the country carried sensational front-page stories describing how thousands of German Latin Americans illegally entered the United States because they wanted a slice of our democracy and freedom and a better life in America. Our newspapers never provided the slightest hint of the truth that they were abducted by the FBI and forced at gunpoint across our border. Propaganda trumped truth.

This is just another example of truth being the first casualty of war, and we were not even at war. This scheme of charging these victims with illegally crossing our border was hatched so that they could be used as pawns. INS inspector Jorre Mangione expressed his outrage in *An Ethnic at Large* (321–22):

> For me, one of the most curious aspects of the internment program was the presence in the camps of several thousand men and women (with their children) from Latin-American countries who at the request of our State Department, had been seized by our own government as potentially dangerous alien enemies and handed over to American authorities. Compounding the bizarreness of the program was the Machiavellian device that was contrived to legalize their detention by the Immigration Service. This consisted of escorting the Latin Americans over our borders, then charging them with "illegal entry" into the country. As an Immigration Service camp

commander told me, "only in wartime could we get away with such fancy skullduggery."

However, we were not at war, not yet. This amounted to nothing more than ethnic cleansing and the elimination of business competition in our southern backyard.

The American Legion official Francis M. Sullivan objected and condemned the practice of importing Latin American aliens to be relocated and detained in American internment camps and requested its continuance be stopped at once. His request was, as expected, totally ignored. Their civil liberties were seriously violated by governmental agencies. What were the real big objectives in this big political world chess game?

On several occasions, before the war, the State Department rerouted ships on international water with German citizens aboard who were traveling home, interning them in American concentration camps while guaranteeing them safe passage. There was no self-restraint to fraudulent deception, intrigue, and lies. Instead of exposing these violations, the media became a willing accomplice.

Top Secret Plan

The US State Department ordered its Latin American activities be kept "top secret." A 1943 State Department memo emphasized, "It is undesirable for the written record to show that the initiative came from US." Be secretive and blame someone else for the dirty tricks. After arriving in the United States, German Latin Americans were conveniently reclassified as detainees and not enemy aliens. The State Department was thus not acknowledging the fact that these people were victims of kidnapping by American governmental agencies. The claim was they were being detained "for their own safety," allegedly also justifying their repatriation as well. There was no limit to FDR's deceptions. Imagine the outrage of our government and our media, providing balanced reporting, if these human rights violations happened in another country.

Kidnapping has always been a crime in America and every other civilized, law-abiding country, even when it was committed by a governmental agency. It is a gross violation of human rights. Even small children in Latin American countries knew that Germans were being kidnapped by Americans and sent to internment camps in Texas. Why don't American children learn these facts in our schools, and why has our government and media totally ignored these injustices and human rights violations? When will historical justice be served, and when will the guilty be held accountable?

The Gurcke Family

Among the thousands of victims of British and US covert actions in Latin America were the Gurckes. Werner Gurcke and his brother Karl Oskar Gurcke became legal residents of Costa Rica in the 1920s. In the 1930s, Karl Oskar married a native Costa Rican woman. In 1936, Werner married Starr Pait, an American citizen born in the United States. They established their homes in San Jose. Werner opened an import business. Werner and Starr were blessed with two beautiful daughters, Heidi and Ingrid, both born in Costa Rica.

Heidi Gurcke Donald took it upon herself to research and document her family's pilgrimage and the agony of thousands of other German Latin Americans subjected to such cruelty because of British and American deceptive operations in Latin America. In her book, *We Were Not the Enemy*, Heidi traces the various aspects of the political turbulence and intrigue and the resulting toll of human suffering, the imprisonment, the deportations, and the loss of their earthly possessions and, not least, their dignity. Heidi shared the story of her family, the story of her parents being accused of and treated as dangerous enemies, as prisoners in Costa Rica and detainees in Texas. Many were repatriated to bombed-out Germany.

Werner, Karl Oskar, and Starr were first blacklisted by the British in 1940 and later by the United States in 1941. Werner realized that this action by the British and later by the Americans would destroy his business. It is important to notice that the United States was not at war. The Gurckes were proud of their German culture and heritage. Why shouldn't they be? Like most Germans, they were apolitical. Goethe said, "Politik ist ein dreckiges Geschaeft" (Politics is a dirty business). The second part of this equation must be that it is also a necessary *Geschaeft*. A look at our history shows that politics is tragically one field that does not attract many German Americans.

Life for the Gurckes became extremely traumatic when in 1942 Werner and his brother Karl Oskar were arrested and held for six long months, never being charged. They were merely being detained. Imagine the terror that these kidnappings and incarcerations struck among the German Latin American population. It was an effective weapon of warfare, except we were *not* at war. By many accounts, this became a nightmarish reality for so many innocent victims. They were considered guilty, and they had no recourse to prove themselves otherwise. The primary reason for their mistreatment was that they were born in Germany. Being born in Germany turned them automatically into dangerous enemies, and they needed to be removed and repatriated.

Starr, Werner's wife, attempted frantically to get Werner out of prison. When she approached the American Council, she was told, erroneously, that the United States had absolutely nothing to do with Werner's arrest and, therefore, did not have the authority to release him. When she talked to the Costa Rican authorities, they told her that they had nothing to do with his arrest. The US State Department was in full charge of generating and authorizing the list for internment and deportation. They had sole responsibility and full local cooperation. There was one more twist; the agents were not shy in letting it be known that they could be bribed with money and sexual favors.

Almost half the German population was blacklisted. The Gurckes' home was raided; their hunting rifle, camera, and radio were confiscated. In 1942, both Gurcke families and many others were boarded onto an old, dilapidated ship and brought to our shores. After being forced to cross the US border, they were charged with "illegally" entering the United States. Along with thousands of others, they were detained at Crystal City, Texas. To increase their level of frustration and their feeling of helplessness, their passports and other documents were confiscated. Without documents, they were virtually without a country. We might be inclined to believe other governments engaged in such despicable acts but not our own. There should be reasons to place our own government on a higher level.

Brother Karl Oskar and his family were repatriated to Germany against their will. If Starr would not have been born an American citizen, Werner and his family would have also been repatriated. Even the agents in the State Department realized that exchanging one American for another American made no sense whatsoever. They were saved the torture of repatriation to a bombed-out and starving Germany. The family continued to be harassed until Werner became a US citizen in 1952. German Americans had forcibly been repatriated well into 1947. The FBI and the State Department often attempted to denaturalize citizens so that they could be interned as enemy aliens and, under duress, would agree to be repatriated. This is contrary to everything that our Constitution and the Bill of Rights stand for. Crystal City became a holding center for FDR's top-secret exchange program.

Ewald and Veronica vom Schlemm

Ewald and Veronica vom Schlemm were friends of the Gurckes, brought together by the hardships both couples faced during World War II in Costa Rica. Veronica was very helpful in putting together the various pieces of the puzzle for Heidi Gurcke Donald. Veronica was British, born in Weybridge, near London, England. She attended school there and after graduation traveled to Costa Rica in 1934 to work as an English tutor. She met her future husband, Ewald, at the German Club in San Jose.

Ewald was arrested as a "dangerous enemy alien" and put in a concentration camp outside San Jose. Veronica and all the other women were rounded up to join their husbands in the camp. They were deported to the United States. When they arrived in the San Petro Harbor, California, most of them were deathly sick, especially the children. After arriving in the United States, Werner's wife, a US citizen, was subjected to a brutal FBI interrogation. It was hours of intense questioning under very bright lights. Starr came out of that interrogation almost hysterical and completely exhausted. It was Veronica who secured a sleeping pill for Starr. Thereafter, they were taken to Crystal City, Texas.

In her correspondence with Heidi Gurcke Donald, Veronica stated, "At my age ... I truly do not want to recall a time when we were beset by so many deprivations and anxieties. I have tried to answer all your questions ... but it suddenly became a burden with which I could not adequately cope." Veronica was a British woman, who fell in love with and chose to marry a

German national. That was her crime. Unfortunately, some of that anti-German hysteria created by the Allies still lingers on.

Heidi is a contributing member of the German American Internee Coalition website (www.gaic.info). Students of twentieth-century history are well served by this website.

Eberhard Fuhr

Back at the conference at Ellis Island, Eberhard Fuhr, one of the organizers of this historic event, chronicled the experiences of his family. The Fuhr family lived in Cincinnati, Ohio. His older brother, Julius, attended college on an athletic scholarship. His father was a baker. In those days, most mothers stayed home to take care of the family and the children. Eberhard was two years old and his brother Julius five when his parents, Carl and Anna Fuhr, immigrated to the United States in 1927. The youngest brother, Gerhard, was born in Cincinnati in 1929. The Fuhrs were law-abiding, tax-paying, and contributing members of the community, who never had any scrapes with the law whatsoever. Throughout our history, German Americans have been law-abiding, hardworking, compassionate good neighbors. The Fuhrs were part of the norm, people anywhere would have loved to have as neighbors.

German pioneers first settled in Cincinnati and the beautiful Buckeye State in the German Belt. Cincinnati has been able to maintain its German culture and heritage better than many other cities in a variety of ways, including annually hosting America's largest Oktoberfest during the third weekend in September, attracting more than five hundred thousand people, close to six hundred thousand guests from near and far. Nationally, there are more than two thousand major Oktoberfests each year being celebrated. J. Edgar Hoover's FBI and the Justice Department would have had a field day collecting names for their secret list of people drinking German beer and singing German songs. Anybody dancing the Schuhplattler would be extremely suspect. It was accepted, even expected, for every other ethnic American group to display affection for the country whence they came but not for German Americans. Tragically, for them to display their pride in their culture, heritage, dance, music, song, and roots became a crime and landed them in an internment camp. That was considered displaying anti-Americanism. How quickly we forgot all the monumental contributions of the German Americans to our great nation. German-American heritage and culture were intentionally destroyed by governmental policy during the twentieth century.

Preceding and during World War II, practicing one's German culture was considered par to promoting Nazi interests. Singing German folk songs, such as "Du, du liegst mir im Herzen" or "Die Lorelei" and enjoying a Stein of German beer with pretzels was sufficient reason to be placed on J. Edgar Hoover's dreaded FBI list, from which there was no escape. All the anti-German hysteria was conducted with FDR's blessings. The usual innocent until proven guilty was turned upside down; the entire judicial system was turned upside down. It was like a twentieth-century Inquisition. Enemy aliens were scrutinized and searched. Government agents were lurking in every corner. It was an unconstitutional persecution of German and German Latin Americans. As some of the agents stated, "We are not prosecuting you; we are persecuting you." The judicial clock was turned centuries back to the Dark Ages.

Maintaining their German heritage, Carl and Anna Fuhr were arrested early in 1942. First, they were taken to Seagoville and then to Crystal City. The youngest brother, Gerhard, joined his parents in the internment camp, rather than being placed in an orphanage. It is incomprehensible why our own government caused such terror in the German-, Italian-, and Japanese-American communities. What was the hidden governmental agenda?

On a dreary and dark day, the FBI hauled Eberhard out of his home, dragging him to the Federal Building, where he was interrogated in a darkened room with a bright light shining directly into his face. The interrogation included questions about his family's loyalty, whom he was dating, and why he was dating her, if he sang in a German-American youth choir, and if he attended a weekend German-language school. He sang in a German-American youth choir, along with Doris Day. Her father was the choir director. It was verboten to preserve their German-American heritage and culture. That was such a tragic and great loss to America, turning the German Americans into the silent majority. Give a small person a little authority and it will go to his head was also true during these wild investigations.

The identity of the informers or accusers was never revealed; they were protected with governmental secrecy. Witnesses or cross-examinations were not allowed, and the request for a lawyer was always denied; these were kangaroo court procedures, sanctioned by presidential decree. Eventually, Eberhard was permitted to go back to their home, but the inflicted terror never left him or his family.

On March 23, 1943, six weeks before graduation, Eberhard was handcuffed by armed FBI agents and humiliated in front of his classmates, teachers, and coaches at Woodward High School. Brother Julius was arrested and handcuffed later that same day. To make Eberhard's disappearance complete, his senior picture was removed from the yearbook. This persecution was worse than the Salem witch hunt, which has since been categorically condemned.

It is not difficult to comprehend the shock and terror that overcame the Fuhr brothers when they noticed the *Cincinnati*

Enquirer front-page head-liner the next day at the Federal Building. The sensational front-page story was "Brothers Want to Help Hitler." The paper must have been desperate for a good story. Our media loves using sensationalism to increase its sales; it's always the bottom line. Allegedly, the FBI finally found some real criminals. The media had them convicted and sentenced even before any show trial. The intriguing part of this deceptive fabrication was the fact that, according to the newspaper, a decision had already been rendered about the two brothers even before a show hearing had been conducted. No one seemed to care that they were erroneously stripped of all their constitutional rights and their earthly possessions. No one listened.

The next morning, the Fuhr brothers were transported to an internment camp. The FBI did not even grant them permission to lock up their home or to turn off the electricity, water, and gas. Shortly thereafter, their home was vandalized. The prevailing attitude was that these criminals got what they deserved because they were Germans. Such was the great power of foxy politicians and media propaganda. If you were German and you were incarcerated, you received what you deserved, because you were German.

For the duration of the transport, the brothers were handcuffed together, facing each other. That made walking very cumbersome. They were denied any bathroom privacy. Eventually, they were united with their parents at Crystal City. By any interpretation of law, they were not criminals but treated like the worst criminals. What purpose did this brutal mistreatment of fellow Americans really serve? Was it merely a sideshow of presidential power, benefitting the elite?

In 1947, more than two years after the end of World War II, Eberhard and Julius were released from Ellis Island. They took the ferry back to the mainland in the direction of the Statue of

Liberty. Everything that our Statue of Liberty represents was denied to them and to thousands of others. Eberhard was now twenty-two years old. Shortly thereafter, Carl and Anna Fuhr were released. When they returned to Cincinnati, they found their boys, but everything else was lost forever. So far, none of the internees were ever compensated for any of their losses. They, like all internees, were never charged with or found guilty of any war-related crime. The Fuhr family, like all the others, were being detained "for their own good and safety"—such an oxymoron and such a total abuse and contradiction of American justice. Sadly, this was our own national reality show with dire consequences.

There were no criminals in the camps, just individuals being treated like criminals. J. Edgar Hoover insisted on having unrestricted authority to ransack, arrest, and intern randomly whomever he chose. The victims were assumed guilty and were not given an opportunity to prove their innocence. Judicial procedures were turned on their head. The internment program was exceedingly capricious. These camps, where thousands of innocent victims were detained, were fear-inspiring concentration camps with two parallel barbed-wire fences, guard towers with spotlights, and armed guards with machine guns, kill zones, and police dogs. FDR got away with this hideous scheme by calling the victims detainees and not prisoners, playing antics with semantics.

Since his retirement, Eberhard Fuhr has been telling his story and the story of thousands of other victims like himself. He also talks about the colossal human cost of these civil liberties violations. Homes were ransacked and lost, families disrupted, lives and reputations destroyed, and years and belongings lost forever. Eberhard was one of the many guests on our German-American radio show. The author had the distinct honor and pleasure of personally meeting Eberhard Fuhr at the Cincinnati

Oktoberfest in 2009. On Friday, April 19, 2013, he was the keynote speaker at the German-American Kulturabend at the Baldwin Wallace University in Berea, Ohio. The lecture hall was well attended by people interested in Eberhard's personal story and our own real history.

National Consciousness

As infants, we have a need to be noticed and recognized, be the center of attention, as we develop our persona. We are active and social creatures. There is a need that our presence be reinforced with various social interactions. We probably do not remember the first time we uttered the words, "Mama, watch me. I can walk. Mama, watch me. I can talk." We develop our personal identity through role-playing and playful competition. We are the product of both our nature and our nurture.

As adults, most still need to feed their personal ego consciousness with the way they walk and talk, their hairstyles, the clothes they wear, the cars they drive, the homes in which they live, their bank accounts, and in a myriad of ways. As we grow up and become part of a group, we acquire the ways of the group. That elevates the importance of the group, and the group mentality gains greater significance. We tend to love what they love and hate whom they hate. Propaganda owes its influence and power to a national group conscious manipulation of the masses.

Abraham Lincoln is credited with the observation that "you can fool some of the people all the time and all the people some of the time." Fortunately, you cannot fool "all the people all of the time." Propaganda and brainwashing have their limits. Our cognitive imperative directs us toward a universal world consciousness, a greater awareness of man's grand humanitarian role in the service of others.

Just like in the atmosphere, there are always different forces and currents of converging interests interacting. The present time in history is no exception. There are powerful forces of special interests keeping the American internment camp program off the radar. Perhaps with God's divine intervention, the biblical David will be victorious over the powerful establishment Goliath. True patriotism shall be served extremely well by unmasking falsehood.

Arthur D. Jacobs

Another proud and upright American patriot of German descent is Arthur D. Jacobs, retired as a major of the US Air Force and professor at Arizona State University. His testament is the legacy of an American boy, born in America, who was betrayed by his government during World War II. His is the story of an innocent American kid caught in the scheme of political intrigue. Professor Jacobs recorded his journey to hell in his book *The Prison called Hohenasperg*.

It is a perilous journey from his home in Brooklyn, New York, to the internment at Ellis Island and then to Crystal City, Texas. The book describes how he survived his imprisonment after the war at Hohenasperg in Germany and how he fought his way back to his beloved homeland—America.

After arriving in bombed-out Germany, in the dead of one of the coldest winters on record, he was transported to Hohenasperg in a frigid, stench-filled, locked, and heavily guarded boxcar usually used to transport livestock. Once in Hohenasperg, he was separated from his family and put in a prison cell. Arthur was only twelve years old; he was a kid, a child, abused and mistreated by his government. The US Army guards called him "a little Nazi" and told him that if he did not behave, he would be killed and hanged from the oak tree, the hangman's tree, in the middle of the prison camp. If that does not get your attention, nothing will.

The nightmare began when Arthur was ten years old in 1943. FBI agents invaded and ransacked his family's home not once, not even twice, but three times because of some baseless, anonymous informer. Each time, the home looked like it was hit by some hurricane. The agents pulled out drawers, threw the contents disrespectfully on the floor, and opened all the cabinet doors, but they never found anything. They created a huge mess, treating their belongings like garbage and with total disregard for the family and their constitutional human rights.

All the constitutional rights of the victims had been violated and trampled on, all because of FDR's abuse of executive power. Power corrupts, and absolute power corrupts absolutely. In America, even convicted criminals have rights. Requesting a lawyer was verboten, a right that even convicted criminals have. Instilling fear and terror was the order of the day. If these injustices happened once, they can happen again. Once governmental powers are expanded, they generally are not given back freely. Government becomes bigger and more powerful at the expense of individual and personal rights.

It took Mrs. Jacobs hours to clean up the mess the FBI agents left behind and put things back in order. None of them ever even apologized for their rude behavior. Remember, these were Germans, and they got what they deserved. After each rummage and pillage, Arthur's mother would be in tears for days on in, frightened and devastated. Even their clergyman refused to intercede on their behalf, because he too was afraid of being arrested and terrorized by association. The beloved Statue of Liberty had turned her back on German Americans. We must remember that these human rights violations did not happen in the Soviet Union, Nazi Germany, or Fascist Italy, but in Brooklyn, New York, and across America. Fear and insecurity rose to a new level. In addition, clearly further violating the constitutional rights of American citizens, governmental agencies would inform the police and their employers about how "dangerous" these individuals were. As a result, finding and maintaining a job became very, very difficult for fellow German Americans.

Some twenty-five years ago, Arthur Jacobs was watching a national television show about the internment of Japanese Americans. What he heard during this program made him sit up and take notice. The announcer, Dan Rather, made the erroneous claim that "During World War II, the US government did not intern German Americans." Arthur Jacobs could not help but wonder if he was dreaming about his nightmarish experiences at Ellis Island and at Crystal City and the hangman's tree at the prison called Hohenasperg. He sent a letter to the program, pointing out the error, but never received a reply, nor did the program ever provide a correction. Why has the media made such false claims and denied all these human rights violations and not truthfully reported these atrocities against fellow Americans? It is no wonder the American people have lost much of their trust in the reliability of the media reporting.

Of course, Professor Jacobs was not dreaming and could only wonder why a reputable national television program would make such a false claim and not attempt to correct it. This was not the only incident of such an erroneous claim. On August 16, 1984, US Representative from California Norman Y. Mineta made a similar false statement in his sworn testimony before a Senate subcommittee, claiming, "We did not lock up German Americans." What would he call the internment program, a paid vacation? Did he perjure himself unknowingly or intentionally?

Furthermore, German-American survivors and their children were shocked to read in the January/February 2017 issue of the *Smithsonian* that Japanese but no Germans were incarcerated during World War II. Why the flagrant denial and persistent revisionism? Shouldn't they have known the facts surrounding this national issue before writing an article?

On October 4, 1987, the *New York Times* reported, "The government never came close to locking up German Americans as security risks." On May 2, 1988, *Time* magazine stated that there were no camps for German Americans. Why this continual denial? Conversely, on October 5, 1945, the *Washington Post* reported the kidnapping program and objected to German Latin Americans wrongly being repatriated against their will to bombed-out Germany rather than being allowed to return home to Latin America, where they had been abducted. Washington, supporting American businesses, wanted to eliminate all German Latin American competition.

There appear to be two realities: the actual devastation, the suffering, and terror that thousands of German Americans and German Latin Americans were subjected to and the revised, sensationalized media version. The suffering of these victims is treated as if it never happened or as totally unimportant, as an illusion or a mirage. As Arthur Jacobs said time and time again, "It may be common knowledge that only Japanese were interned, but that is a boldface lie."

It was his response to the persistence of some interest group in revising American history that inspired Professor Jacobs to write his book. Even history books are guilty of revising and falsifying the facts. Far more than seventy-five thousand German Americans were terrorized and caused great suffering in some sixty-nine concentration camps. Their rights had repeatedly been and are continuing to be violated. They lived in plasterboard and tarpaper shacks, placed into "protective custody," and their mail was strictly censored. Guard towers, barbed-wire fences, and guards with two-way radios and supersensitive microphones at the fences surrounded them.

In 1990, the Seagoville Federal Correctional Institution published an insultingly outrageous claim that German Latin American families "left their home countries to enjoy the freedom of America." This is a boldface, blatant lie! After they were kidnapped, they were forced like a herd of cattle to cross our border at gunpoint and then charged with illegally entering the United States. There appear to be interest groups who want to keep it a secret permanently.

J. Edgar Hoover's FBI acknowledged conducting more than one hundred thousand home searches with or without warrants, mostly without. Most of the victims are still traumatized by their devastating experiences, which disrupted their lives and destroyed their belongings. Many internees still break down and weep uncontrollably when they are coaxed to speak about their sufferings. What was the purpose of this persecution? The FBI and the Justice Department were a constant fear factor in their lives, just like a haunting, ever-present nightmare. Geneva Convention rules were conveniently and intentionally ignored.

The US Supreme Court

Professor Jacobs took his case to court, the Court of Appeals and then the US Supreme Court. The purpose of his lawsuit was to stop the discrimination against German-American internees and to secure a governmental apology for their mistreatment and equal compensation for their losses. Since 1948, Congress has enacted nine separate laws compensating Japanese-American internees, strangely none for German- or Italian-American internees. Might this be the result of differing amounts of clout and influence in Washington? German-American internees have made it clear that they do not begrudge the restitution their

Japanese counterparts received, quite to the contrary. Their compensation did not even come close to compensating for their losses and suffering.

Professor Jacobs's arguments were simple and straightforward and to most students of law legally sound. First, Japanese Americans did not constitute the majority interned, 56 percent of the internees were German and other European Americans. Second, 64 percent of the FBI arrests conducted from December 7, 1941, to June 30, 1945, were German and other European Americans. Furthermore, seamen on German ships in American ports were illegally arrested, an infringement of international law. Third, the arrests of German Americans began on December 7, 1941, four days before the United States was at war with Germany. Fourth, German and other European Americans were detained until July 1948, long after hostilities ceased and longer than their Japanese counterparts. Fifth, the report that the government produced on the internment program, *Personal Justice Denied*, is discriminatory and seriously skewed since it is based only on selective testimony of Japanese internees. All other testimony was excluded, including the testimony of high-ranking officials in the program. That would have also constituted expert testimony, which was denied. There is another serious contention, Public Law 102-248, which designates former internment camps, such as Crystal City, as historic landmarks outrageously claiming only Japanese were detained at the camps. The terror and suffering of German-American internees were treated as irrelevant and unimportant.

Tell the German internees and the children who were born in Crystal City to German-American parents and who came together in 2002 for a reunion at Crystal City that they and their relatives were never there. The motto of the reunion was "And Justice for All." Erika Scheibe Seus, one of the Crystal City children, stated, "It too was heartwarming to hear an apology from the mayor of Crystal City." They all were grateful to hear judges, Texas state legislators, clergy, former internees, and the historian of Crystal City, Richard Santos, speak. They also conducted a memorial service at the swimming pool. Wreaths were laid in memory of the two girls who drowned there. The media chose not to mention this historic reunion on the evening news; it too was killed with deafening silence.

The Court of Appeals ruled against Arthur Jacobs and, therefore, against German and Italian internees, reasoning that the Japanese were interned strictly on racial grounds and that Germans were arrested individually as security risks. Has the court ruled that the government was justified to practice racial discrimination? Where the Japanese not interned and relocated from the West Coast for security reasons?

Arthur Jacobs points out that prior to FDR's Executive Order #9066, the Japanese were arrested individually just like their German counterparts. The court was selective in the evidence it considered and which evidence it excluded. However, it did not deny that German Americans were interned. Arthur Jacobs argued that American German internees were excluded and prohibited from providing testimony in the Civil Right Act. The commission discriminatorily allowed only the testimony and documents of Japanese-American internees, excluding the testimony of German- and Italian-American internees.

It is a documented fact that German Americans were arrested and interned before the United States went to war with Germany. The court ruled that under wartime conditions, the constitutional rights of German-American internees had not been violated, conveniently ignoring the truth. At the time, the United States was *not* at war with Germany. In the fall of 1991, the case was filed with the Supreme Court. The high court chose not to hear the case of *Arthur D. Jacobs v. William Barr et al.* (91-2061).

Jacobs points out German Americans were not interned solely for alleged national security reasons or to silence American German opposition to the war but for the more sinister Machiavellian mission of using them as a commodity to be exchanged. This fact remains: concentration camps were a reality long before the United States officially entered the war. With time, patience, and perseverance, all things shall be accomplished. I pray that justice delayed will not become *justice denied*.

Arthur Jacobs and other members of the German American Internment Coalition (GAIC) are confident that the US government, our Congress, will ultimately address the issue of the mistreatment of German-American and German Latin-American internees and acknowledge the devastation it caused. Government will ultimately pass the Wartime Treatment Study Act, hopefully *before* all the internees have died. We may never forget that *the price of liberty is eternal vigilance*!

Anneliese Krauter

Another traumatized German-American internee who appeared on the German-American radio show was Anneliese (Lee) Krauter, who invited me to come along on her journey. Let us all join Lee on a young girl's journey during World War II. She, like so many other internees, has been telling her story, which she recorded in her book, *From the Heart's Closet*, at schools, civic groups, libraries, conferences, on the air, and anywhere else that anybody is willing to listen.

Lee is an all-American girl, born in America. Hers is an amazingly honest account of life in New York, her father's butcher shop, the internment at Ellis Island, and the subsequent forced repatriation to a bombed-out Germany during the war. It is an eloquently written, awe-inspiring story sincerely from the heart of a little, tiny girl. Lee describes the human cost and devastation to thousands of families caught up in the vortex of J. Edgar Hoover's suspicious conduct, the FBI bureaucracy, and FDR's and Winston Churchill's intrigues.

They were among the thousands who were forcibly repatriated. After arriving at their ancestral home in Bettenhausen, Thuringia, they faced more suspicions there. Everyone was wondering why they returned at such a God-forsaken time. They experienced never-ending Allied bombing, death, and destruction. An overwhelming sense of indifference as to the outcome of all these devastated, unfortunate souls permeated the atmosphere.

The human drive for survival gave these individuals extra-human inner strength. God did not forsake them; humans forsake each other for selfish, egocentric reasons. The most compelling part of the book talks about the betrayal as the family flees to escape from being caught in the *Russian Zone.*

In their flight from the Russian Zone to the American Zone, they came across an American GI who showed compassion and an interest in helping them reach the American Zone. On the way, the American GI violated tiny, little Anneliese. She was only ten years old. By any definition, this was a sexual assault. In any civilized society, this constituted statutory rape of a little, helpless child. These poor victims had no rights. The GI might have had a tiny, little girl of his own at home. Raping women from eight to eighty appeared to be the norm and occurred all too often. Remembering the painful ordeal, she described it as if a sledgehammer was being forced into her tiny, little body. Anneliese has forgiven the GI, but the scars and the wounds have remained. Did the GI violate tiny little "Lee" because he knew he could get away with it? He too was a member of the Greatest Generation.

After all the pain and suffering and several years later, this story does have a happy ending. Lee found the love of her life; it was love at first sight. Joe, also an American, and Anneliese Krauter settled down in Indiana. They were blessed with four sons and many grandchildren.

With the Freedom of Information Act, documents were attainable. After nine months of waiting, Lee received a copy of the arrest warrant for her mom. Francis Biddle, attorney general, stated that her mom was an "alien enemy whom I deem dangerous to the public peace and safety of the United States." Nearing the end of his life, Biddle lamented that his role in the internment and repatriation policy he enforced during World War II was his "greatest regret." Francis Biddle admitted his transgressions against German Americans. When will the US government demonstrate the courage and fortitude to do likewise? The time is long past due.

Another revelation in the document Lee received was her mother's offer to renounce her American citizenship so that she could keep her family together, even if it was in an American concentration camp. Countless individuals suffered needlessly. They are the real heroes of the greatest generation.

Lee recalled in her book that this "set us on a course more adventurous than I could have ever imagined, had I not lived it." This is a story of personal courage, through the eyes of a beautiful little child. For most of her adult life, Lee had a deep, burning inner desire to tell her story. Her friends encouraged her to write a book, but she had to promise her mom that she would not publish it until after her mom was gone. You see, her mom was still utterly afraid that the FBI would knock on their door and arrest them all over again. Those were very deep wounds, causing excruciating pain. Many of the internees went to their graves with that fear hidden deep within them. Lee kept her promise to her mom, publishing her book, *From the Heart's Closet*, after her mom died.

So many internees took their sufferings and torture to their graves, keeping the oath, which they were forced to sign, never to speak or write about their internment experiences. It seems there are interest groups who would like nothing better than to keep it permanently hidden and off the radar. This happened in America, where we pride ourselves in having constitutionally protected human rights and eagerly display our human compassion. These rights have little weight unless they are enforced and applied without discrimination. If all men are created equal, then we all stand equally before the law. Is it not the will of God that men are free, are brothers, and are equal? Our Constitution does not provide for first- and second-class citizens, for master and slave. Why do humans persist in such differentiation?

The Heitmann Family

The British secret intelligence gave the name of Alfred Heitmann to the FBI, which promptly arrested him on the strength of an empty, false British accusation. No one ever checked the accuracy or validity of any claim. At a show hearing, the FBI produced a Chinese laundryman who claimed that Alfred made pro-Nazi remarks in his presence. This was a legal mirage; no charges were ever filed. This was all the justification required for being detained; they were being detained "for their own safety." Due process and cross-examination were never allowed.

It does not take a legal scholar to realize that these so-called "cases" would have been thrown out of any self-respecting court even in a third-world country. However, this was sufficient for J. Edgar Hoover's FBI to arrest and intern him. Had this happened in another country, we would have rightfully complained about human rights violations. Alfred's nightmare journey began when he was sent to Camp Meade, Camp Forrest, Fort Lincoln, and finally to Camp Seagoville.

Indefensible charges were fabricated time and time again, thousands of times, at the expense of our German-American population. The victims were twice victimized, first by being falsely arrested and secondly by having all due process procedures denied. In this legal mirage, no one was ever officially charged with anything. The stress of uncertainty concerning Alfred's whereabouts and the FBI not telling his wife, Caroline, where he was or why he was being detained took its physical and mental toll. Imagine the fear and helplessness these poor victims felt. They were finally reunited when Caroline *voluntarily* joined Alfred at the Seagoville camp. Once she chose to *voluntarily* enter that camp, there was no *voluntarily* leaving it again. Thousands were held against their will, without any legitimate cause.

Their only child was born in 1948. Dr. John Heitmann is professor of science history at the University of Dayton. Similar to the psychological and emotional scars of rape and sexual assault victims, internees were infected with a repressed shame that they carried with them the rest of their lives. In addition, talking about their experiences brought forth an excruciating amount of pain. Alfred, like most internees, took his oath of silence very seriously and ultimately took his secrets to his grave. Fabrications, unsubstantiated accusations, and lies were the norm, not the exception.

The Heitmann's home was no exception. Any discussion about World War II or the internment program was strictly verboten and completely off limits. As John grew up in the fifties and sixties, he ran into a wall of silence. The recollection was much too painful. The devastation of camp life, which may have caused a miscarriage in October 1944, greatly contributed to years of anxiety. Professor Heitmann concluded that the unwarranted shame and everything that was associated with it remained consciously and subconsciously with the family until Alfred's death in 1983. This wall of silence was finally broken down only through Dr. Heitmann's persistence long after his father's death.

Professor Heitmann gradually uncovered glimpses of the past and able to reconstruct the course of events that his parents were forced to endure. A few snapshots and an ashtray inscribed "Seagoville, 1943" stuck with him and kept reappearing in his memory bank. His mother told him that it was a rock that his father hand painted while they were interned. It was etched in his memory from his earliest childhood. Any persistent inquiry into this relic only led to his parents being increasingly evasive. This too was part of the damage that FDR and J. Edgar Hoover, with British secret intelligence guidance, had inflicted on thousands of helpless and innocent people. Dr. Heitmann recalls that it was this wartime experience that was being kept from him that shaped his childhood and family life.

It was 1994, eleven years after his father had died and almost fifty years after the war ended, when Professor Heitmann began the painstaking journey into his own family's past. While he visited his mother, who now lived alone, he looked at the many books she had dating back to the 1930s and '40s. One book in particular caught his attention—a Lutheran catechism dated 1943. It was a gift from the German government to "Kriegsgefangener," or POWs.

Shortly thereafter, he visited the National Archives, a trip he had taken many times as a professional historian and university faculty member. This time, he was in pursuit of his own family history rather than that of others. The question he wanted to answer was "How did it come about that in 1942 his father, Alfred Heitmann, was arrested and interned?"

The Freedom of Information Act made it possible to search

the files that formerly were classified "top secret." However, there were still many stumbling blocks. Often, relevant sections are blacked out, which forces the researcher to cross-reference other documents. Any request for a document takes a very long time. It is not the usual friendly treatment we have gotten used to at our friendly local neighborhood library.

Alfred was a World War I orphan. His father never returned from the war. Alfred landed in New York in September 1939. In June 1942, FBI agents, armed with machine guns, came to the place of his employment, arrested him, and treated him like the most dangerous criminal. That shattered Alfred and Caroline's American dream, of leaving totalitarianism and the war in Europe behind them. That became their tragic American reality show.

For many German Americans, the internment experiences continued well into the summer of 1948. Alfred and Caroline's ordeal ended in the summer of 1945. They settled in Western New York, close to Caroline's family, but it was a life without a real past. Remember, he who controls the past controls the future. Who is controlling and rewriting our past? The stigma of internment remained, because "in America, people don't just get put into jail for no reason at all." That obviously is a false assumption, a mirage, even in America. It simply could not be true, but it was, because it happened to tens of thousands of innocent victims.

Countless innocent individuals, like Alfred and Caroline, are not even relegated to a footnote in American history textbooks. Even with overwhelming documentation, this part of our history is still being falsified and revised by our media and textbook industry. Why? Will it take a lawsuit to bring about the whole truth and nothing but the truth in our history textbooks and everywhere else? Twenty some years ago, the textbook industry promised the German-American community, the DANK Organization, that it would rectify that mistake, but thus far that has remained just another empty promise.

These shattered lives of countless, innocent individuals shout to God in heaven about these grotesque examples of what America the beautiful is *not* supposed to be. If America is to continue shining as the pillar of all the noble virtues of democracy, freedom, and human decency, then we, as a nation, must come clean with our own history; otherwise, our recent history will also tarnish our future. If the largest ethnic group in America was terrorized so viciously, imagine what could happen to another smaller group. We need to be brave to remain free. The rights and privileges of every individual must always be protected unconditionally. Is national guilt and shame preventing us from facing our own past honestly?

Christa Schmitz

All those revisionists denying that such atrocities could have ever happened in America should check the birth certificates of all the German-American children born in the American concentration camps. Like the doubting biblical St. Thomas, "Take your hand and feel the wounds in my side." After Italian Americans were "reprieved" by Attorney General Biddle in 1943, German Americans were J. Edgar Hoover's only target group, and he hunted them relentlessly. Our entire constitutional legal system was turned upside down.

When Christa Schmitz was sixteen, she applied for a work permit so that she could take a job at a dress shop near her home in the Bronx, New York. She was required to provide her birth certificate. That caused her to be ashamed. *Not* she but others should have been ashamed. She recalls that she was rather embarrassed to have to provide evidence that she was born at the "Alien Internment Camp, Crystal City, Texas," a concentration camp in America.

Schmitz, now Christa Schmitt of Vancouver, was one of 252 children born at Crystal City. Time and maturity have helped Schmitt move beyond the shame. Shame is a very debilitating psychological force. What disturbs her and others are the forced silence and coordinated national denial, possibly the result of a national feeling of guilt and shame. True remorse requires action, not denial.

The denial of our internment program has been called a deliberate cover-up. Professor Arthur Jacobs stated, "So many have been so misinformed for so long, including law professors and history professors. When they finally learn of the truth, they turn their heads the other way, or bury them in the sand." In the meantime, the victims suffer while they continue to be forgotten and ignored.

Christa has been unable to ascertain the reason for her father's arrest or why the FBI shipped the family off to a concentration camp. Relevant documents sent to Schmitt at her request have sections blacked out and marked "classified." How ironic, governmental agencies are still resisting providing the requested documents and nothing less than the whole *truth*.

The internment program during both world wars was a blatant violation of human rights, an unconstitutional persecution of German Americans and others? Of course! Our proud national consciousness demands national resolve. We cannot forever keep our heads in the sand. Truth is like oxygen, fueling national vitality and perpetuating freedom and true democracy. Denial is like a cancer eating away at our proud national consciousness. Let our actions demonstrate that we are the land of the brave and the free.

The unique strength of our nation is beautifully summarized on our one-cent coin, our "Pfennig," our penny, "E pluribus

Unum" (out of many one). Our one nation is composed of many diverse ethnic groups. Our stability and prosperity have been achieved by working harmoniously together and learning to tolerate and appreciate our diversity. When any group is discriminated against, as German Americans have been during and following both world wars, the foundation of our constitutional rights is seriously jeopardized.

Truth remains the only remedy, not sensationalism, exaggerations of fabricated allegations, or denials. There are endless stories of terror and of flagrant miscarriages of justice by overzealous government officials operating under the guise of *patriotism.*

The Eiserloh Family

Mathias was a student of engineering when he met his future bride, Johanna, in her hometown of Idstein, Germany, after World War I. They both were dreaming of immigrating to America, which they did in 1922. Mathias and Johanna Eiserloh brought with them the hopes of most immigrants, to live, work, and raise a family in relative freedom and *not* being harassed by any governmental agency.

At first, life was not what they had imagined it to be. Like most immigrants, the Eiserlohs were faced with finding employment, learning a new language, and adjusting to cultural and social differences. Mathias found employment in his chosen profession. The Eiserlohs purchased two acres of land in Strongsville, a suburb of Cleveland, Ohio. They designed and built their dream home. Three healthy children were born between 1930 and 1941. Johanna raised a flock of chickens and began to sell the eggs and hens. Life was good. They attended functions at a German social club, which was mainly comprised other engineers and their families. The club also served as a network for members to find jobs and mutual support, as is often the case in such organizations.

On the day following Pearl Harbor, J. Edgar Hoover kicked his operation into high gear; more than sixty thousand German Americans were rounded up. What did German Americans have to do with Pearl Harbor? Nothing, except it would serve British strategic political interests. The next day, December 9, 1941, without any warning, Mathias was arrested by the FBI at his job in front of his coworkers and jailed in Cleveland, Ohio.

The unannounced, surprise ransacking of homes and the arrests added to the amount of fear the FBI created. Their savings were frozen, and their nightmare began. The Treasury Department categorically froze the assets of the internees. Everyone was looking the other way; upstanding, good Americans were unwilling to get involved. There were no riots or demonstrations against these brutal treatments of fellow Americans.

Without her husband and with their savings frozen, like all the other wives, Johanna was left destitute. There was no governmental safety net to turn to for help. Neighbors and friends began to treat them with chilling coldness. The children at school were harassed with cruel and nasty insults. No one believed that an innocent man could be jailed and most certainly not in America. The prevalent attitude was that he must have done something. Unfortunately, innocence became proof of guilt. Her former customers no longer bought her chickens and eggs. Johanna tried repeatedly to find out the true cause of Alfred's arrest but was never given a reason, because there were no justifiable reasons.

In total desperation, Johanna was forced to sell the home for a pittance of its true value. Fearing that the proceeds from the sale of the home would also be frozen and lost forever, she insisted on a cash sale and had little choice but to sell it to an unscrupulous buyer. Before she moved out of the house, a masked robber attacked her during the night and demanded "the money."

Since the buyer was the only one who knew of the money, it might well have been him who wanted to steal the house outright. Fortunately, she was able to fight the intruder off. A few days later, they were terrorized again when someone shot their two German shepherds. Johanna was left partially paralyzed, and sadly, there was no one there to help them and no criminal investigation. Why, they got what they deserved; they were Germans. Such was the power of massive propaganda fueling anti-German hysteria.

After two years of separation, the family was reunited at Crystal City. They soon learned from other internees that their story of despair was not unique. Thousands of others had been treated the same way, losing homes and possessions and their dignity.

On the train to New York Harbor, to board the SS *Grimsholm* for repatriation, Johanna gave birth to their fourth child, Guenther. Two days after delivery, the Eiserloh family was forcibly repatriated to a bombed-out, starving, and devastated Germany. The Red Cross would have provided appropriate help to Mrs. Eiserloh and her newborn baby. Conveniently, the Red Cross was never informed. Again, no one was ever held accountable.

Like so many others, the Eiserlohs endured the fourteen-day stormy crossing of the Atlantic war zone. Upon arriving in Europe, they received more bad news; the crates that contained all their earthly belongings had been stolen. Maybe they were never sent. They were left with only the clothes on their backs.

The Eiserloh children, all born in America, were exchanged for four other US citizens. One would have had to be a saint not to despair and be utterly bitter at such mistreatment by one's own government. The Germans who had been exchanged included many US-born children, spouses, and naturalized citizens. The FBI, the Justice Department, and the British Secret Intelligence Service raised divisiveness, intrigue, and tragedy to new levels.

After being literally dropped off in a totally bombed-out and devastated Germany in the middle of the coldest winter in Europe, the Eiserlohs began trucking north amid unrelenting Allied bombings and air raids. As often as they could, they took the train, but all too often, they had to walk in snow and ice because the railroads were destroyed.

After a very treacherous journey, they finally arrived in Idstein during the first few weeks of March, starved and exhausted. Their reception was almost as cold as the winter. The relatives were caught by complete surprise and in total disbelief. Why would any sane person return to a bombed-out and starving Germany with a sickly small baby at a time like this? The Eiserlohs suffered from malnutrition. You'd have to be totally out of your mind. If it would have been the Eiserlohs' decision to return at such a God-forsaken time, their relatives would have had just reason to wonder about their sanity, but this was part of FDR's exchange program of human cargo and his demand of unconditional surrender.

Their troubles didn't stop. Under suspicion of being American agents and undercover spies, six SS men severely beat Mathias in their basement home in full view of his terrified wife and children. This time, not the FBI but the Gestapo arrested Mathias and hauled him off to an undisclosed prison. What did they do to deserve such torture and mistreatment? These are stark reminders that all of history is a story of man's inhumanity to his fellow human beings. The names may change, but the stories do remain the same.

After the unnecessary war, the Eiserlohs gradually began

to rebuild their lives. They applied repeatedly for reentry to America but were denied. Finally, in 1947, the two oldest children, Ingrid and Lothar, then twelve and seventeen, were allowed to return to the land where they were born—America. In 1955, the rest of the Eiserlohs returned to America. After high school, Lothar joined the US Air Force and was granted a security clearance to receive nuclear weapons training. He, of course, was no longer considered a "dangerous enemy alien." The question begs to be answered: Who or what changed Lothar or US policy, and who harbored criminal intent?

Lothar was a guest on the German-American radio show. His voice reflected deep emotional wounds due to the suffering his family was forced to endure without even as much as an apology. Saying "sorry" is not a sign of weakness. Now, Lothar and his sisters, Ingrid and Ensila, share their experiences as part of the German-American Internee Coalition's enlightenment program, so that this part of our history may never be forgotten or repeated. Nobody deserves to suffer like this, and no one should be discriminated against because of his or her ancestry. Time and time again, hate and greed raised its ugly head. According to Scripture, the love of money continues to be the root of all evil. The more things change, the more they are the same. Governmental transparency continues to be essential to peaceful coexistence.

The Morgenthau and Kaufman Plan

In Britain, as in the United States, German-phobia reached a feverish level. According to Allied propaganda, the German people were allegedly responsible not only for both world wars but for all the wars since the beginning of recorded history. They were responsible for all our problems; they had to be made to pay the consequences. They have been and still are paying.

The destruction of Germany and the internment program are being justified by conveniently making wartime atrocity propaganda permanent history. Good men and women will not allow insult to be added to injury.

To rid the world of these war-lusting souls, Henry Morgenthau and Theodore N. Kaufman advocated the "eugenic sterilization" of forty-eight million German men. In addition, Germany would be partitioned and divided among its deserving neighbors. Kaufman authored a book entitled *Germany Must Perish*, and Morgenthau wrote a book *Germany Is Our Problem*. They proposed an agenda known as the Morgenthau Plan, which was contemptibly cruel, as it also perverted intellectual history. Even Martin Luther was rendered a Nazi, which rendered all Lutherans as Nazis. Not only Luther but also Kant, Fichte, Hegel, and others were allegedly part of the Nazi development in Germany. The Morgenthau Plan, approved by FDR, was to starve twenty to thirty million Germans in the process of turning Germany into an agricultural and pastoral nation.

The noted author William L. Shirer claimed that Bismarck, who introduced national health care to Germany; Kaiser William II; and Hitler instilled in the German people a "lust for power and domination, a passion for unbridled militarism, contempt for democracy, for authoritarianism." There was obviously no shortage of material fueling hate, lies, and anti-German sentiments. *Will it ever end?*

At the end of the war, Germany was in total ruin. FDR and Churchill stood firm on unconditional surrender. That amounted to total exploitation of and absolutely no rights for Germany. Millions of civilians, old men, women, and children were dead or crippled as a result of the Allied carpet bombing and the slaughter of the Red Army. Sixteen million ethnic Germans were brutally forced out of their homes and their ancestral homeland. Women were raped and then nailed, still alive, onto the side of barns and left to die. Millions were forced into slave labor camps in Siberia; most of them never returned. Millions were brutally killed by Stalin and Tito (Josip Broz). The name Tito stands for Technical International Terrorist Organization. He is responsible for hundreds of thousands of innocent lives. Stalin is responsible for millions of lives. World War II was the greatest ethnic cleansing in human history. Germany was occupied and divided into four occupational zones, which became East and West Germany. Germany is still waiting for a genuine peace treaty, not just a Four Plus Two Contract and not another armistice. When will Germany be granted genuine self-determination and national sovereignty by Washington? Japan was granted a peace treaty shortly after the war. Why not Germany? Who is blocking a true peace treaty for Germany?

At the conclusion of the war, things didn't go the way the British were hoping and planning. Winston Churchill and the British elite allegedly assumed, erroneously, that the United States would revert back into an isolationist attitude and policy as they did after World War I, when 90 percent of Americans were strong supporters of isolationism. That did not happen. FDR had his own plans for a Pax Americana, and in the process, FDR became the gravedigger of the British Empire. However, according to Patrick J. Buchanan, the primary person responsible for Britain losing its empire and the West losing the world is Winston Churchill. These wars of the twentieth century might well go down into history as the greatest lunacy ever committed by the human race.

Fortunately, there is not enough darkness in the world to put out the light of even one candle, the candle of love. Simultaneously, there is not enough silence and denial to kill the voice of truth. This synopsis of our recent history would not have been possible without the untiring work done by the internees and their children and grandchildren—the real victims. We are forever indebted to all of them for their persistence and determination. Their suffering and pain will not and cannot ever be forgotten.

President Wilson's idea that all people are entitled to self-determination is rooted in our Constitution and in Jefferson's proclamation that "All men are created equal." And yet, we allowed ourselves to be dragged into two world wars that never threatened our national security, nor did they really concern us. Tragically, we did not allow self-determination for Germany. Our leadership chose to become involved in brutal persecutions. Brutality and intimidation forced German Americans to become the silent majority.

The time is long overdue; we must step up to the mirror and be totally honest with the reflected image and verdict. Justice emerges from a just government. A tree will not only lie as it falls, but it will fall the way it leans. Let our actions radiate the noble principles laid down by our founding fathers. We can no longer accept shallow excuses and inaction.

Our freedom is continually being challenged by enemies masquerading as friends of democracy. FDR's administration displayed a self-righteous attitude, which he used to justify, among other actions, the internment program and all the suffering that went with it. We attributed our involvement in both world wars to the noble cause of "spreading democracy" but denied it to a large portion of our own population. We preach free trade but practice protectionism, justifying perpetual war for perpetual peace. These are obvious contradictions. We desperately need to find our way back to the spiritual light of 1776, the Declaration of Independence, and what our republic stands for.

Die Deutsche Zentrale

On February 25, 1942, the *Cleveland Plain Dealer* reported that the German Central Farm, a social club in Parma, Ohio, became another victim of the anti-German violence and destruction that swept through many of our communities. The newspaper reported that "more than 1,000 windows (were) smashed in the main building ... not an unbroken dish left in the kitchen ... pianos were destroyed and fires were set." These atrocities were reported in the press, but as usual, nothing was ever done about it and no one was ever held accountable for the crime. Tragically, it too was part of the acute hysteria against all things German. There seems to be no end to the horror stories against German Americans. Sadly, there is still no balance in the media; it is still skewed against German Americans.

In a letter to the editor in the *Plain Dealer* on July 13, 1942, Paul Saubermann demanded that the "Die Deutsche Zentrale sign on York Road (be) removed as an eyesore and a grim reminder of what it represents ... the sign is really an affront to the Americans." He was offended by the name *Deutsch* (German). Obviously, some individuals were of the erroneous and narrow-minded opinion that German Americans were not really Americans. Individuals like that need to be reminded that German pioneers first settled Ohio, and their many contributions are evident throughout the state. More than 44 percent of Ohioans are proud German Americans.

Fortunately, the German Central Organization survived all the atrocities committed against it and its members. It is still an active and vibrant social and cultural center. May it long remain a "home away from home," where its members proudly preserve and perpetuate their German-American heritage.

Frank Ziegler

In the middle 1920s, Frank Ziegler and his future bride, Agetha, arrived in Cleveland, Ohio. Both he and his wife were sponsored by her uncle and aunt, Johann and Sabine Soda. Frank and Agetha were blessed with a son and a daughter. In those days, Cleveland, like most cities in the German Belt, had its various ethnic neighborhoods. Frank and his wife purchased a home in an ethnic German-American neighborhood on East Seventy-Ninth Street and Decker Avenue.

It was a beautiful and well-kept neighborhood. Neighbors were mutually supportive. If someone's house was in need of paint, the neighbors would all join in, and the house would usually be painted in a day. The home owners would provide plenty of food and refreshments. Schnapps and beer would usually be served to celebrate the finished project. It was a great neighborhood spirit, neighbors supporting neighbors.

Frank joined the Bayrische Maennerchor (men's choir), preserving his German heritage. Once a week, they would get together to sing and enjoy a glass of beer. At the turn of the twentieth century, Cleveland was home to some two hundred German American clubs. Many were singing societies. The story went that if five Germans got together, they would form three social clubs and four singing societies. Since then, most of these organizations have been forced out of existence.

The influence of German ingenuity and diligence were evident throughout the region. German restaurants and hotels became centers for German-American social and cultural gatherings. William Richter was the first to serve beer on tap in his tavern on Ontario Street. The well-known Cleveland and American brewing industry was established almost entirely by German Americans.

They established banks, like the Cleveland Trust Company

(now AmeriTrust), founded by George Gund. Jacob Mueller, who also served as lieutenant governor, founded the Germania Insurance Company. They established schools with rigorous programs taught in German. German religious leaders became involved in establishing hospitals, orphanages, and nursing homes, such as the German Hospital (now Fairview Park General Hospital), Deaconess Hospital, Lutheran Hospital, the Methodist Orphanage in Berea, the Jewish Orphan's Asylum, and the Altenheim. German Americans have continuously displayed their culture in the arts, music, and folklore, as they have abundantly contributed color and substance to the rich fabric of our local and national American heritage.

While German Americans enjoyed their sauerkraut, bratwurst, and beer, they also supported higher education. They founded the German-Wallace College in Berea, which merged with Baldwin University and became Baldwin-Wallace University during World War I. All was not well. There was a sinister undercurrent of anti-German hysteria raising its ugly head again.

Frank was a highly trained expert machinist. He worked for Warner and Swasey, located on East Fifty-Fifth Street and Carnegie Avenue. He introduced carbine and diamond tooling, which revolutionized the industry. Frank Ziegler and his work received national notoriety when they were featured in the national *Machine Tool* magazine.

While Frank and his wife lived peacefully, minding their own business, on Decker Avenue, the FBI staked out their house, parking across the street and watching their every move. The FBI's actions were intentionally not inconspicuous. Everyone in the neighborhood became uneasy; many lived through the horrors of anti-German hysteria during World War I. On three different occasions, the FBI ransacked their home, opening everything and throwing the contents on the floor. Each and every time they left the house in a complete mess. Can you imagine this happening in America today?

The Zieglers decided to sell the home on Decker Avenue and purchase another house on West Fifty-Seventh and Memphis Avenue, hoping the FBI harassment would go away. No such luck. A few weeks later, the FBI began staking them out again and ransacking their home, again three times, each time leaving the house a total disaster. They were to create as much terror as possible on every unannounced visit and make the victims feel helpless. The agents confiscated a radio. Everybody was so afraid and scared to even talk, much less to complain. Besides, there was no one to complain to and no one listened.

Frank was arrested by the FBI and taken to the POW prison camp on Pleasant Valley and York Road, in Parma, Ohio, which is the present site of the West Campus of the Cuyahoga Community College. Warner and Swasey were not pleased with the FBI arresting their star machinist. The FBI would bring Frank to work in the morning and pick him up again after work. That went on for about two weeks. To further terrorize the Ziegler family, the FBI would escort their children to and from school. After they met with his employer and checked his work record, they stopped returning him to prison at night, but they never really left him alone.

His friends and fellow members of the choir were also interrogated; among them were Emil Schmidt, Joe Holzheimer and his brother Otto Holzheimer, and others. Frank's wife, Agetha, worked for the May Company. FBI agents shadowed her and informed her employer that she was extremely suspect and dangerous; they were trying to get her fired. The neighborhood was getting nervous. There was no end to this brutal, abusive harassment.

Frank Platzer, who later served as vice president of the Bayrische Maenerchor, dated Herr Ziegler's daughter. After calling on his future bride, Herr Ziegler said to his daughter Anita, "Marry that boy. I like him." And she did. The Platzers lived happily thereafter and were blessed with two lovely daughters.

The FBI continued to terrorize Frank Ziegler and his family. This persistent mistreatment might well have contributed to the stress that caused his heart attack and early death. Frank Ziegler died in 1953.

Constitutional Protection for All

The Fourteenth Amendment guarantees

> All persons born or naturalized in the United States ... are citizens of the United States. No State shall make or enforce any law which shall abridge privileges and immunities ... nor deprive (them of) life, liberty, or property, without due process of the law; to deny to any person ... the equal protection of the law.

German Americans, like all Americans, were supposed to enjoy the full protection of the Constitution and the Bill of Rights. These protections and rights disappeared completely for a large portion of our population; they became null and void. The constitutional procedure was totally reversed. A person was presumed guilty until proven innocent beyond a reasonable doubt. Prejudice was fueled by governmental policy and divisive media fabrications. Unfortunately, for a portion of our population, life, liberty, and property were held at the pleasure of the FBI and other governmental agencies.

We, as a nation, allowed our constitutional and personal

liberties and human rights to be thrown to the wind for political expediency and whims.

Max Ebel

The author first became aware of the existence of American concentration camps shortly after Senators Russ Feingold and Chuck Grassley first introduced the Wartime Treatment Study Act in the Senate on August 3, 2001. Robert Wexler (D-FL) was the lead sponsor of the House resolution. About the same time, an article describing the internment program by Karen Ebel appeared in several German-American newspapers. Karen talked about her own father's internment and the horror that thousands of German-American internees were subjected to.

All internees and their families, all German Americans, are very grateful to Senators Russ Feingold and Chuck Grassley and Congressman Robert Wexler and others for their untiring efforts in introducing and reintroducing the Wartime Treatment Study Act. With perseverance and patience, it shall ultimately pass, and justice shall be finally served.

Karen Ebel, an attorney at law, has been a guest on our German-American radio shows. Her understanding and insight of the issues and her empathy with all the human suffering and experiences of the internees, including her own father, were evident in all her accounts. When I first spoke about these atrocities on the air, some of my radio colleagues questioned my sanity because, according to them, this could have never happened in America. They were sadly not well informed; such is the result of the deafening media silence. Karen is one of the cofounders of the German-American Internee Coalition and a prolific contributor to its website. This website provides a wealth of information about many internees and their agonizing experiences (www.GAIC.Info).

Max Ebel was born in Speyer, Germany, in 1919. He completed his apprenticeship as a cabinetmaker and following in his father's footsteps, immigrated to America. As a youth, Max joined the German Boy Scouts (Pfadfinder) and the Red Cross. He chose to come to live with his father in America in 1937. That was after he was attacked for refusing to join the Hitler Youth. He was left with a scar on his face.

Max Ebel worked with his father, who owned the original Cambridge Woodcraft in Cambridge, Massachusetts, creating church furnishings and fine furniture. They also developed a safer lifeboat for the US Navy. He became active as a junior air raid warden and a Boy Scout.

His friends and family members, people who knew him well, described him as a quiet, gentle, and peaceful man. He possessed patience and inner strength, outgoing warmth, and a genuine kindness that prevailed in spite of the many adversities.

Max Ebel was arrested in 1942 and spent the following two years in camps throughout the United States including Ellis Island, Camp Forrest in Tennessee, and Fort Lincoln in Bismarck, North Dakota. He volunteered to replace rails for the Northern Pacific Railroad. While working, he met Lakotas and came to admire the Native Americans, who like German-American internees had been brutalized and mistreated. One is reminded of the Trail of Tears, on which thousands of them died. While he was still interned, Max was inducted into the US Army, but he failed his physical.

After a lifetime of silence, at age eighty, Max Ebel began to speak out about his internment experiences. Max was no criminal, but he, like all the rest, was treated like a criminal. The crucial point is that neither he nor anyone else was ever charged with or found guilty of any war-related crime, but sadly, he and all the others were forced to suffer.

The *Concord Monitor* first broke Max Ebel's story in

January of 2000. His story also enjoyed US and international media coverage, including the BBC radio and German radio and television. His daughter, Karen, said that her father knew the fear but dared to step forward and publicize his story so that more light would be shed onto that dark corner for the whole world to see.

Karen Ebel and others are committed to having legislation passed that will right the wrongs and bring about some semblance of justice. She emphasizes the fact that her father and so many others were wrongfully imprisoned. She said, "I want him to get an apology. More than that, I want a promise that it will never happen again." Imagine this happening elsewhere. There would be no end to our politicians and the media condemning such blatant human rights violations, but this is something that happened in the United States. Turning off the light does not make anything disappear.

The Schneider Family

Gertrude Anna Schneider was born near Stuttgart, Germany, in 1908. She was the oldest child of Johann and Luise Grokenberger. While walking with her grandpa and looking at the moon, her grandpa told her, "Someday, Trudl, man will walk on the moon." A few decades later, the German-American rocket scientist Werner von Braun and his team of German space scientists turned that prediction into reality.

Her family, along with several other families, accepted the invitation to immigrate to Canada. It was a sense of adventure that filled them with hope. They settled in Edmonton, Alberta. Her parents, Johann and Luise, helped build a Lutheran Church, which they attended regularly.

The cold, harsh winters, however, persuaded the family to relocate to Southern California. Their friends told them that work was plentiful. The children attended German-language school. Johann left for Los Angeles in 1923, and shortly thereafter, the rest of the family joined him. At first, they settled in a house they rented. Gertrude met her future husband, Paul, at a German-American picnic.

They endured the Depression years by raising their own food and meat on a few acres of land. Paul and Gertrude attended many functions at Das Deutsche Haus, where they enjoyed picnics in the summer and the many "fests" in spring and fall. They were justly proud of their German heritage and culture, as they had every right to be.

On December 7, 1941, about 7:30 p.m., after flashing their badges, three armed FBI agents searched the whole house, turning it upside down, as they always did, and then arrested Gertrude. Men were not the only ones arrested. There were also many women placed into American concentration camps. If you were a member of a German social club, you were a target because all German-American clubs were decreed to be "subversive." During the interrogation, she was forced to sit under a very bright light that became increasingly uncomfortable. A matron escorted her to the restroom, granting her absolutely no privacy. What pleasure could this disgusting matron possibly have gotten watching another woman go to the bathroom? Give a little person a little power and it goes to their head.

Reporters took a picture of the arrested American Germans, which appeared the next morning on the front page of the local newspaper with the usual fabricated, sensational story. She was taken to a matron's office, and the matron grabbed her by the arm and hissed at her, "You dirty Nazi spy!" She was ordered to take a shower and given blue prison clothes. She does not remember what happened to her own clothes. Then she was placed in a prison cell.

What was very disturbing and significant was the fact that

they were arrested and imprisoned on the day of Pearl Harbor, before America was at war with Germany and even before the massive relocation of Japanese Americans from the West Coast. The Terminal Island Detention Center began to fill up with more German-American women and, a few days later, Japanese-American families. The headman of the immigration office told her parents that this reminded him of the First World War. He said the British were showing the Americans how to go about interning people. The British "were running the show." Historically, the British were the first to demonstrate the use of concentration camps in Africa. Concentration camps are a British contribution to the world.

The food was very bad. The women refused to eat it. One morning, they were served a rather thin cabbage soup with worms floating around in it. On Good Friday, in 1942, she and her husband were given another ten-minute hearing in front of five men and a judge named Silverstein.

During the next night, the internees were awakened, put on a train marked "FP" (Federal Prisoners), and taken to Seagoville, Texas. Searchlights from the towers were operating all night. In late summer, 1942, her husband and her daughters came to visit her.

Paul was attempting to give up his citizenship so that he could keep his family together, even if it meant being repatriated to Germany. The judge denied his request because he could not allow American-born children to be sent abroad. He also stated that what was happening to Paul and his family was not prosecution but persecution.

While Gertrude was interned, Paul was relentlessly persecuted. He was forced to sell their home because their bank assets were frozen by the Federal Reserve Bank. It should be noted that the Federal Reserve Bank is neither federal, nor a reserve bank, but rather a conglomeration of about ten international banks who control the flow of our money. Thus far, the frozen assets of these victims have not been released and the internees have been afraid to ask for them. The FBI might be knocking at their door again. When Paul wanted some of his own money, he had to itemize exactly what he needed it for and how much he needed. He had to account for every penny of his own money. There was no limit to which the FBI was willing to go to terrorize the German Americans. Imagine our media bouncing on such a story of human rights violations in another country. Sadly, the media and text industry have kept totally silent about our own human rights violations.

When Paul tried to work, FBI agents haunted him from job to job. It was common practice for agents to call his employer and order them to fire Paul and others like him. It was common practice for the agents to call the police and their employers, informing them of how dangerous these enemy aliens were. Even after Gertrude's release, Paul was continuously being hunted out of his jobs.

After they moved to Shasta County, Paul found work with Pacific Gas and Electric. After only two months, the boss asked Paul, "Are you an American citizen?" He replied in the affirmative. His boss told him, "I've been ordered to lay you off, but I'll be damned if I'll do it!" He told Paul that he owed his life to German doctors during World War II, when he was seriously wounded and thanks to them he is still there.

Paul died in November 1982. The injustice of Gertrude's internment and being always reminded that his citizenship meant nothing during and after the war since he was "just a German" was something Paul Schneider never got over. There never seemed to be an end to the fueling of hatred against American Germans, even to this day. Paul was persecuted in a way that was far worse than being interned. The agents did their best to stop him from earning a living.

All suffered needlessly at the hands of overzealous, false "patriotic" agents and federal policy. Unfortunately, such false patriots exist in every country.

Pearl Harbor

Pearl Harbor has consistently been held up as the reason the United States entered the war. The widely read reporter and author Robert Stinnett served in the US Navy from 1942 to 1946, where he earned ten battle stars and a Presidential Unit Citation. In his book, *Day of Deceit*, he discussed American involvement in Pearl Harbor and demonstrated that it was neither an accident nor a total surprise. His research has profoundly altered our understanding of one of the most significant events in American history.

Congress and our nation were never provided the full story and full disclosure concerning FDR's involvement with Pearl Harbor. Robert Stinnett stated, "It may have been necessary for wartime security to withhold the truth about Pearl Harbor until the war ended, but to do so for more than half a century grossly distorted the world's view of American history."

Before he wrote *Day of Deceit*, he served as a photographer and journalist for the *Oakland Tribune*. Bruce Barlett, of the *Wall Street Journal*, said the book was "Fascinating and readable ... Exceptionally well presented." He has demonstrated that ample warning of the attack was on FDR's desk and, furthermore, that a plan to push Japan into war was initiated at the highest levels of the US government.

Richard Bernstein of the *New York Times* book review stated, "It is difficult, after reading this copiously documented book, not to wonder about previously unchallenged assumptions about Pearl Harbor." And Tom Roeser of the *Chicago Sun-Times* said,

"Stinnett has made a sickening discovery through the Freedom [of] Information Act … (about) FDR."

Arthur McCallum, expert adviser on Japanese affairs to FDR, advised him how to get Japan to attack the United States. FDR instigated a policy intended to provoke a Japanese attack, by shutting off their oil supply. Stinnett does much to unmask the awful truth about Pearl Harbor, providing overwhelming evidence that FDR and his top advisors knew that Japanese warships and planes were heading toward Hawaii. FDR died in office in April 1945, four months before Japan surrendered.

The Singular German Attitude

Professor Arthur Jacobs made an interesting observation. He does not understand what it is about the German psychic, their mental attitude, in talking about and remembering their own suffering. Germans were also victimized. There seems to be an inherent resistance to speaking about their suffering and pain. Germans were terrorized, a fact that is usually overlooked. All suffering deserves to be recognized.

A basic question needs to be answered. Has the media been able to unrelentingly indoctrinate and brainwash them so completely that they perceive themselves only as perpetrators and villains? And furthermore, is that behavior an expression of a subconscious imprinted, media-created inferiority complex? If so, how is this rectified? Most people are quite ready and willing to cry and complain and voice their demands for restitution, not so the Germans. During the last century, they suffered far more than anyone else but have rarely complained. Most Germans share the attitude that they lived through the agony; they don't care to open up these wounds by speaking about it. They need to speak about it to initiate real inner healing.

Throughout history, especially recent history, Germans

and German Americans were victims of abuse, whether in American internment camps during both world wars, the concentration camps in Latin America, the slave labor camps in Bolshevik Russia, Soviet concentration camps in former East Germany, the ethnic cleansing in Europe, or Tito's death camps. Most of them, with few exceptions, are exceedingly reluctant to speak of themselves as victims and talk about their suffering. There exists a prevailing attitude: "I lived through it, and I don't want to be reminded of it." And yet, each time an interview with an internee was aired, the victims, stepping out of the long shadow of agony, expressing their gratitude for finally talking about and remembering their suffering, were overflowing with emotions.

We must unite and speak with one united voice on behalf of all who no longer have a voice. We must finally right the wrongs done to our fathers, our mothers, our brothers, and our sisters. Their suffering cannot and will never be killed with silence. At the very least, they all deserve a governmental apology and an acknowledgment of their mistreatment. Convicted criminals on death row receive better constitutional protection than the thousands of innocent victims in our American internment program.

All the victims, alive and dead, call upon all Americans, especially German, Italian, Japanese, Hungarian, Romanian, and Bulgarian Americans; German Jews; Jehovah's Witnesses; and homosexuals whose civil liberties were criminally cast aside. These actions were the result of alleged national security policy. Countless families were destroyed for eternity. *Together we can and will make a difference!*

America must be ready for a greater and nobler national consciousness, firmly anchored upon the solid principles given to us by our founding fathers that are all inclusive and nondiscriminatory. "All men are created equal" still is and must remain "self-evident." Denying a full review of our past will only eat at our national consciousness like a cancer. Our challenge continues to be the *restoration of the truth* and maintaining a government of, for, and by the people.

The United States has long reminded other nations to acknowledge their wartime offenses. Now the US government must fully assess its treatment of German-American and German-Latin-American internees and evaluate the damage caused by its many human rights violations.

Whenever there is a distinction rendered between liberty and justice, for whatever reason, neither is on a solid foundation. Both are required unconditionally to sustain our freedom and democracy. Dwight D. Eisenhower stated, "Though force can protect in emergency, only justice, fairness, consideration and co-operation can finally lead men to the dawn of eternal peace." True justice must remain blind. Under the law, we must all remain equal. Justice is the glue that holds civilized nations together. As long as we honor the temple of justice, there will always be a foundation for individual freedom and security, general happiness, and perpetual improvement of mankind.

All our problems and crises are of our own making. We put ourselves, with British covert manipulations, into this predicament. What we created, we can also change and rectify. It is an act of wisdom to learn from our past and our mistakes. Let us build bridges to our future based upon a solid foundation of truth and justice. All of us united and speaking with one voice *can make it happen*! There is nothing more powerful than a voice whose time has come.

Front cover: Dodd Field 1942, Fort Sam Houston Museum
Background: Train arriving in Kenedy, April 1942
Inset: *Kenedy Advance* clipping, 1942

Texas hosted three confinement sites for enemy aliens, administered by the Department of Justice's Immigration and Naturalization Service in association with the Department of State, at Crystal City, Kenedy, and Seagoville. In addition, two U.S. Army temporary detention stations were located at Dodd Field on Fort Sam Houston (San Antonio) and Fort Bliss (El Paso).

Japanese, German, and Italian Latin American Internment

During the war, the U.S. Department of State—in cooperation with 15 Caribbean, Central American, and South American countries (see map)—worked to increase the security of the Western Hemisphere, especially the vulnerable and vital Panama Canal Zone.

This was accomplished primarily through financial and material support—via programs such as the Lend-Lease Act—to participating American nations. At a conference of Western Hemisphere countries in Rio de Janeiro, Brazil in January 1942, the U.S. called for the establishment of the Emergency Advisory Committee for Political Defense. This new security program was tasked with monitoring enemy aliens throughout Central and South America. The result was thousands of Axis nationals, as well as citizens of these Latin American countries of Japanese, German, and Italian ancestry, were taken into custody by local officials. While a number of those arrested were legitimate Axis sympathizers, most were not. Forcibly deported, these detainees were shipped to the U.S., considered security risks, and detained in internment camps across the country, including the three permanent INS camps in Texas.

Stripped of their passports en route to the U.S., these Latin Americans were declared "illegal aliens" upon arrival, a fact many former internees and historians have referred to as "hostage shopping" and "kidnapping," by the U.S. and Latin American governments. These Latin American internees provided the U.S. with an increased pool of people for exchange with Japan and Germany, each of which held comparable numbers of U.S. and Allied personnel taken prisoner earlier in the war.

By late January 1942, the U.S. began transporting the diplomatic staffs of Germany, Japan, and Italy residing in Mexico through Laredo, Texas and on to predetermined destinations on the East Coast. In March 1942, the U.S. began to negotiate with Japan and Germany for the safe return of U.S. and Allied citizens. The first

German march, Seagoville Enemy Alien Detention Station, 1942

repatriation that included Japanese American internees took place in June 1942. German enemy aliens, German Americans, and German Latin Americans were also voluntarily and involuntarily repatriated in massive movements during the war.

TEXAS HISTORICAL COMMISSION

SEAGOVILLE ENEMY ALIEN DETENTION STATION
Dallas County

Next to historic Ellis Island in New York City, the most architecturally significant INS confinement site was at Seagoville. The Geneva Convention of 1929 prohibited the detention of prisoners of war, as well as enemy alien civilians, in prisons. This eliminated the U.S. Federal Bureau of Prisons from being assigned the responsibility for the internment of civilians during World War II. Originally built by the Bureau of Prisons as a minimum-security women's reformatory in 1941, Seagoville Enemy Alien Detention Station was transferred to the INS on April 1, 1942.

The INS utilized the Seagoville facility for the detention of Japanese, German, and Italian families (briefly), childless couples, and single women detained as enemy aliens arrested within the U.S. and those brought from Latin American to be interned, while awaiting parole or repatriation to their ancestral country of origin. While a small number of families lived at this detention station in 1942 and 1943, this was considered a temporary fix, which the INS resolved with its largest site in Crystal City.

This internment camp included its own hospital with quarantine section, an auditorium, industry and service buildings, and 352 rooms for detainees. Each dorm-esque living quarters was a self-contained housing unit with small kitchen and dining area, and adequate recreational facilities. However, these accommodations did not provide enough living quarters for detainees as the population grew in 1942 and 1943 to its peak population of 650 internees and a staff of approximately 120 INS and civilian employees.

Above: Postwar aerial, Seagoville Enemy Alien Detention Station,1947
Inset: Porcelain traditional Japanese doll presented by Mayaso Iwamura to FCI-Seagoville in October 1990. Iwamura was born as an internee at the facility in 1943. (Malcom Potts, FCI-Seagoville, TX)

Aerial, Crystal City (Family) Internment Camp, 1945

CRYSTAL CITY (FAMILY) INTERNMENT CAMP
Zavala County

Many enemy aliens were fathers, and from the beginning the INS faced an ever increasing number of requests from wives and children volunteering internment to be reunited with the head of their households. Crystal City (Family) Internment Camp is unique because it was the only INS camp established specifically for families. In seeking a location to place this expected large confinement site, the INS looked for a facility that was removed from important war production areas and had quality water and electrical services. Noting the pressing need for the camp to open before the end of 1942, the INS went to a location identified in January 1942 as a good place for an internment camp. During the Great Depression, the U.S. Farm Security Administration had acquired land on the outskirts of the city.

On December 12, 1942, the camp's first internees to arrive were German. On February 12, 1943, the first group of Latin Americans arrived—also Germans—deported from Costa Rica. On March 17, 1943, the first group of Japanese American internees arrived. Before closing, both the Kenedy and Seagoville camps transferred a portion of their internees here. The Crystal City (Family) Internment Camp closed on February 27, 1948, nearly 30 months after the end of the war on September 2, 1945. In addition to the camp's national significance, built to reunite enemy aliens and their families, this confinement site was the largest such wartime measure that brought together enemy aliens and American citizens representing multiple nationalities in one camp.

Although mentioned briefly in this brochure, please contact the THC directly for a free copy of the Crystal City (Family) Internment Camp brochure for a more detailed history of this confinement site.

An Undertold Story

The U.S. implemented three programs to identify and, if necessary, detain civilians considered a threat to the country during the war years: the War Relocation Authority, the DOJ Alien Enemy Control Unit, and the Department of State's Special War Problems Division. In all three programs, citizens of their respective countries, legal resident aliens, and naturalized citizens were targeted alongside individuals legitimately identified as enemy aliens. Within weeks of the Japanese attack on Pearl Harbor, the DOJ took into custody several thousand Axis nationals. Although not legally administered in each case, and often spurred by prejudices, the action was intended to assure the American public that its government was taking firm steps to look after the internal safety of the nation. After arrest and detention, the U.S. looked toward the possibility of exchanging enemy aliens with Japan, Germany, and Italy. Between 1941 and 1945, the U.S. and its Allies suffered hundreds of thousands of casualties to the advancing Japanese and German armies across the globe. In addition to these combat casualties, U.S. and Allied civilians caught overseas were taken prisoner as countries fell to the Axis. In some cases, enemy aliens held in the U.S. were exchanged not only for detained civilians, but for severely injured service members.

The five internment camps in Texas: Dodd Field at Fort Sam Houston, Fort Bliss, Kenedy, Seagoville, and Crystal City each housed Japanese, German, and Italian enemy aliens, and a number of U.S. citizens. Together they make up an undertold part of U.S. and Texas World War II history. For more information on the Texas camps or to download a free copy of this or the Crystal City (Family) Internment Camp brochure please visit the THC's website at www.thc.state.tx.us.

Background: Red box notes the location of the detention station, Fort Sam Houston map; top photo: fence and electric line, Dodd Field, 1942; bottom photo: Japanese registration, Kenedy Enemy Alien Detention Station

11

CHAPTER 4

Camp Survivor Reunion

On a beautiful and sun-filled Saturday, August 28, 2010, many survivors from the American internment program came from all parts of our great country. More than 120 survivors came, some with their children and grandchildren, to Quakertown, Pennsylvania, to an extraordinary reunion and commemoration. Unfortunately, many of their fellow survivors could not be present. Many of their comrades had traveled beyond the level of time to the glory of the everlasting, perfect camp above. The bonds that were formed so long ago were still burning brightly and their friendships kept alive and genuinely sincere.

Mrs. Anneliese Krakau, widow of Alfred, and their daughter, Helen, graciously welcomed fellow internees from across our great nation, as far away as California and Texas. Christa Schmitz came from Vancouver, Washington, with the largest group of eight. Joanna Howell, who kindly volunteered to help in the next reunion and commemoration, came with her family from Texas. It was their endurance and perseverance that was the inspiration for this book.

The Krakau homestead is nestled on a beautiful five-acre spread in rural Quakertown. All were treated to refreshments, extraordinary German home-style cooking, and some very good, heartfelt conversation among dear old friends. They all have suffered so very long in silence. It felt good to talk.

Eberhard Fuhr, whose internment experiences at Crystal City and Ellis Island were described earlier in *Ellis Island Remembered*, orchestrated this memorable, historic event. Pastor Manfred Bahmann of Allentown, Pennsylvania, invoked the blessings of heaven on all present and upon all who were unable to join their fellow internees. Dr. Joe Wendel encouraged all to remain tenacious about their rights and liberties and stay the course.

Mr. Andreas Krauss, first secretary of the political department at the German embassy, brought greetings and best wishes from Ambassador Dr. Klaus Sc018iot. Mr. Krauss displayed genuine empathy and heartfelt interest in the internees and the suffering they were needlessly subjected to. All were grateful to have the German embassy present. All considered the reunion a smashing success, partially due to the large turnout and in part due to the internees sharing their many painful experiences, feelings, brutal human rights violations and sorrows, and an occasional joy, all so compassionate and real. They all were visibly happy to see each other again. They remembered when it was a crime to sing German songs, attend church services conducted in German, and perform music composed by the great German classical composers. In many states, like Ohio, even the instruction of German in public schools was outlawed. Some communities had book-burning ceremonies of German books.

For almost a century, the world has been saturated with atrocities stories committed by the Germans and the Nazis; however, the crimes against Germans, German Americans, and Latin-American Germans have affectively been killed with deafening silence. The media have treated the internees as if they never existed and as if the crimes against them never occurred. This has become such a travesty of justice. The media was invited to this reunion but never showed up. It would have been such a golden opportunity to listen, learn, and report, but the media chose to ignore this historic event with their absence.

This part of our own history has persistently been killed with silence. These crimes did not happen in the Bolshevik Soviet Union or Nazi Germany but in the United States, against US citizens. We all bear a full measure of responsibility for these crimes committed against German Americans and others. The consensus was that we must remain actively involved if these injustices are to be rectified by helping pass the Wartime Treatment Study Act. This unfortunate episode in our history shall then receive the official acknowledgment and condemnation it deserves. Cognitive dissonance shall and will never prevail.

Because of this media blackout, many Americans still believe that this dark chapter in our history never happened, but it did. Even after all these years have passed, our media still denies and kills this dark chapter of human rights violations with total silence. They quoted the Scriptures proclaiming, "Truth shall set us *free*." German Americans were deprived of their constitutional rights and of *due* process. Due process guarantees every American the right to cross-examine their accusers and be represented by legal counsel. Their homes were invaded and ransacked; they were handcuffed, terrorized, and thrown into internment camps, and all their earthly possessions were stolen. Even textbooks are still totally silent about German American suffering. And if anything is mentioned at all it is all too often falsified. It was stated that we as a nation must face our history honestly and bravely, the noble and the ugly.

Thousands of German South Americans were kidnapped, forced across our border, and then charged with illegally entering the United States. What a fraudulent and deceptive scheme.

Many suffered forced deportation to a bombed-out, devastated, and starving Germany, which was part of the British blockade to cause massive starvation. This blockade was finally broken when President Herbert Hoover sent food to the starving and dying Germans, Austrians, Hungarians, and other Europeans.

The internees were reminiscing about their experiences, how they were robbed of their childhood and youth, their dreams, hopes, aspirations, and of all their earthly possessions. One internee recalled how, as a child, he saw armed FBI agents storming into their house and ransacking their entire home, not only once but several times. When his father asked the agents what they were looking for, the agents snapped at him, "We'll let you know when we find it." For a long time, these children and the adults suffered from acute nightmares, and many still suffer as senior citizens.

Violence leads to more violence, hate to more hate, and kindness is repaid with kindness. In spite of all the incredible suffering and cruelty that has been inflicted upon thousands of innocent victims, there was no noticeable bitterness displayed among any of the survivors. Someone once said that wisdom comes by suffering. If one's heart is filled with love and forgiveness, then love and forgiveness will abound. The hearts of these survivors were filled with, not only tested patriotism, but with wisdom, strength, courage, and inner fortitude as they shared their many experiences filled with deep emotions. Prior to being released, they were forced to sign an oath never to speak or write about their experiences in these internment camps. Even their fundamental freedom of speech was usurped.

Tragically far too many kept that oath even unto death. Let us never forget and vigorously defend our First Amendment guarantees of free speech, free press, and peaceful assembly, as they are at the core of all our freedoms. Without the First Amendment, the rest of our rights are in constant peril. Their shared memories bore the imprint of all their suffering and inflicted brutality.

What is totally amazing is the fact that not a single internee was ever charged with or found guilty of any war-related crime. Quite to the contrary, many have distinguished themselves, proudly serving in uniforms of the US military forces. The allegiance of all these victims has been tried, tested, and proven true.

For more than four hundred years, since 1607, German Americans, who comprise far more than a third of our population, have labored for our common good, defending our Constitution and all it stands for. Many paid the ultimate price defending our great nation.

All those revisionists denying that such atrocities could have ever happened in America should check the birth certificates of all the German-American children born in our American internment camps. Their birth certificates attest to the fact that they were born in an American internment camp. The children of all the internees are fully committed to bringing about closure and ensuring that justice shall finally be served. Justice has been delayed much too long.

Dr. Albert Jabs engaged a group of people in a lively dialogue about the Fourteenth Amendment and how the internees were deprived of their constitutional rights. "Nor shall any State deprive any person of life, liberty, or property, without due process of law; nor deny to any person within its jurisdiction the equal protection of the law."

Dr. Nishikawa and Mr. Ekeda, representatives from the Japanese Poston, AZ Internment Camp, showing *solidarity* with their German brethren, were engaged in many conversations about their similar experiences. Barbara Jones Brown from the University of Utah and Jena Devine at Princeton collected information for their research projects about the American internment program.

Anneliese Krauter discussed segments of her book. Professor Arthur Jacobs, who wrote a book about his experiences, could not be present. Another internment coalition member, Karen Ebel, was also unable to be present. Ms. Ebel, along with many others, has been very involved in promoting the passage of the Wartime Treatment Study Act.

The fact that this bill has not yet passed does not speak well of our national moral consciousness. Senators Russ Feingold (D-WI) and Chuck Grassley (R-IA) have repeatedly introduced it in the Senate; Robert Wexler (D-FL) has been the lead sponsor in the House resolution. We all can and should do our part by encouraging our elected officials to finally pass it. There is a great amount of urgency to pass this bill while there are internees still living. They could finally see American justice being served. They have suffered much too long in silence. Let our national rhetoric be reflected in our unanimous actions.

There was discussion of the next reunion and commemoration. It was suggested that next year's event be held somewhere in the north-central part of the country. The reunion commemoration in 2012 could be held at Crystal City, Texas, in conjunction with the opening of an Internment Museum and during the annual Spinach Festival in November, as it draws huge crowds, politicians, and the media.

For all who attended, it was a most memorable and historic day. It was time well spent with very dear old friends, friends who have so much in common to share and tell. We can all learn so much when truth is spoken. By honestly facing the whole truth about this dark part of our history, we, as a nation, can become involved in ensuring that such atrocities will never be inflicted on fellow Americans of any ethnic group and our individual liberties will never again be usurped and violated. So many years later, the time is long past due for an official acknowledgment and condemnation of this unfortunate episode in our history.

There is no better time to act than now. The Internet (www. GAIC.Info) is a great source of further information.

Watchtower and fence at Crystal City, Texas.

W A R R A N T

TO THE DIRECTOR OF THE FEDERAL BUREAU OF INVESTIGATION:

In pursuance of authority delegated to the Attorney
General of the United States by Proclamation of the President
of the United States dated December 8, 1941, I hereby authorize
and direct you and your duly authorized agents to arrest or
to cause the arrest of EBERHARD ERNST FREDRICK FUER, 1907
Baymiller Street, Cincinnati, Ohio.

an alien enemy whom I deem dangerous to the public peace and
safety of the United States.

The said alien enemy is to be detained and confined until
further order.

By order of the President:

FRANCIS BIDDLE

Attorney General

~~PROPOSED/8//1941~~

March 8, 1945.

Note: ① Struck-out date
is Before War between
Germany & U.S.
② Note that March 8, '43
Preceded Hearing of
March 24, 43

163

A Confirmation Class at Crystal City.

CRYSTAL CITY, TEXAS

Anyone who still doubts the existence of American Concentration Camps needs to look at the birth certificates of the children born in the camps. Some 256 children were born in Crystal City.

CHAPTER 5

The Berlin-Baghdad Railroad

Since the beginning of recorded history, wars have been well established. The future of wars shall be well secured as long as wars continue to remain profitable for the elite and the multitude remains willing to answer the call for military service in the name of patriotism. As long as greed and money primarily dictate the direction of forces that govern world events and remain the central driving forces, stopping the war culture shall continue to be elusive and be as easy to avert as an avalanche.

It is therefore imperative that we scrutinize the paradox of how a never-completed railroad might have been a contributing excuse in propelling and being a contributing factor in causing a world war. A greater appreciation of the conditions in the world today necessitates a greater understanding of the political forces, the background, and the various special interests that precipitated World War I and ultimately World War II. The two wars are two acts of the same world tragedy.

As in any political chess game, two sides emerged. One side was the Triple Entente, which included England, France, Russia, and ultimately the United States; on the other side was the Triple Alliance, including Germany, Austria-Hungary, and Italy. Italy, however, switched sides and declared war on the

Central Powers on May 23, 1915, after its leaders were bribed in a secret meeting in London. The Triple Entente persisted in the English attitude of keeping international commerce a British monopoly. Germany's Drang nach dem Osten has been compared to Russia's push into Siberia and Central Asia and America's march to the Pacific.

Germany offered both France and Britain a significant share in the railroad. At first, Britain responded with a counterproposal, expressing her willingness to become a financial partner in the construction of the railroad in exchange for half of the concessions. This British counterproposal would have split the globe into two commercial and industrial spheres of influence, as it would have greatly benefited both countries. Britain would have remained the *primes inter pares*, the first among equals. Sadly, the pro war forces won in London and derailed any further discussions. The stakes then became much larger than merely the Berlin-Baghdad railroad, namely the total destruction of Germany's industrial and commercial prosperity.

Britain's long-range plans were preparing itself for a military confrontation by forging alliances, as she has done for centuries. In 1904, ten long years before the outbreak of World War I, Britain invited France into a joint defense alliance against Germany. France, however, still remembered the Fashoda incident of 1898, which was the climax of a territorial dispute between Britain and France in eastern Africa. France aspired to gain control of the Upper Nile. This maneuver would have excluded Britain from the Sudan and possibly forced Britain out of Egypt. This confrontation was resolved in a diplomatic victory for dear old England. France, still filled with sentiments of revenge toward Germany because of the defeat of the 1870–1871 war, accepted England's offer to form a common front against Germany.

Britain then made a similar proposal of a defense alliance with Russia against Germany. England promised Russia warm-water ports and part of the spoils of the Ottoman Empire. England was always very clever in forming alliances by making promises of sharing the spoils of war. Then England did everything in her power to provoke Germany into committing some act that could possibly qualify as an "act of aggression." No one in his or her right mind could possibly accept the notion that the assassination in Sarajevo was the reason for or a possible excuse for World War I. But vicious British propaganda turned it into such an excuse of justifying a military confrontation against Germany.

Ultimately, Britain succeeded in bringing Japan, Portugal, Serbia, Montenegro, and finally Italy into her alliance, thereby completely encircling Germany. Germany, on the other hand, did not make similar offers to share the spoils of war to persuade countries to join her side against bloody old England. The kaiser was politically naïve and no match for British intrigue; his political ineptitude allowed Germany to be encircled. World War I could and should have been prevented.

The growing prestige of "Made in Germany" and Germany's impressive industrial, commercial, and military growth increased Britain's concern and determination to go to war against Germany before Germany's military power would increase to such a level that dear old England with her alliances would no longer be able to crush Germany. Time was of the essence. Britain premeditated, provoked, and precipitated the bloodiest world wars in human history. The war would solve two problems for bloody old England: it would remove both Germany and Russia as industrial and commercial threats and stop the construction of the Berlin-Baghdad Railroad.

There were several converging factors, including England's persistence in enforcing its influence as the primary world power, the expansionist aims of Russia, the Jewish home state issue, and France's desire for revenge and its national pride.

Germany enjoyed prosperity and did not want a war to spoil its success. It was a known fact that Germany had the least to gain and most to lose from a military conflict. The kaiser and Germany did not want war.

It was a widely recognized fact that the Berlin-Baghdad Railroad would have connected widely separated areas, opened vast natural resources, opened new markets, and created an industrial and commercial boom, the likes of which the entire region had never experienced, particularly Europe, Asia Minor, and Iraq. The old caravan routes that linked the Far and Near East would reach into Western Europe. Its importance was readily visualized, especially after oil was discovered in Iran in 1908, diametrically increasing the importance of the entire region. The big world powers all wanted a portion of the oil.

For some time, Europe had been discussing a railroad that would connect the Near and Far East to Europe. The English and French governments were negotiating the railroad project but then for various reasons, including huge finances and tremendous engineering challenges, abandoned the project. There were no less than thirty-seven tunnels and numerous bridges to construct. That, however, was not the end of it. German financiers with considerable governmental encouragement began to do more than just talk about it. With any political hot potato, it gets thrown around and then is either totally abandoned or someone picks it up and will likely get burned. That someone was Kaiser Wilhelm II. The kaiser was not especially good at building alliances, visualizing the entire political picture, or evaluating all the pros and cons of an issue. Driven by his own fantasies and his huge ego, the kaiser was unwilling to accept the true political climate or fully appreciate all the deceptions and intrigues surrounding him and Germany. He and Germany should have done their due diligence. It was rather obvious that the railroad would not turn a profit in the near future, so what was the rush? The kaiser was the wrong man at the wrong time and place. The kaiser excelled in parades, pomp, and circumstance; he wanted to make his mark on history with the Berlin-Baghdad Railroad. It ultimately proved to become far costlier than the kaiser and Germany could digest.

The Suez Canal, the Trans-Siberian Railroad, and the Berlin-Baghdad Railroad were the three great modern versions of the trade routes of the Middle Ages. The railroad was to run from Berlin through Austria, Hungary, Serbia, and Bulgaria across the Dardanelles into Turkey and to Baghdad. A rail was planned that would connect Paris to Vienna. The main line would connect local lines from virtually every country in Europe. Extensions were also being considered to Armenia, Kurdistan, and Alexandretta on the Mediterranean Sea. The railroad linking Central Europe with the Persian Gulf offered a three-to-five-day-faster trade route, which was huge. One serious concern was the fact that the rail line would run through several countries, some friendly and others rather unfriendly, some unpredictable and others riddled with corruption.

How could any European government possibly be opposed to a railroad that would be such a blessing to so many? Corporate greed and national pride were the primary forces that drove the opposing forces. Every action has an opposite reaction. Bankers who financed steamship lines and other nonrailroad modes of transportation were protecting their financial interests and swiftly voiced their strong objections. It was not so much a question of what was best for most of the people or what would provide fair competition but what would bring the greatest amount of profit to the special interest groups. English and French steamship company agents began to agitate against the project. They forcefully flexed their muscles, doing everything they could to effectively block the road to prosperity for millions of people. The kaiser, accepting the present financial conditions, could have put the railroad project on the back burner until the climate was more favorable.

There is no question the Berlin-Baghdad Railroad would have been, without equal in comparison and magnitude, of all the various projects, bigger than the Santa Fe from Chicago to Los Angeles or the Union Pacific from Omaha to San Francisco lines. Also, the railroad was being planned at a time when the Orient was still full of mystery and seen as a slumbering economic frontier.

International bankers, headquartered in London at the time, joined forces with the English government, demonstrating their opposition to the railroad project. Fears that the railroad would seriously limit English control and dominance of world commerce and finance, in addition to Germany's rise as a major world power, sparked England's determination to demonstrate her power and control at all cost, including war. The English were the predominant trading power in the Persian Gulf, and they intended to keep it that way. The British had worldwide responsibilities but were unable to back them up; they formed alliances as needed and dissolved them when convenient.

Times were changing. The railroad—the iron horse— was quickly becoming the major means of transportation. Even though England and France abandoned the project, they were also not willing to allow Germany to proceed with the construction of the railroad. National financial interests outweighed human benefits and prosperity for the many, the middle class.

Following the Franco-Prussian war of 1870–71, Europe, Japan, and the United States experienced an unprecedented industrial and commercial growth. This expansion generated not only competition but deadly rivalries. The concept of a European Union, benefiting the whole of Europe and working together harmoniously for the common good of the many, had not entered the vocabulary of the European and world leaders. Their superegos plus the willingness of politicians to accept bribes proved to be a serious and destructive stumbling block.

At first, England and France displayed considerable interest in participating in the construction of the railroad but after considering all the financial and engineering challenges, plus weighing all the financial interests of nonrailroad modes of transportation, abandoned the project. If they would have chosen to work together in this rail project, they would not have gone to war. This is just one of many examples in history where war could have been averted.

Paradoxically, however, when Germany demonstrated some interest in and received the green light from the Ottoman Empire to proceed with the construction of the railroad, England and France put up every roadblock to stop Germany from building the railroad, even though Germany offered them a major financial stake in the project, which they arrogantly turned down. France was offered 40 percent in the project. Both governments viewed any involvement on their part as contributing to Germany's bid to become a world power, and that could not be tolerated. Germany was getting too big and powerful; it needed to be cut down in size, which became their obsession.

France was still recovering from its defeat by Germany and gravely concerned about the dramatic increase in Germany's power. French politicians pushed France into an alliance with England against Germany.

The satire of this development was that the longtime chancellor, Otto von Bismarck, made no secret of his opposition to Germany's involvement in the Berlin-Baghdad Railroad. In 1875, he proclaimed in the Reichstag that Germany's interests in the Turkish-Balkan area "were not worth the bones of a single Pomeranian Grenadier." Bismarck persisted on the side of caution and strongly advised not to become entangled in an area where Austria and Russia were at odds with each other. In 1886, Bismarck warned that since Germany could not appease one of these nations without offending the other, it would be extremely advisable not to get involved at all. Prince Otto von Bismarck enjoyed great respect and admiration, which, sadly, Kaiser Wilhelm II wanted. What Berlin was lacking was a government with checks and balances, rather than an absolute monarch with a severe ego problem.

The kaiser wanted to get away from under Bismarck's shadow and make a name for himself with the Berlin-Baghdad Railroad. In order to take Bismarck out of the equation and to silence the opposition to the project, Kaiser Wilhelm II released the wise old chancellor Otto von Bismarck from his duties. The timing could not have been worse. This single act would prove to become a major mistake with serious, tragic consequences. The monarch, like most leaders blinded by power, wanted to be surrounded by like-minded people who were more agreeable to his personal fantasies and who were eager to fuel his ego.

Count George Leo von Caprivi, Caprera, and Montecuccoli followed Baron Otto von Bismarck. Germans loved and were easily impressed with titles, almost as much as their English cousins, fueling their hubris. All too often, titles appeared to be more important than substance. Caprivi served as German chancellor from March 1890 to October 1894.

During that time, Germany promoted bilateral treaties for the reduction of tariff barriers. This, however, angered the conservative agrarian sector, especially the Junkers. The Catholic Center Party was promised educational reforms, but they were never delivered. For centuries, the Roman Catholic Church has been a most formidable and powerful political force. Kaiser Wilhelm II's so-called "New Course" in foreign policy abandoned Bismarck's military, economic, and ideological cooperation with Russia. The kaiser desperately attempted to forge a closer relationship and cooperation with England but failed. Kaiser Wilhelm II refused to comprehend that his English relatives were not about to share their world dominance with anyone, especially with Germany. It appears that William wanted to be both British royalty and the monarch of Germany. He could not be both; he failed on both accounts. The kaiser should have solidified his relationship with the czar of Russia, which he grossly neglected.

Over the centuries, Catholic Austria battled Protestant Germany. Germany's religious schism has been a curse since the Reformation and Counter-Reformation. No other nation has suffered so much and for so long because of religion as the German people. The Jesuits battled Protestant Germany. Twice Otto von Bismarck led Germany to military victories, defeating Catholic Austria in 1866 and France in 1870. Bismarck outlawed the Jesuit Order for meddling in Germany's political affairs with the Kulturkampf Law in 1872, which severely angered Rome. World War I provided an opportunity for payback. The effects of Germany's religious divide have for centuries had very tragic and deadly results. For centuries, Catholic Austria and Protestant Germany were fighting each other rather than defending their common interests. Religion and religious fervor proved far more important and binding than mutual national unity and national political and economic interests.

Wilhelm was Queen Victoria's oldest grandson. Czar Nicholas II of Russia, Princess Sophie of Greece, and King George V of England were his first cousins. Some of the European wars were in reality some kind of family feud. Wilhelm was born after an agonizing ten-hour delivery, which his mother and he barely survived. During the delivery, Wilhelm suffered neurological damage that crippled his left arm. In adulthood, his left arm was six inches shorter than his right arm and functionally useless. There has been speculation that this burden might have been a foreboding sign of his royal kaisership.

Wilhelm blamed his British mother and her English physicians for killing his father, maiming him, and crippling his left arm. His mother did not tolerate any German physicians in her presence. They were, according to her, inferior to her British physicians. The youth also suffered severely because of the absence of any maternal affection and love. All sorts of positive encouragement, which are so vitally important in a child's emotional development, were completely lacking in his childhood and youth. After his ascension to the throne, his mother, Victoria, left for dear old England, never to return. There was an estranged relationship between mother and child. After Victoria left for England, the contact between them was virtually nonexistent.

A letter written at the start of 1890 speaks volumes about their relationship, or lack thereof. In part, the letter reads,

> Ein Wort der Warnung. Du bist jetzt jung, gesund und erfolgreich, und arrogant und ueberheblich im Stolze Deiner neugewonnenen Macht, ... ein egoistisches Misachten der Gefuehle und Wuensche anderer immer frueher oder spaeter, die egoistische Person selbst schwer straft und Mangel an kindlicher Demut bleibt nie ungeraecht.

His mother should have communicated with him in a loving and caring fashion more often when he was growing up.

His physical handicap weighed heavily on him. He was unable to handle any weapons or be the soldier he aspired to become. He was even unable to cut the meat on his dinner plate.

He needed constant reassurances and was easily influenced by flattery. He enjoyed being the center of attention. He needed to be the bride at every wedding.

Wilhelm did not ascend to the throne as a consequence of a popularity contest or a national election. A national election would have served Germany's interests much better than Kaiser Wilhelm II, especially keeping foreign interference at bay.

The kaiser's behavior demonstrated that all too often his decisions were made impulsively rather than reflectively. He appears to have been poorly prepared for the political chess game on the world stage. He was rightfully proud of and he appears to have been swept away by Germany's impressive industrial and commercial growth. The German people deserved all of the credit, not the kaiser. He flaunted it wastefully with huge parades and expensive gifts.

At the time, Russia covered an area larger than all other European countries combined and larger than the United States, but she was not in possession of even a single ice-free, warm-water harbor that was open to shipping all year round. Russia made several attempts to gain an ice-free port in the Far East but had to abandon that idea following the defeat by the Japanese fleet and army in the Russo-Japanese War of 1905. In that conflict, Japan received support from Britain, which angered Russia. Russia had been demonstrating an interest in the Dardanelles, but Turkey was not about to roll out the welcome mat and let them just walk in leisurely.

In November 1910, Czar Nicholas II visited his cousin Kaiser Wilhelm II at Potsdam to discuss their mutual interests and concerns, relative to the escalating climate of war. The relationship between the two monarchs was exceedingly friendly. The kaiser voiced no objections to Russia acquiring a year-round seaport, and the czar was agreeable to Germany proceeding with the railroad. They had an amicable relationship of mutual cooperation to prevent a war, if at all possible. What both failed to realize was the fact that Russia was being infiltrated very secretively by false Russian patriots who turned Russia against Germany.

The two monarchs agreed that the railroad project would benefit all of Europe, including Russia. Russia would abandon her plan of the Dardanelles and Berlin could proceed with the railroad project without any objections from Russia. In return, Russia would gain a "sphere of influence" in Persia and then run a railroad through the country to the Persian Gulf and the Arabian Sea, establishing a warm-water, year-round seaport. This was a win-win agreement, without spilling a single drop of blood. However, that would unfortunately change swiftly. There were hidden powers and special interests in Russia, as there are in every country, who were strongly opposed to this arrangement. In 1899, the Russian press, not the czar, issued warnings against the project, clearly demonstrating that the czar was no longer in charge and in control of his country.

The old devil—greed, envy, and jealousy—reared its ugly head again and poisoned the political atmosphere. Strong opposition came from bloody old England, poised to destroy Germany's industrial and commercial strength. France, still recovering from its defeat, was fearful of Germany's increasing military power. There were also highly placed false Russian patriots agitating and beating the war drums, pushing Russia ever closer into the English-French camp, thus encircling Germany. Both Kaiser Wilhelm II and Czar Nicholas II should have been very concerned about the political developments and climate within Russia and provided each other mutual support before that window of opportunity was permanently closed. Czar Nicholas II and his family were murdered in 1917 by Bolshevik agitators, who now had control of the country. The

Bolsheviks wanted to establish a new world order, which has proven to be a huge failure.

In 1871, a short section of railroad was built, but it was not until 1888 that the Baghdad rail project began on a more serious level. That was when Dr. Siemens of Deutsche Bank founded the Anatolian Railway Company. The company took over an existing English rail and extended it into the southern part of Anatolia.

On November 27, 1899, Germany was given concessions for extending the railroad. Included were guarantees of revenues per kilometer of track laid and the establishment and operation of irrigation projects, harbors, and various industries on both sides of the rail. Included in these concessions was an agreement to consider an extension to Baghdad in the future.

At this time, there was virtually no serious opposition to the project by other European powers, including England and France, This picture, however, changed drastically. During these early years, the project was a relatively quiet commercial venture. Germany ran its railroads efficiently and punctually. The Turkish government was impressed, as was everyone else. The proposed route was from Haidar Pashe (the Asiatic side of Constantinople) through Angora, Adana, Mosul, Aleppo, and Baghdad, on to Asra, and further to the Persian Gulf.

In 1897, the Turks won a war against Greece in which the German-built railroads played a contributing factor in the outcome. The sultan then asked for the continuation of the construction of the railroad. It was commonly held that the railroad would help Turkey unite and promote its progress, which England and France were attempting to prevent.

In an attempt to appease English objections and concerns, Germany turned the concessions of the Baghdad Railroad to the Basra section back to Turkey in 1908, but that was not enough. The meeting between the kaiser and the czar at

Potsdam in 1910 and the English fears of a German-Russian rapprochement clearly shows that the window of opportunity to prevent the encirclement of Germany was still open, which the kaiser and the czar unfortunately failed to see. The kaiser was blinded by his personal phantom, his *Trugbild*.

Germany's sphere of influence was recognized in an agreement between the Deutsche Bank and the French-dominated Ottoman Bank. As late as June 15, 1914, England agreed to recognize Germany's rail monopoly in most parts of Turkey. They agreed that the rail would stop in Basra, and England would retain control south of Basra. Tragically, these negotiations and agreements were nothing more than delaying tactics. With these deceptive tactics, England delayed the construction of the railroad sufficiently to interrupt and disturb Turkish troop movements in the war. England proved to be diplomatically the winner. Germany needed Bismarck more than ever.

German-built railroads are still operating and are still the backbone of the railroad system in modern Turkey, Syria, Jordan, northern Arabia, and in parts of Israel and Palestine.

Already in 1899, England was blocking the railroad to the Persian Gulf as part of its tactics as protectorate over Kuwait. Further, England and France refused to allow Turkey to raise customs to pay for the railroad. They refused to be part of the railroad management, and they denied any railroad shares to be traded on their stock exchanges. Any genuine support or cooperation for the railroad was sadly missing. The kaiser was blinded by the web of intrigues and deceptions. He remained receptive to false prophets and insincere flattery, fueling his fantasies.

After the encirclement of Germany, the strategy was that England, France, and Russia would force war upon Germany by attacking Austria-Hungary. Austria-Hungary had many Slavs within its empire. Aggressive agitation, including terrorism, was implemented primarily in Poland, Romania, and Serbia. These countries, bordering on Austria and Hungary, were believed to be politically unstable and supposedly easily influenced. For example, a Catholic bishop in Hungary received a package with a time bomb. It killed and maimed several people, including the bishop.

Every entity has both a legitimate and a hidden power structure. An extremely aggressive and poisonous propaganda campaign against Germany was led under the banner and battle cry that was referred to as "pan-Slavism." This campaign instructed all Slavs to unite under the protection of the czar of Russia, urging all Slavs to unite into one great Slavic empire. The primary political objective of all this agitation was to bring the Dardanelles and all the eastern Balkan countries on the Black Sea under Russian control and to build a united Slavic front against Germany. These were some of the first rumblings of the Bolshevik Revolution.

This anti-German terror campaign was carried out by professionals, financed by international bankers in New York and Russia and implemented by Serbia. That is where the Black Hand Society was headquartered.

In France, there were two main movers and shakers, spearheading all the covert activities. Raymond Poincare, prime minister of France, and Alexander Izvolski, Russian ambassador to France, were very creative in their craft. They did everything in their power to persuade the French people to become actively involved in the conspiracy to force a war on Germany. Tragically, Bismarck was removed from the political scene to guide Germany and Europe away from another military conflict and the unnecessary bloodshed and destruction. At Versailles, Raymond Poincare spearheaded the efforts to exact the harshest terms on Germany.

Huge sums of money were funneled through Russia, promoting war. There appeared a bottomless supply of bribe money, which was distributed generously to influence and corrupt the members of government, as well as the press corps in France. The power of money was exerted upon the French press to fabricate and print news stories and editorials for the sole purpose of influencing and misleading the proud people of France about the true conditions in the Balkan states.

Poincare resigned from his position as prime minister and had himself elected president of France, thereby gaining greater control and influence on French foreign policy. Corruption appeared to be the order of the day. Poincare applied every conceivable method, attempting to convince the French people that life was hardly worth living until Alsace and Lorraine were again part of greater France. Conveniently, he chose not to ask the people of Alsace and Lorraine what they would have preferred themselves. Most preferred just to be left alone and not be used as a political football.

Poincare was provided with an endless supply of bribe money. Poincare and Izvolski were exceedingly generous with bribe money. Much of it was flowing into the Balkan countries, fueling the agitation and intensifying the prejudice and hatred against Germany. The Balkans were chosen for the opening scene of the next war. Serbian leaders eagerly accepted huge sums of money and in return applied every conceivable means to keep the intrigue against Austria-Hungary boiling.

Poincare and Izvolski's plot was partially realized in the first and second Balkan wars of 1912 and 1913. However, these conflicts did not gain any amount of traction and did not develop into anything major. More bribe money was pumped into the mix to generate more fabrications, lies, and deceptions. Their actions not only totally betrayed France but destroyed every opportunity for peace in Europe and the world.

It is interesting to note that England and France opposed Russia getting a foothold in the Dardanelles, fearing that Russian commerce on the high seas would seriously undercut English and French financial and commercial interests. Special interests, working against the czar, created unrest in Russia. While offering Russia nothing substantive in return, England, France, and false Russian patriots conspired to bring Russia into their alliance, encircling Germany.

During all of this, Kaiser Wilhelm II seems to have been focused on spectacular pomp, oblivious of all the intrigue surrounding him, as he appeared to be poorly prepared for the immense challenges of the political chess game and the intrigues on the world stage. He needed to be aware that the cheerleaders don't win the game. He compounded the mistake of Austria-Hungary by failing to immediately invade Serbia successfully after the assassination in Sarajevo. The heir to the Austro-Hungarian throne, Archduke Franz Ferdinand, and his wife were assassinated in Sarajevo on July 26, 1914, as they made their way through the crowded streets in an open carriage. Unfortunately, they chose to ignore warnings of an assassination plot.

Germany was not involved in the Balkans during Bismarck's time. That changed after Wilhelm's ascension to the throne. Having an absolute monarch is perhaps the best form of government but only if the monarch is blessed with the wisdom of Solomon. Tragically, William was no Solomon and no political genius.

The impressionable young kaiser's vanity, his sense of insecurity, and his emotional need for attention were something that Germany could ill afford at this juncture. He enjoyed showcasing and parading Germany's industrial and commercial growth and displaying its military strength. The German people deserved all the credit for these successes. His pompous behavior made Germany's neighbors not only envious and jealous but also nervous. The kaiser needed to practice humility and modesty, which is always virtuous and acceptable to the Creator. Kaiser Wilhelm II enjoyed putting his pompous arrogance on full display.

Just one year after Kaiser Wilhelm II ascended the German throne, he traveled through the Dardanelles to Constantinople. A jubilant crowd received the distinguished visitors. All over, German flags were hoisted, military bands played the German national anthem, and a 101-gun salute received the monarch. This trip did more diplomatic damage than good. The kaiser would have represented Germany's interests much better had he stayed home in Berlin.

Young Kaiser Wilhelm II's political ineptitude contributed to the rift that emerged among the European powers, culminating in the encirclement of Germany. The kaiser should have made every effort to renew Bismarck's Reinsurance Treaty, rather than allow it to expire. Everything possible should have been done to strengthen the relationship with Russia. Having Russia on Germany's side would have significantly altered the course of events and possibly saved Europe and the world from two wars.

The kaiser had a need to be popular and to be everybody's friend, which made him susceptible to flattery and caused him to commit serious diplomatic and strategic errors. Trying to be everybody's friend, he was no one's. For example, he dedicated the new German Protestant church in Jerusalem, the Church of the Redeemer. He also declared his and the empire's protection of the "Dormitto beatae virginis," in an attempt to appease the German Catholics. During his first visit to Jerusalem, he befriended Theodore Herzl, the Viennese journalist considered to be the father of modern Zionism.

At the time, Germany was the spiritual and political fatherland of Zionism and the incubator of the State of Israel.

Theodore Herzl easily recruited the kaiser to the cause of Zionism. He was even persuaded to do Herzl's bidding in the Middle East. Kaiser Wilhelm II received Herzl again during his second visit to Jerusalem. It was during this meeting that Herzl asked the kaiser to charter a company to initiate German-Jewish settlements in Palestine. The kaiser was just full of surprises; he also asked the sultan's blessings for the Jewish settlements. Herzl easily persuaded the kaiser to promote Zionism in the holiest city of Christianity. German Zionism even became the midwife of the Balfour Declaration. Wilhelm II lacked a solid and reliable compass to guide his political and ideological convictions.

There were good and friendly relations between Germany and the World Jewish Organization. Until 1915, the headquarters of the World Jewish Organization was located in Berlin. For centuries, Germany was a refuge for Jews from Russia and Poland because of the frequent persecutions of Jews. In 1812, Germany issued the Edict of Emancipation, which gave Jews equal civil rights with Germans. As expected, this edict attracted Jews to Germany. At that time, no other country had granted Jews full civic equality like Germany. Many German Jews married German Gentiles and lived happily after.

Jews prospered in Germany and enjoyed many special liberties. Kaiser Wilhelm's Germany was the spiritual and political home of World Zionism. Max Bodenheimer, president of the German Zionist Federation, proclaimed that the interests of the Russian Jews and those of the German Reich were identical. On August 17, 1914, Bodenheimer, with several other German Zionists, established the German Committee for the Liberation of Russian Jewry. They supported those powers that were lined up against Russia and would bring about a Russian revolution. Czar Nicholas II was perceived as an enemy of world Jewry, and they believed that he would stand in the way of the

Zionist agenda in the creation of the State of Israel. In 1914, the International Zionist Executive was located in Berlin.

Ronald Graham wrote to Arthur Balfour, "We might at any moment be confronted by a German move on the Zionist question and it might be remembered that Zionism was originally if not a German Jewish at any rate an Austrian Jewish idea."

To circumvent a German-Jewish alliance and a German-Jewish connection, Arthur Balfour announced on October 31, 1917, the following: "His Majesty's Government view with favor the establishment in Palestine of a national home for the Jewish people." The Balfour Declaration was designed to win world Jewry for the Allied cause against Germany. It pulled the carpet from underneath the kaiser's feet. However, the Balfour promise was perceived as insincere, because London had intentions of establishing an Anglo-Arab Empire. For Zionists, the creation of the State of Israel was understandably uppermost on their agenda. It gained religious status.

The sultan's foreign minister made a special point to warn and emphatically impress upon the insensitive Kaiser Wilhelm II the fact that the sultan was not favorably disposed to Zionism and an influx of Jewish settlements. Instead of graciously accepting the advice, Wilhelm II chose to totally ignore it, displaying arrogance and being callous toward his host. Unfounded fantasies contributed to the political and human wreckage of the Middle East and far beyond.

All the European conflicts, except one, involved only one of the Entente Powers, namely Alsace and Lorraine, Bosnia, Herzegovina, and the increasing German navy. Only one, the Berlin-Baghdad Railroad caused hostilities with all three powers all at once. Realistically weighing all options would have been a far better course of action, but the kaiser continued accepting poor counsel from individuals who fueled his ego and fantasies rather than provided reality. In addition, he promised far more than Germany was able deliver; all too often he spent money like a drunken sailor.

War has been described as failed diplomacy or diplomacy at the most brutal level. Could Germany have avoided getting sucked into a military conflict by displaying much greater sensitivity to Russia's national concerns and forestalling the implementation of the Berlin-Baghdad Railroad until greater cooperation and support was achieved? To every problem there is a solution, and it does not need to be war and bloodshed, unless the war is a sideshow to some other objective. The Ottoman army attacked Russia, which further contributed to the hostilities.

Contributing factors to the military conflict were the expansionist policies of Russia, the well-financed movement of revenge in France, England's unbending determination to destroy Germany as an economic and industrial competitor, and the Jewish question. Diaspora Jews, understandably, wanted a homeland of their own, and Israel appeared within reach.

What has been glowingly absent from historical accounts of the creation of the State of Israel is the extraordinary physical legacy of the role Kaiser Wilhelm II and Imperial Germany played. Wilhelm's political aptitude or lack thereof proved to be no match for the intrigues and deceptions of the world political chess game that surrounded him.

Kaiser Wilhelm II wrote in his memoirs,

> While on my summer cruise in the Norwegian Fjords, I learned about Austria's ultimatum to Serbia, and the Serbian reply to Austria. I immediately returned home, only to find the Foreign Office at odds with the chief of the General Staff, who felt war was sure to break

out. It took the Russians setting red mobilization notices for the Wilhelmstrasse diplomats to comprehend that war was upon us. In November 1918, I learned that when asked about his summer plans, in the spring of 1914, Nickolas had replied "I shall stay at home this year because we shall have war." This same Czar had given his word of honor that, owing to his gratitude for my stand in the Russo-Japanese War, he would never draw his sword against Germany—least of all as an ally of England. He hated England for having incited Japan against Russia.

Wilhelm spent much too much time sailing and being entertained on his yacht when he should have been concerned with the affairs of state.

Germany was economically and industrially doing exceedingly well. It had the least to gain and the most to lose. A war would only disrupt and weaken its economic and industrial growth. Germany's mistakes were Kaiser Wilhelm II's abandoning Bismarck's policies, especially with Russia, his misguided fantasies, and him letting himself become entangled in the intrigues of the Austrian foreign office. The kaiser should have kept his nose out of the Sarajevo powder keg and not allowed himself to become a tool in Herzl's objectives.

Kaiser Wilhelm II was very generous. He presented the Ottoman people a huge and ornate fountain, which still stands as a testament to Kaiser Wilhelm's generosity. On October 29, 1898, the kaiser rode, flanked by his chancellor Bernhard von Bulow, high on top of a white stallion into Jerusalem. A jubilant crowd received him as if he were the savior of the Ottoman people. He rode into Jerusalem as if he were the sultan, rather than his guest.

Timing is everything. For some time, the dialogue concerning the railroad had been current in all European countries. Bismarck had been acutely aware of and concerned about the various political minefields. Unfortunately, his concerns were ignored. The driving force for the construction of the railroad was the increasing demand for imported metals, minerals, and food to feed the growing German and European population. It would have been a display of wisdom to let the demands for these goods propel the construction of the railroad in a timely cooperative fashion.

Turkey was in possession of everything Germany and the rest of Europe needed, such as copper, chrome, lead, zinc, and oil. From that perspective, the railroad was viewed as having the potential of unlimited possibilities. Time, patience, and perseverance are virtues that were in short supply which the kaiser needed to emulate.

The historic tours of Kaiser Wilhelm II fueled his personal fantasies and his ego but did little to benefit Germany. Feeding his fantasies, some Muslims went as far as claiming that the kaiser had been ordained by God to free Muslims from infidel rule.

For some time, the Ottoman Empire had experienced unrest, which had been cleverly exploited by foreign powers. The sultan had struggled to get out from under European control. Converging forces between the orthodox Muslim teachings and a wave of liberal concepts added to the internal unrest. Little has changed; some of the names have changed, but the stories and struggles remain the same.

Part of the displeasure with traditional Muslim practices is related in a letter written by Anmed Riza while he was visiting Paris. In part, the letter read,

> Were I a woman, I would embrace atheism and
> never become a Muslim. Imagine a religion

that imposes laws always beneficial to men but hazardous to women such as permitting my husband to have three additional wives and as many concubines as he wishes, houris awaiting him in heaven, while I cover my head and face as a miller's horse. Besides, I would not be allowed to divorce my husband who prevented me from having any fun, but would be required to submit to his beatings. Keep this religion far away from me!

This was a Muslim man writing to his sister, after he observed how women were treated differently in Europe.

Many of the kaiser's advisers displayed a great amount of talent fueling the emperor's childish fantasies, saturating his ego and his need for flattery through the allurement of self-serving advisers. Tragically, Wilhelm II was totally blind to it all.

One such self-appointed adviser was Max Oppenheim, who succeeded to endear himself to and gain the kaiser's trust. He fueled the kaiser's fantasies, telling him that he was well on his way to becoming a liberating force in the Ottoman Empire. Oppenheim, like the kaiser, saw the world through rose-colored glasses. On July 30, 1914, he wrote a letter to Kaiser Wilhelm II, stating, "(England) must … have the mask of Christian peaceableness publicly torn off her face … (unite) the whole Mohammedan world to a wild revolt against this fateful, lying, conscienceless people of shopkeepers." Neither Oppenheim nor the kaiser stopped to ask how that might possibly serve Germany's interests.

Max Oppenheim was a dreamer and a self-proclaimed Oriental authority, fueling the kaiser's fantasies. Max added the title of baron to his name on his calling cards, claiming to be Baron Max von Oppenheim, displaying his need for personal importance.

Based upon his self-professed expert knowledge and reliable sources, Oppenheim promised the kaiser "that the world of Islam would be fighting with the Central Powers in the greatest war that has ever erupted on this earth with Germans and Muslims fighting shoulder to shoulder ..." He was correct in predicting that it would erupt into a major war. The modern Middle East was created out of the defeated Ottoman Empire. Intrigue and corruption reigned supreme. For some time, there were plots to dismantle the Ottoman Empire. The kaiser was completely misguided to believe that he could, without additional support, save the Ottoman Empire and expel England from Egypt.

Neither the kaiser nor Oppenheim had a realistic concept of the Arabian power politics. They were dealing with primitive tribesmen who knew little of the world beyond the desert and couldn't care less. Germany and the kaiser began gradually to realize, but much too late, that the Islamic holy war was far costlier than Baron Max von Oppenheim predicted. His predictions turned out to be costly self-deceptions. Without control of the seas or the railroad, it is difficult to fathom how the Germans could have been successful in restoring Egyptian independence from English misrule and exploitations.

The Bedouins were not jihad (holy war) material. Whenever they could, the Bedouins were double dealing, demanding and accepting bribes from both sides. In order to sell their false loyalty, they skillfully created a bidding war between the English and the Germans, with both sides hoping to purchase worthless political influence with clerics and other individuals.

Deception and betrayal by clerics against each other and against the outside infidels were rampant. The Ottoman Empire was unable to speak with one voice. No one was really in charge or had total control of the country. The Empire was cursed with many internal conflicts. Bismarck was an anti-Orientalist for good reason. Oppenheim's promised holy warriors had to be dragged into the war, and they fled at the first sight of conflict.

Kaiser Wilhelm II vowed to be the protector of three hundred million Muslims with unending shipments of German gold and cash, competing with English bribes. Oppenheim was exceedingly generous with German gold, without any accountability whatsoever or knowing what the mountains of gold purchased. Many individuals enriched themselves with German gold and money. Germany paid for the entire war, more than $125 billion in today's money and nothing to show for it. Der Kaiser hatte keine Kleider.

The kaiser and Berlin much too slowly began to realize that their colossal investment in the Ottoman Empire was a bottomless pit and would likely go up in smoke. The hope of retrieving any of it swiftly evaporated. Besides, the Ottoman Empire itself contributed mighty little to its own war of liberation.

Kaiser Wilhelm II had much to learn from "die Goetterdaemmerung." His actions in pan-Islam proved to be a total strategic failure. It was one more failed obligation and unnecessary involvement that Berlin could ill afford, but the kaiser stubbornly persisted while living his fantasies.

The Ottoman Public Debt Administration had control of all monies raised through customs and taxes from duties collected on salt, silk, tobacco, alcohol, and stamps. Eighty percent of the money collected went to pay the huge interest on the Ottoman debt. High interest rates were levied. France dominated and controlled the Ottoman Public Debt Administration. England did not allow the duties to be raised, because it would have helped subsidize the construction of the railroad, which was seen as being at the expense of English trade and benefiting Germany.

In November 1920, two years after the end of the war that did not end all wars, several international bankers convened in London to discuss the possible completion of the Berlin-Baghdad Railroad. This meeting proved, beyond a shadow of a doubt, that all the bloodshed and suffering solved absolutely nothing. From the very beginning, the railroad was an ice-cold calculated business proposition. It had absolutely nothing to do with pan-Slavism, France regaining Alsace and Lorraine, or making the world "safe for democracy," sacrificing millions of lives as mere cannon fodder. But it had much to do with England insisting on its economic and political world domination and the creation of the State of Israel.

On December 2, 1921, the former Cleveland Press had this to say, "When Germany went to war the main thing she wanted was to complete the Berlin-Baghdad Railroad. Seven years elapse. The curtain rises on Act II: Hugo Stinnes, Walter Rathenau and other big Germans visit London. It leaks out that they are arranging to complete the railroad from Berlin to Baghdad. That is the usual way. After the dreadful war is over, both sides try to settle the original issue as they should have—peacefully." However, the meeting in London did not arrive at a consensus. The window of opportunity was shut, and the Berlin-Baghdad Railroad was never completed. It would have been a benefit to so many, and it would have been, without equal, the most important and far-reaching transportation route. When we listen to politicians speak, it is imperative to know whose payroll they're on.

On October 6, 1922, four years after the end of all the destruction of World War I and the loss of millions of innocent lives, Vaillant Conturier, a member of the French parliament, accused Poincare of being the primary scoundrel that caused all the destruction of France. With intense emotion, he stated, "M. Poincare, it is you and your politics we have to thank for the fact that French soil for 600 kilometers has been converted into a ghastly cemetery. You may therefore claim the renown of being Europe's supreme gravedigger."

The French ambassador added his own personal condemnation: "That man Poincare is the blackest scoundrel and the greatest criminal of the century." People do know the truth when they hear and see it.

The Berlin-Baghdad Railroad was a display of Germany's dramatic commercial and industrial growth and economic power. It escalated into the English-German deadly trade rivalry and the ensuing political chess game. In this part of the world, few of the players have changed, but the interactions and strategies reflecting economic interests, shifting alliances, and the diplomatic chess games by the dominant world powers continue. The sons of the poor have been sacrificed on the altar of war.

After the kaiser's fantasies fell apart, he blamed everyone but himself, displaying total denial. On December 2, 1919, he wrote in his memoirs that the Germans had been "egged on and misled ..." Neither Kaiser Wilhelm II nor Germany wanted war, nor did they want to hurt the English people; after all, they were relatives. Basically, he was naïve and a coward and not a ruthless Prussian militarist as he was portrayed by all that British anti kaiser propaganda.

Germany could have very well done without the war, and the railroad could have waited. However, if the railroad would have been completed and would have been able to operate without the various national and financial interferences, it would have been such a huge blessing to the entire region and the world. In contrast, a very small number of people benefited financially from this river of blood that was caused by the love of money.

As much as das Volk der Ditcher and Denker excels in science, literature, music, industrial creativity, and production, the kaiser lacked all comprehension and any *"Tuchgefuhl"* for politics on the world stage. Adding to the kaiser's childish need for attention and constant recognition, his venture into the global scene was doomed to failure from the start. What Germany needed was a democratic government with checks and balances, not an absolute monarch, which was simply an inherited dictatorship. The kaiser was full of contradictions; he could not support both a Muslim majority and a Jewish-Christian minority all at the same time, but he did not know that.

This is a tragic story of how a project with the potential for so much good and prosperity for so many people led to such devastation and the slaughter of millions, driven by naked greed and power. It could have become, without equal, the most important transportation route, linking the old caravan routes and connecting the Far and Near East to Western Europe.

If we are to be masters of our human destiny and not become helpless victims of an avalanche of military destruction, then we have a responsibility to fully focus and refocus our energies to peaceful endeavors and peaceful solutions.

The disparity between military power, the power of atomic destruction, and our moral and ethical sensitivity has widened catastrophically. Humans have been described as the most dangerous animals on earth. We have the power to self-destruct and contribute to our extermination. The forces of good and evil are within us. We do have a choice; let's pray that we also have the inner fortitude to do what is good and righteous. Let us hope that people go to their churches, not just to be seen, but more importantly, to seek divine guidance.

The Creator of the universe gave us the ability to trace nature through her various windings to her most concealed recesses, revealing the great proportions of the universe. He also gave us the innate ability to know right from wrong, good from evil, which has been referred to as the categorical imperative by the great German philosopher Immanuel Kant. We have been given a choice; let us choose wisely, for ourselves and the future of humankind.

Dr. Werner von Braun and his team of scientists knew the war was over. Here they surrender to the US Army. Pictured are Charles L. Stewart (left) from the Army Counterintelligence Corps, Lt. Col. Herbert Axter, Dieter Huzel, Werner von Braun, Magnus von Braun, and Hans Lindberg. Gen. Dornberger was also present.

As secretary of the treasury, Henry Morgenthau was able to wield considerable influences over FDR, the JCS, and the occupying forces in Germany and Europe. The JCS 1067 became the policy of American and Allied forces in Germany and Europe. The Morgenthau Plan was to reduce and degrade Germany and German living standards. In the Morgenthau folder in the FDR library, there is a picture with a handwritten note from FDR that reads, "For Henry from one of two of a kind."

President Truman expressed reservations about many of FDR's administrative personnel, including Morgenthau. About Morgenthau, he said "that he would not appoint someone like Morgenthau as dog catcher." Morgenthau demanded a public statement of confidence, when Truman refused, Morgenthau resigned.

CHAPTER 6

Versailles Treaty—Justice Denied

During the first two years, the fortunes of war were against England and her allies. In 1916, the British War Cabinet began discussions about considering accepting the German offer for a negotiated peace on the basis of the status quo ante, the status before the war. No nation would lose or gain any territories or legal or commercial rights. England's situation was desperate. German troops were occupying much of France and Belgium. Italy was suffering at the hands of the Austro-Hungarian army, the Russian giant was crumbling, and the French army was rioting.

The Germans and others were convinced that without the Balfour Declaration, the English government would have accepted the German peace proposal, and the war would have ended in 1916. The Balfour Declaration promised establishing a "national Jewish homeland" in Palestine. With America's entry into the war, the slaughter and killing continued another two years. Millions of lives would not have been sacrificed had America remained neutral and never entered the European military conflict; the world would be different.

At the onset of the war, soldiers were made to believe that they would be home when the first leaves began to fall in autumn, at the very latest at Christmas. In the front lines were soldiers in foxholes, avoiding getting killed, dredging through mud up to their ankles, and doing everything they could to stay alive. In the no-man's-land between the opposing sides were corpses from both sides partially covered by the newly fallen snow. These were the real victims who paid the ultimate price; they would never again enjoy a sweet embrace from a loved one.

All at once, out of nowhere, as if guided by an invisible hand, a miracle happened. From the North Sea to Switzerland, the shooting and the war stopped. This was the Christmas miracle on Christmas Eve of 1914. After five long months of war and hundreds of thousands of casualties, as the dead are euphemistically referred to, the slaughter and killing stopped, at least for one short memorable moment.

Cautiously, Christmas trees, decorated with real burning candles, appeared in front of foxholes. On the German side, banners went up with the inscription "Frohe Weihnachten," and on the English side "Merry X-mas." Christmas carols and not the sound of guns and cannons resounded throughout the war zone. The significance of the Christmas miracle of 1914 was that the soldiers stopped the war and refused to continue killing each other, even if it was only for a miraculous short moment, fulfilling the true spirit of Christmas, a display of brotherly love in action.

One English soldier wrote home to his wife, "Imagine while you were enjoying Christmas dinner at home, I was chatting out here with men whom, just a few hours ago, I was trying to kill."

Another soldier wrote, "Both sides are exhausted and eager to put an end to this war. All suffer from lice infection, freezing cold temperatures, rats and acute fear of death."

A little while later, their angelic voices joined in singing the old familiar carols in both languages. They played soccer, drank Belgian beer, and celebrated the holiday. An English soldier rode his bicycle to the supply depot to fetch a real soccer ball. Suddenly, an English soldier is face-to-face with his longtime German barber, who was forced to leave London at the onset of the war. The Englishman immediately received a fresh trim as a Christmas present. If only for a very short moment, brotherly love was replacing mass murder in uniform.

Leslie Wilkinton expressed his exuberance over what he had just witnessed: "Never have I seen a more beautiful and angelic picture of Peace on Earth." One of the officers took pictures of all the soldiers celebrating Christmas together. Then they discussed another Waffenstillstand, another ceasefire, for New Year's Eve, because they wanted to see how their pictures turned out. These men were not enemies. Wars are not started by nations but by greedy individuals, who usually have been bribed and care little about human casualties and suffering.

Arthur Conan Doyle, creator of Sherlock Holmes, described this moment of genuine human compassion as an "episode of true humanity in the midst of utter human brutality." This clearly demonstrates the power people have; the people stopped a war, turning impersonal troops into real *Menschen*, who got along quite well. They really did not want to kill each other. This was the Christmas miracle of 1914; the world needs more examples of people power. Like the literary Christmas Scrooge, the miserly old man in Dickens's story, the English military elite was enraged.

Only one day later came the cold and chilling orders from the high impersonal command from London that the slaughter and mass killing would continue. The next soldier who came up with such a crazy notion as singing "Stille Nacht" or "Silent Night" with the opposing troops was to be executed. The soldiers knew that this was just another unnecessary war, an artificial conflict dreamed up by the war profiteers.

By the time the United States officially entered World War

I, a virtual stalemate existed because of the exhaustion of the combatants. They would have likely settled for peace as they had done so many times before if Wilson and the United States had stayed out of the war completely. President Wilson was pushed into the war; he was indebted to the bankers who bankrolled his election, and there were groups interested in expanding American imperialistic objectives. Sadly, our involvement in Europe created only chaos and misery.

In 1916, the sanctimonious Woodrow Wilson sent Colonel House, one more time, to dear old England to inform the English government that the United States would definitely enter the war on England's side as soon as he was able to persuade and drag the American public into the war.

Had he followed purely constitutional and Christian principles, he would have pressed for peace rather than manipulating America into the war. At home, Wilson spoke from both sides of his mouth. He lied to the American people, espousing assurances that America would not get involved in the European war. He persisted with his slogan, "He kept us out of war," which was a well-calculated political deception. He never actually claimed that he would continue to keep us out of the war. There are historians who portray Wilson as a man possessing high ethical virtues, but his actions soundly contradict such claims. He was no Nelson Mandela or Albert Schweizer.

When Wilson addressed the US Senate on April 2, 1917, seeking a declaration of war against Germany and her allies, he described the peace after the war as a "peace without victory." He stated, "Only a peace between equals can last; only a peace the very principle of which is equality, and a common participation in a common benefit." Wilson's actions, unfortunately, contradicted his rhetoric.

President Woodrow Wilson started a tradition; he obligated

America to enter every military conflict to ensure its desired outcome. However, if America continues to be the international policeman, then America must also accept the moral obligation of ensuring that justice is served to the defeated; otherwise, it acts like the proverbial bully on the elementary school playground. In any dispute, there are always two sides and varying degrees of fault and responsibility. Versailles was a dictated peace in which *justice* was *denied*.

In January 1918, President Woodrow Wilson presented an open and public overture, an invitation to stop the slaughter. Wilson drew up a document, which he called his "Fourteen Points," which he presented to Germany and her allies. He assured Germany, Austria, Hungary, Bulgaria, and Turkey that their countries would not be torn apart and divided among the victorious allies as it had been agreed upon in the secret meetings in London, if Germany and her allies would only agree to stop fighting and lay down their weapons. That proved to be a lie and a cruel deception.

President Woodrow Wilson in an address to Congress on June 8, 1918, elaborated his "Fourteen Points" as a blueprint to peacefully ending World War I. His main points were a non -vindictive peace, national self-determination, government by the consent of the governed, an end to secret treaties, and an association of nations strong enough to check aggression and keep peace in the future. These were truly noble terms proposed by Wilson, who, tragically, extended the war by forcing America into it. Based upon these noble terms, Germany and her allies signed an armistice. The parties agreed to this pre-armistice contract that supposedly bound the Allies to make the final peace treaty conform to Wilson's "Fourteen Points," which it never did.

What was accepted at face value and in good faith, as a binding agreement, justifying an armistice, ended up as a grand scheme of deceptions and lies. Woodrow Wilson was being blackmailed and the armies of the Central Powers tricked into laying down their arms. The governments of the Central Powers tried to avoid war from the start, so they welcomed the armistice. Kaiser Wilhelm II's overriding problem was that he did not want to hurt his English relatives, while the British elite did everything in their power to destroy him and Germany. Kaiser Wilhelm was Queen Victoria's oldest grandson, and he appears to have been confused as to his primary allegiance and responsibility. Was he part of the British royalty or the German monarch? He tried to nurture friendly relations with England, which were not returned.

It was common knowledge that Germany had very much to lose and very little to gain by this war. The English and French, however, did have much to gain. The armistice appeared as a no-brainer. And besides, Wilson's pledges seemed reasonable: "Peoples and provinces shall not be allowed to be bartered away from one sovereignty to another, as if they were lifeless subjects, or pawns in a game … nations may be ruled and governed only with their consent … self-determination is no hollow phrase." Based on Wilson's pledges, the German, Austrian, Hungarian, Bulgarian, and Turkish governments agreed to the terms of the armistice, and the "war to end all wars" came to an end but not the suffering.

When the German government accepted the agreement, an armistice was declared for the eleventh hour of the eleventh day of the eleventh month. That was November 11, 1918. This armistice is still being celebrated in parts of the United States as a noble human gesture.

The Paris Peace Conference was convened about two months later, on January 18, 1919. Its stated objective was for the world to return to "normal" conditions of peace and tranquility and to national and individual prosperity—after the Allies just destroyed Germany's prosperity. Wilson's pledges and noble promises were totally ignored, a direct insult to Wilson and the United States. However, Wilson voiced no serious objections. The Versailles Treaties were born of injustice and became the basis of further injustice.

Versailles is a beautiful suburb of Paris, France. On June 28, 1919, England, France, and the United States forced upon Germany and her allies the most ungodly, brutal, inhumane, unjust, and ill-conceived indictments. Their good faith was betrayed. These greedy treaties cast a curse over the entire world and were the primary cause that led to the Great Depression, to Hitler, and ultimately to World War II and beyond.

The conditions that were created by these indictments led to worldwide economic chaos and grave social upheaval, first in Europe and then in America. The stock market crashed on December 29, 1929. In addition, the Federal Reserve, which Wilson signed into law, tightened the supply of money, which also became a contributing factor to the Depression.

English brutality knew no limits. More German, Austrian, and Hungarian women, children, and elderly were starved to death after the armistice, because of England's blockade of German ports than died during the entire war, and Wilson and America did nothing. Bloody old England threatened to starve the German people from the surface of the earth if her leaders refused to sign the suicidal Versailles Peace Treaty, which has been referred to as a process to "crucify Germany."

Writer L. Broad reported, "As a consequence of the Allied blockade, which was not lifted until mid-1919, Hunger was Lord in Germany. The people lost their resistance to disease and infections. Malnutrition resulted in mental paralysis among the grown-ups and was known to induce hunger madness in children." The English dismissed their loving and caring Jesus.

It is important to be cognizant of the various hidden forces of international commercial and industrial interests that drove the world to the most destructive wars in history. It is always important to know why our sons and daughters were sent to foreign soil to engage in deadly military conflicts. We should never ignore President George Washington's warnings to keep out of foreign alliances and entanglements.

It behooves all upright individuals to actively participate and take ownership in both the internal and external affairs of our great republic. Apathy is never an option. We should always be willing to accept it as our duty to safeguard our nation from invisible and hidden foreign and domestic powers. Like Germany, we too have much to lose and little to gain in foreign entanglements.

To keep out of other people's and nation's affairs and focus on our own business is always great advice both individually and nationally. Never lose sight of the fact that international forces, the movers and shakers that drive and move world events, are very powerful and well financed and their efforts well organized. Agents and lobbyists, representing international and foreign interests, must never succeed in curtailing or derailing true patriotism. In our pursuit of happiness, always demand both liberty and justice; there never can be one without the other. Why would the British, French and American working, blue color, class fight and kill the German working class?

Germany's cardinal sin, as far as England was concerned, was that she became too powerful industrially and commercially. England's obsession and determination was to reduce her in size and eliminate her as a serious competitor. The leadership of Germany's neighbors was very pragmatic in their own national interests and national gains. England displayed a self-serving approach and was not about to share its spot in the sun with anybody, especially Germany. Kaiser Wilhelm II was unwilling to accept British political reality. All of Germany's requests and gestures for peace did little to deflect England's determination for war.

England persisted to ensure that no nation became so strong that it could challenge the supremacy of the British Empire. England had worldwide obligations but no way to maintain them. She would enter alliances to further her objectives. Her second mission was to expand and spread the influence of the British Empire over as much of the world as possible. Since Germany was perceived as a serious detriment and threat to both of England's objectives, England became the primary driving force behind both world wars.

As soon as Germany was disarmed and defenseless, all the pledges and promises of the armistice agreement were summarily withdrawn and ignored. The kaiser was rather naïve and foolish to agree to this one-sided disarmament. Even Wilson's much-heralded principle of self-determination was betrayed by Wilson himself, as he participated in denying and ignoring the human rights of Germans living in Poland, the newly created Czechoslovakia, and Yugoslavia. He did nothing to stop the ethnic cleansing and expulsions in these regions.

Point 5 of Wilson's Fourteen Points provided Germany assurances that Germany would retain its colonies and no territories of Germany, Austria, and Hungary would be amputated. Tragically, they were annexed by bloody old England and France. Japan took control of Germany's North Pacific colonies. England wanted the South Pacific islands for herself. Germany and her allies were ruthlessly exploited by greedy, unscrupulous politicians, behaving like vultures.

The Treaties of Versailles have been referred to as unmitigated fraud. The US Congress rightfully refused to ratify them and drafted a separate peace treaty. However, the United States reserved all the rights granted to her in the Versailles Treaties. The Council of Four, of which Wilson was a member, acted as judge, jury, and executioner. The other members were Clemenceau of France, Lloyd George of England, and Orlando of Italy. The process and content of the proceedings were kept secret. The treaties were not the result of open negotiations between equals, as Wilson promised.

Both Clemenceau and Lloyd George arrogantly announced to their respective citizens that the Germans would be forced to pay for everything. The Reparations Committee never changed the reparation demands, which they had the power to do. Other nations had their debts forgiven but not Germany.

George Clemenceau, prime minister of France, arrived saturated with hate and revenge toward Germany. He was determined to completely and permanently wreck Germany. Lloyd George, who was known in Ireland as "Black and Tan George," came with two objectives: grab as much as possible for England and see to it that France did not walk away with too much.

Since Russia surrendered to Germany prior to the armistice and signed the Treaty of Brest-Litovsk, all the promises made to Russia became null and void. France's territorial gains were immense and second only to those of England. These treaties, intentionally or otherwise, laid the groundwork for the resumption of the war twenty years down the road. Wilson supporting the secret meetings negated any opportunity for his "Fourteen Points."

The Versailles Treaties were a grandiose attempt to legitimize international grand theft and provide justification for their enormous economic gains and the gigantic amputations of territories, most of which had been decided far in advance at a secret meeting in London. It was the intention of the Allies to keep Germany prostrate and in bondage virtually forever. Bismarck was fully cognizant of how Germany would be treated once it suffered defeat, but the kaiser was blind, naïve, and unwilling to accept good counsel.

The eminent American historian Professor Fay asserted, "One must abandon the dictum of the Versailles Treaty that Germany and her allies were solely responsible. It was a dictum exacted by the victors upon the vanquished, under the influence of blindness, ignorance, hatred, and the propagandistic misconception of which war had given rise. It was based upon erroneous, fabricated evidence. It is generally recognized by the best historical scholars in all countries to be no longer tenable."

The treaty, which Germany was forced to accept, was signed on June 28, 1919, in the Hall of Mirrors. The treaty imposed on Austria was signed on September 10, 1919, in Saint Germaine, and the treaty forced upon Hungary was signed on June 4, 1920, in the Trianon Palace. This palace was a "love nest" built by the French king, Louis XV, for his lady friend Madame Dubarry.

The reparations were temporarily postponed from the treaties' proceedings to be addressed at a later date. That was equivalent to handing over a blank check, the amount to be filled in at a later date by the victorious allies. Germany was never consulted about anything, including its ability to pay. The treaties gave the Reparations Committee the right to change any of the harsh conditions, but the committee chose not to change anything.

The treaties were severely skewed. They were not the result of open negotiations; they were a display of brutal revenge and excessive greed. The vanquished were declared guilty as charged and no defense permitted. Germany and her allies, Austria, Hungary, Bulgaria, and Turkey, were collectively and individually found guilty for the outbreak of the war as well as responsible for all the losses and damages caused by and resulting from the war.

All the agitations, bribes, and corruption permeating from Paris and precipitating the war were not mentioned. The intent of the verdict was to inflict upon Germany, Austria, Hungary, and their allies economic and national ruination and death. England and France found themselves not guilty of any crime or the minutest blame relative to the war. They asserted that the kaiser and his allies, totally unprovoked, one day started a war. That was total fiction, even according to their records.

In Article 231, for example, the indictment stated,

> The Allied and Associated Governments affirm, and Germany accepts, the responsibility of herself and her allies, for causing all the loss and damage to which the Allied and Associated Governments and their nationals have been subjected as a consequence of the war imposed upon them by the aggression of Germany and her allies.

Germany had a choice to either sign this monstrous document or the British starvation blockade would continue and more Germans, Austrians, and Hungarians would be starved to death.

The indictments against Austria and Hungary contained similar language. The emphasis was on Germany and her allies being forced to accept sole blame as the aggressor. Germany and her allies were found guilty as charged, no defense allowed. This antagonistic kangaroo court behavior assured the continuation of the war at a later date.

To add further insult to injury, the indictments contained language that the accusers *affirmed* and the accused *accepted* the truth of the indictment. Germany and her allies were forced to accept and plead guilty as the sole aggressors and to accept *sole* responsibility for the outbreak of the war; this was a clear case of self-incrimination. That was like a legal plea agreement based upon fabrications that were total fiction.

With threats of torture, more suffering, privations, and further starvation, Germany and her allies were forced to accept the guilty verdict and sign this monstrosity, known as the Versailles Peace Treaty. The fact remains that these kangaroo-style proceedings would have been laughed out of any self-respecting American, French, or English court of justice and the advocates would have been ordered to a psychiatric examination.

As to Germany's *sole* guilt accusations, we are reminded of the statement by Lloyd George in the House of Commons on March 3, 1921: "For the allies, German responsibility for the war is fundamental. It is the structure of the treaty of Versailles which has been erected, and if that acknowledgement is repudiated or abandoned, the treaty is destroyed ..."

The claim that it was allegedly a German plot against the peace of the world is a preposterous claim; it is based upon a false claim of a fictitious crown conference that never took place. The construct of the "sole guilt" clause is on very shaky, sandy ground that would not withstand the slightest rebuttal. The "sole guilt" claim must be re-visited for justice to be served.

Lord Buckmaster shared his observations about the Dictate of Versailles: "It is dishonest and despicable to induce a nation ... to lay down its arms on the basis of certain conditions, and then, when she has become defenseless, to impose other and additional conditions on her. That can never be forgotten!"

The Allies crushed Germany beneath the burden of unrealistic reparations, stole vital German territories, and rendered Germany defenseless against internal and external enemies. Lloyd George warned us, but he was ignored, that the terms of the treaty "will be the source of a new war." History proved him and others to be right.

J. W. Kershaw, representative of the Labor Party, stated in 1920 at the party convention in Scarborough, "If we had been the defeated nation, and such conditions had been imposed on us, we would prepare our children in our schools and homes for a war of retaliation to shake off the victors' loathsome intolerable yoke instead of bearing it patiently. These conditions were not only a conspiracy against Germany, Austria and other defeated nations, but also a blow against the entire construct of civilization."

There is no known international law or Geneva Convention rule that possibly would sanction such fraudulent, greedy, vengeful, and ill-conceived behavior among nations. When an individual or a nation is forced to sign an agreement under threat of torture and physical abuse, then such a contract is null and void because it lacks the element of free consent. England, France, and their allies had the burden of proof that Germany, Austria, Hungary, and their allies were indeed the "sole aggressors," which they failed to even attempt to prove because there was no basis to such a claim.

If Germany, Austria, Hungary, and their allies would have been granted an opportunity to debate the issues fairly and openly, as they should have, according to international law, the proceedings would have taken a different form and produced a greatly different outcome. Perhaps World War II could have been averted. The Versailles verdict was a display of nothing less than muzzling and ruthlessly exploiting the vanquished.

As discussed in a previous chapter, the German kaiser and the Russian czar worked feverishly to avert a war. They encouraged each other to do everything in their power to avert a war. On June 29, 1914, Kaiser Wilhelm II sent Czar Nicholas II a telegram to ask the Russian government to remain neutral in the Austria-Serbian conflict. The czar, in turn, sent his trusted general Titistchev to Berlin to confer with the kaiser personally. The purpose of this meeting was to discuss a plan of what the two monarchs might or should do to avert the war. Unfortunately, the trusted general was arrested by Sazanov, the minister of foreign affairs, as he was about to board the train to Berlin.

The Russian monarch was no longer in charge; he was surrounded by false patriots, and subversive forces infiltrated his country. Imagine the president of the United States sending the chief of staff on an assignment and the secretary of state arresting him or her as he or she attempted to board a plane. Unscrupulous agents infiltrated not only France and England but also Russia.

Kaiser Wilhelm II published an article in the *London Morning Post* entitled "Efforts Toward Peace," in which he stated in part, "The whole war is plainly arranged between England, France and Russia for the annihilation of Germany, lastly through the conversation with Poincare in Paris and Petersburg, and the Austro-Serbian strife is only an excuse to fall upon us! God help us in this fight for our existence, brought about by falseness, lies and poisonous envy!" Tragically, the kaiser realized this much too late.

When war broke out, Izvolski, the Russian ambassador to France and coconspirator with Poincare, rubbed his hands and gleefully exclaimed, "This is my war!" There was rejoicing in Paris and London, but the kaiser was greatly distressed and the German ambassador to Russia broke down and wept. Good men wept, and violent men rejoiced. According to international law, "the mobilization of the military forces of one country against another country is equivalent to a declaration of war on the country against which the mobilization is directed." It was like a pack of wolves, scheming to bring down a big animal. They initiated a war instigated by Serbia against Austria, and then Germany would come to the aid of Austria.

After the war, on September 5, 1919, Woodrow Wilson declared that "the war was purely an economic and trade war." Of course, Wilson knew that already when he asked Congress to declare war against Germany. The primary cause of World War I was the unadulterated perpetuation of imperialism, eager to advance their own selfish imperialistic interests.

The Council of Four rewarded themselves and their allies lavishly, while brutally beating up on the vanquished, whom they coined the bad guys. Adding deception, lies, and hypocrisy, the peace that could have been tragically slipped from the world's grasp because of a few narrow-minded and greedy individuals.

Kaiser Wilhelm II foolishly held on to the notion that the controversy brewing was between Serbia and Austria-Hungary and should be settled between them, not spill over into other countries. What Wilhelm II did not want to accept is the fact that England, France, Russia, and Colonel House had been working long and diligently creating a climate of war against Germany.

Because the kaiser was not convinced that this conflict would spill over to any other country, he confidently went on a cruise on July 6, 1914, while diplomats in England, France, and Russia were feverishly preparing secretly for war. The kaiser spent far too much time on cruises, living childish fantasies, when he should have been in Berlin attending to pressing governmental affairs.

At this time, Germany and Austria-Hungary had not issued orders for the mobilization of their armies. Austria was still attempting to resolve the conflict through diplomatic channels. England and France wanted to catch Germany and Austria-Hungary totally by surprise. Thus, neither Germany nor Austria and Hungary can legally be found guilty of aggression. The kaiser was unwilling to accept the fact that his English relatives would treat him any differently than he would treat them, namely with love, compassion, and care. Serbia had already mobilized, as she was ordered by the Entente powers.

The upright people of France, England, Russia, Germany, Austria, Hungary, and America did not want war. The people never do, unless they are attacked and are forced to defend their homeland. So, who were the special interest groups who pushed and brainwashed the people for war? The people would not have been so willing to fight and give their lives if there would have been governmental transparency and if they were given all the facts. Transparency is always essential to peace. Political leaders betrayed their people. The people were not given a choice. Sadly, as the lyrics go, "theirs not to reason why, theirs is but to do or die."

The governments of England and France, along with false Russian patriots, were scheming to force war upon Germany. But the only way to get Germany involved in war was to have Serbia instigate a war against Austria-Hungary. As described in an earlier chapter, international bankers supplied tons of money to bribe and corrupt politicians and the media. It was calculated that a Serbian military conflict would bring Russia to Serbia's rescue. The American entry into the European theater of war would turn it into a world war, serving imperialistic interests.

The French ambassador to Russia assured Russia that France was ready to fulfill all its obligations of the alliance and move ahead as secretly as possible, so as not to afford the Germans any excuse for mobilization. The English were fully committed to align themselves with France and Russia, but, like Wilson, needed to find a pretext that would justify military action.

The media in England was not yet as corrupt as it was in France. For example, the *Manchester Guardian* reported,

> Of all the small powers in Europe, Serbia is quite decidedly, the one whose name is most foully daubed with dishonor. The record of her rulers and her policy in recent years is an unmatched issue of cruelty, greed, hypocrisy and ill-faith …

If one could tow Serbia to the edge of the ocean
and sink it, the atmosphere of Europe would be
cleared.

The question should be asked, were the good Serbian
people victims of its corrupt leaders and the world political
power establishment? A secret meeting between Poincare and
some members of the French government marks the beginning
of World War I.

The French ambassador in London was instructed by
Poincare to give the German ambassador personal assurances
that the French government had not taken any warlike steps and
it also was doing everything in its power to preserve peace by
diplomatic means, which was a blatant lie. Poincare had been
distributing large sums of bribe money to instigate a war. The
kaiser and the German government should have been much
better informed about the internal activities and true intensions
of its neighbors.

Sir Grey, the English secretary of foreign affairs, spoke with
a forked tongue. In one breath, he told the German ambassador
that Austria was totally within its rights to obtain satisfaction
in the assassination of Archduke Franz Ferdinand and his wife,
and in the next breath, he instructed the Russian government
that the English fleet was ready for war against Germany and
Austria-Hungary. Lord Welby, the former head of England's
Treasury Department, expressed his frustrations, "We are in
the hands of an organization of crooks. These are politicians,
generals, manufacturers of armaments, and journalists."
Germany wanted to maintain peace and continue its commercial
and industrial growth, not war.

The French writer Georges Demartial wrote, "The French
people were thrown into the war as helpless as a bound
chicken destined for the spit." Upright and honorable French

people strongly opposed to war held peace meetings in Paris and elsewhere. The French government broke up these peace meetings by police force. The French leader of the peace movement, Jean Juares, was assassinated by the Russian Secret Service, ordered by Izvolski.

On the night of July 31, 1914, Poincare met with Viviani and Messimy in Poincare's residence. The purpose of the meeting was to "officially" declare war on Germany. Austria was regarded as a negligible military quantity. The English government, as a pretext, claimed it had a diplomatic obligation to defend Belgium, even though there existed really no such agreement. Both England and France planned to invade Belgium illegally to attack Germany. Moreover, Belgium did not ask England to assist her militarily to preserve her neutrality, but Belgium did ask Lord Grey of England to mind his own business, which he ignored. However, Grey was determined to go to war under any pretext. He needed to appease the war hawks in England.

England had been meticulously preparing for war. It is very revealing that there existed detailed plans for war against Germany at the end of 1910. The kaiser refused to accept the reality that his relatives in England wanted to destroy Germany and him. England's plans for war were so complete that within few hours after England declared war on Germany, her troops were on the continent engaging Germany in a military Blitzkrieg. It is exceedingly unfortunate that Germany was saddled with a pompous, naïve monarch.

On August 3, 1914, Sir Grey, secretary of foreign affairs, vehemently denied that any agreement for war existed with France. However, this same agreement emerged mysteriously the following day, on August 4. Frederick Cornwallis Coneybeare wrote on August 4, 1922, stating, "Grey was doubtless as much of a hypocrite in the week before the War as he had been eight years before ... We attacked Germany for three reasons: (1) to down her navy before it got any larger; (2) to capture her trade; (3) to take her colonies." This statement turns the sole guilt clause into a baseless farce. Russia declared war on Turkey on October 30, 1915; England and France on November 5, 1915; and Italy, changing sides, on Austria-Hungary and Germany on August 27, 1916.

The only thing that remained was how to get the United States into the war. President Woodrow Wilson and Colonel House, the hidden power behind Wilson, decreed that the United States would enter the war on England's side. America really had no common cause with any of its allies. So, why did America declare war on Germany on April 8, 1917, and turn it into a world war? Americans were told that they were sacrificing their lives on foreign soil to "make the world safe for democracy." This was one hellish way to pay them back. The government of Wilson betrayed the American people, especially the German Americans. Wilson's hands were tied by the thread of blackmail.

Wilson used the sinking of the *Lusitania* as an excuse to enter the war. The American people were not told that the Lusitania was loaded with six million pounds of ammunition and explosives and equipped with high-powered naval rifles destined for England. It was more profitable for the financial interest groups of the United States to be on England's side. It was not an ethical or moral issue, as claimed by the political establishment, but an ice-cold business calculation for which our boys, our GIs, were sacrificed.

The English blockade also cut off American shipments of materials and goods to Germany and her allies. America entered the war to protect the investments of the bankers and enrich the war profiteers. The military theater also distracted Americans from their own economic troubles.

The underlying reasons of the war were to defeat and economically ruin Germany and Austria-Hungary and to obstruct the construction of the Berlin Baghdad Railroad. French politicians, Poincare, and false Russian patriots misled their people; England's politicians resorted to fraud and deception to bring England and America into the war. Americans were deceived into the war by the sinking of the *Lusitania* and under the slogan "to make the world safe for democracy." It is rather paradoxical that since World War II, the United States has been involved in more military conflicts than any other nation. Perpetual war for perpetual peace is an oxymoron, a total contradiction, but that is what we got.

In 1917, Lord Balfour explained the reasons for the war rather succinctly: "This war has been described, and quite accurately I think, as a war against the world domination of Germany ... The practical destruction of the Turkish Empire is undoubtedly one of the objects which we desire to attain." There are many secret documents locked up in our archives for good reason. The American people have a right to know the contents of these documents.

On April 30, 1915, there was a secret meeting in London, in which Italy was promised large parts of Austrian territory if she switched sides, which Italy did. Russia was promised the Dardanelles if she did not make a separate peace treaty with Germany, which she did. Wilson had full knowledge of this meeting and the secret covert agreements before he asked Congress to declare war on Germany.

The Paris Peace Conference was convened on January 18, 1919. Its stated and advertised objective was to return the world to normal conditions of peace and prosperity. However, this was anything but a peace conference. The reparation issues were postponed to a later date. The people of Germany and its allies believed that the president of the United States would not engage in deception. The governments of Germany, Austria, Hungary, Bulgaria, and Turkey agreed to an armistice, based upon Wilson's Fourteen Points of self-determination, and the war to end all wars finally came to an end.

After they laid down their weapons, the Central Powers were not allowed to be present at the Paris Peace Conference. Those who were invited to this "peace" conference included the British Empire and all its colonies, France, Italy, the United States, Japan, Belgium, Brazil, the British Dominions, India, China, Cuba, Greece, Guatemala, Haiti, Panama, Hedjaz, Honduras, Liberia, Nicaragua, Poland, Portugal, Romania, Serbia, the new Czechoslovak Republic (which until this time was part of Germany), and Guam. The Allies displayed their self-serving generosity by stealing as much as they could from Germany and her allies. They committed grand theft.

In April, a German delegation was ordered to come to Versailles to receive and accept the terms of the peace conditions. The delegation was subjected to outrageous and humiliating treatment. John Foster Dalles, a member of the American delegation, reported that "the Germans were ordered into a barbed-wire enclosure, exposed to gawkers like animals in a zoo. Any and all personal contact with Allied delegates was forbidden." This is not how international agreements are usually finalized, but there was nothing usual about how the entire Versailles Peace Treaty was conducted; most of it was kept top secret.

On May 7, they were led into the Trinian Palace Hotel. In a large hall, some two hundred delegates sat in a large hall, including Woodrow Wilson, Lloyd George, and Clemenceau. At this point, the Germans did not know if they would be handed a negotiated peace, like that which had been granted to France in 1815 by the Congress of Vienna, or a dictated peace awaited them.

Count Ulrich von Brockdorff-Rantzau expressed the German reaction, "We know of the intensity of the hatred which meets us … That as the vanquished we shall be made to pay and as the guilty we shall be punished. The demand is made that we shall acknowledge that we alone are guilty of having caused the war. Such a confession in my mouth would be a lie." He also went on, stating, "The hundreds of thousands of non-combatants (German) who have perished since the eleventh of November by reason of the blockade were killed with cold deliberation, after our adversaries had conquered and victory was theirs." After this short speech, Lloyd George impulsively snapped a letter-opener in half and Wilson called the Germans a stupid people.

Felix Fechenbach, president of the German National Assembly, stated, "The inconceivable has happened; the enemy has given us a treaty that by far exceeds the most pessimistic predictions. It means the destruction of the German people. It is incredible that a man (Wilson) who promised the world a just peace could become an accessory to this work guided by hate." The Treaty of Versailles was signed by Foreign Minister Hermann Mueller on June 28, 1919, and the world has not seen peace since then.

Hindenburg commented that it would be more honorable to go down in battle than to accept the enemy's intolerable conditions. Under threat of the Allied total invasion, the German government did bow to the dictated treaty on June 23. On the same day, the German navy, which had been detained in the British port of Scapa Flow, sank itself on the order of Admiral von Reuter: nine battle cruisers, five heavy and seven light cruisers, and fifty destroyers.

London and Paris invited literally everybody to the grand feast, attempting to legitimize this international grand theft. This made a total mockery of Wilson's guarantees and promises. Justice was forcefully denied, and therefore, the whole world was betrayed. Several books have been written about this spectacle, including the book by Dr. E. J. Dillon entitled *The Inside Story of the Peace Conference*. The prevalent attitude was grab what you can while you can. Part of Wilson's guarantees stipulated, "Peoples and provinces shall not be allowed to be bartered away from one sovereignty to another ..." but that is precisely what happened. The newly formed Czechoslovak Republic was formed by giving it large territories from Austria and Hungary. The Allies were the victors who not only wrote the history but also made up rules as they pleased. Such tactics always have adverse consequences.

The Germany that England and France referred to in the Versailles Treaties did not exist until 1871, when Bismarck was able to unite all of Germany into one nation with one central government. Germany's former glory and power was lost as a result of the Thirty Years' War and the Treaty of Westphalia in 1648. The war of religious freedom raged in the land of Luther. Religious freedom was denied to the German people. The pope ordered the Catholic Hapsburg kaiser in Vienna to mobilize the imperial army under General Wallenstein and force the Protestant Germans back into the Roman Catholic Church. During this religious strife, 1618 to 1648, more than a quarter of Germany's population lost their lives and many left seeking religious freedom. Many immigrated to the United States and other parts of the world.

The great religious struggle and its many adverse effects on Germany played such a major part in its history. For centuries, the Roman Catholic Church exercised authority and control over its members. Austria has for centuries been a strong bastion of Catholicism. Even the Catholic kaiser in Vienna was ever obedient to the absolute power of the church, calling out the army to subdue the Protestants of the empire. Without that action, Germany would most likely be religiously united and mostly Protestant, but Rome needed money.

The Treaty of Westphalia reduced Germany into a conglomeration of some three hundred small states, each with self-autonomy, making Germany easier to control by its neighbor France. Each minor monarch had been granted the authority to determine the religion in his domain. This religious schism has been a curse to Germany and Germans ever since.

For far too many Germans, religious affiliation has proven more important than national affiliation. Many Catholic Germans took up arms against their Protestant brothers and sisters. Catholic Bavaria fought on the side of Napoleon against Protestant Prussia. The religious division has remained a curse and burden for all Germans. There still is no division between state and church in Germany and some other European countries; they still pay church taxes. The concept of separation of church and state is still absent from German policy. Many books have been written about the role of the church and Germany's religious schism in German history because it has played such a monumental part in its history.

It is imperative to understand history to comprehend present conditions. Balfour stated that England was not engaged in the war for the promotion of democracy or "to make the world safe for democracy" nor "to end all wars" but to eliminate a powerful commercial rival, Germany. The *Chicago Herald and Examiner* reported,

> This document proves the Versailles Treaty was not in reality a peace treaty but a mere ratification of the spoils of war, divided by the allies in secret pacts prior to the spring of 1917, fully two years before the end of the war. At Versailles, the allied diplomats merely "rubber stamped" in public what they had pledged each other years earlier in secrecy.

Poland was promised huge slices of German and Austrian territories, just to keep her from sending an army to help Germany. That is how dear old England operated. Bohemia and other Austrian territories gave birth to Czechoslovakia. The Turkish Empire was destroyed by wholesale annexation of her territory. Bosnia and Herzegovina, which were part of the Austrian Empire, were promised to Serbia. Parts of Hungary were promised to Romania. Balfour promised over half of Hungary to Serbia and Romania. What would we do if we found out that foreign interests were attempting to divide us up, as they tried to do during our Civil War? To that end, both Paris and London provided financial aid to the southern independence movement. The Russian Czar sent a fleet in support of Lincoln to keep the union together.

After the secret treaty in London, Italy switched sides and declared war on Austria-Hungary in April 1915 and on Germany in 1916. For switching sides, Italy received the southern part of the Austrian Tyrol, Suedtirol, home to 200,000 Germans and very few Italians, and areas in Asia Minor and Africa, including the harbors of Fiume and Valona in Albania. The Sykes-Picot Treaty in 1915 allowed France to carve up Southern Turkey, basically dissecting the Ottoman Empire and giving France Syria, Citrus, and southern Armenia. England grabbed Acre, Haifa, and Lower Mesopotamia from Baghdad to the Persian Gulf.

Georges Clemenceau, prime minister of France, wanted Germany to be cut down into a series of small states, as she was as a result of the Treaty of Westphalia following the Thirty Years' War in 1648. Cutting down Germany in size and then encouraging a separatist movement in the western German states was part of Clemenceau's plan. He was determined to turn Germany into a second- or third-class power.

The reparation dictates allowed France to annex the Saar region, with a plebiscite for the area to decide its own fate at a later date. France was to indoctrinate the residents to become part of France. France received the Saar coal mines and the right for its military to occupy the Rhineland for fifteen years. France's land gains were immense and second only to those of England. Italy fared relatively poorly. Both Clemenceau and Lloyd George resisted granting Italy what she had been promised in their secret treaties. Wilson also agreed to grant Italy South Tyrol, contradicting his policy of self-determination.

Italy and other nations learned that agreements with England and France meant little when their own imperialist interests were at stake. France made a treaty in 1917 with Russia, expressly allowing her to gobble up Poland. A section of Schleswig-Holstein was given to Denmark, and a plebiscite was ordered. However, the Danes recognized that the area was predominantly German and rejected the plebiscite and any additional annexations. That was noble on the part of Denmark. Unfortunately, other Europeans did not act so honorably.

Allied propaganda showed the kaiser as a fat butcher cutting up the world, when in reality it was the Allies who cut up and divided among themselves Germany, Austria, Hungary, and Turkey. Edward Benes bragged at the Paris Peace Conference that he was given much more than he asked for. Thomas Masaryk, another Bohemian, voiced his objections to being given territories with 3,500,000 Germans to form a Czech Republic. England and her allies financed a few Czech leaders to make demands for Czech freedom and to tell the world that they wanted to be independent of Austria and Germany, while thousands of Bohemian soldiers were fighting in the Austrian army.

Arthur Ponsonby reported that England enriched itself with new territories covering some 1,415,929 square miles, which is slightly less than half of the area of the United States. France increased from 207,054 to 212,659 square miles. What did the United States get? Millions of Americans out of work and the Depression. Florence E. Marshall summed it up, "A pretty penny we paid for war! Let's make an honest confession; $45,000,000,000 spent and what did we get? The Depression!"

In March 1938, US Senator William E. Borah summed it up this way:

> When the so-called peace treaties were signed at Versailles, ancient states had been dismembered, national boundaries re-established, vast colonial possessions given over to the victors, people shoved about from sovereignty to sovereignty, with no more choice upon their part than have cattle which are prodded from one corral to another. All of Europe and parts of Asia had been redistributed, divided up, parceled out largely in accordance with the terms of the secret treaties made while our American boys were being conscripted to fight in foreign countries for the preservation of democracy! ... And like Mark Antony over the body of bleeding Caesar, we quickly seized the bloody hands of those who assassinated liberty!

US Congressman Raymond J. Cannon, speaking on the floor of Congress, said, "The Treaty of Versailles has many crimes and bloodshed to account for." The Versailles treaties assassinated democracy. Lloyd George, prime minister of England, bowed his head in regret and shame, stating, "The religion of Jesus Christ is the only thing that can save this world from another catastrophe." Why the mutilation of Germany and her allies? What did it really accomplish and who benefited?

A treaty that a president of the United States signed is not binding upon the American government until our Senate ratifies it by a two-thirds vote. The Versailles Treaties were rejected by the US Senate for all the right reasons. On July 17, 1928, the Paris *Figaro* stated, "Germany is not guilty, the peace is unjust." The indictments of the treaties are false and totally untrue, because World War I was plotted by France, England, and false Russian patriots and provoked by their agent, Serbia. If the claim of "aggressor" fails, then the indictments fail.

The self-righteous Allies attempted to conceal their unjust dealings by their proclaimed morality while ethical principles were absent. Wilson's point 1 provided for "open covenants openly arrived at." Tragically, Wilson's Fourteen Points were summarily withdrawn and totally ignored as soon as the talks began on January 12, 1919. The victorious Allies insisted on top secrecy for good reason.

Wilson agreed to be part of the secret meetings, thereby losing all credibility to demand adherence to his noble Fourteen Points. England, France, Japan, and Italy were hustling secret treaties among themselves. The Allies continued their hateful, aggressive mode of operation at the expense of Germany and her allies.

The redrawing of borders, huge land grabs, international theft, ethnic cleansing, starvation blockade, rapes, and murders led directly to Hitler and World War II. The Allies rewarded themselves lavishly; there is no honor among thieves. Religious and moral principles, whenever they got in the way, were merely pushed aside for the sake of greed and gain, which is always self-serving and void of anything noble.

Such was the nature of their hypocrisy, elevating themselves to the status of calling themselves the good nations and punishing the so-called bad nations, whom the Allies decreed were unfit to play any major part in any future affairs of Europe and the world. When con artists sit in judgment, good men sit in jail. What the treaties displayed was false moral arrogance and a total absence of a genuine desire for lasting peace. Their actions contradicted the armistice agreement.

Czechoslovakia was newly created with land stolen from Austria and the Sudetenland. This area was highly developed industrially and populated almost entirely by Germans and was also congruent to Germany. The Germans of the Sudetenland appealed for relief to the newly formed League of Nations and to the victorious Allied powers but were rebuffed and their concerns ignored. The victorious powers were blinded by their greed.

The apex of injustice regarding the German people was the provision against Anschluss (union) of the German people of Austria with Germany. Historian H. G. Wells called it "an ubiquitous breach of the right of self-determination." The Catholic Hapsburgs in Vienna ruled the German Empire for over six hundred years, forming one nation for centuries.

Those in power, passing judgment, should have seriously reflected upon all the possible consequences of their shallow, ill-conceived decisions. To secure respect for the Versailles Treaties, the treaties needed to be respectable, fair, and just. Tragically, any and all positive and noble qualities were totally absent from the treaties.

Poland had ambitions of territorial expansion; it was infested with a spirit of imperialism. Besides the land grab from Germany, Austria, and Hungary, Poland also took advantage of the chaos created in Russia by the Bolshevik Revolution and grabbed large territories of western Russia, in which very few Poles lived. Poland also severed land from Lithuania and became involved in a conflict with the newly formed Czechoslovakia over the district of Teschen.

At Versailles, Poland made territorial demands that were so extreme that Lloyd George, prime minister of England, was outraged. But Georges Clemenceau, prime minister of France, motivated by hate and revenge, endorsed their demands. As a result, Posen, West Prussia, and Eastern Upper Silesia were annexed and became "the Polish Corridor." This corridor became the trigger mechanism of the second act of this tragic thirty-year war.

The territory that was amputated from Germany and annexed to Poland included highly developed industrial and commercial areas, which, over centuries, were developed by Germans. Almost the entire population was German. The people's wishes, wanting to remain part of Germany, were denied. In Silesia, after the population voted to remain and be part of Germany, the entire territory was awarded to Poland. All expressions of self-determination were forcibly overruled. Poland then engaged in brutal ethnic cleansing.

German schools in Poland were closed, medical assistance was denied, the homes and businesses of Germans were destroyed or confiscated, and Germans were no longer given licenses to operate businesses. In the Polish town of Lotz, a German school and the German stores and banks were demolished on Palm Sunday in 1939. All German inhabitants were forced to wear armbands with the number 206. In 1919, there were concentration camps in Potulice, Poland, for Germans. Many Germans were brutally beaten on the streets and in their homes. Many were killed. Later, Hitler ruled with equal brutality. The media, however, focused only on Hitler's brutality, totally ignoring the suffering of the Germans. Hence, the world knows what the Germans did, but little or nothing is known about what was done to the Germans.

Both sides were ignorant of the fact that the best way to avenge revenge is not to behave and act revengefully. Friedrich Schiller, the German dramatist, stated, "Revenge is barren of itself; itself is the dreadful food it feeds on; its delight is murder; its satiety despair." With time, revenge turns more bitter. Nothing debases a person or a nation more than revenge.

The ancient city of Danzig and the area surrounding Danzig, some eight hundred square miles, was mercilessly torn from Germany. For centuries, this city and the entire area had been part of the German Reich, populated by Germans. It was designated as a "free city" under the control of the League of Nations. That was a misnomer, since it was under the control of foreign powers. That was just one of many contradictions. It was not *free* to reattach itself to Germany. This was an intentional permanent amputation and intended as a source of irritation to the Germans. In order for the Germans to reach their own East Prussia, they had to travel through the newly created Polish territory and be subjected to newly created Polish regulations and humiliations.

Poland built a seaport in the corridor, close to Gdynia (Gdansk). The seaport at Danzig gave Poland a measure of control over its German population. By building the seaport of Gdynia, the greater part of the old port of Danzig was neglected. Memel had been founded as a German city by the grandmaster of the Teutonic Order of Knights in AD 1252. The surrounding area was populated by Lithuanians, but the city itself was German in language and character.

It has so often been stated that war is a firmly established human institution everyone claims to hate. However, it is so profitable to the establishment that its future is well assured. Profit trumps human compassion and human suffering. Over the centuries, the methods of war have changed from rocks and swords to the atomic bomb and chemical warfare. President Dwight D. Eisenhower warned his countrymen that disaster was at hand if the "military-industrial complex" succeeded in institutionalizing war as a permanent condition of American society. What the leadership has created is permanent war for permanent peace.

Greed and brutality at Versailles reached a new level of hypocrisy. The treaty confiscated the private property of all

Germans who resided in Allied countries. Millions of ethnic Germans lost everything—their ancestral homesteads, their livestock, and their art collections—and millions lost their lives. They were forced to leave all their earthly possessions behind. Millions were murdered. That was the new standard dictated by the Versailles Treaties.

As part of this ethnic cleansing, they left with what they could carry, and most of that was stolen on the way by partisans. Many were brutally beaten. The raping of German women was rampant, and no one cared or did anything about it. The debts that Allied nationals owed to German nationals were forgiven and canceled, but the reverse was not true. The debts owed by Germans had to be repaid in full. The Reparation Commission confiscated German properties in Allied countries. German nationals were stripped of all their property in Poland and the newly created states of Czechoslovakia and Yugoslavia.

At the Versailles Peace Conference, the previously accepted principles of international law were pushed aside and ignored. The clock of human justice was turned back to the brutality of the Dark Ages. Individual damages sustained because one had the misfortune of residing in the path of the war were no longer compensable, even to the citizens of the victor. The victors decreed that Germany and her allies were *solely* responsible for all damages.

The formula of indemnity was not only skewed but altered significantly. Previously, even citizens of a vanquished country could bring suit against a victor nation. At Versailles, even the leaders of Germany were stripped of all proper decorum and treated like the worst criminals, while being forced to sign the treaty. These actions made a total mockery of President Wilson's claims. Wilson professed that the peace that would follow would be a "peace of equals," which was turned into a farce. The rules that were applied were a rude example of "Might makes right."

There are endless reasons why these proceedings were held in absolute secrecy.

The victorious powers concocted schemes to humiliate and eliminate Germany as an economic competitor for a very long time, hopefully forever. This was done under the false pretense of a so-called higher morality by the good guys. It was a display of venomous hate, greed, intrigue, and deception in all these ill-conceived reparation claims against Germany. Germany finally paid off these outrageous claims in 2013.

In Section V of the Property Rights Article 297 and 298, Germany not only lost all its colonies but also its national property and the private property of German nationals in Allied countries.

The English economist, John Maynard Keynes, who resigned as a delegate of England in total disgust over the shallow blindness and hypocrisy in the proceedings, stated in his "Economic Consequences of Peace,"

> The German Empire has been built more truly on Coal and Iron, rather than on Blood and Iron ... The skilled exploitation of the great coal fields of the Ruhr, Upper Silesia, and the Saar, alone made possible by the development of the steel, chemical, and manufacturing industries which established her as the first industrial nation of Europe. In striking therefore at her coal supply, the French politicians were not mistaking their target. The judgment of the world has not recognized the transaction of the Saar as an act of spoliation and insincerity.

He also predicted that these reparation demands were impossible to comply with. They would lead to Germany's and Europe's economic demise and, ultimately, to the Great Depression.

The amputated parts of Silesia and the Saar regions accounted for more than one-third of Germany's total coal production. Upper Silesia had always been a part of Germany and accounted for 25 percent of Germany's hard coal production.

The reparation provisions included twenty million tons of coal or its coke equivalent to be delivered annually to France for the first five years. For the next ten years, France was to receive annually the difference between the coal mined in Northern France and the prewar coal production of the German mines. Germany was also obligated to deliver eight million tons to Belgium and up to eight million tons to Italy and continue the prewar shipments to Luxemburg. These demands were painfully unrealistic.

Germany was greatly concerned about the demands on its coal production and its effects on its steel industry. Germany was dependent upon the mines in Alsace and Lorraine, which were now part of France. In order to inflict as much damage as possible to the German industry, shipments of iron-ore were sporadic and unpredictable, aiming to impoverish Germany. These cold, calculated measures created not only uncertainty but resentment. A feeling of revenge began to raise its head. Remember, Alsace and Lorraine were amputated once from Germany as part of the Treaty of Westphalia, as were other parts.

This created a cycle heading toward a major catastrophe. Since the German industry was unable to export its goods, Germany could not obtain the needed gold to meet its reparation obligations and to purchase the needed raw materials. This brought the entire process to a halt, which is what Clemenceau had in mind. In the beginning of 1920, Germany defaulted on her reparation payments to France.

In addition to all the above reparations, Germany was ordered to turn over all her ships larger than 1,600 tons, a quarter of the ships between 1,000 and 1,600 tons, and a quarter of all trawlers and fishing boats. Germany was also ordered to turn over all the vessels sailing under foreign flags but owned by Germans and all the vessels under construction. Furthermore, Germany was stripped of its entire merchant marine fleet and, therefore, had to purchase merchant marine transportation service from other nations, payable in foreign currency, which was in short supply. This service was provided previously by its own vessels. The income from this service and what the ports provided was lost for many years.

What these individuals of average ignorance did not realize and John Maynard Keynes predicted was that their own economic health was predicated upon Germany's economic health. The League of Nations was created, which was a country club of the privileged victorious powers, the "good guys." Because it was an instrument to benefit the select, it seriously clouded the future of world peace.

It was composed of two chambers, the assembly and the council. The council was open to a select few, giving them control of the body, because they were holding permanent seats. The assembly was open to all victorious nations found acceptable. The permanent seats were reserved for France, England, Italy, Japan, and the United States, which declined membership. Russia, Germany, and her allies were excluded. This was a misnomer; it should have been called the League of the Victorious Nations.

The conference inserted a most favored nations clause, which only favored the victorious nations. The essence of this clause was to provide a customs advantage for the good nations and an additional disadvantage to the bad nations. Thus, Alsace and Lorraine could export to Germany without the burden of customs for five years, but Germany's exports into these provinces were subject to whatever customs the French chose to impose. Such lopsided advantages were also granted to Luxemburg and Poland. The Saar, a highly industrialized region, was put under the control of the League of Nations, which meant it was under French control. France insisted on a clause that would allow the Allies to impose special customs on the occupied Rhineland. This clause could be used at will against Germany.

After the war, Germany's railroads were in deplorable condition; however, she was ordered to surrender 5,000 locomotives and 150,000 railroad cars all in good working order. This became a serious burden and handicap to the recovery of the German economy. To add additional insult to injury, the Allies established an international commission to control all the transportation and the management of all German shipping on all its major rivers. John Maynard Keynes expressed his personal disbelief: "They constitute an unprecedented interference with a country's domestic arrangements, and are capable of being operated so as to take from Germany all effective control over her own transportation system." The victorious powers were continuously thinking up new methods and schemes to harass, discriminate, and humiliate Germany, while feeding their own egos and shallow, self-serving interests.

Germany surrendered not knowing the cost of the reparations that the reparation committee would levy later. The committee set the reparations that were to be paid by Germany at the horrendous sum of 132 billion gold marks, plus 26 percent of all export earnings, as well as additional other revenues. An Allied committee was set up, which had the authority to move freely anywhere at will within Germany and conduct unannounced inspections. Germany no longer was a sovereign nation.

It seems that the Allies, especially England and France, did everything they could to keep Germany powerless forever. It is incomprehensible that there were not more individuals who realized that these harsh measures could not be enforced for very long and that they would lead to war to undo the harshness and unfairness of the treaties. There were special interest groups scheming to bring about the second act and the continuation of the war.

The brutality; the injuries to Germans and to their pride; the loss of her colonies; the great loss of German territories; the ethnic cleansing of her people; the theft of virtually the entire German Merchant Marine; all the stumbling blocks on the way to Germany's recovery; the theft of 21 percent of her cereal and potato crops, a third of Germany's coal, three-quarters of her iron-ore, and three-fifths of its zinc; and the mistreatment of the German people, as well as the reduction of the German military to a mere skeleton had predictable consequences.

John Maynard Keynes, and others with sound and responsible minds, predicted that the reparation demands would fail and inflict serious damages to the German industry and the German morale because they were fraudulent. President Herbert Hoover, one of our few presidents of German roots, saw the reparation demands this way: "The preposterous sums levied at the Treaty, at once started forces that ended by bringing economic degeneration to the worlds. And from this collapse came a part of the forces which created Hitler." President Hoover further observed, "During the whole period from 1919 to 1939 France was to the advancement (of peace) constantly demanding guarantees for her own security, as the price for economic cooperation with other nations in any direction."

The primary causes of inflation, mass unemployment, and the rise of the Communist Party in Germany were a direct result of the hideous Versailles Treaties. Neither the Germans nor the kaiser ever wanted this war, as they have been falsely accused. And finally, the treaties erroneously branded Germany and her allies as the *sole* aggressors. In addition, the Allies stole thousands of industrial secrets. This was the political chess game on the world stage, for which Kaiser Wilhelm II was poorly prepared. He failed his people. It seems that the financial establishment has been attempting to create a world system for financial control, dominating the financial system of each country and the economy of the world.

By any standard, the Versailles Treaty was a deliberate violation of the pre-armistice contract. Article 231 of the treaty erroneously placed sole responsibility upon Germany. The "war guilt clause" was not only exceedingly unfair but legally, morally, and ethically unfounded. It caused deep-seated resentment among virtually all Germans. Germany was forced to pay reparations that were totally outrageous, while they also were being starved to death.

The brutality of this war and its aftermath took on biblical proportions. The archives of the Allies are slowly opening, but tons of documents are still locked up in Virginia and East European archives. Does the public not have a right to know what is being hidden? Transparency is an integral part to attaining world peace. There were numerous reasons why the more than two thousand telephone conversations between FDR and Churchill prior to the United States officially entering World War II are permanently under lock and key, never to be made public. Political secrecy is a form of public manipulation and political intrigue, which always defies constitutionality and serves only the elite few.

Contrary to all the anti-German fake news, Germany has never been a threat to its neighbors. All the fake news in the press will never bring peace; transparency and truth will and so will the re-attachment of all the amputated German territories. The European Union will long endure only if all the countries exist in their historical borders. Trust is destroyed if even one country retains territories that rightfully belongs to its neighbor.

In Koenigsberg, East Prussia, Emmanuel Kant said the following in 1795 about perpetual peace:

> Since this peace cannot be effected or be guaranteed without a compact among nations, they must form an alliance (foedus pacificum), different from a treaty of peace (pactum pacis) in as much as it would forever terminate all wars, whereas the latter only finishes one.

Peace will not suddenly appear, but it may become attainable when all nations genuinely strive to eliminate the roots and conditions of war in earnest, and war no longer is profitable.

The Nemmersdorf massacre of October 21, 1944. Countless other massacres would follow. On October 19, 1944, the first Soviet troops broke into German territory. The farming population did not flee and were brutalized. The Red Army went on a murder spree. The streets and alleys were filled with corpses of adults and children. Women were nailed against the sides of barns after they were gang raped. A few days later, after the German forces regained this region and saw the result of Soviet brutality, they invited the International Red Cross and the media to show the world what the Russians had done. That was the beginning of brutality against German civilians. The media kept silent.

What is the Morgenthau Plan? The Morgenthau Plain is a scheme hatched by FDR's secretary of the treasury Henry Morgenthau Jr., along with Theodor Nathan Kaufman and Harry Dexter White, an alleged Soviet agent. They set out to reduce Germany and the German population to be a threat to England, France, and Russia. Theodor Nathan Kaufman wrote a book in 1941 called *Germany Must Perish*, in which he advocated mass murder and sterilization of the German people. Kaufman wanted to exterminate the Germans, and the Soviets wanted to impoverish them, thereby turning them into Communists. Morgenthau wrote a book *Germany Is Our Problem* (pictured), which became FDR's blueprint for his demands for unconditional surrender. Fortunately, the Western Allies realized in time that Germany was needed in the defense of Western interests.

CHAPTER 7

Judea Declares War on Germany

These days we are bombarded with wall-to-wall media coverage of the atrocities committed against individuals and civilizations around the world, but Americans still know very little about the crimes and all the human rights violations committed against Germany, German Americans, and Latin German Americans. The world knows what the Germans did, but very few know what was done to the Germans. The media chose to pick and choose what is and what is not newsworthy. While it produced tons of anti-German news stories, it killed with deafening silence the atrocities committed against Germany, German Americans, and Latin German Americans. Fortunately, information is gradually becoming more available and has become more balanced in dealing with this segment of our history. A more factual and truthful picture of Germany and German Americans is slowly emerging.

The entire twentieth century was and remains one big holocaust, of which the Jewish suffering is a fraction. The big question remains did Judea arbitrarily decide, in an unprovoked act of anti-German hostility and without justification, to proclaim total war on and the destruction of Germany? There are always two sides to every story as there are to every coin. The harsh verdict of the Versailles Peace Treaties and the unfair treatment of the German people following World War I predictably contributed to the rise of National Socialism and Hitler. As discussed in an earlier chapter, it really did not matter who was in charge of Germany, whether it was Hitler or a Jesuit priest. The expressed mission was the destruction of Germany's industrial and commercial power. According to Morgenthau and FDR, Germany was to be reduced in size and population. The Germans were to become an agricultural society of no more than twenty million people, which would be less than the population of either England or France.

There were anti-Jewish sentiments not only in Germany but in neighboring countries as well. The Polish government in exile, for example, insisted on removing 3.5 million Jews from the New Poland. Before World War II, Poland abused not only Germans but also Jews and Ukrainians. Thousands of Jews and Germans were placed into Polish concentration camps. Jews were mistreated and murdered because their loyalty to Poland was regarded as suspect. Furthermore, Poland demanded to increase its territory considerably at Germany's expense. The Allies willingly agreed.

It is significant to point out that FDR was seeking papal intervention in ending the war against Japan but then changed his mind. As a result of FDR's demand for unconditional surrender, Germany was rendered voiceless. Japan was the backdoor to justify a war to the American people against Germany. The Allies were focused on Germany's industrial and commercial destruction. Japan was given a peace treaty shortly after the end of World War II. Almost a century later, Germany is still waiting for Washington to act. The Two Plus Four Agreement is not a peace treaty, just a new arrangement. The US military is the only force still stationed on German soil. FDR and Churchill stated in the Atlantic Charter in 1941, "Respect the right of all peoples to choose the form of government under which they will live." It must be stated that in 1941, America was still not officially in the war. FDR was, however, eagerly demonstrating his allegiance and support to England. Germany, however, was discriminated against by denying her this basic right. The political chess game became very intense. Churchill voiced his concern not to "become the King's First Minister who would preside over the liquidation of the British Empire."

FDR possessed a deep desire to liberate the colonies, which, in turn, unraveled the British Empire. He observed,

> If we really believed our own propaganda, we would have to declare war on the British, for they have set themselves up as the master race in India. British rule in India is fascism. The colonial peoples deserved something better to look forward to than simply the return to their old masters.

Ultimately, FDR has been credited for being the grave digger of the British Empire. Tragically, FDR's and Churchill's policies secured a long period of perpetual war for perpetual peace, which is a total contradiction. It is true that violence leads to more violence and fueling hate will lead to more hate. The media and Hollywood have functioned superbly well skewing public opinion.

Germany has been the most maligned of all nations and the German Americans the most terrorized of all ethnic Americans. Mr. Wiesel first coined the term *Holocaust* in 1967. Nobel Prize winner Elie Wiesel encouraged, "Every Jew, somewhere in his being, should set apart a zone of hate … healthy, virile hate … for what the German personifies and what persists in the German." This is very similar to Kaufman's assertions in his book *Germany Must Perish*. Anti-German propaganda remained relentless. There is nothing more powerful than a voice whose time has come. Hopefully, people acting in unison and with faith can not only move mountains but also correct such biases.

The suffering and slaughter of Germans has hardly, if ever, been mentioned or covered, as if German suffering and German lives do not matter; neither were the fire-bombings of the German cities and the expulsions of some sixteen million Germans at the end and following the war. They were brutal, malicious, and premeditated criminal acts. Patrick J. Buchanan told us, "The world knows what the Germans did, but no one knows what was done to the Germans." *Justice Denied* will bring further balance to this huge void and misrepresentation. The Allies bear much of the responsibility of inflicting the suffering on the civilians and the total destruction of that cultural pillar in Central Europe and Western civilization. Even as late as 1990, England's iron lady, Margaret Thatcher, demanded that President Gorbachev not allow that West and East Germany be united. It was a blessing for Germany and the rest of the world that Mr. Gorbachev ignored her self-serving British demands, which were completely void of human compassion.

Fabrications, fake news and propaganda leading up to and during the war were produced by the tons. The herculean challenge now is correcting these lies and this massive amount of propaganda. Thomas Jefferson told us that "information is the currency of democracy." Lincoln said, "To sin by silence, when one should protest, makes cowards of men."

Today, it has become an issue of repetition of telling the same story over and over again. It is the persistent repetition that sinks into our subconscious mind that collectively develops our individual and national cognitive dissonance. A just verdict vindicates the rectitude of all human conduct. History is perpetually unfolding. We need to engage in critical discussions, maintain an open mind, and always question everything. The mind is like a parachute; it only works when it is open.

It is hoped that we will learn from history, else we may be condemned to repeat it. We read in our textbooks that Jews were expelled from England by Edward I in 1290 and readmitted by Oliver Cromwell in 1653. Jewry gradually began to play an important role in British business life in the mid-eighteenth century. Their numbers were relatively small; there were about twenty-five thousand Jews in Britain at the end of the eighteenth century. They were concentrated in London as merchants, bankers, stockbrokers, and financiers. During the nineteenth century, in London, Jewry became increasing German, due to their migration from Germany.

Until the nineteenth century, British Jews kept largely to themselves. Practicing Jews were barred from the House of Commons until 1858. Disraeli, the only Jew in English politics at the time, was baptized as a teenager. Until the late nineteenth century, practicing Jews were barred from attending Oxford or

Cambridge. During the twentieth century, the Jewish presence and influence increased dramatically.

Prior to 1914, the German Jewish financial, commercial, and cultural elite were more influential and successful in Germany than the Jews in England. The Jewish population in Germany was composed of long-established German-speaking residents of Germany.

Until the twentieth century, the American Jewish community was relatively small and assimilated. The Jewish elite was primarily comprised of Sephardic German-speaking Ashkenazis from Germany, who faced little or no hostility. American Jewry did not begin to flex its political muscle until the turn of the century. The American establishment remained white, Anglo-Saxon, and Protestant (WASPs). Between 1881 and 1924, some three million impoverished, poorly educated, Yiddish-speaking Jews arrived from Russia. Within a generation, this small Jewish minority gained significant influence in America.

It should be mentioned that in America, the non-Orthodox Jewish elite was opposed to the Zionist agenda and a separate Jewish national identity. Ninety percent of the Jewish electorate voted for FDR, thereby gaining three *velten* (worlds): die velt (this world), yene velt (the next world), and Roosevelt. Jewry was split between Zionism and assimilation.

Many people were surprised and confused by bold headlines in the *Daily Express* of London and other newspapers around the world, including some in America, announcing on March 24, 1933, that "Judea Declares War on Germany." The article promised that "Jews of all the world will unite in action" against Germany. That was considered the first bullet fired in World War II. The bigger question that many were asking was what caused this complete reversal of Judea declaring war on Germany? The report detailed how Jewish leaders around the world in combination with powerful international Jewish financial institutions launched a boycott of Germany to cripple its already precarious economy. This action set destructive forces, at all levels around the world, including America, Canada, and the United Kingdom into motion.

This declaration went on to admonish "Jews of the World (to) Unite! (called for the) Boycott of German Goods! (and) Mass Demonstrations!" Furthermore, it demanded that "the Israeli people around the world declare economic and financial war against Germany. Fourteen million Jews stand together as one man to declare war against Germany. The Jewish wholesaler will forsake his firm, the banker his stock exchange, the merchant his commerce and the pauper his pitiful shed in order to join together in a holy war against Hitler's people." This called for a worldwide orchestrated effort to punish and teach the German people a lesson. No one spelled out what lessons the German people were supposed to learn and for what reason? This was one huge political move on a giant world political chess game promulgated by the Balfour agreement.

Understandably, this call to action on the part of all the Jews of the world was somewhat perplexing, since, throughout its history, Germany welcomed Jews and provided them with equal civil rights before any other European country. For centuries, Germany was a refuge for Jews from Russia and Poland. The headquarters of the World Zionist Organization until 1915 was located in Berlin. Kaiser Wilhelm II actively supported the Zionist ideals before and during World War I and then found himself betrayed by world Zionism. Moreover, Kaiser Wilhelm II personally appealed repeatedly to the sultan on behalf of the Zionists to create a Jewish state in Palestine. His efforts continued until 1916 when the Balfour statement appeared. Benjamin Freedman described the London agreement as a "stab in the back" of Kaiser Wilhelm II by the World Zionist Organization. The Germans were surprised and so were many others.

An overview of the Balfour agreement is critical in understanding the shift. Let's look at what was going on in America and Europe. America's neutrality in World War I was by far the most important issue in the 1916 presidential election. The Republican platform called for "a strict and honest neutrality in the European war." The Democratic platform condemned the efforts of every organization that has for its object the advancement of the interests of a foreign power." Americans were poised for true neutrality and about 90 percent most definitely wanted no part of a European war.

How did Wilson's administration end up pushing for war and then end up in the war if Americans were so strongly opposed to a military involvement in Europe? History is often made by chance and coincidence rather than by great people and momentous battles and by visualizing opportunities and acting upon them. In the case of Palestine, its future may well have been sealed when Woodrow Wilson began a long, romantic extramarital affair with Mrs. Mary Peck, later Mrs. Hulbert. She was the beautiful wife of a Princeton University professor when Wilson was president of that institution. Wilson's indiscretions opened him up to blackmail, which forced him into the war and also established a road map for the creation of the state of Israel.

When Mrs. Wilson became aware of her husband's transgressions, she filed for divorce. This affair threatened to derail Wilson's political career. He was running for governor of New Jersey. His handlers effectively covered up the divorce request, and Wilson won the race. Grover Cleveland's support secured Wilson the presidency at Princeton in 1902. By 1908, Wilson's behavior had alienated Cleveland and others, who branded Wilson intellectually dishonest. Wilson's immoral lifestyle had become so well known that he was asked to resign. Wilson's extramarital behavior was kept out of the news. A man of integrity would have resigned and saved the nation from war. Imagine such explosive material being kept out of the national evening news today.

At the time that Wilson received the nomination for governor of New Jersey, Mrs. Wilson filed for divorce on statutory grounds. Wilson's political backers asked Mrs. Wilson to withdraw the divorce request and have it expunged from the court records. If Mrs. Wilson's divorce application had become public knowledge, his political career would have been over. In hindsight, that would have been a blessing because Wilson was then being blackmailed. The divorce request was kept from the public, and Wilson was elected. He served as governor from 1911 to 1913. Wilson's indiscretions cost America and the world dearly. In Washington, the relationship was continued. Wilson was often referred to by newspapermen as "Peck's Bad Boy." There was a book published with the same title. Mrs. Wilson died of a broken heart because of Woodrow's unsavory affair and the disgrace and humiliation it brought upon her. He proved to be nothing more than a common womanizer.

The overshadowing and exceedingly persuasive carrot dangling in front of the Jewish world leadership was the Balfour Declaration. The world Zionist leadership claimed that the Balfour gave them "legal right to a homeland in Palestine." Balfour was prime minister in the early 1900s at the time when the British offered Uganda as a possible Jewish homeland, which was refused. The big challenge was gaining American support for England's postwar goals of dividing the Ottoman Empire. English intrigues in the Middle East and elsewhere are still being felt today. It was not hard to persuade Wilson into the scheme because he was overeducated, lacked common sense, and was handicapped by his lose morals. The honorable thing for Wilson to have done would have been to resign, but he stubbornly refused.

An insightful paragraph from Anatole France's *Penguin Island* illuminates the picture rather well. We read in part,

> The sofa of the Favorite ... on it were decided the destinies of a great people; nay on it was accomplished an act whose renown was to extent ... over all humanity. Too often events of this nature escape the superficial minds and shallow spirits who considerately assume the task of writing history. The fall of empires and the transmission of dominions astonish us and remain incomprehensible to those of us who have not discovered the imperceptible point or touched the secret spring which, when put into movement, has destroyed or overthrown everything.

This is a well of material for classical literature. Wilson's indiscretions directly influenced American and world history.

This is how we were pushed into World War I. Now let's look at the developments pushing us into World War II. The Balfour Decree put various forces into motion. A speech was delivered by Samuel Untermeyer in a radio broadcast on August 6, 1933, over WABC in New York. The following day, the *New York Times* printed the contents of this broadcast. Samuel Untermeyer encouraged Jews and Gentiles alike to enlist in a holy war against Germany. He stated in part,

> Each of you, Jew and Gentile alike, who has not already enlisted in this sacred war should do so now and here. It is not sufficient that you should buy no goods made in Germany. You must refuse to deal with any merchant or shopkeeper who

> sells any German-made goods or who patronizes
> German ships or shipping ... we will undermine
> the Hitler regime and bring the German people
> to their senses by destroying their export trade
> on which their very existence depends.

This was a very tall order to turn this war into an American and world war. He was filled with confidence that there was enough political and financial muscle worldwide to accomplish this mission. The target was the German people, i.e., the implementation of the Morgenthau / FDR Plan. The political aim was to eliminate Germany as an industrial and commercial competitor, hopefully forever.

Another event was the release of two books. *Germany Must Perish* was published by Theodore N. Kaufman in 1941, and Henry Morgenthau published a book *Germany Is Our Problem*. Therein they laid out their plan of how to deal with Germany and what to do with the Germans. The book was dedicated "To all those men and women who, inspired by the efforts, hopes and aspirations of mankind place its needs before their own ..." He laid down a blueprint of how to implement the gradual and total destruction of Germany. In September 1944, FDR asked Morgenthau and others to outline for him a detailed program for the treatment of Germany after her defeat. FDR, with whom Morgenthau had worked on terms of intimacy and confidence for many years, knew Morgenthau's leanings and interests. FDR wanted to take and did take the plan to the Quebec Conference. A tree will fall the way it leans; FDR's leanings became clearly visible.

The plan, which was marked "Top Secret," was titled "Program to Prevent Germany from Starting a World War III." Morgenthau spelled out how to deal with Germany. The Kaufman / Morgenthau / FDR plan included the demilitarization of

Germany, new boundaries for Germany, the amputation of German territory, partitioning of Germany, the exploitation of Germany's industrial Ruhr region, restitution and reparations, the reeducation and propaganda for the German people, and instilling in the German people a feeling of national guilt for many generations to come. It also spelled out some of the responsibility of the United States, such as full military and civilian representation.

On occasion, FDR revealed his own personal point of view, stating,

> We shall not leave them a single element of military power ... The German people are not going to be enslaved—because the United Nations do not traffic in human slavery. But it will be necessary for them to earn their way into the fellowship of peace-loving and law-abiding nations. And in their climb up the steep road, we shall certainly see to it that they are not encumbered by having to carry guns. They will be relieved of that burden—we hope, forever.

Contradicting himself, FDR sent millions of Germans following the end of the war to Joe Stalin as slaves.

Attempting to persuade the public, Kaufman stated in his book "should circumstances decree that the American public cast its ballot in favor of war as a measure of self-defense it would become paramount that the lives of our native sons not be sacrificed in vain as were their fathers' lives a generation ago ... If our soldiers must go forth to kill or die in battle, at least let them be given not alone a Slogan but a Solemn Purpose and a Sacred Promise. Let the Purpose be an Enduring Peace!" He used patriotism to wear down any and all resistance against

America going to war. Why did Kaufman consider the lives that were lost during World War I to have been "sacrificed in vain"? Understandably, most veterans of World War I strongly disagreed with Kaufman's callous assertions.

Kaufman stated that the war was not to be against Hitler or against the Nazis but that it was "a struggle between the German nation and humanity." He tried to convince his readers that there was a "centuries-old inbred lust of the German nation for conquest and mass murder." He set himself up as an expert on the Germanic people, passing judgment. He provided no support or evidence of any kind for his assertions. He further claimed that they and they alone were born with this character defect. He said that not the leadership but the German people were responsible for the war and, therefore, "must be made to pay for the war. Otherwise, there will always be a German war against the world." His propaganda further asserted erroneously that "Germany has forced a Total War upon the world. As a result, she must be prepared to pay a TOTAL PENALTY. And there is one, and only one, such Total Penalty: Germany must perish forever!" According to Kaufman and Morgenthau, this "character defect" justified the mass murder of Germans by starvation, fire-bombings, expulsions, and other means. It should be noted that at this time, America was not officially at war. However, both Kaufman and Morgenthau were doing everything they could to persuade Americans to enter the war at once.

Kaufman failed to mention the fact that World War I was forced upon Germany, and the Versailles Treaties ensured the continuation of that war, which became World War II. He makes the claim "that regardless of what leader or class rules Germany war will be waged against it by that country, because the force which compels it to action is an inseparable part of the mass-soul of that nation." He further claims, "We are paying today for the lack of experience of the last generation with dealing with the peoples of the German nation." He professes to be that voice of experience. He makes another ludicrous and shocking claim "that as much as 20% of her population is entirely guiltless of complicity in her crimes …" He, therefore, justifies the murder of the remaining 80 percent of the German people. He did not differentiate between Germans in Germany, German Americans, or Germans in the rest of the world. He was unabashedly arguing for mass murder.

What is amazing is that Kaufman, without any political authority, spells out how Germany would be reduced in territory and population and how *Germany must perish*. He turns it into a "definite obligation which the world owes to those who struggled and died against the German (people) yesterday, and … it is the bounden duty of the present generation to those yet unborn, to make certain that the vicious fangs of the German serpent shall never strike again. And since the venom of those fangs derives its fatal poison not from within the body, but from the war-soul of the German, nothing else would assure humanity safety and security but that that war-soul be forever expunged, and the diseased carcass which harbors it be forever removed from this world … Germany Must Perish!" (10–11). He viciously stereotyped the German people and provided a blueprint for FDR's demands for "unconditional surrender." Germans are suffering and will continue to suffer from this vicious plan and FDR's "unconditional surrender."

Kaufman wrote in his book extremely uncomplimentary comments about Germans. He stated that Germans were the most primitive, vulgar, uncaring, and criminal people on earth. It has been stated earlier, far more than one-third of all Americans proudly profess their German roots. Kaufman and Morgenthau were filled with extreme hatred. By spewing such sickening hate, they placed their integrity and any personal human integrity into serious question. Their thinking was extremely twisted. This set the stage and tone for all the anti-German hate propaganda that followed. Kaufman and Morgenthau might have been hallucinating when they promised that the destruction of Germany would ensure world peace. This would be considered insanity if it were not the blueprint for FDR's "unconditional surrender."

Kaufman states that (page 21), "Germans are an execrable people (deserving of being execrated, eliminated)! They think and dream of nothing but chicanery ... The German does not live on the heights; he avoids light ... They are capable of little else but hating and lying ... They meddle in everyone else's affairs ... they ... breathe in an atmosphere of haughty contempt for their neighbors ... Hate is sacred ... this race has been elected by God to order the modern world." Furthermore, he describes Germanism as a "monstrosity" about which, according to him, supposedly Adolf Schickelgruber talks about in *Mein Kampf.* Kaufman displays total ignorance about the fact that in the last century or so, six out of ten new inventions and so much more came from Germany and Germans were instrumental in building the great United States and many other parts of the world.

He states, "It would be impossible ... to list and describe the daemonic brutalities practiced by the Germans upon innocent peoples ..." He gives the sinking of the *Lusitania* as an example of German brutality, claiming they "boiled those women and children alive in oil!" He fabricated hatred toward the Germans to minimize any feelings of guilt and to justify mass murder.

He claims that the teachings of "Kant, Nietzsche, Hegel, von Bernhardi, Rohrbach, Treitschke and Spengler," amalgamated this, what he calls, German war-soul and, furthermore, is at the very roofs of the German soul." He claims, "Hitler is merely the agent decanting the poisonous fluid from its bottle, which is the

German war-soul, into the jug that is world humanity." He also accuses the Germans of "world conquest and domination ..."; therefore, he postulates, we must strike first and destroy Germany. He ignores the fact that throughout its history, Germany has been involved in fewer military conflicts than England or France.

Kaufman argues, on page 90, "When an individual commits premeditated murder, he must be prepared to forfeit his own life in consequence. When a nation commits premeditated murder upon its fellow nations, it must be prepared to forfeit its own national life ... An eye for an eye, a tooth for a tooth, and a life for a life." He further reasons that "the death-penalty is postulated as the ultimate punishment on earth, the indispensable keystone of every ordered system of criminal law ... the sword is an expression which runs deep in the blood of the honest man ... blood is atoned by blood ..."

Legal scholars may wish to analyze the faulty reasoning in his book. He justifies mass murder.

One solution in reducing the German population was mass sterilization. Kaufman states, "By preventing the people of Germany from ever again reproducing their kind ... Eugenic Sterilization, is at once practical, humane and thorough ... Sterilization has become ... the best means of ridding the human race of its misfits: the degenerate, the insane, the hereditary criminal." And, according to him, the Germans fit all those descriptions. On page 94, he states, "to immunize itself (the world) forever against the virus of Germanism," he wanted to sterilize all German men under sixty and all women under the age of forty-five. He claimed that this would take no more than a month, and within two generations, the world would be rid of the Germans. On page 97, he states, "Mass sterilization of the Germans is the best means of wiping them out permanently." Is this the lesson the Germans were supposed to learn? What is amazing is that no one pointed out the criminality of his demands for mass murder.

The World Jewish Congress elevated this war against Germany to a "holy war." Dr. Franz J. Scheidl wrote in his book *Geschichte der Verfemung Deutschlands* the following: "Diese Erklaerung nannte den Krieg gegen Deutschland, der nun beschlossen sei, einen heiligen Krieg. Dieser Krieg muesse gegen Deutschland bis zu dessen Ende, bis zu dessen Vernichtung gefuehrt werden." Translated that reads, "This declaration has called for war against Germany, which was determined to be a 'holy war.' This war is to be carried out against Germany to its end, to her total destruction." The overarching objective was the total destruction, the unconditional surrender, and the total exploitation of Germany.

FDR's agenda and demand of an "unconditional surrender" are a direct implementation of the Kaufman / Morgenthau demands.

Woodrow Wilson was portrayed by the media as a paragon of virtue, which was contrary to the actual facts, because he had at least one skeleton in his closet. Samuel Untermeyer, a New York lawyer, threatened to publish Wilson's love letters to Mrs. Peck. Untermeyer told Wilson that Mrs. Mary Peck-Hulburt wanted $250,000. Wilson replied a week later stating that he could only raise $100,000. Untermeyer offered Wilson a deal, namely that Untermeyer would select the next Supreme Court justice when that seat became available. Unless Wilson agreed to Untermeyer's terms, his love letters would be published. In due time, Louis Brandeis sat on the Supreme Court, Mrs. Peck received $30,000, Untermeyer ended up with the rest of the money, and the Peck incident was forgotten in political Washington. That seems how political intrigue in high places works.

Wilson's ego caused his refusal to resign and ultimately cost us millions of lives and billions of dollars. On January 18,

1916, President Wilson submitted Louis Dembitz Brandeis to the Senate for confirmation. Strong opposition delayed his confirmation until June 5. This occurred about five months before James Malcolm was engaged in discussions with Sir Mark Sykes at the British War Cabinet about getting the United States into the war on England's side. Justice Brandeis guided Wilson toward getting America into the war. At a meeting, at which Dr. Weizmann was present, Mr. Malcolm came up with a gentleman's agreement. It was agreed that the Zionists should work to activate Jewish support for the war cause, especially in America, and in return the British Cabinet would help Jews to gain Palestine. (See Malcolm, *Origin of the Balfour Declaration*).

On January 22, 1917, President Wilson addressed Congress, asking, "Is the present war a struggle for a just peace, or only for a new balance of power? Who will guarantee the stable equilibrium of the new arrangements? There must be, not a balance of power, but a community of power, not organized rivalries, but an organized common peace … A permanent peace must be based upon equality of nations and national rights. It must be a peace without victory." He concluded by stating, "We do not desire any hostile conflict with the imperial German government. We are the sincere friends of the German people and earnestly desire to remain at peace with the government that speaks for them." Were these his sincere sentiments or merely political rhetoric?

It needs to be mentioned that in 1916, Jews in America were overwhelmingly pro-German. The British War Cabinet was doing everything it could to get the United States into the war on England's side. James A. Malcolm, the intermediary in London between the Zionist leaders and the British, stated, "Reports from America revealed a pro-German tendency among the wealthy Jewish bankers and bond issuing houses, nearly all of German origin, and among Jewish journalists who took their cue from them."

The secret 1916 agreement between the World Zionist Organization and the British provided the Zionists in America the "green light" to start working on Wilson, to take all the necessary steps to change the American sentiments from neutrality and totally staying out of the war into an all-out brutal attack on Germany. The mission was to create anti-German hysteria. Wilson owed the bankers who bankrolled his election a favor or two, and he was also being threatened with blackmail. He really was not given much of a choice.

On March 4, 1919, Rep. Julius Kahn submitted a memorandum to Wilson signed by three hundred top American Jewish leaders from all over America, which was published in the *New York Times* on March 5, 1919. This memorandum stated in part, "As to the future of Palestine, it is our fervent hope that what was once a 'promised land' for the Jews may become a 'land of promise' for all races and creeds ... We ask that Palestine be constituted as a free and independent state ... We do not wish to see Palestine, either now or in the future, organized as a Jewish state." That attitude has changed during the following decades.

In January 1934, Vladimir Jabotinsky, the founder of the Jewish group Irgun Zvai Leumi, reported,

> For months now the struggle against Germany is waged by each Jewish community, at each conference, in all our syndicates, and by each Jew all over the world. There is reason to believe that our part in this struggle has general value. We will trigger a spiritual (propaganda) and material war of all the world against Germany's ambitions to become once again a great nation, to recover lost

territories and colonies. But our Jewish interests
demand the complete destruction of Germany.
Collectively and individually, the German nation
is a threat to us Jews.

These assertions against the German people are another
example of the complete reversal. Many German Jews married
German Gentiles and lived happily ever after. The Rothschild
dynasty had its beginnings in Germany.

Chaim Weizmann, president of the World Jewish Congress
and later president of the newly created State of Israel, is
reported in the *London Times*, September 5, 1939, and also in
the *London Jewish Chronicle*, September 8, 1939, affirming,

I wish to confirm in the most explicit manner,
the declaration which I and my colleagues
made during the last months, and especially
in the last week that Jews (of the world) stand
by Great Britain and will fight on the side of
the democracies. Our urgent desire is to give
effect to these declarations. We wish to do so
in a way entirely consonant with the general
scheme of British action, and therefore would
place ourselves, in matters big and small, under
the coordinating direction of His Majesty's
Government. The Jewish Agency (of which
Weizmann was the head) is ready to enter into
immediate arrangements for utilizing Jewish
manpower, technical ability, resources, etc.

In a speech on December 3, 1942, in New York, Mr.
Weizmann proclaimed,

> We are not denying and are not afraid to confess
> that this war is our war and that it is waged for
> the liberation of Jewry ... Stronger than all fronts
> together is our front, that of Jewry. We are not
> only giving this war our financial support on
> which the entire war production is based, we are
> not only providing our full propaganda power
> which is the moral energy that keeps this war
> going. The guarantee of victory is predominantly
> based on weakening the enemy forces, on
> destroying them in their own country, within
> the resistance. And we are the Trojan Horse in
> the enemy's fortress. Thousands of Jews living
> in Europe constitute the principal factor in the
> destruction of our enemy. There, our front is a
> fact and the most valuable aid for victory.

Mr. Weizmann stated that the liberation of Jewry and the creation of the State of Israel were synonymous. However, most of the Reformed Jewry and much of Orthodox and Conservative Jewry were opposed to the Zionist agenda and activities.

German Jews in Germany strongly objected and expressed their displeasure concerning the actions of the World Zionist Organization, stating that the leadership of World Jewry cared nothing about the well-being and safety of Jews in Germany, persisting in their agitation and defamation of Germany. On March 24, 1933, the National Union of Jewish Front Soldiers sent a letter to the American embassy in Berlin, voicing their strong objections:

> It is also our decision to reject the irresponsible
> anti-German agitation of so-called Jewish
> intellectuals overseas. These men, who were

never known as German Jews, gave up their right to be our self-styled defenders when they abandoned us at the critical moment and fled the country. They have no right to meddle in German-Jewish affairs. From their safe cover they dishonorably shoot their arrows of exaggeration to injure German Jews as well as Germany.

Two days after the declaration of total war against Germany, the Zionist Union for Germany sent a telegram to the Jewish leadership in America dated March 26, 1933. It read in part,

In regard to foreign misinformation about the German Jews for the purpose of making anti-German propaganda, the Zionist Union for Germany declares with great resolve we have informed the entire Jewish World Press via the Jewish Telegraph Agency, already on March 17, of our declaration against all anti-German propaganda. We have publicly repeated our protest against all untruthful atrocity announcements and baseless sensationalism. We protest against every attempt to place Jewish interests at the service of other countries or groups. The defense of Jews' civil rights and their economic position cannot and must not be coupled with anti-German political actions.

We are reminded, the overwhelming majority of all Americans, some 86 percent or more, wanted absolutely nothing to do with another military entanglement in Europe. They were misled once before in the war that did not end all wars. Americans were now hoodwinked with the help of British

OSI agents. Their covert activities and getting us into World War II are discussed in an earlier chapter. Our political leaders opted for Communism, Bolshevism, atheism, and Joe Stalin. Only by understanding the mission of FDR's advisers can FDR's demand for unconditional surrender and total destruction of Germany be understood. There is nothing quite like it in our history, except perhaps the deafening silence of any outcry and condemnation against these atrocities by any religious, civic, or political leader.

Bernard Baruch wrote on page 347 in his book *The Public Years,*

> I emphasized ... that the defeat of Germany and Japan, and their elimination from world trade, would give Britain a tremendous opportunity to swell her foreign commerce in both volume and profit ... I know that she (England) would need financial assistance to make the transition to peace, and I believe that America should give it.

This statement adds further credence to the fact that the root cause of all wars is economic. Permanent transparency is the key to permanent peace, but governments continue to be reluctant to provide any transparency; they continue to function in top governmental secrecy. Whistleblowers are not welcome.

Henry Morgenthau, secretary of the US Treasury, stated, "War in Europe in 1934 was inevitable." This was quoted in *Palestine Post* by B. Jenson on page 11. Emil Ludwig Cohn, in his book *The New Holy Alliance,* stated, "Hitler will have no war, but we will force it on him, not this year, but soon." Arnold Leese in his book *The War of Survival* quoted a statement by David A. Brown, chairman of the United Jewish Campaign, "We Jews are going to bring a war on Germany."

Bernard Lecache, president of the International League Against Racism and anti-Semitism, stated in his newspaper *Dreit de Vivre* (Right of Life), on November 9, 1938, "Germany is our enemy number one. It is our object (ive) to declare war without mercy against her. One may be sure of this: We will lead that war."

The *New York Tribune* reported on March 29, 1939, Brigadier General Van Horn Mosely stated, "The war now proposed is for the purpose of establishing Jewish hegemony throughout the world." The *Central Blad Voor Israeliten* in the Netherlands, on September 13, 1939, included the following declaration: "The millions of Jews who live in America, England and France, North and South Africa, and not to forget those in Palestine, are determined to bring the war of annihilation against Germany to its final end."

The Zionists promised total war and total destruction of Germany. Schalom Asch on February 10, 1940, in *Les Nouvelles Literaires* affirmed, "Even if we Jews are not physically at your side in the trenches, we are morally with you. This war is our war and you fight it with us."

Ludwig Emil on page 113, in his book *The Holy Alliance*, made the following assertions:

> When one has followed the development of the German warlike spirit from its earliest days right up to the eugenic use made today of aerial bombardments, by means of examples such as these which here have to take the place of whole books, one asks oneself: should a man with this type of mentality be given a license to drive a car ... can those nations ... be given the same privileges as others ... or, their moral rights be limited?

The German people have never been so brutally trashed and harshly dehumanized as during the twentieth century. On page 114, he continues, "The Holy Alliance ... by daily and ineffectual emphasis of its love of peace ... rendered deaf and dumb in the German fortress ..." Continuing with total contradictions, he wrote, "the heroes of Wilhelmstrasse, who were ready for war ..." They professed that the good guys loved peace and bad guys loved war. Sadly, good Germans were nowhere to be found in the media. It sounds as if the Germans firebombed their own cities and killed their own people, which is fiction.

Remember, Morgenthau and FDR wanted to reduce Germany into an agricultural country and reduce its population to one-fifth of its size. The plan was also to reeducate the German children who were left after all the destruction of the German cities and the confiscation of all German industry. On September 10, 1944, FDR and Churchill met in Quebec. They signed a memorandum stating that Germany was to be converted "into a country primarily agricultural and pastoral in its character."

In order to begin to comprehend the Zionists' complete reversal and subsequent declaration of war on Germany, it is necessary to take a closer look at World War I. Both wars, World War I and World War II, are really two acts of the same deadly tragedy. The war of 1914 became a world war after the United States entered the war. There were huge efforts to bring America into the European military conflict a second time. The bloodshed would have remained a European military conflict without Wilson's and FDR's assurances to England of entering the war on England's side. The economic ramifications and benefits to the bankers have been discussed in an earlier chapter. Without America's involvement, England would have tolerated Germany's commercial and industrial rise and accepted it, as it appears to have done so reluctantly since the end of World War II.

A very huge carrot dangling in front of the leaders of Jewry was the Balfour Declaration. This declaration during World War I became a reality as England became increasingly concerned about a German-Jewish alignment. The Allies could not allow that. England was under pressure to produce this declaration, which it did rather reluctantly. Balfour promulgated his declaration while he was British Foreign Secretary from 1916 to 1919. Israel became a state in 1949. Had Israel become a reality in 1919 rather than 1949, the push for another war would have become superfluous.

The purpose of Judea's declaration, also issued to American Jewry, was to inspire them to use their sizable worldwide influence in the banking, commercial, intellectual, news media, and political arenas to bring America into the war on the side of England. Until then, American Jewry generally favored Germany because of their history of profitable and friendly relations with the Germans.

America's "neutrality" laws stated, "During a war in which the United States is neutral, it is unlawful to send out of the jurisdiction of the United States any vessel armed or equipped as a vessel of war with any intent or with reasonable cause to believe that it shall be used by any belligerent nation." This language was very strong as the result of the overwhelming sentiment of Americans about getting involved and getting tricked into another European war.

For our democracy, or any democracy, to serve the good of all and survive, it is imperative that we, the people, remain vigilant in directing our domestic and foreign policies and affairs "to establish justice, ensure domestic tranquility, provide for the common defense, promote the general welfare, and secure the blessings of liberty to ourselves and our prosperity, for the purpose for which it was ordained." Special interest lobbies representing big corporations and special interests make that mission ever more difficult. Plato stated thousands of years ago that what will destroy a great system are its excesses.

Great injustices were placed upon the German people because of the conditions of the armistice following World War I, based on promises that were not kept and the Versailles Peace Treaties. The greatest injustice was the verdict of Germany's sole responsibility for the war. Any verdict must be based upon actual facts rather than "official" misrepresentations of some conference that never happened. The theory of Germany's sole responsibility must be vacated. This theory must be reexamined in light of all pertinent evidence.

On January 30, 1933, Adolf Hitler was democratically elected, defeating the heavily supported Communist Party candidate. German Jewry heavily supported the Communist candidate. Judea declared total destruction on Germany and the boycott of all German-made goods. On March 28, 1933, Hitler responded with a counter of his own. On March 29, 1933, the *Voelkischer Beobachter* carried his entire proclamation. He said, in part, "A clan of Jewish intellectuals, and businessmen agitate hate against us." He was specific in his order: "The boycott starts exactly at 10:00 o'clock in the morning on Saturday April 1 ... it always must be emphasized that this is a defensive action forced upon us ..." He limited the employment of Jews in the professions to reflect their actual percentage of the total population on "three spheres: 1) German middle schools and high schools (universities); 2) physicians, and 3) lawyers." He stated further that "they abandoned the masses they led astray and fled to foreign countries with their coffers stuffed ... now (they) unfold from there an unscrupulous, treasonous hate campaign against all the German people ... the poverty in Germany is not severe enough, they want it to be worse."

Had the Germans opted for Communism and joined forces with Stalin, European and world history would have been very different and Western Civilization and culture might have become a distant memory. To what extent did the Germans sacrifice themselves for the preservation of Western Judo-Christian culture and civilization?

Many books have been written about Jewish contribution to the world in every discipline. On February 8, 1920, the Rt. Hon. Winston Churchill published an article in the *Illustrated Sunday Herald* discussing "A Struggle for the Soul of the Jewish People" and the preeminent Jewish role in Bolshevism and the agenda of Zionism. He stated, "It created a schism, as it proved as harmful to the world as Jewish Bolshevism." He continued, "At the present fateful period there are three main lines of political conception among the Jews, two of which are helpful and hopeful in a very high degree to humanity, and the third absolutely destructive ... In violent opposition to all this sphere of Jewish effort rise the schemes of the International Jews ... This movement among Jews is not new." The third sphere is Zionism, which "has such a deep significance for the whole world at the present time." As to the creation of Israel, which would "be beneficial" and "which will be a symbol of Jewish unity and the temple of Jewish glory ..."

The Rt. Hon. Winston S. Churchill penned another scholarly article, "Zionism Versus Bolshevism—A Struggle for the Soul of the Jewish People." The article was published on February 8, 1920, in the *Illustrated Sunday Herald*. He provides an overview of the national and the international Jews and their national and international activities. He states, "It would almost seem as if the gospel of Christ and the gospel of Antichrist were destined to originate among the same people ... both the divine and the diabolical." He states that they and all others should be judged on their "personal merit and conduct. In a people of peculiar genius like the Jews, contrasts are more vivid, the extremes are more widely separated, the resulting consequences are more decisive."

Producing written material fueling and benefitting from anti-German hysteria prior to, during, and following the war has been very profitable; the more gruesome, the better it seemed to sell. One such story became a best-selling Holocaust autobiography, *Misha: A Memoir of the Holocaust Years.* At just six years old, Misha Defonseca trudged across three countries to find her Jewish parents, who had been carted off to Auschwitz by the Nazis. She collapsed in a forest but was rescued by a pack of wolves who adopted her as their cub. Her story became a best-selling Holocaust autobiography. There was only one thing wrong with this autobiography. It was a pack of lies. The revelation that this story is mere fabrication and fiction has generated an angry outcry from all who feel hoodwinked and betrayed by Monique De Wael. You see, she is not Jewish at all but Roman Catholic.

Whenever one sees persecution and people bashing, it is most likely that truth is on the persecuted side. Anti-German hysteria, anti-Semitism, oppression, racism, and all forms of slavery can and should never be justified. Germany has been demonized as being super-militaristic and barbaric. Anti-German propaganda portrayed them as Huns, Krauts, and by many other derogatory names. However, throughout its history, Germany has been the heart of Continental Europe and influences and blessings have gone forth from her which deeply affected every one of her neighbors.

In August 2015, spokeswomen Adi Farjon for the Israeli embassy in Berlin told Israeli journalists that it was in their country's best interest to maintain German guilt feelings about the Holocaust, and that it is not seeking full normalization of relations between their governments. She further stated that "without them that Israel would be just another country as far as they're concerned." Ambassador Yakov Hasad-Handelsman was present at this meeting as were embassy employees who don't speak Hebrew. One journalist commented, "It was so awkward. We couldn't believe our ears…, and behind the spokeswoman there were two German women sitting there who don't understand a word of Hebrew – and the embassy staff is telling us they're working to preserve the German guilt feelings and that Israel has no interest in normalization of relations between the two countries."

During the last few decades, the American government has coerced Germany into building three nuclear-armed submarines of the latest design for the Israeli Navy—absolutely free—as part of Germany's never-ending restitution to Israel. Professor Norman Finkenstein wrote an authoritative book about the flow of money to Israel, *The Holocaust Industry*. His parents met while they were inmates at Auschwitz. His book is a "reflection on the exploitations of Jewish suffering" and examines various Holocaust compensation agreements. The book is an international best seller.

The Versailles Treaty left Germany in a totally bankrupt state. Faced with either Communism or National Socialism, the German people chose National Socialism in a national democratic election in 1933. Germans were put back to work. They found employment in public works, repairing public buildings and private residences. They constructed new roads, such as the Autobahn, bridges, canals, and port facilities. They built ships and gave the workers paid vacations on holiday cruises. Ferdinand Porsche was commissioned to design and build the prototype of the people's car—the Volkswagen, a car that the average worker could afford. All Germans enjoyed universal health care. Life was good and continuously improving.

Even a stop clock is right twice a day. All of us are checkered with failures and successes. Why should many of the Germans not be proud of their leader and their successes, just like many Americans, English, and French were proud of theirs? Let's look at some of the accomplishments of the National Socialists. In about two years of Nazi rule, unemployment was virtually eliminated. They enjoyed a stable currency, without inflation. Germany engaged in a brisk foreign trade, using the barter system, exchanging products, materials, and equipment directly without any money being exchanged, cutting out the financial middleman. In about five years, Germany went from being the poorest to the richest nation in Europe. They printed their own money and were not part of the international banking system. Dr. Henry Makow, a Canadian, stated that one of the primary reasons of World War II was the fact that the National Socialists dared to sidestep the international bankers, depriving them of their profit, thus creating an economic confrontation with them.

Hitler radically reformed the German economy after the Depression, which was caused by the Versailles Treaty and the flow of money, or lack thereof. His reforms increased German production, decreased unemployment, and promoted technical development. He demonstrated that an economy could be built outside the gold standard and the international banking system, solely on the trust of the people. Several scholars claimed that the National Socialist economic system was the primary cause for a declaration of war, because it was seen as a danger to the gold standard system, which is founded upon compound interest charged. It was viewed as serious competition against capitalism.

Because it was gaining in popularity, it was decided that the National Socialist economic system could be destroyed only by war. Churchill admitted in 1946 at Fulton that "the war was not only waged to defeat Germany, but to conquer the German export market. We could have, if we wanted, prevented the war in 1935, without firing a shot, but we didn't want to." The war was fought to bolster the value of gold and the profit margin of the international bankers. The German economy increased its GNP during the period of 1933 to 1939 by 100 percent. The struggle against international finance capital and loan capital is how Germany gained independence from the bankers and also brought the wrath of the international bankers upon herself.

Because Germany was no longer on the gold standard, her foreign trade was based on a barter system that eliminated interest being paid to international banks. Countries that were not solely dependent on the United States and England became willing trading partners. Goods were being traded for goods. The big banks were agitated because they did not benefit from commercial transactions by charging interest. Usury, charging interest for the use of money, is seen as creating something out of nothing. Throughout history, many theologians and thinkers have been strongly opposed to usury, including Jesus of Nazareth, Dr. Martin Luther, and Father Charles Coughlin.

Physics tells us that to every force there is a counterforce. Not everyone in Germany supported Hitler. Germany's World War I hero General Erich Ludendorff sent a telegram to President Paul von Hindenburg, stating, "By appointing Hitler as Chancellor of the Reich, you have handed over our sacred German fatherland to one of the greatest demagogues of all times. I prophesy to you that this evil man will plunge our Reich into the abyss and will inflict immeasurable woe to our nation."

Another citation provides significant light on the issue of the military conflict. The world-renowned military writer Britain's General Fuller wrote in his book *The First War of the League of Nations,*

The present financial system is not based upon the strength of production, but upon the means of its distribution—the money. It was converted into a product / ware, which one can buy and sell ... the illness from which the world suffers is Usury (profiteering). France is built upon the power of money and England is the headquarter of international loan-capitalism; therefore, an entente exists between the two. Both are internationally oriented, because both are the dominance of international banking. Since Germany is an outsider ... it comes under suspicion. Germany is already beginning to operate with a concept of working ... This concept must be stopped at any price. For that reason feverish preparations are made for its destruction. The financial institutions have nothing to lose, but everything to gain, when they stir for a war as to destroy such a German reform. And that happens today, and Germany becomes the selected victim.

The following citations under the title "Voices of Others" appeared in September 1989 in the German newspaper *Frankfurter Allgemeine Zeitung*. In connection with the German East and West reunification, the correspondent of the *British Sunday* suggests that the German question be finally answered truthfully. He stated,

We must now be honest in matters with the German question, even as uncomfortable it may be for the Germans, for our international partners or for ourselves ... In essence, the question

remains the same. Not how we can prevent it that
the German tanks roll over the Oder or Marne
(rivers), but how Europe can tolerate a people
whose population, talent and efficiency can make
it to become our regional Super Power. We did
not enter the war in 1939 to save Germany
from Hitler, the Jews from Auschwitz nor the
continent from Fascism. As in 1914, we entered
the war in a not less noble mission, (namely)
that we cannot tolerate a German domination
in Europe. The war of economics had already
begun, long before the (first) shots were fired.

After his visit to Germany in 1936, Lloyd George, former
prime minister of England, reported in the *Daily Express* in
London the following:

> I have just returned from Germany. I have seen
> the famous German leader, and also some of the
> great changes he has brought about. Whatever
> one may think of his methods, which are certainly
> not parliamentary, there is no doubt that he has
> brought a wonderful change in the thinking of
> the German people. For the first time since the
> war (WWI), there reigns a general feeling of
> confidence. The people are happier. Throughout
> the land there is a genuine outpouring of joy. It
> is a happier Germany. One man has achieved this
> miracle. The fact is that Hitler has freed his land
> of its fear of constant despair and humiliation,
> which has given him, in today's Germany,
> unfettered authority. It is not merely for his
> popular leadership that he is admired. Hitler is

honored as a national hero who has rescued his land from total hopelessness and degradation. He is Germany's George Washington, the man who won independence from his country's oppressors.

He fostered a people-oriented economy. He started the charitable Winter Help Campaign. "None shall hunger and none shall freeze." The poorest of the poor were being helped. Germany built the Autobahn using only German materials, no imports. The Volkswagen became the most produced vehicle in the world. Its original cost was a mere 995 reichsmarks ($249) and could be purchased on installments. Synthetic fibers combined with German wool were produced to clothe the people. In order to bring some optimism and joy into the life of the average German, holiday cruise ships were built; they enabled German workers to go on cruises for little money. These cruise ships were most modern in design and comfort. Among them were the *William Gustloff*, the *Robert Ley*, and the *Cap Arkona*. Frequent destinations were the Portuguese islands of Madeira and the Spanish islands and port cities.

The former rabbi in England Jonathan Sacks wrote in his book *Not in God's Name: Confronting Religious Violence* that all "too often in the history of religion, people have killed in the name of the God of life, waged war in the name of the God of peace, hated in the name of the God of love and practiced cruelty in the name of the God of compassion." Each year, the world continues to mock the promise of Christmas—"Peace on earth and good will to all men"—while the killing and brutality goes on in the name of the God of peace. All too often, religion finds itself a source of violence. Religious blessings are often invoked as a cover to justify murder in uniform and violence for the purposes of politics, economics, and earthly power that have nothing to do with God. When religion turns men into murderers, God weeps.

When individuals and nations walk the talk, when rhetoric is also reflected in their actions and behavior, then shall appear a purity of life and rectitude of conduct. Nations must aspire to a never-ending commitment for nobler deeds, for higher thoughts, and for greater achievement, benefiting all equally and without discrimination.

The framers of our Constitution wisely guaranteed individual rights. However, our society has and will continue to be deeply influenced by group allegiances. Since our nation's birth, this reality has been clouded by misconception and myth. All groups have a legitimate place in our society, and their interests must be protected as well as their individual rights. However, precautions must also be taken to ensure that competing group demands do not foster polarization, negativism, or destructive group chauvinism.

The way of peace is the way of truth. World peace will only be maintained by truth and through transparency, with a healthy amount of mutual and verifiable trust.

What a pity that we cannot begin to live by the law of love. The munitions and armament plants could become apartment buildings. Jesus said, "All men are equally the children of God."

Dich schliesst der Feind von allen Seiten ein!
—Johann Wolfgang von Goethe–Egmont

CHAPTER 8

The Dresden Holocaust

Patrick J. Buchanan told us in his groundbreaking, scholarly and well researched book *Churchill, Hitler, and the Unnecessary War* that the "whole world knows what the Germans did, but no one knows much about the suffering of and what was done to the German people." This discourse shall serve as a modest attempt to rectify and bring more light and greater balance to this huge imbalance of public perception. To continuously remain silent no longer is an option. Light always provides greater clarity than darkness.

Because of its world-renowned baroque architecture and for centuries being a cultural showplace, Dresden had enjoyed a reputation as the "Florence of the North" and as one of the greatest cultural centers of Northern Europe; it was a precious jewel in the cultural tapestry of Europe. Music, literature, art, architecture, and education flourished in this island of tranquility. It was a city of refined leisure, recreation, museums, theaters, and sporting events. Dresden china, which is delicately and precisely executed detailed porcelain, is world famous and a symbol of the city. Dresden, the capital of Saxony, was a city of artists and craftsmen, of actors and dancers, of tourists, merchants, hotels, and stadiums for sporting events.

Venerable churches and centuries-old cathedrals were gracing her skyline.

Contrary to all the propaganda, what Dresden was, was defined during the war by what she was not. Dresden was not a city with military or industrial installations. The few factories were outside the city limits and produced toothpaste and baby powder. There were no factories producing poison gas or military gear, as the London and Allied propaganda so profusely and falsely claimed. Dresden became a city of children, of women, of refugees, of the injured and maimed recovering from their wounds, and of the elderly and the sick. During the war Dresden became a Sanitaetsstadt, a hospital city.

Due to its military insignificance, Dresden was considered virgin target and believed to be safe from all the destruction and death that descended from the sky on the rest of the country. The city was open and undefended. All its flak batteries were, sometime earlier, taken to the Eastern Front. A rumor was circulating that Churchill had a niece living in the city, which added to the misconception that this Florence of the North would be spared the Allied fire-bombs, that is if Churchill cared enough about his niece. Arthur Harris, of Bomber Command, gave Dresden hardly a second thought, at least not until Churchill ordered him to destroy this cultural jewel.

All that tranquility changed abruptly on the evening of February 13, 1945, just a few weeks before the end of the war when FDR's unconditional surrender was forced upon Germany. Within fourteen short hours, Dresden, with its splendor, was reduced to ashes and turned into a huge cemetery, a scene straight out of hell.

A. H. M. Ramsey shared in his book *The Nameless War* that while he was a member of parliament, he asked Neville Chamberlain in 1940 about England's policy of bombing Germany. Prime Minister Chamberlain assured Ramsey that

England would never resort to attacking and killing women and children. He considered such brutality terrorism. Unfortunately, the pro-war forces in England pushed him out of office and had him replaced by Winston Churchill, who relished killing civilians—children, women, the elderly, the sick, and the wounded.

Contrary to the mountains of propaganda, the fire-bombing and destruction of Germany was not a spontaneous military necessity but was planned well in advance by the British government years before World War II. Churchill shared his thoughts in an article written in 1925, stating,

> Everything that happened in the four years of the World War, was only a prelude to what the fifth year would have brought. The war of 1919 (that) we never fought, but the idea lives on ... Death stands at the ready, it only waits for the word (command). Next time perhaps, it may be a matter of killing women and children, or the entire population.

J. M. Straight, principal assistant secretary of the British Air Ministry, adds further light to the destruction of Germany. In his book *Bombing Vindicated*, a 1944 publication, he wrote, "These bomber-planes place their descent to a brain wave which came to British experts in 1936 ... while Germany was thinking only in terms of short-range bombers, and particularly of dive-bombers for employment with the army ... It is we who started the strategic bombing offensive."

After Churchill became prime minister on May 10, 1940, he ordered the fire-bombing of Aachen on May 12, Dusseldorf on May 13, Eschweiler on May 15, Hamburg on May 16, and on and on to the very bloody end. Hitler issued a warning to the

English about the bombings and killings of German civilians. He warned that if they did not stop, he would retaliate. British military historian Liddell Hart stated, "The Germans were completely justified in calling those attacks reprisals, especially since they had announced prior to our sixth attack on Berlin that they would resort to such measures if we did not put a stop to our night raids on Berlin. England continued her bombing war against German cities and towns."

On May 23, 1940, only thirteen days into Churchill's prime ministry, hundreds of upright Englishmen were arrested and incarcerated for the duration of the war, because they were rather critical of Churchill's agenda and murderous methods.

To the question of stopping the war, the senseless slaughter and killings, a German official was told, "You must understand that this war is not just against Hitler, or against National Socialism, but against the strength of the German people, which must be crushed once and for all, regardless whether it lies in the hands of Hitler or a Jesuit Priest." Tragically, that was the primary reason for all the killing, slaughter, and fire-bombing; every other claim was merely political hype.

February 13, 1945, was Shrove Tuesday. On Shrove Tuesday, it was and remains customary to celebrate before the start of Lent and the traditional fasting a carnival celebration. But in 1945, the climate was very dismal at best, and no one was in the mood to pretend that there was any reason to celebrate at all. A handful of beautiful little girls, in blond braids, dressed up, unaware of the looming catastrophe, tried to cheer up the adults. They too died an excruciating, painful death.

Refugees fleeing from the advancing Red Army, only sixty miles away, brought fearful accounts of Soviet atrocities, of murder and death, of extreme brutality, of rape, and of women being nailed against the sides of sheds and left there to die after they were gang raped. Raping women of the vanquished is not only animal-like but vulgar and brutal and as old as history itself, a sick and totally unacceptable human behavior in civilized societies. It was and remains a crime.

At the turn of the century, two million German women spoke out against their rapists and tormentors. It was the end of July 1945, when nineteen-year-old Ruth Schuhmacher was raped by four Russian soldiers. It was the fate of millions of women in Germany at the end and following the war. In former East Germany, people were not allowed to talk about Soviet abuse, and in West Germany, the topic was taboo, because the Germans were told by the occupying forces that they alone were guilty of all war crimes. That was all part of FDR's unconditional surrender. Germans were forced to accept all blame; they had no rights. No one focused on German suffering. However, over the years, women gradually started to talk about their trauma. What happened then is now slowly being brought to light. The trauma of Ruth Schuhmacher, who was not able to have children because of the rapes, was typical.

All the buildings in the city were overflowing with refugees. Thousands upon thousands were forced to camp out on the streets, in railroad stations, and anywhere there was a little space. In addition to Dresden's regular population of 650,000, there were an estimated additional 600,000 plus refugees cramped into the city, in the middle of the coldest winter in over a hundred years.

On January 12, 1945, the Russians sent a communique informing their Western Allies that the Red Army had resumed its offensive up and down the eastern front and was advancing into Prussia and Silesia. An elevated level of Allied concern came with this communique. This also became somewhat of an embarrassment to General Dwight D. Eisenhower, FDR, and Churchill, because Eisenhower's forces were still recovering from the humiliating results of General Karl von Rundstedt's Christmas offensive in the Ardennes.

On January 26, Churchill asked Archibald Sinclair, his secretary of air warfare, what he had in the pipeline for "basting the Germans in their retreat from Breslau." Churchill and the English elite had absolutely no compassion for the German civilians. Sinclair's primary job was to lie about British Bomber Command bombing *only* military targets.

The following day, Sinclair responded, stating that "intervention in winter weather at very long range over Eastern Germany would be difficult." This is not what Churchill wanted to hear. Churchill fired off a memorandum, ordering Sinclair to include the American Eighth Air Force and to coordinate an offensive to completely wipe out Leipzig, Chemnitz, and Dresden. Dresden was not a special case; it was simply the last major city left intact. This was Churchill's cowardly method of conducting war against helpless civilians.

During the last year of the war, Dresden became a major "Sanitaetsstadt," a hospital city with many of its schools converted into temporary wards. Of the nineteen hospitals, which were filled to capacity with patients, sixteen were badly damaged, and three, including the main maternity clinic, were totally destroyed.

Without equal, the most gruesome, brutal, and barbaric genocide in all of man's history was the apocalyptic holocaust of Dresden, Germany, on February 13 and 14, 1945. Thousands upon thousands of God's children were incinerated; they were burned to death. The English firebombs proved that they were far more destructive and possessed a far greater capacity of incinerating more people than even an atomic bomb.

It is significant to note that the British government and its RAF began developing and perfecting this satanic weapon of mass destruction already in 1918, prior to the armistice that marked the end of the first act of England's thirty-year war against Germany. What motivated Churchill and the English government was the firestorm's capability to decimate more human beings than any other weapon known to mankind.

Researching, developing, and perfecting the firestorm prior to the end of World War I and subsequently stockpiling five million firebombs amply supports the claim that bloody old England was preparing for World War II long before World War I was even over.

The English and their RAF observed that incendiary bombs, rather than explosives, were far more effective in obliterating entire cities and their human populations. Imagine burning your little finger on a hot object; then multiply that pain a million times. The English meticulously researched the combustibility of the civilian neighborhoods of all German cities with a population of fifty thousand or more. They also studied the structural materials of the homes in the city centers and the flammability of human beings. The British and others need to be reminded that the most flammable kind of wood is the chip on your shoulder.

Churchill and the English elite were determined to inflict maximum devastation on the civilian population. To that end, the flammability of cities in both Germany and Japan was researched to determine the greatest devastation to their residential neighborhoods and the defenseless civilian population. Dense historical old towns, built primarily of wood, have proven especially vulnerable. Kaiser Wilhelm II and Hitler refused to inflict pain and harm upon the English. That was militarily naïve and suicidal.

Churchill was afflicted with a rather strange affinity to war; plus, he also possessed a strong attachment to the most lethal weapons. He also fancied himself somewhat of a military genius, which his bloody and sadistic record amply disproves. Churchill's military ineptitude was overshadowed by his ability to engage in intrigue and deception. Few question his oratorical abilities.

Since the English army proved to be no match for the German army on the front line, the English government chose to ignore Geneva rules and kill defenseless German civilians. Mass murder became the order of the day. Churchill claimed that an enemy city might be hit hard by flying objects "without a human pilot" able to deliver a plague, anthrax, or a small pox virus. The English made no secret of their foremost mission, namely to kill as many Germans as possible and reduce the German population to a mere twenty million.

The English were not the only ones who fermented such hatred toward Germans. Elya Ehrenburg, Stalin's propaganda demon, for years filled the Red Army with hate propaganda in articles and millions of leaflets: "Kill. Kill. Kill. Nobody is innocent. Neither the living, nor the yet unborn ... if you have not killed a German a day, you have not done your duty to the Soviet motherland." A disturbing question remains, namely, what were the hidden forces that were engaged whereby the pillars of Western democracies became agents for the most brutal, senseless, and sinister act of mass murder?

The Dresden holocaust may have happened decades ago, but for the survivors of that crime, the recollection of that horror is firmly embedded. All have, for all these years, suffered emotionally with nightmares and various physical and emotional problems and afflictions. Thus far, nobody has offered to help these poor victims.

The Allies justified going to war and the destruction of Germany with a barrage of anti-German propaganda, claiming that Hitler and the Nazis were such vile, heel-clicking, brutal and bloodthirsty gangsters that bloody old England was under nothing less than a moral obligation to plan and initiate a war of total destruction, to crucify Germany. In addition, FDR and the United States were compelled to enter the war to aid bloody old England.

Professing such noble causes and claiming such a moral high ground, necessitated a total war as it also became unavoidable because of political, social, economic, and cultural interests. The Allies had to save the world from Prussian militarism, the same Prussia that aided the United States in our struggle for independence from the British Empire. So much has been said by Hollywood and the media about those evil, warmongering, heel-clicking Germans, and there seems to be no end in sight to this German-phobia. When will it finally end, and when will the Germans finally be treated objectively as real human beings, as real Menschen?

In and around Dresden, there were some twenty-six thousand US POWs. Kurt Vonnegut Jr. was one of them who barely escaped with his life; most of the other POWs were not so fortunate. He had this to say about the Dresden Holocaust: "You guys burnt the place down, turned it into a single column of flame. More people died there in the firestorm, in one big flame than died in Hiroshima and Nagasaki combined." The land of Luther and of the Reformation was again in ruin, in total ruin.

British and Allied spies were sneaking in and out of Germany, almost at will. There was no iron curtain keeping anyone in or out of the country. Spying is the second oldest profession in history. The Old Testament and the Torah name twelve spies Moses sent to Canaan. George Washington engaged in espionage, gaining intelligence about the English. He observed that "one good spy is worth a regiment of troops." The value of a good spy has been well established.

The dead admonish us to resist the denial of the Dresden holocaust. The English claimed, lying to their own people, that the targets of their Bomber Command were of military significance. Their barbarous acts and directives contradict their deceptive and fake news claims. Truth renders liars harmless.

History relative to both world wars has unfortunately been turned into a propaganda enterprise, rather than an objective, truthful, balanced, and honest historical inquiry of all the pertinent facts. Americans and the free world have much at stake in understanding the causes and forces of how and why the United States was drawn into two world wars. It was America's entry into the European theater of wars that turned them into world wars.

At the unveiling of Arthur Harris's monument in London, with the Queen Mother in attendance, the English claimed that more than 500,000 and according to the Pentagon almost 600,000 helpless human beings perished. These were God's children who perished needlessly. Tragically, the media did not and still does not spend much time or space covering this carnal crime. Since when has it been the function of the media to write or rewrite history by either sensationalizing an event or killing it with silence?

Churchill provided credence to that typical English characteristic of a stiff upper lip, fuming with a condescending arrogance, proclaiming that all enemies of the British Empire could hardly be punished severely enough for daring to defy the supremacy of the British Empire. Churchill viewed all enemies of the British Empire, whether Huns, Kurds, Africans, Indians, or Iraqis as uncivilized tribes that needed to be punished severely enough to teach them a lesson not to defy the British Empire.

The audacity of Germany daring to challenge England's coal and steel supremacy and furthermore, daring to plan the construction of a railroad from Berlin to Baghdad culminated in the necessity of bloody old England declaring war on Germany. Those plans and Germany had to be destroyed, completely destroyed.

There is no doubt that the Baghdad railroad, with all its economic ramifications, would have been an economic blessing, bringing prosperity to all the people of that entire region and beyond. But that was not to be.

The developments leading up to both world wars demonstrate clearly that all wars are motivated by economics, ice-cold economics. War is politics by other means. The future of wars is guaranteed as long as wars remain financially profitable to the elite, the war profiteers. Follow the money trail to arrive at the instigators, the movers and shakers. Patriotism, honor, fervor, religion, national pride, and claims of defense are profusely employed by foxy politicians and the media to embolden the masses with ecstasies of war, which the media glorifies.

We, the living, have an obligation to all who were needlessly sacrificed on the altar of war and profit. They deserve nothing less than that we, the living, speak and write the truth for all who no longer can speak and write. The truth may well be unpleasant and embarrassing to all who try to hide it. Political correctness is all too often nothing more than masqueraded propaganda, fueled by greed and superegos. Propaganda poisons and fills the hearts and minds of the citizenry, as it emboldens soldiers with heroism and enough hate to kill and slaughter fellow human beings.

While Churchill was a correspondent during the Boer War, he advocated the use of gas warfare, the so-called "scorched-earth policy." It was also during this war that England introduced the world to the use of concentration camps. In the land of the Boers, the English tormented and tortured old men, women, and children to force them into submission. These brave people were fighting for their freedom and independence, which England was denying them by applying brutal military force.

A German officer Colonel Wilhelm Siegert described a heretofore unimaginable weapon of mass destruction, the firestorm. He delineated this satanic method of incinerating entire cities and cremating their human population in an article published in 1927 in Berlin. This article did not escape Winston Churchill's attention. Siegert stated,

> It is possible to start numerous sources of fire in a city such that the existing fire departments cannot extinguish all of them at once; the seeds of catastrophe are thus sewn. The individual fires merge into a major conflagration. The superheated air shoots upward like a giant chimney. The air that rushes in along the ground creates the "firestorm," which in turn causes the smaller fires to unfold completely.

Every city in Germany had been systematically firebombed and burned to the ground and their helpless civilian population turned into pillars of ash. The most brutal, sadistic massacre since the beginning of time was the Dresden holocaust. The Dresden holocaust is no secret to the rest of the world; why have Americans so far been kept in the dark? Perhaps it could be an element of shame and an admission of guilt. The media has made every attempt to kill any part of this story with deafening silence. Pretending that it never happened is not an option, contrary to all the facts, and totally un-American. We are still the land of the brave and the free. We are obligated to provide historical truth.

Turning Germany into a pastoral agricultural country, drastically reducing its size and its population, and eliminating it as an economic competitor was part of the so-called Morgenthau Plan. Henry (Heinrich) Morgenthau, as stated earlier, migrated from Mannheim, Germany.

After he arrived in the United States, FDR appointed Henry Morgenthau to the powerful position of secretary of the treasury. However, Henry was more interested in being involved in the current political affairs and how to reduce Germany and its population. It was no accident that he was FDR's neighbor on Hyde Park. As part of the Morgenthau Plan, Germany was demonized and portrayed as the common enemy of the entire world, fueling intense hatred toward Germany.

Shortly after Churchill became England's prime minister, on May 11, 1940, the British cabinet officially abolished the Geneva rule of protecting enemy civilians. That legalized waging war against helpless civilians. The cabinet thereby subjugated itself to Churchill's murderous intentions. Proud English soldiers were now legally authorized to kill old men, women, and children. Churchill's legacy remains turning war into mass murder. The term *holocaust* was first coined by Elie Wiesel in 1967, being consumed by fire, which is what happened in Dresden and throughout Germany.

For some time, Churchill, Charles Portal, and Arthur Harris worked closely together as a team. They worked closely together during the English colonial wars in the Near East, India, and Africa during the 1920s and 30s and again during World War II, raining down brimstone and damnation on all who dared to defy British worldwide supreme authority. The English viewed themselves as the supreme power of the world, extending into all corners of the world. Now it was Germany and the Germans who needed to learn a lesson. It was England's fervent, entrenched belief that no punishment could possibly be severe enough; the Germans had to be punished. Such was the arrogant attitude of Churchill and the English elite.

In February 1942, Portal's directives as to the bombers' mission and England's objectives were rather clear: "It has been decided that the primary objective of your operations should now be focused on the morale of the enemy civilian population ..." meaning that henceforth civilian enemy neighborhoods were officially the primary target of the proud English Bomber Command. The English objective was maximum suffering and devastation to human lives. Churchill arrogantly added his own personal instructions that Germans did not need to live in their cities anyhow; they should travel out into the countryside and watch their homes burn from the hills.

A short time after the war started, already in 1939, England demonstrated its strategy by firebombing seven northwestern German cities. The English dropped their first firebombs on Freiburg; among the casualties were forty kindergarten children. After the civilian neighborhoods in Moenchengladbach were firebombed on May 10 and 11, 1940, Churchill jubilantly proclaimed that the use of air and the sky made it absolutely possible that "death and terror could be carried far behind the lines of the actual armies to women, children and the aged, the sick ..."

Churchill and FDR had a callous side that they and the media tried to keep hidden from the public. Both expressed a desire to bomb all Germans straight to hell with pilotless, remote-controlled bombers that would be loaded with twenty thousand pounds of high explosives, but the English chiefs of staff reneged because of fear of possible retaliations. FDR, on the other hand, could risk not being bombed; the distance was beyond Germany's capabilities.

Germany retaliated for the English fire-bombings on September 7, 1940, bombing the aircraft factories in Coventry. Germany, contrary to massive Allied propaganda, followed the Geneva rules not to primarily attack and bomb civilian and residential areas. What remains a puzzle is the fact that rather than destroy England's factories, Hitler again ordered the bombing be halted.

Why did Hitler order not to destroy England's war machine at a time when Germany had both ground and air superiority?

Churchill did not expect to have air superiority until at least late 1942, perhaps 1943, counting on FDR and the United States to enter the war. Was Hitler so naïve as to believe that England would stop the war, after it went to such extremes to justify going to war against Germany a second time? England made it clear that it wanted to eliminate Germany as an economic competitor. Was Hitler so shallow, or was he obeying orders from a hidden source? There is nothing quite as self-destructive as stubborn arrogance, which Hitler displayed profusely, die deutsche Krankheit. He too was a very good actor. What an irony: Hitler was doing everything he could to save the British Empire, and Churchill and the Allies were trying to totally destroy Germany and ruthlessly reduce the German population. Because of his many strategic military errors, many have wondered if Hitler was the ultimate Trojan horse?

It would not take a military genius to figure out that Hitler made too many fatal tactical mistakes. The British government thought the German invasion was imminent and ordered all the church bells to ring. But Hitler refused to invade England. The invasion would have likely ended the war and kept FDR out of the war. Churchill was counting on Hitler making two major tactical, fatal mistakes, namely not invading England and starting a second front against Russia before the war with England was over. At the defeat of Dunkirk, Hitler allowed the English soldiers to safely return to dear old England rather than have them be taken prisoners, as his generals were about to do. Unfortunately, Hitler again overruled his generals.

Was it naïve or merely stupid for Hitler to ask the English government to stop waging war against defenseless civilians, only to be ignored and laughed at? Why did he accept such insults? Churchill responded by stating that he was not on speaking terms with Hitler. Was Hitler really that naïve, or was there another hidden power giving him orders? Wall Street and others financed Hitler's rise to power, and it was implicated in the organization and operation of Hitler's dictatorship.

After the first few fire-bombings, Churchill boasted to the House of Commons that all German cities "would face a test so unremitting, severe, and extensive such that no country has ever before experienced." The German press described the English as "British gangs of murderers who are waging war against the defenseless." How did he, or did Churchill have knowledge and assurances that Hitler would not retaliate in kind? Why did Hitler commit so many fatal military errors, and why was he ordering a self-destructive, treasonous course?

Since the English army demonstrated it was no match for the German army, Churchill and the English government opted to ignore Geneva rules, which they agreed to. It applied terror tactics against defenseless German civilians. Allied airpower was turned into terror operations. Mass murder became the order of the day.

The good people of the British Isles were lied to. They were told that the targets of the RAF Bomber Command were all of military significance, such as factories and intra-structure. But their terror acts, as well as their directives to the pilots, completely contradicted their false claims. They demonstrated that the first casualty of war is *truth*. Churchill liked to boast; he exclaimed, "We will make Germany a desert, yes, a desert."

Churchill's and FDR's callous brutality reminds one of the savagery that we read about in Joshua 6:21–25, about the capture of Jericho: "And they took the city and they utterly destroyed all that was in the city, both men and women, young and old … In those days, the enemy was slaughtered, forty and two-thousand, at one time."

Churchill was acutely aware that he had nothing to fight the Germans with, other than intrigue, deception, lies, and most important, allies willing to do his fighting. On rare occasions,

Churchill even spoke the truth. He stated, "There was no continental army that could defeat the German military power." Why did Hitler squander German military power?

There was only one way to defeat Hitler: trick him into making enough fatal military mistakes. Hitler appeared to be more than willing to cooperate. Might he have been guilty of committing high treason? It is known that he was supported with millions of dollars from Wall Street, and wealthy Americans. Like Wilson, was he indebted to them?

Churchill's uppermost priority remained getting the United States into the war. This was the only scenario in which he could be on the winning side. The United States would win the war for him. He was acutely aware that FDR was itching to officially enter the war but needed to create the appearance of being attacked. FDR needed an excuse, a crisis that justified a claim for national defense to the American people, so he could officially enter the war and turn the European war into a world war and thereby also expand American imperialism.

Deceptive propaganda was designed to turn Germany into a common enemy. As mentioned before, more than seventy-five thousand German Americans were kidnapped by the FBI, mostly under cover of darkness, and placed into American internment camps to diminish and silence German-American opposition going to war again. Eighty-six percent of all Americans were strongly opposed to America again entering the European theater of war and turning the European war into a world war.

The hypocrisy of all the various ways of justifying the destruction of Germany is an area of research in itself. FDR, Churchill, and the Allied elite intentionally ditched all German efforts to preserve peace in Europe and the world and then blamed them as the aggressor. The Versailles Peace Treaty was a major misstep in preserving peace. Without the Versailles Treaty, there would have been no World War II and the massacre of millions of human beings. They were considered mere collateral damage.

England became the new home of many German Jews. One of them was Friedrich Alexander Lindemann, who subsequently became Lord Cherwell, as a reward for his service to the English Crown. Lindemann left Germany with his Russian-born wife in 1914 to become director of the RAF Physical Laboratory.

During World War II, Churchill appointed Lindemann to chair the British Scientific Intelligence and to the position of his personal scientific adviser. Lindemann became the gray eminence behind the RAF's terrorist firebombing campaign. He was bursting with unrestrained hate and possessed with an utter determination for the destruction of Germany.

Sir Charles Percy Snow, also expressing the opinions of others, stated that Lindemann was possessed with "a deep rooted, sadistic impulse that drove him to destroy German workers' neighborhoods, to kill thousands of women and children." Churchill described him as "the scientific lobe of my brain."

Professor Alex Nathan, another Jewish immigrant from Germany, was of the opinion that Lindemann's hatred of Germans knew no limits. The total destruction of Germany had become his passion and life's mission. Nathan observed that both men, Lindemann and Churchill, were well suited for each other.

After the United States officially entered the war, the USAAF and its scientific staff were ordered to join the efforts in the perfecting of the firebomb. One of the numerous immigrants from Germany was Erich Mendelsohn. He was assigned the task of reproducing a replica of a Berlin working-class neighborhood in the Dugway Proving Grounds in Utah. Experimental raids were carried out on Mendelsohn's model Berlin neighborhood to test and improve the effectiveness of the various firebombs.

The Allied elite expressed disappointment in not being able to incinerate Berlin. However, Mendelsohn's replicas later proved very useful in the bombing attacks of Japanese civilian neighborhoods.

Churchill appeared eager to express his own dislike for Germans in his notorious fashion. "There are 70 million wicked Huns, some of them are curable and others killable." Such was the verbiage of England's prime minister. He conveniently forgot that the majority of the English are German, i.e. Anglo-Saxons. For centuries, the British royal family has been German. One king even refused to speak anything but German.

Shield and defend us from the evil intentions of our enemies. Help us to forgive them for their transgressions against us, but do hold them accountable for their crimes. To the recklessness and imprudence of two world wars, lead this lost world out of the danger of adding the stupidity of not ever ending them. Continuous wars for continuous peace is a total contradiction, a perpetual, never-ending oxymoron.

In World War II, England and the United States engaged in terrorism against Germany. The Allies chose to call it euphemistically "strategic bombing." Contrary to such claims, "strategic" was not strategic at all but blind, blanket area saturation bombing. The bombs were dropped indiscriminately and randomly on residential neighborhoods, creating maximum terror and destruction to human lives.

Today, the United States and England are engaged in a worldwide war on "terrorism." What is terrorism? It is creating fear, disorderliness, and confusion; scaremongering; and the disruption of civil order. Operation Gomorrah was an Allied terror campaign; terrorism from the air was to force Germany into "unconditional surrender." Germany was left with no rights at all, and it still is without a peace treaty.

Mother Nature granted Bomber Harris a full, bright moon

on the evening of Palm Sunday. The Bomber Command was ordered to destroy the city of Luebeck. The raid started at 10:30 p.m. The Allied media reported that the bombers' mission was a total success. In a short time, 1,500 historic, high-gabled houses and eight miles of street facades were ablaze. Two hundred acres of the old town were gutted by fire. Three hundred and twenty civilians were incinerated. Firebombing, by definition, was and remains a holocaust.

On May 30, 1942, Hamburg was chosen as the next target, but because of weather conditions, the bombers were ordered to drop their destructive firebombs on the cathedral city of Cologne. The firestorm, however, did not develop as Bomber Harris and Churchill had hoped for.

Cologne lay like a three-dimensional textbook picture with its medieval history and architecture. Its churches, buildings, artwork, and cathedrals from the Middle Ages had inspired people from around the world. Cologne was also a more modern city with wider streets. Because the water lines remained intact and functioning, the city was able to defend itself. During this raid, 3,300 buildings were destroyed and 9,500 damaged. This was classic British warfare, incinerating innocent, helpless civilians.

It took Harris and the Bomber Command 262 additional air raids before the jewel that was Cologne was 95 percent destroyed and burned to the ground. The English claimed they killed six thousand civilians. On June 2, the *New York Times* reported that there were twenty thousand casualties and described the raid as a brutal act of revenge on the German civilian population.

Churchill issued another of his infamous proclamations predicting that Cologne was a "forewarning of what one German city after another would have to endure from now on." He then cabled FDR, stating, "I hope you were impressed with our mass air attacks on Cologne. There is more to come."

Bloody Old England brought destruction and death to city after city. The list is endless: Bonn, Hamburg, Munich, Krefeld, Muenster, Essen, Kiel, Dortmund, Frankfurt, Karlsruhe, Stuttgart, Nuremberg, Hanover, Bremen, Cologne, Dusseldorf, Berlin, Leipzig, Mannheim, and the list goes on and on. Every city had been firebombed and burned to the ground, and their helpless civilians were incinerated. The most hideous crime of them all was the Dresden holocaust, a war crime of untold proportions. Thus far, no one has been publicly held accountable for these crimes. The world knows what the Germans did, but knows little or nothing about what was done to the Germans.

The Dresden holocaust was a war crime by any definition, because the Allied objective was not to win the war but to totally destroy the city and incinerate its human beings. This holocaust had been planned with meticulous forethought and malicious intentions. Furthermore, Churchill and company did not even try to conceal their delight in the cold-blooded bombing and killing of thousands of helpless German civilians.

During the Berlin campaign, on August 23, 1943, there were 149 bomber casualties. The Germans lost three fighters. After repeated Allied bombings, all the major railroad stations and 50 percent of the buildings were destroyed. The airport was in shambles, entire sections of the city were destroyed, and tens of thousands of its civilians were killed. In March, the Allies killed 40,000 Polish and Russian workers. Hitler retaliated again by bombing Coventry and London, but then, he again ordered the bombing halted. Who was giving him orders to halt the bombing of England's factories?

Arthur Harris reacted, "What Hitler wreaked against London and Coventry, our bombers would repay 1,000-fold, until the inhabitants of every city in Germany had been 'de-housed' and pulverized into surrender." Actually, they were willing to surrender for some time but were being totally ignored. It became increasingly obvious that the Allied mission was not victory but the destruction of Germany and killing as many Germans as possible.

Allied bombs did not kill only German civilians indiscriminately but their own allies. Fifty thousand English prisoners were killed at a train crossing near Orvilto, Italy. Allegedly, these casualties were the result of "friendly fire." There was nothing "friendly" in their deaths.

During World War II, the Bomber Command had a combined force of more than 125,000 men, of which 73,741 were lost in action. The German flak created its own reverse carpet bombing, bringing down many planes. On some raids, half of the Wellingtons did not return. They lacked self-sealing fuel tanks, caught on fire, and became flying coffins.

A bomber crew consisted of a pilot, a copilot, a bombardier, a radio-operator, a mechanic, and two gunners. Most of the crew was around twenty years old. Staying alive was all that really mattered. The temperature up in the air dropped to minus 50 degrees. Many suffered frostbite. The RAF flew 389,809 sorties on 1,481 nights and 1,089 days. Dresden would have never become the brutal reality had FDR accepted an armistice and not stubbornly persisted in unconditional surrender. His obvious mission and objective was not the end of hostilities or victory, but the total destruction of Germany and the reduction of its population.

As one of the final displays of English brutality, Churchill ordered the destruction of Dresden. On February 13 and 14, 1945, the city, with its splendor, was reduced to flaming ruins and ashes, and half of its population perished. The actual number who perished will likely never be known; they remain nameless.

As soon as Harris received orders for the total destruction of Dresden, he invited the Americans to split the available bombers into three separate attacks, thereby dramatically multiplying the destruction and devastation to human lives.

At 9:55 p.m., the sirens announced the beginning of fourteen hours of pure hell, something that could have come out of a Hollywood horror movie. The people went reluctantly to their shelters, as they had done before. The thunderclap came to Dresden; the code name of this operation was "Clarion." Since Dresden had no air-raid shelters, cellars and basements served as air raid shelters.

Bomber Harris and Bomber Command perfected the incendiary attack. Highly trained special crews led the attack delineating a clearly defined and predetermined target area with marker flares, which the Germans nicknamed *Weihnachtsbaum* (Christmas tree). After the area was clearly marked, the bomber squadrons dropped their bombs so densely as to create a bombing carpet so that any fire defense would be overwhelmed.

The Bomber Command used a procedure they called the "fan." The fan was a quarter of a circle. The vertex in Dresden was the soccer stadium. From its pivot point, the fan spread out to 45 degrees; one leg went to the Slaughterhouse and the other to the city center. The red and green markers were laid down with precision on either side of the target.

At 10:03 p.m., the illuminators began to light up the Elbe River and the city center with white cascading flares. Two minutes later, green markers were dropped on the soccer stadium. Because there was no defense, the marker aircraft dove down low to precisely outline the area to be incinerated. First red markers to the left and then green markers to the right were dropped. For ten whole minutes, the lead plane flew undisturbed, illuminating and marking the target. The master bomber swooped down, penetrating the thin cloud cover, to thoroughly inspect his target. The people in the overcrowded city were literally sitting ducks, waiting to be roasted.

The lead bomber called in his first squadron, delineating the western edge leading to the Slaughterhouse. The second wave of bombers, following the right edge, came in on the southern route leading to the city center. The third wave, consisting of four squadrons, flying between the two legs of this triangle, rolled the inferno over the entire inner area. The left leg crossed the bend in the Elbe River twice; the right leg ended at the train tracks at Falkenbruecke. The connecting arc ended in front of the main train station.

The stated mission of the first wave of bombers was to create a firestorm. Half an hour later, the inner city was ablaze. The glow of the fires looked like a red sunset from even 150 miles away. The buildings were primarily made of wood, and all that wood in the wooden structures, roofs, floors, walls, and furniture were feeding the blaze. Thousands of individual fires were transformed into a huge conflagration, an ocean of flames. The flames worked themselves into a firestorm, an inescapable extermination raid. The heat and gas turned the cellars into execution chambers. The people in the basements and cellars rarely emerged alive. Those who were seeking refuge in underground shelters suffocated as the oxygen was sucked from the air to feed the fires.

Tens of thousands of people who survived the first attack crowded onto the Grosser Garten, a park nearly one and one-half mile square, to get away from the heat. Out of desperation, many survivors of the first attack jumped into a concrete emergency water reservoir to escape the heat. The reservoir measured 100 by 150 meters and was a meter deep. What these unfortunate people did not realize was that its sides were sloped and slippery and there were also no handles to assist people in getting out again. The non-swimmers sank to the bottom and dragged the swimmers along with them.

When the rescue team reached the Altmarkt five days later,

they found the tank filled with bloated corpses. Furthermore, the whole square was littered with incinerated bodies; thirty of them could fit into a small bathtub.

This was only the first stage of this barbaric madness. Exactly on schedule, three hours after the first attack, at 1:22 a.m., a second massive English armada of bombers arrived. Since the power system was destroyed during the first raid, there was no forewarning of the second attack.

Half of the bombers during this attack concentrated on the city center to maintain and intensify the fires. The other half concentrated on the edges of the firestorm to significantly increase and multiply the devastation and dramatically increase human casualties. It was timed to catch the German medical and defense units totally off guard. The Germans did not expect a second attack three hours later. There were no limits to British brutality. The second raid was timed so that the surviving civilians would have emerged from their shelters and the rescuers and firefighters would have arrived from surrounding cities. Both proved to be true. For many miles around, military detachments and rescue and fire brigades were on their way to the stricken city, making their way through the suburbs when the second attack started the devastation all over again. Most who came as good Samaritans did not survive the Dresden holocaust.

Many civilians were still huddled in cellars and tunnels, anywhere they could get away from the heat. At the start of the second attack, they were waiting for the fires from the first attack to die down. But it was not to be. One survivor described the unfolding scene: "The detonations shook the cellar walls. The sound of the explosions mingled with a new sound of a thundering waterfall; it was the sound of the mighty tornado howling in the inner city. People burned to death; they glowed bright orange and blue in the dark. As the heat intensified, people disintegrated into ashes." Survivors reported seeing young women carrying babies, running, their dresses and hair on fire, screaming until they fell down or the collapsing buildings fell on top of them.

Tens of thousands of God's children were sucked into the blast of white heat, heat that was intense enough to melt human flesh. Those human bodies turned bright orange and blue, and as the heat intensified, they either were totally incinerated or they melted into thick liquid, which was three to four feet deep. The heat was so intense that even kitchen utensils melted. Let us not forget that death is ultimately the great equalizer that all will face.

The German people did not want to believe that Churchill, FDR, Lindemann, and Morgenthau would stoop so low as to firebomb a city of art and culture, with absolutely no military significance, and at a time when the war had long been decided just for the sake of killing, incinerating old men, women, children, and babies—born and unborn. They wanted to teach the Germans a lesson that they would never forget; the Allies turned Dresden into a ghost town.

Medical staff and firefighters did not need a telephone to tell them they were needed. The inferno could be seen for two hundred miles. The force that the firestorm created carried human body parts, tree branches, and huge quantities of ash and various other debris onto the surrounding countryside, as far as eighteen miles away. This was terrorism and mass murder with an exponential dimension.

An unstable atmosphere is the result of temperature differences. For the same reasons, the firestorm created a man-made tornado, which was far more destructive. The fires developed winds of hundreds of miles per hour. The force that was created was so intense that it ripped off roofs, uprooted trees, and tossed trees and cars into the air. The wind sucked men, women, and children into a glowing inferno from whence there was absolutely no escape. Such destruction of defenseless, helpless human beings and on such a scale has never been witnessed on planet earth. Hundreds of thousands were consumed by fire in the Dresden holocaust.

The firebombs started thousands of fires, which both created and were aided by strong winds. The individual fires joined into an unimaginable huge conflagration of fires. These firestorms to exterminate the German people were man-made and were not a natural phenomenon. Few people, other than the survivors, have any idea of their destructive force and human devastation.

The intense heat generated by the huge column of flames and smoke, miles high and covering thousands of acres, created a powerful updraft of the air in the center of the column. This, in turn, created an extremely low-pressure area at the base of the column. The surrounding fresh air rushed in to fuel the fire at speeds in excess of thirty times that of an ordinary, natural tornado. In an ordinary tornado, the winds are the result of temperature differences of 20 to 30 degrees at most. In the Dresden holocaust, the temperature differences were between 600 and 1,000 degrees Centigrade.

The absence of any air defense allowed the bombers, with no danger to themselves, to drop to very low altitudes and thereby achieve a relatively high degree of precision, creating greater devastation to humans. They visually identified their targets. They could clearly see their targets; they knew they were destroying residential areas and the city center. To justify their actions, it was the usual defensive argument; they were only following orders, bombing schools, hospitals and ignoring the Red Cross signs, which were in clear view.

As if firebombs were not destructive enough, shrapnel bombs with timed fuses were also dropped on Dresden and other German cities. They lay on the ground, detonating and hurling their bullet-like fragments for hours and days after the bombers had left the scene. These shrapnel bombs kept the firefighters and medical personnel from doing their job, preventing them from attending to the wounded.

Blockbuster bombs tore away entire buildings, causing facades and roofs to collapse. Then the firebombs would quickly turn building after building and mile after mile of residential streets into a huge inferno. The individual fires merged into a firestorm, drawing everything into an oven from which there was no escape. The fire spread quickly through all the floors from the top down, building after building. There was nowhere to go; people were trapped and surrounded by fire. All those wooden roof structures developed fires from the top down.

The caustic smoke made it hard to breathe; flames shot out of windows from all sides of the streets. People got stuck in the melted asphalt. There was destruction and death all around them. Hospitals, with the Red Cross symbol prominently displayed, were not spared. According to Churchill, FDR, Morgenthau, and others, there were Germans inside of these hospitals and they did not deserve to live. One survivor described the horrific scene:

> I saw women from the clinic lying all over the meadow ... sick women, pregnant women, women giving birth ... groans, screams and newborn babies crying ... all perished in the inferno ... corpses of people who burned to death shrunk down to the size of dolls ... bodies with totally blackened skin ... all over ... hell ... Some of the people lay there totally at peace, as if asleep ... they had been asphyxiated due to a lack of oxygen. Most had been completely incinerated, the charred bodies measured about twenty inches ...

The Dresden holocaust stands uniquely apart from all other massacres in man's history.

Churchill gave the order to unleash the worst massacre in man's history. In the first wave of bombers, from 10:09 p.m. until 10:35 p.m. 3,000 explosive bombs and 400,000 firebombs were dropped. During the second attack, from 1:22 a.m. until 1:54 a.m., more than 4,500 explosive bombs and in excess of 170,000 firebombs were dropped upon helpless civilians. The first two attacks were carried out by England's Royal Air Force. This brutality cannot be one of the RAF's proudest moments; this was a premeditated crime.

Medical personal from all over Germany had converged on Dresden. They did not suspect that yet another wave of bombers was on its way to completely disrupt all humanitarian efforts. The last attacks were conducted by the Americans and had been carefully synchronized with the first two attacks.

On the following day, which was Ash Wednesday and Valentine's Day, the third and fourth raid blanketed the city. From 12:10 p.m. until 12:25 p.m., more than 1,500 explosive bombs and 50,000 firebombs were dropped by the American Army Air Force. Then, in a separate and fourth raid, which lasted from 12:15 p.m. until 12:50 p.m., an additional 900 explosive bombs and 50,000 firebombs were dropped on Dresden. For thirty-eight minutes, American bombers pounded what was left of Dresden. As part of the final attack, to finish the job, low-flying Mustangs shot at anything and everything that moved and still had any signs of life. When the last planes left the skyline, Dresden was a scene straight out of hell. Dresden was a scorched ruin. Her streets and cellars were filled with corpses. Never in the history of mankind were so many murdered so satanically in such a short time.

The British General C. M. Grieson stated at a press conference in Paris that the Allied Air Forces decided to firebomb and totally destroy all major German cities, regardless of human considerations, and to instill as much terror in the German civilian population as possible. Geneva rules were totally ignored, the Red Cross emblems were ignored, and the sick and wounded in hospitals were subjected to a most torturous death.

The English and the Allies dehumanized the Germans so excessively as not to cause any feelings of guilt among the pilots and members of the armed forces for the mass murder and the terror they created. Hate generates violence. Butcher Harris ordered the double and triple attacks on Dresden. The double and triple raid not only doubled but significantly multiplied the devastation and loss to human lives. Most of the dead were liquefied into a yellow mass that melted into the asphalt of the streets, or they turned up as piles of ashes.

British journalist Vivian Brown stated,

> Although the war had already been decided militarily in favor of the Allies and the victorious conclusion was now only a matter of weeks, at most months, the Anglo-Americans nevertheless started the joint "Clarion" attack, in which a total of 9,000 bombers and fighters took part ... The Allied air attacks on Dresden were almost exclusively against the civilian population ...

Everybody knew the war was over. Already in January 1945, Dr. Werner von Braun and five thousand of his coworkers had left the Penemuende Research Center and arrived with their research material in Bleicherode im Harz. They were brought to the United States under Operation Paperclip. The majority of the German scientists arrived in December 1945 and February 1946.

Out of 28,410 buildings in the inner city, 24,866 were totally destroyed, and an area of more than eleven square miles was burned to the ground. For five days and six nights, the city kept on burning. No one could safely enter the city. Gradually, they were able to assess the human losses and destruction. The unanimous verdict was that the city was devastated, eradicated, snuffed out, obliterated, and totally ruined. Of 54 churches, nine were totally destroyed, including the Frauenkirche, and 38 seriously damaged. These were the churches in which the people got married and the newborns were baptized. Of the 139 schools, which were turned into hospital wards, 69 no longer existed and 50 suffered major damages. The city symbol, die Frauenkirche survived the air raids but collapsed two days later because of the intense heat, which reached 1,100 degrees Fahrenheit.

During the second firebombing, the Dresden Zoo was struck and severely damaged. Many of the spooked animals escaped and mingled with the desperate survivors. It should be noted that the marshaling yards were untouched, as were the few factories, because they were located outside of the city and away from the civilians.

In December 1944, Kurt Vonnegut Jr. was an American soldier who had been captured by the German army. He experienced the firebombing of Dresden as a prisoner of war. In 1969, Vonnegut shared his experiences in an antiwar novel, *Slaughterhouse Five*. The novel enjoyed considerable success. He, along with some 26,000 Allied POWs, experienced the destruction of Dresden from the prison camp. He talks about how he narrowly escaped death during the air raids and the Dresden Holocaust. Vonnegut writes,

> The death toll was staggering. The full extent of the Dresden Holocaust can more readily be grasped if one considers that well over 250,000 ...

possibly as many as half a million ... persons died within a 14-hour period, whereas estimates of those who died at Hiroshima range from 90,000 to 140,000.

One person who lived through the Dresden holocaust was Margaret Fryer. She shared her recollections:

> The firestorm is incredible, there are calls for help and screams from somewhere but all around is one single inferno. To my left I suddenly see a woman. I can see her to this day and shall never forget it. She carries a bundle in her arms. It is a baby. She runs, she falls, and the child flies in an arc into the fire ... Suddenly, I saw people again, right in front of me. They scream and gesticulate with their hands, and then—to my utter horror and amazement ... I see how one after the other they seem to let themselves drop to the ground. Today I know that these unfortunate people were the victims of a lack of oxygen.

Otto Sailer-Jackson was a keeper at the Dresden Zoo. He shared his experiences:

> The elephants gave spine-chilling screams. A baby cow elephant was lying in the narrow barrier-moat on her back, her legs up in the air. She had suffered severe stomach injuries and could not move. A cow elephant had been flung clear across the barrier-moat and the fence by some terrific wave, and stood there trembling.

Lothar Metzger was a child living in Dresden during the war. In May 1999, he wrote about his experiences:

> At about 9:30 p.m. the alarm was given. We children knew that sound and got up and dressed quickly, to hurry downstairs into our cellar which we used as an air-raid shelter … There were nonstop explosions. Our cellar was filled with fire and smoke and was damaged, the lights went out and wounded people shouted dreadfully. In great fear we struggled to leave the cellar. We did not recognize our street anymore. Fire, only fire wherever we looked. Our 4th floor did not exist anymore. The broken remains of our house were burning. On the streets were burning vehicles and carts with refugees, people, horses, all of them screaming and shouting in fear of death. I saw hurt women, children, old people searching a way through ruins and flames … explosion after explosion. It was beyond belief, worse than the blackest nightmare … Dead and dying people were trampled upon … We saw the burning street, the falling ruins and the terrible firestorm.

Tons of horror stories were fabricated, creating an intense and savage propaganda scheme against Germany in order to justify and excuse the fire-bombings and slaughter of German civilians, the starvation blockade, the raping of German women from eight to eighty, the total destruction of Germany, and the reduction of its population. Germany still suffers from FDR's unconditional surrender. After almost a century, the Allies still have not granted Germany a Peace Treaty, einen wirklichen Friedensvertrag. World War II was Churchill's war and part of

England's thirty-year war against Germany. Hitler appeared to be willing to sacrifice millions of German lives needlessly to save the British Empire. Hitler was concerned about saving the British Empire, and Germany is still paying for his treasonous acts.

Gerhard Hauptmann, one of Germany's Nobel Prize laureates, admonishes the world:

> A person who has forgotten how to weep, learns how to once more at the sight of the destruction of Dresden ... I know that there are quite a few good people in England and America, to whom the divine light of the Sistine Madonna was not unknown, and who now weep, profoundly and grievously by the extinguishing of this star ... From Dresden, from its wonderfully sustained nurturing of the fine arts, literature and music ... glorious streams have flowed throughout all the world, and England and America have also drunk from them thirstily ... God should love and purify and refine more than heretofore—for their own salvation.

The Zwinger housed several museums, including works by the old masters, such as Rubens, Rembrandt, and Raphael. Raphael's *Sistine Madonna* was added to the collection in 1754 and destroyed during the Dresden holocaust.

Churchill marveled at how fortunate England had been at the loss of a relatively small number of human lives, especially when compared to the horrific loss of lives in Germany. He stated, "In two years struggle with the greatest military power ... barely 100,000 of our people have been killed, of which nearly half are civilians." The Swiss newspaper *Die Tat*, on January 19, 1955, estimated the German casualties, due to firebombs, far in excess of two million people.

Hitler professed he delayed a blitz on England out of sentiment for the English people. Others believed him to be a bumbling fool, willing to commit high treason. He repeatedly intervened on England's behalf. England's brutality turned them into liars and hypocrites. The question has been raised: Where did the bloody English keep their loving Jesus? For more than a year, Berlin and Tokyo made repeated requests to stop the war, the destruction, and the senseless killings, but FDR and Churchill were not interested. They claimed they were not on speaking terms with Berlin or Tokyo.

Winston accused Eisenhower of being soft on the German civilians and ordered him to use terror tactics so that they would leave their homes and block the roads for the German retreat. Referring to Dresden as a unique atrocity, General Eisenhower stated on February 16, "The Allied Air Commands have made the long-awaited decision to adopt a deliberate terror bombing of German population centers as a ruthless expedient to hasting Hitler's doom." He also conveniently forgot that there were formal requests from Berlin and Tokyo to stop the war. Tragically, it was unconditional surrender FDR and the Allies insisted upon, totally disregarding the human loss and leaving the defeated nation with absolutely no rights and endless exploitations.

Eisenhower's comment received some media coverage in the United States but was censored in England. Tragically, the issue was not victory, because the war was virtually over, but the destruction of Germany and the slaughter and the submission of its people. The fire-bombing of Dresden had been planned not only with meticulous forethought but also with malicious intentions.

Churchill made another false statement; he may have again been intoxicated. He claimed that the Dresden holocaust was

to create the best impression possible on Uncle Joe Stalin at
the Yalta Conference. That is another lie, because the Yalta
Conference preceded the Dresden holocaust, hence, the
Dresden holocaust could not have had any influence on Stalin
at the Yalta Conference whatsoever.

There is a lot of noble talk by the media, professing our
sincere opposition of bombing innocent civilians, especially
hurting innocent children, but that did not apply to German
civilians or German children. The public has sadly become
skeptical of what it sees, hears, and reads; the media and
politicians are no longer trusted. For this great democratic
experiment called the United States to survive, we must wage a
battle for honesty, truth, and justice. This glorious experiment
shall long endure, as long as all are truly equal under the law.

Giving in to special political pressures from the occupying
Allies, Dresden city tour guides and school textbooks are
whitewashing this horrific crime of the century by claiming
that *only* thirty thousand died in the Dresden holocaust. That
is a far cry from the truth, a bold-faced lie and a callous insult
to the dead.

A documentary of the Dresden holocaust was commissioned
by the German government, which fell into Allied hands. The
mountains of dead corpses filled the footage. This was later
edited and spliced into Allied propaganda films about Nazi
"concentration camp atrocities." These were displayed to the
world and to Germans as evidence of German collective guilt.

The police president filed a report about the Dresden
holocaust. He stated,

> As the result of the confluence of a number of
> fires, the air above is heated to such an extent that
> in consequence of its reduced specific gravity, a
> violent updraft occurs which causes great suction

of the surrounding air radiating from the center of the fire ... The suction of the firestorm in the larger of these area fire-zones ... One effect of this phenomenon was that the fire in the smaller area fire-zones was fanned as by bellows as the central suction of the biggest and fiercest fires caused increased and accelerated attraction of the surrounding masses of fresh air. In this way all the area fires became united in one vast fire ...

This report also fell into Allied hands.

Estimates of the dead in Dresden range from 350,000 to 600,000. A German newspaper *Eidgenossen*, on January 3, 1986, listed 480,000 dead. Among the dead were 37,000 babies and toddlers, 46,000 school-aged children, and 55,000 wounded and sick in the hospitals, as well as doctors, nurses, and other hospital personnel, 12,000 rescue workers, and 350,000 simply listed as "men and women." These figures do not reflect all the refugees killed fleeing the Red Army.

In the bombing raids on the English munitions and aircraft-producing town of Coventry, 380 people died. This small number partially explains why the Allies are downplaying the casualties of the Dresden firebombing. The dead admonish us to resist diminishing or denying the full extent of the Dresden holocaust.

Certainly not all the crimes committed against humanity during World War II were the work of Hitler and the Nazis. There was plenty of guilt to go around, as there usually is. However, that was not the impression created by the Nuremberg Trials or the Allied media. The perpetrators of the Dresden holocaust should have been arraigned at the Nuremberg Trials, if that court would have applied American Constitutional standards. To add further insult to injury, these atrocities are not even mentioned in American high school or college history textbooks.

The official London propaganda persisted in their false claim that the RAF Bomber Command bombed *only* military targets. The emphasis was, as usual, on *only*. London further claimed that the reports of the atrocities of the Dresden holocaust were nothing more than Nazi propaganda. As may be expected, the London newspapers failed to print any pictures of the destruction of Dresden and the mountains of corpses to support their false claims. A picture would have been worth a thousand words and would have contradicted London's erroneous claims.

At least for a few days, this massacre was publicized. The attack caused acute embarrassment to FDR's administration; they were astutely sensitive to public opinion. As a result, the air force spokesperson never failed to point out the huge difference between the indiscriminate RAF blanket, saturation firestorm attacks and the far more selective and precise bombing by the US Army Air Force.

In order to stop any further inquiries of this massacre, General George C. Marshall fabricated the story that bombing Dresden was the result of Stalin's request. However, no evidence has ever been produced either then or since to support the validity of this statement.

The naked truth can be silenced for only so long. The sadistic destruction of the Florence of the North and the mass murder of so many innocent old men, women, and children, as well as Allied POWs and foreign workers, rightfully caused a revulsion of sentiments. On March 28, Churchill felt compelled to write to the chief of the RAF Bomber Command, saying, "It seems to me that the moment has come when the question of bombing of German cities simply for the sake of increasing the terror, though under other pretexts, should be reviewed."

Tragically, the damage had already been done and the crimes

had been committed. Now the politicians were running for cover, like rats on a sinking ship, and leaving the RAF to take all the blame. Politicians are notoriously very good at shifting the blame away from themselves and onto someone else. It has been noted that in bloody old England, the nickname of its commander changed from "Bomber" to "Butcher" Harris. Arthur Harris accepted the blame and insults with that typical, notorious British stiff upper lip. On February 19, 1946, Butcher Harris sailed into exile to South Africa. Er hatte ausgedient; he was no longer of any use.

The case of the American Eighth Air Force first blatantly lying was then replaced by self-deception. The myth that the Flying Fortresses aimed exclusively at military targets is still part of the official American legend of World War II. There were no military targets, but the media has been perpetuating this myth. No one likes to be reminded of their brutality and inhumane cruelties. The media and the textbook industry still do not realize that World War II has been over for a very long time. The public is usually willing to accept that other governments lie to their people but not our own. We should be able to hold our own government accountable to higher standards.

Mustangs chose as their targets the terrified survivors on the roads leading out of Dresden and people who were huddled on the banks of the Elbe River and on the Grosser Garten. No one has an accurate count of the women and children killed by the Mustangs. Among the many children slaughtered were choirboys of Dresden's churches. This mission of mass murder was carried out maliciously in cold blood.

There is a meadow on the left bank of the Elbe River. The people in cellars near the meadow went to the meadow to get away from the heat and the smoke. The nursing staff of the Johannstaedter Hospital carried their patients to the meadow and laid them on the grass. Thousands of crippled survivors were dragged out to the banks of the river by their nurses, where they lay in rows on the grass, waiting for the next morning to arrive. The last thing on anybody's mind was the third attack, this time by the Americans. Scores of Mustang fighters were diving down low, so low that the survivors could see the whites in the pilots' eyes. They were picking off and shooting at the bodies down below huddled on the banks of the Elbe River and anyone else who was still moving and had any sign of life. This was another example of utter inhumanity exacting utter brutality.

For five long days and six nights, Dresden kept on burning. No one could safely enter the city, because shrapnel bombs continued their destruction. The disposal of the staggering number of dead bodies gained uppermost importance in order to prevent an epidemic. Throughout the war, German authorities demonstrated great respect for the dead, enabling relatives to identify and bury their dead. Weeks after the firestorm, there was an increased urgency, because there were still thousands of unopened cellars under the smoldering ruins, and the odor of rotting flesh permeated the city.

To prevent a plague, the remaining corpses had to be disposed of quickly. The Allied POWs held in Dresden, who survived and were well enough were included in the clean-up efforts. They constructed huge funeral pyres in the Altmarkt. Layers of bodies, or what was left of the bodies, were piled on a gridiron with straw between each layer, soaked with gasoline, and then set ablaze. In this way, thousands upon thousands of bodies were cremated. The ashes were loaded into containers and buried in a graveyard outside the city. The mass grave was 25 feet wide, 15 feet deep, and 150 feet long. There was no other choice but to incinerate the corpses. The funeral pyres burned for five weeks and continued burning after the Russian troops occupied Dresden. Russian troops were still burning the charred corpses on large wooden pyres weeks after they occupied Dresden. May all the nameless dead who perished needlessly in the Dresden holocaust *never be forgotten.*

Until February 1944, Hitler strictly forbade mass graves for the burial of the bombing victims, because it painfully resembled the tragic fate of the German people. Hitler, like FDR and Churchill, was concerned about public opinion. However, the huge number of corpses forced the issue; there was no longer any choice. As stated, the corpses were cremated at the Old Market, where iron girders were built into huge grates on which about 500 corpses were stacked into a funeral pyre, drenched with gasoline, and burned.

On May 16 and 17, 1942, the RAF carried out Operation Chastise on German suburbs and provinces. Included in these raids was the destruction of the six dams across the Ruhr River, which supplied the entire area's drinking water and was also the source of the electricity. The Eder and the Moehne Dams were seriously damaged, flooding the river valleys. Twelve thousand two hundred lost their lives, as well as their homes and livestock. This operation met all the criteria of a war crime, yet no one was ever held accountable.

On March 16, 1945, the RAF destroyed 90 percent of Wuerzburg. The red crosses on top of hospitals were again totally ignored. The patients and the medical staff were incinerated. Two days later, on March 18, 1945, just days before the end of the war, the city and its inhabitants suffered further bombings by the US Air Force.

FDR died April 12, 1945. It was so indicative of Churchill that he did not attend FDR's funeral. Churchill's enthusiasm for FDR had dramatically diminished, since FDR was no longer of any use. Many believe that FDR's death might have been a blessing of sorts, because FDR was determined to implement unconditional surrender completely.

This crime of the twentieth century is even more repulsive because there has been and still is no outcry against these atrocities by Christian and non-Christian leaders alike. Where are the Christian and religious leaders? Where are their voices? Is there no world conscience? Greed and political gain dominated those who hypocritically claimed they waged a "crusade" against Germany in the name of humanity. Truth is never well received, especially by those who want to kill it with silence. Greed and profit kills the conscience.

Dresden has been called a Phoenix. This legendary bird allegedly lived several hundred years, burned itself to ashes on a pyre, and rose youthfully alive from the ashes to live another period. It has been stated that justice is the glue that holds civilized human beings, as well as civilized nations, together. As long as we honor and respect the temple of justice, mankind will always find a foundation for individual security and the opportunity for man's happiness, tranquility, and social order.

Her opa, her grandpa, called her his precious little angel. Thirteen-year-old Jackie shared her feelings:

> I don't think of myself as someone special, but do know that I have a heart and a soul. Both my heart and my soul have been crushed. I am afraid. I am afraid of life ... all because of a fire. That fire consumed my parents and left me here all alone with nothing. Perhaps it would have been better if I also were dead. It was good-bye to my parents and all my friends. All my memories went up in a flame. I wish I could change that day, and save my parents and my friends. But, that will never happen.

Since the unification of the former West and East Germany in 1989, much has been done in restoring this once great cultural center to its former glory. In the rebuilding of the Frauenkirche, more than ten thousand sandstone fragments have been carefully reassembled. This is a testament to German persistence. The Frauenkirche is Germany's largest Protestant church. It has a capacity of some two thousand people. It was ceremoniously re-consecrated on October 30, 2005. October 31 is Reformation Day. Many dignitaries and many heads of state were in attendance, including Queen Elizabeth II of England.

During the 1960s, a group of young people went from Coventry to help in rebuilding a hospital in Dresden that was completely destroyed. In June 2006, a golden cross was raised to crown the rebuilt cathedral, the Frauenkirche. It was a gift from the people of England, including the queen. The British Dresden Trust commissioned a London goldsmith whose father took part in that horrific Dresden holocaust.

People from around the world have joined and contributed generously in the efforts of rebuilding the Frauenkirche. A German American, Dr. Guenther Bloebel, winner of the Nobel Prize for Medicine in 1999, donated most of the prize money, almost a million dollars, toward the rebuilding of the Frauenkirche and the new synagogue in Dresden. If Dr. Bloebel would have patented his discovery, he would have been able to rebuild all of Dresden, not just the Frauenkirche and the synagogue. Through Friends of Dresden, Inc., which Dr. Bloebel helped to found, he has been able to raise millions of dollars for the rebuilding of historical architectural buildings. Dr. Bloebel witnessed the Dresden holocaust from about thirty miles away. Dr. Bloebel and his family were thirty miles away from Dresden. He stated that the fire was so bright that he could have read the newspaper.

It has been claimed that music heals wounds and touches the most tender human chords and sentiments. In November of 2006, the world-renowned New York Philharmonic Orchestra presented a musical gift to the people of Dresden. The musical salutation was expressly "a symbol of reconciliation." At the opening of the concert, Lorin Maazel said, "Es ist eine grosse Ehre fuer uns hier zu spielen" (It is a great honor for us to play here). Then the maestro continued on a more personal note about his mother-in-law, who survived the firestorm and also about his brother, a military physician during World War II, who attended to soldiers of different nationalities, including German.

Germany has been apologizing for its actions during the war and continues to pay huge sums of restitution. On the fiftieth anniversary of the attack, German President Richard von Weizsacker spoke of his country's guilt in Coventry, England. Conversely, when the Queen of England visited Dresden, she failed to lay a wreath at the cathedral ruins, the Frauenkirche. A rare and golden opportunity to heal wounds and build bridges was sadly missed. The typical British stiff upper lip trumped human compassion. After so many years, the time is long past due to tell the whole story, the truth and nothing but the truth, about Churchill and FDR's Valentine's present to Uncle Joe Stalin.

When will we pause long enough to allow God, the Great Architect and Creator of the universe, to speak to all of us through his creation? When will we begin to speak and act as if we were the crown of His creation in a universal environment of His truth, justice, brotherly love, relief, and freedom for all, at peace with one another? The doctrines of "an eye for an eye and a tooth for a tooth" and "forgiveness and turning the other cheek" are not synonymous; they are contradictory.

There are individuals who have accepted the fact that in war, however just the cause may be believed to be, *no one* emerges with clean hands. Saying sorry is not a sign of weakness. It is morally the right thing to do. When will those criminals responsible for these crimes be held accountable? When will Germans be compensated for all their losses or at least receive public acknowledgment? Justice shall be served when all will be equal under the law and treated without discrimination.

The archives of the Allies are slowly opening, but tons of German documents are still locked up in Virginia and East European archives. Transparency is an integral part of world peace. The more than two thousand telephone conversations between FDR and Churchill prior to the US officially entered World War II are permanently under lock and key, never be made public. Germany is still struggling under the American imposed Article 130. When will Germany be granted its deserved sovereignty and a real peace treaty rather than an armistice? Does the world insist on real peace, or will it be satisfied with continuing to only talk about it?

For decades, this catastrophe has been kept off the media radar and treated as if it never happened. Revisionists and apologists have been actively minimizing the actual death toll. They have erroneously claimed that less than twenty-five thousand innocent people died in the Dresden holocaust. That denial could only be attributable to a collective shame and guilt. The Dresden holocaust pales all atrocities committed in human history. As Kurt Vonnegut said in his book, between 250,000 and 500,000 died in "a single column of fire."

The fire-bombings of Dresden remain one of the deadliest and ethically the most problematical raids. It was a premeditated act to cause the greatest amount of destruction to the residents and the refugees fleeing from the Red Army. What turned this into mass murder is the fact that Dresden had no military significance and the war had been decided for some time.

Marshall de Bruhl relates in his book *Firestorm: Allied Airpower and the Destruction of Dresden,*

Nearly every apartment and house was crammed with relatives and friends from the east; many other residents had been ordered to take in strangers. There were makeshift campsites everywhere. Some 200,000 Silesians and east Prussians were living in tents or shacks in the Grosser Garten. The city's population was more than double its prewar size. Some estimates have put the number as high as 1.4 million ... the open spaces, gardens and parks were filled with people.

The USAF Historical Division Research Studies Institute Air University reported that "there may probably have been about 1 million people in Dresden on the night of the 13–14 February RAF attack."

The two waves of bombers, three hours apart, followed the next day by a massive daylight raid by more bombers and escort fighters, made the Dresden holocaust extremely deadly. Some of the estimates claim that perhaps as many as 50 percent of the people perished. By the end of February 1945, only 369,000 inhabitants were left in the city. To add further damage, Dresden was attacked again by American air strikes by 406 B-17s on March 2, and again by 580 B-17s on April 17, contributing to an additional 453 dead.

The incineration of the corpses at the Altmarkt, the city square, was not the only means of disposing of the dead. An English soldier reported on May 5, 1945, in the London edition of *Stars and Stripes* about the removal of the bodies,

They had to pitchfork shriveled bodies onto trucks and wagons and cart them to shallow graves on the outskirts of the city. But after two weeks of work the job became too much to cope with and they found other means to gather up the dead. They burned bodies in a great heap in the center of the city, but the most effective way, for sanitary reasons, was to take flamethrowers and burn the dead as they lay in the ruins. They would turn the flamethrowers into the houses, burn the dead and close off the entire area. This whole city is flattened. They were unable to clean up the dead lying beside roads for several weeks.

The Dresden holocaust has been described as a most cowardly attack on a civilian population, a war crime of untold proportions. It was the worst massacre and slaughter of helpless civilians in the history of the world. In addition to the great loss of human lives, a massive amount of irreplaceable art and architecture was destroyed. With all the crimes committed during World War II, the Dresden holocaust will go down in history as the day of abysmal human dishonor. If England and America shall live another thousand years, this shall be recorded as their darkest hour. May the noble principles of the Statue of Liberty and all it stands for and the foundation of the Constitution be forever reflected in man's behavior.

The Frauenkirche, with its rebuilt splendor, again welcomes the faithful from around the world. The thoughts and prayers take us back to that horrific Shrove Tuesday and Ash Wednesday, which was also Valentine's Day, in 1945. May the blessings of heaven continue to rest on all who have joined in remembrance and devotion with a deeper appreciation of life and the human attributes of brotherly love, relief, and truth. May the media stop killing the truth with deafening silence. The dead admonish us to do no less.

The ruthless hand of ignorance, driven by greed and power and viral hate, and the devastation of war have laid waste and utterly destroyed cultural centers and monuments, on which the utmost exertions of human genius have been employed. These monuments, constructed by so many celebrated artists, did not escape the cruel ravages of barbarous forces. Man's hate reached the depths of man's inhumanity to man.

The restoration of Dresden and the rebuilding of Germany is a stunning testament to the resolve of the German people. Many of the baroque treasures that were left in rubble have been painstakingly restored. The Zwinger is a grandiose baroque structure, the Semper Opera is one of the most famous opera houses in Europe, and the New Synagogue was the European building of the year in 2002.

There is an accelerating urgency to our understanding a basic technological truth: namely, if we are to be our own masters of our human destiny rather than remain helpless victims of an avalanche of continuous military destruction, we must refocus our combined energies to peaceful cooperation rather than confrontation, death, and destruction.

All the deaths, the devastation, and the destruction shall have been in vain and meaningless unless they serve and provide a lesson to the living. Only God knows how many innocent dreams and lives were buried in the Dresden holocaust. Let us remember that light is always more convincing than darkness, and so is *truth*. It is written that "the fruit of righteousness is sown in peace of them that make peace."

The Dresden holocaust on February 13 and 14, 1945, stands as one of the worst war crimes in the history of mankind, especially since there was no military reason for the firebombing of this cultural jewel. Some 722 heavy bombers of the British Royal Air Force and an additional 527 of the US Army Air Force dropped more than 3,900 tons of highly explosive and incendiary bombs, killing about half of the residents and refugees squeezed into the city. Mainstream media still downplays the actual number killed. Several reliable sources claim that between 240,000 and 500,000 suffered an excruciating death.

Victims of the Dresden Holocaust. Russian troops are still burning the charred corpses on large steel pyres in the center of the city after they overran the region. Thousands upon thousands of people were burned to death during the fire-bombings in the Dresden holocaust on February 13 and 14, 1945, even though it was virtually the end of the war. According to the English, half a million people perished.

Scars of War. The result of man's inhumanity to man. Civilians-
women, children and the old were consumed by fire.

CHAPTER 9

Ethnic Cleansing

We need to pause and reflect upon the fact that without World War I, England's determination to eliminate and destroy Germany as an industrial and commercial competitor forever, France's drive for revenge, and the unjust and brutal Versailles Treaties, Hitler and World War II and all the atrocities of the twentieth century would not have happened, and millions of lives would have been spared. The root cause of World War II is World War I and the greed reflected in the abominable Versailles Treaties.

Some fifteen to sixteen million Germans suffered brutal expulsions, deportations, and evictions from their ancestral homeland. In addition, there were some five million Volga Germans rounded up and forced into Siberian slave labor camps. They were robbed of all their earthly possessions, of their very identity, and millions were brutally and mercilessly killed. While Germany has been paying billions upon billions in restitution, no one has even considered the possibility that these sixteen million Germans were also victims of the war and are justly entitled to fair compensation for all their suffering and losses; at the very least, an apology should be forthcoming. Surely their lives and deaths matter. These Germans are the victims of expulsions, deportations, rape, starvation, and murder; they were the primary targets of all the brutality and hatred of the war after the war was over. They shall not remain nameless statistics; the injustices they were subjected to can never be reversed, nor can or will they be forgotten. They were not Nazis or criminals; they were victims of the war. Most of them were apolitical and could care less about politics. Putting all Germans or any group of people into a "collective guilt" designation dehumanizes their individual suffering and their personal identity as human beings and is legally baseless.

The euphemistic term *ethnic cleansing* is relatively new and a complete contradiction, because it implies an act of sanitation and purification of the ethnic Germans and others. Ethnic cleansing appears to whitewash a crime by associating it with the idea of "cleansing" a territory of undesirables. The term became part of our vernacular when Serbs forcibly evicted tens of thousands of Bosnian Muslims, Croats, and Serbs from their homeland in the mid-1990s. This practice was again reignited in 1999 when Serbia chose to expel the Kosovar Albanians. They represented 90 percent of the region's population. These criminal acts were finally stopped when the strategic-bombing campaign by the United States commenced. This broke Serbia's stronghold and put an end to Serbia's dreams of a Greater Serbia. Thereafter, the Kosovar Albanians returned to their homes. Expulsion, deportation, and murder are never a solution to prejudice and hatred; it is merely a revengeful human criminal reaction that is generally repaid in kind. It perpetuates negativism.

One of the earliest expulsions and relocations was the Babylonian captivity, from 586 to 538 BC. As a consequence of the Jewish uprising in Jerusalem, King Nebuchadnezzar II evicted all Jews from Judea and took them to Babylon. Five centuries later, from AD 69 to 79, during a period that is generally referred to as the Second Destruction of King

Solomon's Temple, the Roman Emperor Vespasian forcibly removed the Jews from Judea again. There is no greater loss and pain on earth than being forced from one's home and homeland.

Another reshaping of the European ethnic landscape took place when Ferdinand and Isabella of Spain expelled Jews and Moors from the Iberian Peninsula in 1492, about the time Columbus sailed the Atlantic Ocean. During the Spanish Inquisition, the Roman Catholic Church failed to force Jews to Catholicism. Louis XIV of France revoked the Edict of Nantes in 1685, ending the peaceful coexistence of Protestants and Catholics. The Protestant Huguenots were mercilessly expelled from France. The Huguenots were given a choice; they could recant their "heretic" religious convictions and publicly profess their allegiance and subjugation to Roman Catholicism. All who refused were either killed or escaped and settled in neighboring Brandenburg, Germany. Christ's only commandment of loving thy neighbor as thyself was being ignored by church politics. Confession cleanses the soul not only of an individual but also of a church.

The nineteenth and twentieth centuries saw ethnic cleansing elevated to a new level when it became an official state policy. In 1830, the US Congress passed the Indian Removal Act, which granted legal justification for the expulsion of all Indian tribes from their historical hunting grounds. These Native Americans were forced across the mighty Mississippi and the Great Plains. Disastrously, all those noble principles proclaimed in our Constitution conveniently did not apply to our Native Americans, who inhabited this continent for thousands of years; they were the original proud and brave of this great land.

The act was followed by confrontations and tragedy. The Black Hawk War of 1832 drove the Sauk and Fox tribes into Iowa and Kansas. The Trail of Tears of 1838 to 1839 expelled the Cherokee, Creek, Choctaw, and Chickasaw tribes from their ancestral homelands. The Seminole Wars of the 1830s and 1840s drove Florida Indian tribes unto the Southwest territories. The noble principles of our Constitution were, sadly, tarnished by the white man's selfish greed.

By far the most gruesome and deadliest display of man's brutality and barbaric animal-like behavior occurred during the twentieth century. World War I; the Versailles Treaty; the fire-bombing of every German city; England's starvation blockade; Hitler's brutality; FDR's insistence on Germany's unconditional surrender, which led to the total destruction of Germany; the massive expulsions of Germans from Eastern and Central Europe; and America's incarcerations of innocent people raised man's ruthless brutality to a new level.

The expulsion of some sixteen million Germans from 1944 to 1950 remains the greatest and most ruthless calamity in man's history. The ethnic Germans, die Volksdeutschen, bore the brunt of all the hate and revenge and the inhumanity of the war. Nothing so debases man as revengeful ruthlessness. While the media has perpetually devoted its attention to Auschwitz and the Jewish Holocaust, it has practiced a blackout on the other genocide against the ethnic Germans.

Professor Dr. Alfred-Maurice de Zayas, an astute lawyer and a professional historian, points out, "None of the ethnic cleansing operations come close to the monumentally brutal ethnic cleansing that Germans were subjected to." These monumental expulsions and deportations are the exhaustive study of Professor de Zayas's books, such as *Nemesis at Potsdam* and *A Terrible Revenge and the Ethnic Cleansing of the East European Germans*.

A historical overview is necessary for a better understanding of the events. The Ottoman Turks crossed the Bosporus and established themselves in Europe in 1361. They pushed into the

Balkans and left a trail of death and destruction. In 1389, they decimated the Serbian army in Kosovo. Many of the Christian Serbs were sold into slavery or killed. The young boys were taken from their parents and raised as Janissaries, soldiers of the Sultan.

Sultan Suleiman II defeated the Hungarian army on August 29, 1526, under King Louis II at Mohacs. Half of the Hungarian army and many members of the Hungarian nobility were slaughtered. To avoid getting captured, King Louis II of Hungary fled the battlefield but drowned in the swollen waters of a nearby creek. Since he left no heirs, the surviving Hungarian nobles awarded the crown of Hungary to his brother-in-law, Ferdinand of Austria, emperor of the Holy Roman Empire of the German Nation. With Ferdinand as king of Hungary, Vienna began the four-hundred-year alliance of the Hapsburg dynasty with Hungary. At that time, only a narrow strip of Hungary was not under Turkish control and rule.

A hundred and fifty years of Turkish misrule turned this entire territory into a virtual wasteland. It was inhabited by nomadic herdsmen who lived in dugouts on the plain. The land was barren; it lacked roads and bridges, a virtual no-man's-land.

The Turkish army kept advancing. Ferdinand believed himself to be a man of peace and was not willing to stop the advancing Turks, at least not until the Turks laid siege to Vienna. The siege of Vienna was lifted, and the entire territory recovered from the Turks. The decisive battle that turned the course of events around took place at the gates of Vienna on September 12, 1683, when the combined forces of the Holy Roman Empire, which included Germany and Austria, supported by Polish troops under King Jan Sobleski, and Hungarian, Venician, and Croatian contingents, defeated the army of the Ottoman Empire.

This victory put an end to the gradual encroachment of the Islamic expansion into Christian Europe. The German troops were commanded by the legendary Prince Eugene of Savoy, a Frenchmen in the service of the Hapsburg double monarchy. At present, there is a new wave of Turkish invasion into Germany and Europe with millions of Turks and their families seeking political asylum. This has again raised new cultural, security, political, economic, and religious issues.

After this territory was cleared of the Ottoman Turks, Emperor Charles VI issued an edict inviting and persuading German farmers and craftsmen throughout the southwestern German-speaking areas of Europe. The government agents succeeded in persuading people from the Palatinate, Lorraine, Alsace, Luxemburg, Wuerthenberg, Bavaria, and Austria. The prospective settlers were promised personal freedom in perpetuity, land grants, credits, and ten years of tax exemptions. Centuries later, they were rewarded by being driven away and having all their earthly possessions stolen.

At first, only German Catholics were invited and allowed to settle this region. It was not until Emperor Joseph II promulgated his Edict of Tolerance in the 1780s that Protestants were also invited. However, the villages and towns were kept religiously pure; they were either all Catholic or all Protestant towns. True religious tolerance and harmony was not practiced. This religious intolerance and schism has plagued Germany and the Germans for many centuries. This schism and differentiation gave the Catholic Germans in the Catholic Hapsburg Empire a feeling of superiority over their Protestant German neighbors. This created an emotionally and psychologically unhealthy national climate, perpetuating distrust and a lack of true national unity. The church preached religious tolerance but practiced religious exclusivity.

The new settlers first traveled to embarkation points along the Danube River, such as Ulm, Donauworth, and Regensburg, to begin their two-week river cruise on specially built barges.

Once they arrived at their destination, the wood from these barges would provide the lumber for their new homes, or it was sold for other construction purposes. Since they traveled within the empire from one end to the other, they remained subjects of the Hapsburg Dynasty. It has been observed that since none of the land these settlers received had previously belonged to anyone, no one was displaced. This happened at a time when western Germany suffered from repeated French incursions, crop failures, and ever-increasing demands from greedy landlords.

They settled along the Danube River and its tributaries. Over time, they came to be known as Danube Swabians, Dounauschwaben, even though they did not all come from the Schwabenland. They tamed the land by building levies along the great rivers to keep them from overflowing; made rivers navigable; dug many canals; drained the marshes, the swamps, and a lake; and turned it all into fertile and productive land. They introduced the steel plow and the scythe, planted orchards and vineyards, and mulberry trees along the village streets, and sustained a thriving silk industry. They grew hemp to produce linen and rope and introduced crop rotation and selective livestock breeding. They brought cuttings of Riesling grape to the region and planted vineyards in Karlowitz, at Weischetz, and at Weisskirchen in the Banat. In due time, this territory, the Danube Basin, became one of the great breadbaskets in the world. They produced 67 percent of the country's total agricultural exports and 94 percent of the hemp as well as manufactured goods, such as articles for the household, farming implements, tools, and wagons.

The Banat was a fertile and mineral-rich region located in northern Romania and included areas of Serbia and Hungary. It was settled by Germans after the Turkish devastations. It became a highly progressive area, in some way perhaps even more so than Germany proper. However, at the end of World War II, it was shamefully devastated and depopulated, with the blessings of the victorious Allies. Germans were forced into extermination and starvation camps. More than 240,000 died a torturous death, part of Tito's ethnic-cleansing program. Tito was honored at Buckingham Palace by Queen Elisabeth II for his service to England.

The new settlers in this region were not only German farmers but also demobilized soldiers from Prince Eugene's army; later, prisoners from the Seven Year's War as well as Italians and Spaniards were settled in this region. The town Betschkerek was originally called New Barcelona. Germans drained the swamps and turned them into fertile, arable fields. Mathias Hammer found coal near Steierdorf, which started again the coal mines around Reschitz, Steierdorf, Anina, and Orawitza. These coal mines had been known already to the Romans. Some of the silver coins of the monarchy were coined with silver mined from this region.

Already in 1788, Empress Maria Theresia yielded to Hungarian demands and handed the Banat over to the administration of Hungary. Until then, the Banat had been imperial territory. With that move, the "magyarization" of the Banat Germans began. The Hungarian language became the language of instruction in all German elementary schools. Germans became victims of magyarization. As a result of the Versailles Treaties in 1919, the Banat was divided up among Romania, Yugoslavia, and Hungary. An additional burden to the Germans was that they were unfairly taxed at a higher rate.

The Germans established many farming villages and designed and laid-out many cities. In 1880, almost 40 percent of the population of Budapest was German. Hungary is greatly indebted to its Danube Swabians. Engineers and architects like Haussmann, Emmerich, Steindel, Lechner, and Hild laid out the city, its main streets, and the square. They designed the parliament buildings, the National Theater, the opera house, the Millennium Monument, and the beautiful bridges spanning the Danube River. Many Danube Schwabians, Donauschwaben, achieved lasting international renown, such as Franz Liszt and Joseph Pulitzer.

To restore peace and harmony within Hungary, Emperor Franz Joseph agreed to an Ausgleich (*equalization*) in 1867, in which the Hungarian half of the dual monarchy became virtually independent. This was the beginning of the end of the double monarchy. One of the results of this Ausgleich was that henceforth Hungarian, rather than German, became the official language of communication. Beginning in 1905, children in towns that were 100 percent German, Croatian, or Serbian were taught only in Hungarian. This was part of the drive to magyarize non-Hungarians. There was great pressure put on the 52 percent of the population of Hungary who were not Magyars to adopt Hungarian names. No one was able to get a government job or represent Hungary in the Olympic Games unless he or she had a Hungarian name and thus appeared to be Hungarian. The soccer championship of 1954, between Germany and Hungary, included several Danube Swabians. Supp Posipal played for Hamburg SV; Puskas, Kocsis, and Hidegkutti played for Hungary. Prior to the magyarization, their German names were Purzeld, Wagner, and Kaltenbrunner. This was part of a movement to display and showcase Hungarian accomplishments and national pride.

Through the centuries, the Danube Swabians maintained their language, which is a unique dialect similar to the German spoken by the Amish in America. They preserved their culture and promoted their colorful heritage, as they also contributed greatly to the agricultural, commercial, and industrial success of the country. They established schools and promoted and supported education. Every town had a school. The Germans in Hungary, as they have been in every other country, were positive, law-abiding, upright, and contributing members of the society.

Then something cataclysmic happened. The Trianon Treaty amputated two-thirds of Hungary's territory; it was now only a shadow of its former self. The Allies arbitrarily created Czechoslovakia, Romania, and Yugoslavia from the land it took from Hungary, effectively destroying the Austro-Hungarian Empire. Yugoslavia was created to reward the Serbs for their role in starting World War I. Redrawing the European map was Churchill's method of controlling Europe and beyond.

These newly drawn borders also affected the Danube Swabians, as they now became residents of these three countries. Because of these new borders, some 700,000 Danube Swabians were still part of Hungary, 350,000 were now Romanians, and more than 600,000 became the German minority of the artificially created Yugoslavia. The new Yugoslavia, which was governed by brutal force, had seven ethnic and five religious faiths and as a result was considered politically extremely volatile.

The new borders created difficulties that did not exist before. In some towns, the borders ran right through the middle of the town. As a result, some of the people were no longer able to attend their former parish church, nor were they able to send their children to the same school as before. This made life much more complicated, and it was a total mockery of Woodrow Wilson's principle of self-determination. Self-determination became only a good-sounding, empty political propaganda slogan.

All the traditional and historic tranquility and harmony between the Germans, the Serbs, the Croats, and the Hungarians totally vanished in 1941 when Hitler overran this territory. War came to the Danube Swabians without any input on their part. They became the victims of this war that they wanted no part of. The young and not-so-young men were conscripted into the German army. They became part of the thousands of Volksdeutsche missing in action.

In October 1944, the Soviet troops marched in, and life changed drastically. They raped German women from eight to eighty, and many women were gang raped and then left to die. In December 1944, women from seventeen to thirty-two were rounded up and sent to Siberia as slave laborers. When the Soviet troops left, Tito and his partisans took over; that was when life really became a living hell.

Anna Welker, née Gussmann, remembers her childhood in Tito's Yugoslavia. On October 2, 1944, Anna's family and all the families of Neu-Schowe were ruthlessly driven out of their homes at gunpoint. With gunfire all around, they were marched out of town as it got dark. They heard the dogs howling from their empty homes. It was an eerie feeling of foreboding. At about midnight, the townspeople reached Stepanovicevo. There, they were crowded into a three-story school building. On December 6, St. Nicholas Day, the march continued until they came to Tito's extermination camp, Jarek.

In Jarek, the Gussmanns were housed in a three-room house with dirt floors and whitewashed walls. The house was void of all furniture, but on the wall hung a framed verse. Their bedding consisted of straw on the floor along both sides of the room, with a path down the middle. The nine members of Anna's family, plus eight other people, were crowded into that room—seventeen people in one room. The kitchen in the middle was empty, and the small room in the back had seven people in it. Nine of the twenty-four people were children. Ten of the original people in the house died, including three of the children. Four of Anna's family members died.

In January 1945, right after her twenty-first birthday,

Anna's cousin Elisabetha Filippi was torn from her three-year-old daughter Liselotte and shipped to the Soviet Union, where she was forced to work in coal mines for nearly five years.

In the spring of 1945, many of the younger people were taken from Jarek and placed into labor camps. Children ten and older were put to work in the fields around Jarek. What was served as food was terrible and without salt. They had no soap to keep clean, and lice and fleas were totally out of control. The people started to die in increasingly greater numbers.

Anna recalls,

> My little sister Gerhild started to walk in Jarek. My grandfather found a right sandal and a left shoe that fit her. My aunt Elisabetha sewed a dress for her by hand. Toward the end of May, my sister came down with a high fever and diarrhea. My aunt carried her up and down the path in our room. On June 3, 1945, my darling sister Gerhild died. My grandfather found enough wood to make her a coffin. I looked at her in that box, her rosy cheeks turned pale. I had to touch her. To my surprise, her once soft cheeks felt cold and solid. For several weeks, I could not get rid of that feeling.
>
> Shortly after my sister died, my aunt Elisabetha was taken away to a labor camp. Liselotte was now in the care of her great-grandparents. The fleas pestered Liselotte a great deal at bedtime and she screamed "the fleas, the fleas" until she fell asleep. Now that I didn't have a sister any more, I turned my affection towards Liselotte. When I could find something edible, while out at work, I shared it with her.

Evenings we talked mostly about food. People said that if they got out of this hell hole alive, they would spend their money on food. We sang hymns at night before we went to sleep. My grandmother often said to my grandfather that if they survived this ordeal they would join their son Adam in Cleveland, Ohio.

Beginning August my grandmother Luisa took ill. She lost control of her bowels and didn't wish to be among us in the room. She asked to have a bed made in the stall. We put a pile of straw on the floor of the stall to serve as her bed. Mother and I took turns looking in on her during the daytime, but at night she was all alone. In the morning of August 8, 1945, we found grandmother had passed away. The people in the room next to the stall said that she called for my mother all night. My mother and her friend, Elisabetha Lick took one of grandmother's skirts apart and sewed her body up in it.

Beginning September, Katherina Steinmetz, an elderly woman who was in the room with us, got diarrhea. She didn't want to go to the stall where my grandmother died and she didn't want to stay with us. In the yard stood a one room house and that is where she wanted to go. We took turns caring for her. I remember looking in on her when she asked for water. Her voice was gone but I could read her lips. I lifted her head and tried to give her some water, but the water ran out on both sides of her mouth. Within an hour she died.

When Katherina's few belongings were divided, my grandfather asked for her eye glasses. Grandfather didn't go to work that day because he fell ill. He came down with a high fever and was out of his mind for a week. Friedrich Schnur died on September 19, 1945. His body was laid out in the one room house on a bench. Grandmother asked me to come and say good-bye to grandfather before she covered his face.

My grandmother Elisabetha and Liselotte were suffering from malaria. Liselotte sometimes sat for hours staring at the wall. When grandmother's body shook from malaria, I sat on her to calm down the shaking. Around the 10th of October I became very sick. By now the back room was less crowded, so my mother asked if I could stay there. On October 19, 1945, my mother called me to say good-bye to my grandmother. By the time I struggled to my feet, it was too late. I just saw how the men closed the gate behind them. Now I had no more grandparents that loved me and whom I loved so much.

Towards the end of October, we received word that my aunt was brought back from the labor camp and that she was very sick. I went to get her and she could hardly walk. She had to lean on me for support. When we came home, my aunt laid down on the straw and did not get up for weeks. When she was better again she could not walk because she could not straighten her legs. The main thing was that the four of us were together again.

The winter of 1945/46 was very hard for all of us. There was no fuel to heat with and the food was worse than ever. My mother had traded away her wedding band, her earrings and my earrings for food. Now we had nothing left to trade. Mother suffered from an undiagnosed, disabling illness and therefore we remained in Jarek. People who were able to work, got out of Jarek from time to time and thus were able to get some food.

On April 17, 1946, Jarek was closed and the remaining survivors were transported in boxcars to Kruschevlje near the Hungarian border. Life in Kruschevlje was better than in Jarek. I didn't have to go to work there and from time to time I could sneak out at night and beg for food. Even while life was a little better, I became very sick. I had such a craving for an onion. Somehow my aunt got me an onion and after eating that whole onion I got back on my feet. Liselotte was taken from us as an orphan. The communists gathered the children to form an orphanage so they could ask for foreign aid. Liselotte was in the neighboring camp of Gakovo. With the help of Michael Teschner, my aunt presented herself as Liselotte's mother and we got her back at Christmas 1946.

My uncle Adam Schnur, who came to Cleveland, Ohio, in 1929 was able to get a couple of packages to us with food and clothes. In spring of 1947 my uncle sent $200.00 to a woman who was able and free to give it to us. My aunt and I snuck out of the camp at night to get the money.

That amounted to 13,000 dinars. We paid 1,000 dinars per person to get us out of Kruschelje. On May 2, 1947, we left the camp. We made our way through Hungary to Austria, through the Russian, English and American zones in Austria. We reached my father, Andreas, on September 7, 1947, in Munich, Germany. Liselotte Filippi was reunited with her mother Elisabetha in November 1949 and with her father in 1950.

Frank Engelmann, a professional educator, was a highly respected and caring teacher of German at a renowned high school in Ohio. He shared his experiences in Tito's Yugoslavia. His family settled in Novoselo (Neudorf) in the state of Batschka at the behest of the Austrian empress, Maria Theresia. This was all part of the Austro-Hungarian Empire.

Frank recalled that his father was drafted into the Yugoslav army, just before the German takeover and as a result ended up being a German POW in Augsburg, where he had to work in the Messerschmidt aircraft plant. Because the family had traveled extensively during his younger years, his dad was fluent in several languages, including German, Portuguese, Hungarian, and Serbo-Croatian and knew some Italian. Through his contacts with Ukrainian coworkers, he could learn Russian rather quickly, because it too is a Slavic language and he already knew Serbo-Croatian. As an interpreter for the Ukrainians, he gained a higher status among the workers. He sent for his family and secured an apartment for the his family. He stated,

Due to the incessant bombing of the Messerschmidt works, my parents decided to escape on their uncle's riverboat, which carried us down the Danube River and past Novoselo.

We were lucky to escape, but fell into the claws of Tito's partisans. After a joyful reunion with my grandparents and a few weeks of relative quiet, the war was declared over and the partisans ran roughshod over us unarmed civilians.

On Christmas day, partisans ordered all of us out of our homes. In the village square they killed the town policeman, the doctor and his son, and the mayor. After severely beating the village priests, they barked their orders. We were to go home, pack what we could carry, and report the next morning to the village square. House keys were to be left in the door locks, and no cameras were permitted on anyone. Pictures and any documentation of Tito's atrocities was strictly verboten.

After waiting fearfully throughout the night, the next of many tragedies followed, namely the separation of the families. The military-aged men were marched out of town to the hemp factory, where they were interrogated and tortured for days without food and water. Those that survived had to run to the next town, followed by partisans on horseback. Those that could not keep up were shot and their bodies were dumped into the Danube River. Dad survived the trek to the planned building site of an airport, run by the Russians. This was hard manual labor. Dad used his knowledge of Russian to ingratiate himself with the Red Army supervisors. Later he jumped on a train, loaded with Russian soldiers, and escaped.

Able-bodied women, and those without small children were loaded onto trains and shipped to Russia as an expression of gratitude to Stalin for his help to Tito. The screaming and crying of the family members was overwhelming. Of the ninety eight people shipped away, as human restitution, only four survived, one of them was my aunt Johanna, who was enslaved for ten years.

The partisans feared no resistance, since they guarded only children, old people and women with young children. They were given "Carte blanche" to exterminate us by Churchill's own decree at Yalta: "All Germans living outside of the new German borders must be eliminated."

The bestiality of the partisans became more gruesome on our trek to Jarek. Most of our people had to walk, but the old, infirm and mothers with babies were permitted to ride on horse drawn wagons. Stragglers were picked up by empty wagons, which slowed down until they were out of sight, whereupon we heard gunfire. After a while the wagons appeared again, but empty. The guards on horseback were goading more of the old people to ride on the death wagon, but no one accepted their invitation.

Due to over work, undernourishment and disease, we lost a third of our village population. We were crowded together into small houses, twenty to thirty in a house. Lice and fleas plagued us. To wear us down, we were forced to work from dawn to dusk. What they called food was watered down barley soup and maize cakes made from roughly ground cow corn, which would tear up one's insides. The old people died first. They lost their desire to live; most contracted dysentery, dehydrated and died. The children without parents died next.

I survived because my grandmother would steal food from surrounding farms while on work detail. She would show the older children where to sneak through the barbed wire fence and beg for food. The guards would not shoot us, but locked us up in dark cellars when we were caught.

After some time, the partisans turned Jarek into a camp for orphans, to indoctrinate them into becoming Yugoslavs. The rest of us were moved to Gakovo, from where we escaped, only to be caught and taken to a smaller, more secure camp. By 1948 the camp commanders realized the value of their prisoners as hired-out laborers, whose services could and were sold for a price. They saw to it that fewer people died. They also were known to accept bribes.

As with German camps during the war, the Red Cross had access and was permitted to inspect camps to assess casualties. However, Tito and his partisans demanded a condition to this practice. They had to be notified beforehand before the inspection team was to arrive.

The camp was emptied on inspection day. We were marched into the woods far away from the camp. Guns were pointed at us and we had to remain totally silent until word came that the Red Cross inspectors had left. Seeing nothing and no one, they had nothing to report, and Tito kept receiving his foreign aid. Actually, enough people had escaped and brought the news of our Holocaust to the West, but their report was ignored. The media was not interested.

In time of our most dire need, when mom was pregnant with her third child, grandmother found a compassionate Hungarian family, who sent letters to our American relatives. They sent us money, American cigarettes and coffee. In a black-market economy, coffee and cigarettes were worth their weight in gold.

Eventually Oma was able to save enough to be able to bribe the commandant to let us go. Being fluent in English, she played her trump card, claiming she was American. It would be prudent for the commandant to play ball, because her American relatives knew where she was. We were released unscathed; we were even given a wagon and an escort to the border.

Churchill had ordered it, Tito and Moshe Pilade planned it, and Vid Dodic and the partisans carried out the death sentences. The stories remained the same for thousands of victims.

The root cause of these atrocities can be traced back to World War I and the Versailles Treaty, the greed and inhumanity of the victors. By design, World War I brought the destruction and mutilation of the Hapsburg Austro-Hungarian Empire, the German Empire, the Russian Empire, the Ottoman Empire, and ultimately the British Empire. The creation of a dozen or so small, allegedly "national" states, which were in reality multinational states, contributed greatly to the state-sponsored ethnic cleansing. Rhetoric was one thing and reality something completely different.

The leaders of the victorious powers gave their approval and consent to the horrendous expulsions, deportations, and evictions at the Yalta and Potsdam Conferences in February and July of 1945. Furthermore, they also agreed to amputate major German-inhabited territories, such as East Prussia, Eastern Pomerania, Danzig, Eastern Brandenburg, and Silesia. Furthermore, they also agreed to expel more than 3.5 million Sudeten Germans from their ancestral homeland, the mountainous regions of Bohemia and Moravia. A similar agreement was passed relative to the German minority in Hungary, Romania, and Yugoslavia. These were ill-conceived agreements, without any concern or consideration for the German minorities. The prevailing attitude was that the Germans got what they deserved, which is morally and legally totally unacceptable.

A Terrible Revenge—The Ethnic Cleansing of the East European Germans, 1944–1950 by Alfred Maurice de Zayas is a groundbreaking scholarly treatment of the fate of fifteen to sixteen million Germans. Included in his book are many personal accounts of the victims who miraculously survived.

The climax of the brutal ethnic cleansing came at the end and following World War II, when fifteen to sixteen million Germans were ruthlessly expelled from their ancestral homeland in Eastern and Central Europe. Although the Germans were the main target and victims of this terror, Hungarians were also tragically subjected to Edvard Benes's ethnic cleansing and ordered out of the newly founded Czechoslovakia. Over 200,000 were driven across the frozen Danube River in the middle of a very cold winter without proper clothing.

The question has been raised: Is ethnic cleansing ever legal and by whose laws? The right not to be expelled from one's homeland is a fundamental human right. Dr. Alfred M. de Zayas was the secretary of the United Nations Human Rights Committee. He maintains that, according to international law, mass expulsions are doubly illegal. It gives rise to a state's responsibilities, as well as personal criminal liabilities. If laws are to be meaningful, they have to be consistent, nondiscriminatory, and nonselective in their application.

Dr. de Zayas points out that at the Nuremberg tribunal several German Nazi leaders were condemned and executed for "war crimes" and "crimes against humanity" in connection with the expulsions at the beginning of the war of one million Poles from Warthegau in 1940 and around 105,000 Frenchmen from Alsace. He asks the critical question, "How much more of a crime was the expulsion of fifteen times as many Germans from their homelands in eastern and southern Europe?" He also questions sending far more than a million Germans as "reparation in kind" to Siberia into Uncle Joe Stalin's slave-labor camps. It appears that justice at Nuremberg was not only not blind but furthermore discriminatory in its application. Most of the German victims who were sent to Siberia never returned or were never heard of again. It was a virtual death sentence. They vanished from the surface of the earth. Justice for millions of victims was tragically denied.

In the summer of 1945, the Big Three, consisting of Josef Stalin, Henry S. Truman, and Clement R. Attlee met at Potsdam to divide the spoils of war and pass judgment about "collective punishment" for the German people for their alleged transgressions. They sanctioned the cruel and ruthless ethnic cleansing, which totally disregarded the principles proclaimed in the Atlantic Charter. The deportations had a sanctimonious proviso that the expulsions be "orderly and humane." That is a contradiction in terms, because an expulsion is never orderly and humane.

There is no such a thing as a humane transfer of a population; that is a huge contradiction of terms. The loss of one's homeland is and can never be humane. Expulsion is primarily an act promulgated by racism and terror. It is a crime and can never be anything else, nor can it be justified.

Therefore, the Czechoslovakian Benes Decrees, the Yugoslav AVNOJ decisions, and the Polish Bierut Decrees fall short of acceptable international and European minimum standards of human rights. They should be internationally condemned as being totally dishonest. These expulsions violated international law and treaty obligations protecting minority rights, which were accepted by Poland, the new Czechoslovakia, Yugoslavia, and Hungary in 1919.

The international military tribunal at Nuremberg that condemned the expulsions by the Nazis of Poles and Frenchmen condoned the far greater crimes of expulsions of millions of Germans. Those who were expelled by the Nazis could return home after 1945; the Germans were not given the same opportunity. Chancellor Konrad Adenauer wrote, "Misdeeds have been committed loathsome enough to stand alongside those committed by the German National Socialists."

For centuries, the ethnic Germans enjoyed friendly, harmonious, and mutually beneficial relations with all their neighbors. They had their festivals, celebrated weddings and baptisms, gave thanks for the bountiful harvest, and enjoyed life with its many joys and sorrows. They cultivated the land and contributed greatly to the industrial and commercial output of the country. They all lived peacefully in a multiethnic state.

Perhaps we need to remind ourselves, were it not for the Germans, who liberated this huge virtual wasteland from the Ottoman Turkish Empire, there might still be an Ottoman Turkish Empire in Europe but no Yugoslavia, Romania, or Hungary. It is the legacy of the Germans who bestowed this land to those who centuries later refused to share this part of the earth with them. Even though these states were created or reshaped upon the principle of national self-determination, tragically this same principle of self-determination was regrettably denied to millions of Germans and to thousands of Hungarians.

The Western media has been accused of managing the news to reflect favorably on some events and groups while denigrating or ignoring others. There is a strong tendency to be politically correct, hence the news seems to be lacking balance and appears skewed with only partial information or total omissions. The total silence on the deportations, expulsions, rapes, and murders are just one example of the media attempting to be politically correct rather than provide accurate and unbiased news.

The absurdities and injustices of the Treaties of Versailles, St. Germain, and Trianon of 1919, the pan-Slavic "Drang nach dem Westen," Stalin's power politics, the imperial expansion of the West, and England's determination to destroy Germany forever as an industrial and commercial competitor have all contributed to the multitude of human rights violations. These are crimes against humanity. The suffering of millions of innocent victims cannot and never will be dismissed or killed with silence. This silence, in and by itself, constitutes a crime against humanity. Dr. de Zayas stated that the discrimination against German victims in the media, in textbooks, in museums, and in political dialogue is fundamentally an assault against basic norms of human rights and dignity. Even downplaying these crimes violates the honor and reputation of the victims.

At the Yalta Conference on February 11, 1945, Stalin, Churchill, and FDR signed an agreement, authorizing the deportations of millions of ethnic Germans from Poland, the new Czechoslovakia, Romania, Yugoslavia, Hungary, and the Reich, including East Prussia, Pomerania, and Silesia. Millions were transported to the Soviet Union as some kind of living reparations. Expulsions and deportations to forced labor camps have been defined as war crimes and crimes against humanity. This ethnic cleansing occurred mostly after the end of the war as some kind of collective punishment.

In the fall of 1944, Tito and his Anti-Fascist Council met

at Jaice in Bosnia and passed a resolution containing three main points. After the forced establishment of Yugoslavia, the ethnic German minority was to be disposed of and deprived of all human rights, including the right to live, just as Kaufman demanded. This was to be accomplished through mass liquidation, mass deportations, and extermination through starvation and forced slave labor in concentration camps. Tito told the world what crimes he and his willing executioners were going to commit, and the world did nothing, tacitly condoning his crimes. As stated earlier, Tito even received an official reception with Queen Elizabeth II in London for his sinister service to the crown.

Tito established some thirty-two death camps in Yugoslavia. Survivors have organized conferences and come together at meetings to remember the hundreds of thousands in Tito's extermination and starvation program. These survivors share their personal experiences, often deeply emotional recollections, their suffering, and what they saw, heard, and experienced. These atrocities will not and cannot be forgotten, nor will they be shoved under the carpet, as if their suffering, torture, and deaths did not matter. The conscience of the world will remember and never forget.

Gakovo was one of many German Catholic towns that prospered for centuries. It was also turned into one of Tito's death camps. One morning, all three thousand residents were ordered to report to the town's square. After all reported, they were surrounded by heavily armed guards. A fence was erected surrounding the town, with armed guards stationed all along the perimeter; it was turned into one of many concentration camps. The healthier younger adults were herded and pushed into cattle cars and shipped to Siberia as slave labor. This was a present from Tito to Stalin. Daily, thousands continued to arrive in Gakovo in cattle cars from other towns. At times, there were more than twenty-one thousand German prisoners in Gakovo destined to be killed.

Tito's brutality and the ruthless torture by his willing executioners knew no limits. Death by unspeakable torture became the norm. The victim's hands were tied with wire that cut deep into their skin and flesh. They were herded into buildings where they were brutally beaten and slaughtered by totally inebriated partisans. They took turns stabbing their victims to death, while relishing their moans and screams. Partisankas (female partisans) took special delight in cutting off the genitals from their male victims while they still showed signs of life. The slaughter would continue into the wee morning hours. After the tormenters had slaughtered and beaten their victims into an unrecognizable mass, the torturers themselves would slump onto the blood-soaked floor in a drunken, unconscious stupor. Tito was very generous with Vodka and Sligovitz, keeping his willing executioners intoxicated. Only drunken wild savages could commit such atrocities.

Tens of thousands were brutally slaughtered, murdered, and buried in unmarked mass graves that they were forced to dig before they were riddled with bullets. They were ordered to hand over all their earthly belongings—everything they owned. Women had their earrings ripped out of their ears. Anyone who hesitated or dared to refuse was severely beaten and made an example of. They were forced to completely undress before they were shot. Used clothing full of bullet holes did not sell well on the black market. Many were buried in shallow graves; during the spring thaw, hands, legs, and skulls would stick out of the ground.

For centuries, the German minority had been upright, law-abiding citizens. They were proud of their colorful heritage and their many contributions to their country, which they loved. Following the war, they were summarily classified as

Germans and as traitors. The Communist puppet regimes used the victims being German as sole justification for their expropriation, deportation, and extermination.

The majority of the Germans were farmers, toiling on the land, minding their own business, and being acutely politically naïve—apolitical. The surviving victims of Tito's death camps have come together to share their experiences, their personal stories, and their suffering, which left so many deep physical and emotional scars of this bloody bondage. Perhaps the present-day leaders of the states that were part of this fabricated former Yugoslavia will apologize, acknowledge the guilt of these atrocities, and offer reasonable restitution. Germany has been apologizing and paying billions in restitution; the time is long overdue for others to do likewise.

In May 2017, Serbian Prime Minister Alexsander Vucic unveiled a memorial dedicated to the hundreds of thousands of Germans, Donauschwaben, who were abused, expelled, raped and murdered in the former Yugoslavia at the end and following World War II. Inaugurating the memorial in Jarek, Vucic stated that "Only through respect for the foreign victims will we have the right to demand respect and rights for our own victims." These atrocities were kept off the radar in the former Yugoslavia. German Chancellor Angela Merkel personally advocated this memorial to Tito's German victims.

Barbara Minster was fifteen when the fences suddenly encircled her town on November 23, 1944. Her family, like all her neighbors, had lived there for centuries. They had no intentions of leaving their hometown; this was the home they knew and loved. Because Minster spoke some Serbian, she was granted some modest privileges. She painfully recalled, "They slashed the throat of my best girlfriend, because she had hidden some items in the hems of her clothes. But they let me wipe her neck and her wrists and kind of say good-bye." These ethnic

Germans had a choice, either stay and suffer a slow death of starvation or risk the dangers of escaping. In 1947, Barbara Minster and her family escaped. These were war crimes and crimes against humanity, and yet no one raised a finger and the media kept and still is keeping totally silent. The media has an obligation to talk about these crimes and expose the brutality of Tito's death camps.

Hans Kopp was nine years old when he witnessed how partisans dragged his grandmother, Apollonia Oeffler, out of the house in Gakovo a few days before Christmas. On Christmas Eve, she came back to her family after being raped multiple times and, because she fought off her tormentors, she was beaten beyond recognition. She died that Christmas Eve surrounded by those who loved her. Downplaying these crimes is dishonoring the dignity and honor of all these victims and tacitly approving the crimes. After surviving two years in Tito's death camp, Hans and his family escaped. When and where, if ever, will these criminals be held accountable?

Danube Schwabian towns like Gakovo and Rudolfsgrad were designated as concentration camps by Tito's adviser Moshe Pijade. He is credited with the systematic extermination of the Danube Swabians, the ethnic German minority. The German homes had been stripped of all furniture and valuables. All money, gold, and jewelry was stolen. They had to sleep on straw-covered floors, thirty to a room. Often, there was only space enough for them to sleep standing. There was no fuel for heat; after all, why waste heat for dead and dying bodies?

They were able to stay alive by sneaking out of the camp at night at the risk of getting shot. They begged for food from the local Serbs and Hungarians, former neighbors who were compassionate people and sympathetic to their plight. These were good and generous people. Had these former neighbors not been so generous, no one would have survived Tito's death camps. And most likely, no one would have ever known anything about these crimes.

After the partisans took over a town and turned it into a concentration camp, they would select the most beautiful young German women, preferably blondes, who were then torn from their families and taken to a compound at Pancevo, across the river from Belgrade. They were kept like caged animals to satisfy the sexual lusts of Tito's elite. They were assaulted by foul-smelling savages. If they resisted, they were shot. In a short time, they were all infected with syphilis. To stop the spread of syphilis, the remaining 150 women were taken to a pasture, ordered to undress, shot to death, and buried in unmarked mass graves.

On October 1, 1945, more than eight thousand people in Sekic were assembled—mothers with small children, the sick, the elderly, invalids, and cripples. All were shipped to the extermination and death camps at Gakovo, Krushevlje, and Radjica, and thousands starved to death. Children were housed separately; they were severely beaten when they tried to return to their mothers. Little children behind barbed wires were a horrifying sight; they were forced to look into the eyes of death. Angst, fear, and confusion were reflected in their eyes.

In addition to the starvation and typhoid fever, the partisans engaged in large-scale executions of German men; that horror began during the night of October 22, 1944. Executions took place in Sarcha, Deutsch-Zerne, the Banat, and the Batschka. A liquidation commando rounded up about 350 men in Filipovo on October 25 and shot 240 men, execution style. This genocide against the German minority was never worthy of the evening news or even the last page of the daily newspaper.

Feketic had around six thousand Hungarian and two thousand German residents. Justina Hoffmann recalls that on October 7, 1944, Russian troops marched into their town.

A few days later, the local partisans took control. Businesses and homes were totally looted. Women and girls were brutally raped, even during the daytime, while a Russian soldier stood guard outside the house. To keep the women from screaming for help, a rag was stuffed into their mouths. Because Sofia Dietrich refused to divulge her daughter's hiding place, she was beaten terribly and permanently disfigured. These were the actions not of men or honorable soldiers but of wild, out-of-control savages.

The names of German towns like Gakovo, Rudolfsgrad, Jarek, Mitrovica, Molidorf, Kruschevlje, and others will remain burned into the memories of Danube Swabian survivors and their descendants forever. Annual memorial services are being held in Cleveland, Philadelphia, Toronto, and as far away as Brazil. May those who perished and their tortures never be forgotten. The Germans were herded like cattle and forced into cattle cars like sardines, without any sanitary facilities and then sent to the Gakovo death camp, which was near the Hungarian border. At times, Gakovo had as many as twenty-one thousand prisoners destined for a torturous death.

Many were taken to the starvation death camp in Jarek, Batschka. There were over twenty-five thousand children and old people in this camp. Young and old were dying in great numbers. The Red Cross would have come to aid starving children, but they were intentionally not informed and were not allowed to come into the camp. There is still a media blackout on this part of our history. Half a million people were wiped off the former Yugoslavia's history. These victims lost their lives, their identities, and their history, as if they never even existed.

After the deaths of the adults, the parents and grandparents, there remained some forty thousand orphaned German children. They were shipped to Communist homes for children throughout Yugoslavia and given Slavic names.

There is no equal to the ruthless brutality of Tito and his willing executioners. This butcher ordered all Germans in Yugoslavia to be exterminated, to be shipped to Siberian slave-labor camps, or to be carted off into Tito's death camps, where they were destined to starve to death. In these death camps, they were kept without sufficient food, supplies, doctors, or medicine. Hundreds of thousands suffered an excruciating death at the hands of Tito and his inebriated executioners. Only intoxicated animals with a mob mentality could possibly commit such horrendous atrocities. Nicolai Tolstoy wrote an exhaustive and scholarly book, *The Minister and the Massacre*, in which he describes Tito's crimes and English intrigues, as well as the many human rights violations. There has been a blackout about these crimes for far too long. Genocide is a crime against humanity and extremely reprehensible. Genocide is a crime; ethnic cleansing is genocide.

Katherine Flitz was only nine when she witnessed people getting shot and tortured and children being separated from their families. Her mother died of typhoid fever. Because of a total lack of medical attention, thousands died of typhoid fever. She spent three years in the death camp at Gakovo before she was able to escape with an aunt and an uncle. Her sister escaped with another aunt. These unfortunate victims attempted to escape at the risk of getting shot. Some escapees were caught and punished or shot. Some guards would accept bribes to lead them to the Hungarian border and then double-cross them. Many of the Germans would end up back in the camp.

To add insult to injury, when Tito died, he was praised by the Western media as the last of the great Allied heroes. There was absolutely no mention of his crimes. This mass murderer was never held accountable for his crimes. When lust for power and lust for wealth marry, tragedy is certain to be a wedding guest. Will justice ever or finally be served, or will intrigue, murder, lies, and deceptions continue to prevail?

Many of these partisans ended up moving to Germany for a better life and many also migrated to America. They have not been held accountable for their crimes in any court of law, because only Germans can be tried for war crimes. That is such a travesty of and a total contradiction to justice; that is no justice at all. Some of these criminals even bragged about committing murder. One immigrant, a former partisan, settled in Kent, Ohio. He went by the name of Vicmeg. He bragged that he killed hundreds, may be thousands, of Germans. He explained that he would hit the Germans with a steel ball attached to a short rope at the bottom of their skulls and break their necks. He bragged that he would never be held accountable for his murderous crimes and that no American court would ever touch him. He was spitting into the face of justice. The American and world legal system has failed, when criminals brag about getting away with mass murder.

For decades, Hungarian officials placed the cause of all the brutality of the expulsions and deportations on the Big Three Allied leaders ordering all that terror against the ethnic Germans, vehemently denying the fact that their Communist puppet government requested the authority for the expulsions. In part, it was obeying Stalin's orders and in part also the push for the magyarization of Hungary. There was a large concentration camp in Budapest, run by the Hungarian Communists, where many Donauschwabens were murdered. There are numerous survivors of all the concentration camps, who suffered excruciating torture, nursing the unchristian wish that these criminals would forever suffer and burn in hell for ordering and authorizing the ethnic cleansing and reparation in human slavery.

Were these decisions the result of political pressure, ignorance, and indifference to the consequences of their actions, sentiments of revenge, or a misguided sense of justice that imposed this horrific fate on millions of innocent human beings, minding their own business and harming no one? These decisions unleashed the most grievous violations of human rights.

Theresia Wagner, née Redling, recalls her childhood in Marko, Hungary. It was a beautiful small farming village near Veszprem. Of the 801 residents, 703 were German. Life was good. They joyfully celebrated their annual Schuetzenfest, weddings, baptisms, Christmas, Sylvester, and Easter and mourned their losses at funerals. Life in Marko and all other German towns centered around their daily chores, church, and various social functions.

They faithfully perpetuated their colorful German heritage in language, song, music, dance, and various other cultural activities. They shared their joys and their sorrows. One of the many activities was harvesting poppy seeds and baking Mohnstrudel. The dried poppy shells were steeped in hot water, and the tea derived would be used as a narcotic against pain and to help in putting sick and crying children to sleep. Theresia also remembers how her father in springtime, after working in the fields, would bring home sweet, wild strawberries for the children.

This tranquil lifestyle, as they knew it for centuries, changed abruptly. Theresia recalls how, on March 15, 1945, "an old man came to warn us that the Russians are coming, the Russians are coming." They hurried to their summer homes in the vineyards to hide from the Russian soldiers. When they arrived, they found that the people from Veszperm had already forced their way into the huts. So they went to the hayloft to sleep.

The reputation for ruthless brutality of the Russian soldiers preceded their arrival. The girls were rightfully afraid of being raped, thus they dressed like old women and hid in the hay.

The Russian soldiers pushed their sabers into the hay to find hiding girls. They did not care if girls were injured or dying while being raped.

A few days after Easter in April 1945, they returned to Marko and found many dead German and Russian soldiers. Theresia remembers, "It was a horrible and devastating scene with a terrible odor … While the Russians were there they dumped things into the well, spoiling our drinking water. Due to the lice that were brought in by the Russian soldiers, typhus broke out." Theresia's aunt died of typhus fever. Conditions quickly became deplorable.

At the end of the war, Josef Redling came home and saw his youngest son, Stefan, for the first time. He was also told of the tragic news that his son Tony would not be coming home from the war. At night, two Hungarian Communist policemen arrested Josef and threw him into a jail in Budapest. The situation in Hungary was difficult and confusing, because Hungary, like Italy and Romania, had switched sides. Hungary was no longer on the German side and part of the Austro-Hungarian Empire. That empire no longer existed.

Josef Redling served in World War I in Galizien, now part of Slovakia, from 1914 until 1918. During World War II, he was conscripted in 1944. From January 6, 1946, until October 10, 1947, he was incarcerated in Budapest, and then he was deported to East Germany. He died on August 16, 1984, in Cleveland, Ohio.

After Josef was incarcerated, Elisabeth was on her own again, shouldering the burden of caring for her children. Life was very, very difficult, and food was extremely scarce. The Communists in Hungary broke into their home and stole everything that they could carry and that was not nailed down. They took all the food, china, silverware, pots and pans, clothing, and furniture. All they could do was silently watch or get shot.

These were some of their former Hungarian neighbors who now were mistreating them.

On January 13, 1948, the Germans were rounded up and taken to the Herend railroad station. This became their final farewell to their ancestral homes. They were lined up and loaded into boxcars. Then the boxcars were shut from the outside. Slowly, the train began to move. When the train rolled through Marko, they heard the old familiar church bells ringing their final good-bye; it was their final Godspeed. It was already dark when the train with its German captives arrived in Budapest. They were filled with fear of being shipped to Siberia to one of Stalin's slave-labor camps.

The next day, the train stopped.

> The doors opened and we were let out onto an open field somewhere in Czechoslovakia. The men and women, everyone was very embarrassed when they pulled their pants down or their skirts up, because nature called. The soldiers did not even have the decency of looking away. After about ten minutes we were ordered back into the boxcars. The train ran all night. At seven in the morning we were in Pirna, East Germany. I saw a war-wounded man on crutches begging for some bread. We were taken to a big building, where we were registered and sprayed with louse powder. We were taken to a place called Kraupa and put into a little house without any heat. Brother Stefan contracted pneumonia. Through the Red Cross, mother was able to locate dad at a cabbage factory in Erding, near Munich.
>
> We were put on a train again en route through Dresden to Plauen. Dresden was a bombed-out

cemetery with most buildings totally destroyed. There was no sign of any life, not even a mouse could have survived. Refugees were trying to leave for West Germany.

Frau Redling really had no choice, if she did not want her family to die of starvation, but to also move westward. After several attempts, they succeeded in escaping; things improved a little.

At fourteen, Theresia found work on a farm milking cows and cleaning chicken coops. A year later, she worked for another farmer in Bavaria spreading manure with a pitchfork. She was left out on the field all by herself. It was November, and it was cold; she was not dressed warmly enough. When the farmer picked her up in the late afternoon and noticed that she was shivering, he had the audacity to tell her that if she worked harder, she would be warmer. He also lacked some basic human compassion.

Like so many others who lost their homeland, the Redlings left Bremerhafen on board the military ship, *General Harry S. Tayler.* They saw the Statue of Liberty in March of 1952. In September 1952, they ended up in Cleveland, Ohio, where Brother Josef and his wife and Brother Frank were already living. Cleveland had several German-American cultural and social clubs, which were quite active in perpetuating German-American cultural and social activities. They made many new friends.

Theresia found the love of her life, Adolf Wagner. They raised a loving and caring family and soon became active members in some of the German-American organizations. Theresia was blessed with an exceptionally beautiful voice. She and Rose Thuma sang and yodeled and entertained for many appreciative audiences. For several decades, Theresia has been researching the history and ancestry of her people.

Mother Elisabeth was extremely homesick. She always wanted to return to her beloved Marko. And exactly twenty-eight years to the day, she got her wish; she died on January 13, 1976, in Cleveland, Ohio.

Centuries from now, future generations will look at the 1940s and World War II as a decade when bigotry and barbarism reached a feverish pitch. Much of the ruthlessness, the savagery, and the intrigues of the war will continue to be an unfolding story, patiently waiting to be told. The expulsions cannot be regarded as punishment for a collective guilt. That would be a totally misguided sense of justice. Furthermore, there is enough guilt to go around.

Furthermore, there is no such thing as collective guilt. English writer Victor Gollancz stated that it is "a nonsensical, illiberal, anti-Christian and lamentable Nazi idea." In these Soviet puppet states, Germans were forced to make public apologies for their "collective guilt." Guilt, innocence, and merit are always personal and never collective. The key question is always who are the responsible individuals? The aim should always be historical truth and the enforcement of international law without discrimination.

Some of the towns in former Yugoslavia that were turned into death camps include Gakovo, Esseg, Jarek, Krushevje, Novisad, Ruma, Sombar, Srem, Temesvar, Vukovar, Weisskirchen, Karldorf, and Grosskikinda. In 1950, the Walter Commission of the US House of Representatives reported that no phase of the expulsion could be considered "humane." Since 1989, documents have been released from Russian, Polish, Czech, and Serbian archives documenting and detailing the brutality and the suffering by the German victims. World War II was neither the cause nor the result of all the expulsions and the deportations of the German minority. The causes were the imperial expansion and interests of the victorious participants, England's desire to weaken Germany, and pan-Slavic nationalism.

Yugoslavia was the most gruesome killing field in Europe. "The killings that took place here have no comparison in Europe. In two months after the war, more people were killed here than in four years of war," said Joze Dezman, a historian who heads the government Commission for Concealed Mass Graves. So far, no indictments have been filed against any of the murderers. A particularly gruesome discovery was the mummified remains of the approximately three hundred pro-Nazi soldiers from Croatia and Slovenia in a mining shaft in Huda Jama, believed to have been killed with gas, because there are no signs of visible wounds.

University professor Mitja Ference has unearthed more than 570 hidden grave sites from World War II. His discoveries have shattered a psychological barrier in Slovenia and sparked new political debates about the sins of the war, in which thousands of Germans, Croats, and others on the losing side were brutally slaughtered.

In 1999, he found 1,179 skeletons in a trench near the city of Maribor, where a road bypass was being built, which halted his research. He believes there are far more than twenty thousand corpses buried under the new bypass. It is also believed that if these were other than German corpses, the project would have been stopped until the research was completed. The government in Ljubliana persisted on the continuation of the road construction, rather than finding more suitable resting places for the many dead. The trench was big enough to line up POWs and civilians, shoot them with machine guns, and cover their corpses up with earth.

This is just more of Yugoslavia's authorities persistently refusing to acknowledge that these mass executions ever took place, and they also refused to inform the relatives where these victims were buried. This is more cover-up and denial of guilt for Tito's exterminations.

Romania, under Communist rule, totally neglected the beautiful German cities and farming villages, allowing them to deteriorate and become virtual ghost towns. The family farms were turned into collective farms, and their ancestral villages were leveled to clear the area for agro-complexes. This Communist experiment was a complete failure. The borders were sealed, and no one was allowed to leave the country, which became a huge concentration camp.

Germany experienced its Wirtschaftswunder, its economic miracle, and was in need of competent workers for its booming economy, so the Communist dictator Ceausescu turned "his" Germans into monetary capital. Since his Germans wanted to leave anyway, Ceausescu sold his Germans to Germany. Germany paid 14,000 D-marks for professional people and 8,000 D-marks for everyone else. It also paid an additional 2,000 D-marks under the table as bribe money to the local Communist henchmen to release their "Romanian citizens." This became a profitable swindle for communistic Romania. Ceausescu got rid of his unwanted German minority, confiscated their earthly possessions, and received solid currency for every German who left. This is a solid reminder that not all criminals are in jail; some have become politicians. This human-being trade stopped when Ceausescu was overthrown and killed.

The once flourishing Banat, which was the agricultural jewel of the Austro-Hungarian Empire died a slow death. The once lush and fertile fields lay dormant and overgrown with weeds. The homes and churches slowly crumbled as they fell into disrepair. What took the Germans generations and centuries to build was destroyed in a few short years. The Danube Basin no longer was the land of milk and honey.

In Hungary, the land and the homes were taken away by the Communist regime. In Romania, the beautiful and orderly farming villages were bulldozed, their farms collectivized. In

Yugoslavia, they were treated the worst. Tito's orders were to exterminate, slaughter, or starve them to death. No one raised a finger or protested in any form. The media killed it with deafening silence in the land where we pride ourselves on having constitutionally protected rights of freedom of speech and the press. Remember, without freedom of speech and the press, all other freedoms are in constant peril.

With the Germans gone, Romania disintegrated into a social and economic abyss. Yugoslavia first became a beggar nation, and then it disintegrated from within. Since the fall of the Communist regime, so far, Hungary has emerged as the only country where there is real hope for a decent life for the Germans in their ancestral homeland.

It should not be forgotten that the Hungarian people helped the Germans in their escape from Tito's death camps, giving them food and a safer route to Austria and Germany. During the 1956 Hungarian uprising, when Russian tanks massacred Hungarian freedom fighters, the Danube Swabians living in Austria and Germany were also the first to help the Hungarian escapees. One good deed deserved another.

How can any nation face its future without coming to terms with its past? Perhaps the media can rectify its past omissions. Giving due acknowledgment to these atrocities does not minimize the suffering of Hitler's victims. The victims of the greatest ethnic cleansing in human history will not and cannot be forgotten. It is a necessary first step toward real reconciliation. Many governments of European countries that engaged in ethnic cleansing have made gestures of sympathy and have admitted the expulsions were unjust. Some of the countries have expressed a willingness to discuss the topic of restitution.

The end of the war did not bring about a new era of human rights and an end to human rights violations. Most historians were afraid to handle this subject. One exception was the English human rights activist Victor Gollanz, who demonstrated his fortitude to speak up and to condemn this ethnic cleansing: "If the conscience of men ever again becomes sensitive, these expulsions will be remembered to the undying shame of all who committed or connived at them."

Ann Morrison, an American, produced and directed a complete six-film series entitled Millions Cried … No One Listened. She takes us through the history, horror, and terror of the expulsions and deportations of some sixteen million ethnic Germans and millions of Volga Germans. Ann states in her documentary, "It is only when we know and remember our past that we truly gain awareness of who we are. It is then that we dare to dream of our future." For further information about this great documentary, one may go to www.annfilms.com.

Now the Danube Swabians, the ethnic Germans, are scattered around the world. They have assimilated and become upright and contributing members of at least a dozen countries. They did not and do not seek revenge, nor do they bear grudges or hatred, even toward their tormentors. They were robbed of all their earthly possessions, millions were murdered, thousands were raped, and they were buried in unmarked graves. They were the victims of the other genocide. They cried, and no one listened. They maintain their abiding faith that justice will be served. Nothing debases man more than revengeful ruthlessness and the mockery of justice.

Those who have nothing to hide need not fear the truth! We are reminded that the Creator is a sure paymaster. He will reward us according to our merits. There is no ethical aspiration higher than the desire to deliver us from the ruination we have brought on ourselves willingly or tacitly by world wars. It appears that the financial establishment is attempting to create a world system for financial control, dominating the financial system of each country and the economy of the world. We owe respect to the living and truth to the dead.

Queen Elizabeth II is pictured with dictator Josip Broz (Tito) of Yugoslavia, hosting him at a tea for Tito party in 1976 at Buckingham Palace. At his death, the media praised him as the last of the great leaders of that period; many considered Tito to be a cruel, cold-blooded mass killer.

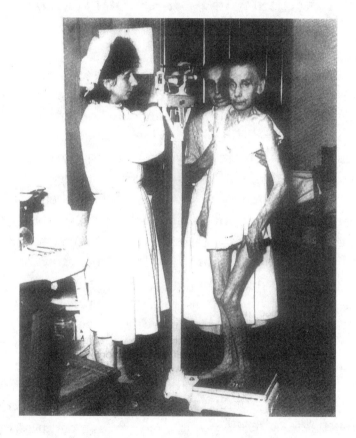

One of thousands of malnourished Germans, on the verge of starvation, in a Berlin hospital.

CHAPTER 10

Expulsions and Deportations

Religions and national politics thrive on and are perpetuated by fear. Nothing in life is to be feared. It is only to be understood. Religious fear is infused by the unknown, the need for salvation, and the hope of everlasting life. While most, if not all, religions preach brotherly love, relief, and truth, most practice religious exclusivity, lacking tolerance. Governments instill fear and anxiety by claiming that there is a risk factor of being attacked by some enemy, while politicians and the media fill the populace with the ecstasy of heroic patriotism, a willingness to kill or be killed. No one loves a man whom he or she fears. If you fear God, how can you love Him?

It has been written that truth shall set us free. Without historical truth, the world shall continue to fight one war after another. Transparency and accountability are essential for peace on earth and the peaceful coexistence of the human race. This historical cycle of perpetual war for perpetual peace is otherwise unstoppable, and millions of lives will continue to be sacrificed on the altar of war and profit. Fear grows in darkness. If you fear there is a bogeyman around, turn the light on, and the bogeyman will disappear. Learn to be tolerant, and make a real effort of understanding the beliefs, practices, and habits of others, not necessarily having to accept them.

It is common knowledge that the military industry and the bankers benefit greatly from wars and, therefore, have a vested interest in its perpetuation. Dwight D. Eisenhower warned us about being dependent upon a wartime-driven economy. Unfortunately, historians and academics are all too often obsessed about being politically correct, and the primary concern of most politicians is being elected or reelected. Who really cares that our military hospitals are overcrowded with maimed and crippled soldiers and that thousands of our veterans are homeless and don't receive proper care? Too many have become the forgotten heroes of the greatest generation. It has been stated before that all wars are economic and motivated by greed and lust for power. In centuries past, monarchs displayed an appetite for riches and territorial gain, driven by their personal egos. Now, imperialistic expansions, greed, and the spoils of war are the driving forces that benefit the very few at the top.

At the Nuremberg war trials, Hermann Goering stated,

> Naturally the common people don't want war: neither in Russia, nor in England, nor for that matter in Germany. That is understood. But, after all, it is the leaders of the country who determine the policy, and it is always a simple matter to drag the people along, whether it is a democracy or a fascist dictatorship or a parliament or a communist dictatorship. Voice or no voice, the people can always be brought to the bidding of the leaders. That is easy. All you have to do is tell them they are being attacked, and denounce the peacemakers for lack of patriotism and exposing the country to danger. It works the same in any country.

For the military industry to thrive anywhere, the country needs a real or perceived enemy. Sadly, all too often, the agents of the war industry seem all too willing to create one, and the media has been all too willing to sensationalize the news to increase their ratings.

There is something wrong in our democracy, our academia, and the mainstream media if a genocide of such a magnitude as the ethnic Germans experienced at the end and following the war and the incarcerations of thousands of German Americans and Latin German Americans can simply be brushed under the carpet and killed with deafening silence. Where is our moral conscience? Has our justice system failed and allowed human rights violations against millions of victims? Think of the energy and intrigue that was generated to turn German Americans into the silent majority. The narrative in the media is unfortunately still stuck in the war and postwar rhetoric. A truly objective dialogue about German suffering occurs all too seldom, and when ithappens, it is turned, all too often, into a discussion about Nazi atrocities, totally ignoring the massive genocide against Germans. The lives of Germans do matter.

More and more concerned people and a growing number of the descendants of the victims of the condoned ethnic cleansing of Germans, die Volksdeutschen, are actively seeking information and searching the archives for answers to the brutal expulsions and deportations, the starvation blockade, slave labor, the countless rapes of German women from eight to eighty, and the mass murders. The truth always emerges to the light of day.

At the end of and following the war, some sixteen million ethnic Germans, were forced out of their homes and their homeland and were corralled like cattle to what was left of Germany, the four occupational zones. There was a degree of reciprocal ignorance: the Germans in Germany knew little of the brutality, the suffering that the refugees were forced to endure, and the refugees knew even less of the fire-bombings and the total destruction of Germany and the results of FDR's "unconditional surrender." The Germans made room for the refugees. Now, about a third of Germany's population is comprised of German refugees and their children.

The Polish government in exile nursed dreams of a greater Poland and not of becoming a country occupied and controlled by the Soviet Union. They were scheming of a westward expansion into German territory and regaining the eastern Polish territory occupied by the Soviet Union. These dreams lacked realism. The eastern part of Germany was put under Polish administration, and the eastern part of Poland is still occupied by Russia. The Polish communist chief Boleslav Bierut ordered all German property confiscated and all ethnic Germans ruthlessly evicted from their homes; this constituted grand theft, but no one cared or objected. International law and minority rights were completely ignored and trampled upon.

During the final three months of the war, more than three million refugees fled the Red Army. The first large wave of refugees began in January 1945 and lasted long after. In the summer of 1944, Stalin promised the Polish National Freedom Committee (what a misleading, promising, fancy name) that the western Polish border with Germany would be the Oder and the western Neisse Rivers. That meant that more than eight million Germans were to be brutally expelled or murdered. The Soviet-Polish plan was to deal with the Germans so severely and ruthlessly that they would be eager to leave "willingly" on their own. Germans were threatened by the Polish army with death if they did not "voluntarily" leave. This happened after the war was officially over. Polish generals publicly proclaimed, "The German vermin should thank God if they still have their heads on their shoulders." That was part of the new world order in Poland and the implementation of the Morgenthau Plan.

Anthony Eden of England visited Stalin on December 16, 1941. At that meeting, Stalin insisted that the Polish western border be moved to the Oder River and the Soviet western border should remain according to the Hitler-Stalin agreement. Stalin was able to expand the Soviet Union. This was again a topic of discussion at Teheran on December 1, 1943, with Stalin, FDR, and Churchill in attendance. Churchill insisted that Polish interests had to be satisfied at the expense of Germany. Churchill and FDR were no friends of Germany, and Stalin was no one's friend. The Polish border was to be moved to the Curzon Line, i.e., the Oder River. The Curzon Line was named after England's foreign minister George Curzon, who first suggested it after World War I.

The father of the present Oder-Neisse Line is Josef Stalin, who was baptized as Josef Wissarionowitsch Dschugaschwili. On December 3, 1941, Stalin told Wladyslaw Sikorski, president of the Polish government in exile, that the Polish border would be moved westward and the Soviet border would also be moved westward. At the time of this discussion, the German Wehrmacht was a mere twelve miles outside of the Kremlin. What did Stalin know that the German people did not know? Hitler sent the Wehrmacht into the icy Russian winter in summer uniforms. Was this another of Hitler's treasonous acts?

What or who caused Hitler to invade the Soviet Union and begin a second front, after Hitler and Stalin signed a nonaggression pact. Stalin provided Hitler with millions of tons of material. Hitler knew the futility of fighting a war on two fronts. Hitler knew that starting a war with Russia would be the beginning of the end; yet he ordered this treasonous, militarily suicidal act. Was he committing high treason knowingly?

That was not Hitler's only military mistake. Hitler did not want to defeat Britain at a time when his forces might have been able to accomplish that. He prevented the invasion of England when his forces had the upper hand. Churchill expected the invasion and ordered all the church bells to ring in anticipation of the invasion. His generals had plans ready, but Hitler again overruled his generals. At the defeat of Dunkirk, Hitler allowed the English forces to return to England rather than take them captive as POWs. They did come back, obeying orders, to destroy Germany. Considering the steps that England had taken to justify a war against Germany, this act was not only exceedingly stupid but military suicide. Hitler acted either as a total fool, or he was receiving orders from someone else, making him the ultimate treasonous traitor within Germany.

The victorious powers authorized and were instrumental in the expulsions and deportations of some sixteen million ethnic Germans. This was a deliberate and malicious policy executed on an astronomical scale. Millions were starved, brutally beaten to death, and died being pushed toward what was left of Germany, the four occupational zones. Like wild animals, they were chased out of their homes, and all their worldly possessions were stolen. This brutality and grand theft was condoned by all the victorious allies, except France. Hate propaganda did not end with the official end of the war. Never have a people been more severely mistreated than the Germans during the twentieth century. They were exiled and prevented from ever returning to their homes.

The Czech government in exile and the Polish provisional government demanded and received permission to expel their German minority. Their demands were willingly granted. Edvard Benes opportunistically ignored more than a thousand years of harmonious coexistence that bonded Germans, Moravians, and Bohemians. The German emperor, Otto the Great, established his governmental seat in Prague and built the first German university in Prague. This region was an integral part of the German empire. The elector of Bohemia was one the seven electors of the empire. Poisonous, sickening anti-German hysteria was fueled especially by Elya Ehrenburg, who demanded that "We shall kill. If you have not killed at least one German a day, you have wasted that day ... for us there is nothing more joyful than a heap of German corpses."

Already in 1941, Benes set forth his plan of cleansing the new Czechoslovakia from the undesirable Germans, to denaturalize them, steal all their possessions, and ruthlessly expel them. He stated, "In our country, the end of the war will be written in blood. The Germans will be paid back mercilessly and multiply for everything they have done to our country since 1938. The whole nation will participate in this fight. There will not be a Czech who does not participate in this mission and there will not be a patriot who does not take revenge for everything the nation had to endure." Benes, who suffered from an acute case of hate, also suffered from selective amnesia. Many Czechs disagreed with him diametrically, and thousands of Czechs served heroically in the German army.

Ruthless brutalities toward Germans were carried out already prior to and during the Potsdam Conference. Tragically, the Allied leaders gave willingly their blessings to this brutality. To add to the horror, German victims had no rights, no voice, and no one to protect them; no one would listen. Tragically, murdering or raping Germans and stealing everything they had were not punishable crimes.

In the fall of 1945, Robert Jungh reported from the land of the dead in the east, "Wer die polnische Zone verlassen hat und in russisches okkupiertes (Mittel-deutsches) Gebiet gelang, atmet gerade auf. Hinter ihm liegen leergepluenderte Staedte, Doerfer, Konzentrationslager, oede unbestellte Felder, leichenbesaete Strassen, an denen Wegelagerer lauern and Fluechtlingen die letzte Habe rauben." The German army did not retreat until the beginning of May 1945, almost the very end of the war. That left some three million Germans behind, who did not flee and were totally unprotected. Many Germans did not leave because they saw no reason to leave and were not about to leave everything behind.

In the new Poland, the Nazi concentration camps became Polish concentration camps, where tens of thousands of Germans were systemically tortured and murdered. They were beaten, raped, robbed, tortured, and driven forcibly westward with what little they were able to carry on their beaten backs, and most of that was stolen along the way. The Germans had no one to turn to for protection. Uncle Sam turned his back and could not be counted on for help. Those who were still alive and could move were loaded onto open cattle cars and forced to the west. Many Germans survived this terror because there were many compassionate and caring Poles and Czechs. Many Poles and many Czechs were married to Germans.

Poles that were on the German "Volksliste" were subjected to a rehabilitation training, prior to being accepted back into Polish society; they were considered traitors. However, many Poles were denied this mandatory rehabilitation; they were brutally expelled just like their German neighbors. Many of these Poles were threatened with a death sentence. The expulsions from Poland continued to the end of 1946, when most, if not all, had been either murdered or forced to leave "voluntarily".

One of the many atrocities was committed on December 17, 1946, in the town called Stolp, where 1,800 Germans were forced out of their homes. At 7:00 a.m., they were ordered to come to the county seat and bring along their luggage. Most of their luggage was then promptly stolen. They had no rights, no recourse, no one to complain to, and no voice; they called for help, but no one listened. Anyone who dared to object about their mistreatment was severely whipped and beaten, and many were shot. Jewelry, watches, and anything of value was stolen. Many of the men and women were ordered to completely undress in freezing, ice-cold 20-degree Fahrenheit temperatures. They were then told to stand there until midnight; thereafter, they were pushed into open cattle cars and delivered to Germany. That was one display of "orderly and humane" in the new Poland.

How many Germans were left in East Germany and were placed under Polish administration at the time of the Potsdam Conference? Churchill, who began to be concerned about the Bolshevik expansion into Europe, spoke of eight million who would return after the hostilities. Stalin insisted that they did not want to return anymore, and besides, the Poles themselves did not want them back anymore either. Stalin spoke of only two million in East Germany who still did not get it that they were no longer welcome in their own homes. He considered them homeless who should be willing to leave voluntarily or be killed.

During the discussion of the new Polish western border, the Big Three were willing to agree on the Oder River but not on which Neisse River. There are two Neisse Rivers, the Lauritz Neisse River, which flows north and south, and the Glatz Neisse River, which flows further southeast. Both rivers flow into the Oder River. That was a major issue. If the Glatz Neisse River became the border, Breslau and parts of Silesia would have remained as a part of Germany.

Since the Big Three could not reach an agreement, Stalin made a well-calculated suggestion that they listen to the provisional Polish government. Since he had already discussed the western Polish border with his puppet Polish leaders, he was certain that their argument would reinforce his. They easily convinced the western allies that the new Poland needed the larger territory for the millions of Poles who were being displaced by the Soviet Union in the eastern part of Poland. Churchill was in full agreement with this argument, since one of his objectives was to reduce the size of Germany. Blinded by an acute case of German-phobia, the western allies refused to see the long-term ramifications of this agreement. Stalin won the argument, and the western Neisse River was agreed upon. Even before the Potsdam Agreement, Polish agents placed demarcations of the new Polish border along the western Neisse River, as it had been decided in secrecy with Joe Stalin.

There was a proviso to this arrangement, namely that this was a temporary border. The final border would not be agreed upon until Germany was granted a peace treaty. The Allies, especially Washington, had been rather reluctant to move forward on a German peace treaty, perhaps because of the border issue. Margaret Thatcher, the former British prime minister, strongly objected even to the unification of former East and West Germany.

Almost a century after World War II, Germany still does not have an official peace treaty. The Four Plus Two agreement is not a peace treaty, nor is the unification of the two parts of Germany. The real East Germany is still under Polish administration. Stalin knew that no self-respecting western state would accept the Oder-Neisse Line in perpetuity; he skillfully used that reasoning to keep the Poles in line.

Both FDR and Churchill knew that the slaughter of thousands of Polish officers and Polish intelligentsia in the Katyn Forest near Smolensk was committed by Stalin but chose to blame the Nazis, because it served their political agenda, and they did not want to offend Uncle Joe Stalin. If Churchill and FDR lied about the Katyn Forest massacres, what else did they lie about?

Anyone in the communist block who dared to question the legality of the Oder-Neisse border was imprisoned and taken out of circulation. Stalin kept complete control over his puppet states; all were marching "willingly" to his cadence. The communists gave the Germans virtually no choice: you either will be terrorized, raped, starved, and murdered, or you will willingly and voluntarily leave everything behind. Thus, they reasoned that no one could claim anything was stolen.

How times had changed. It is difficult to fathom that the ancestors of these victimized survivors were invited and persuaded with perks and privileges to settle and develop this land. For centuries, Bohemia, Moravia, and the Sudetenland were considered part of Germany and as such a protectorate of the German empire.

The Polish, Czech, and Soviet official account of the expulsions was that the Germans left voluntarily and were treated humanely. According to the millions who suffered and were murdered, this was a bold-faced lie and nothing was further from the truth. All occupying forces tried to reeducate, or brainwash, the Germans, convincing them that they received what they deserved. How can any policy be so callous and cruel and continue to inflict insult to injury?

Dr. Konrad Adenauer, first chancellor of West Germany, voiced his hope that the refugees would be able to return to their lost homes, die verlorene Heimat, but he was also realistic enough to know that it would not happen in his time. No one can really expect the Germans to accept the present border arrangement in perpetuity. Hope shall provide an amicable and fair solution to a problem that was created by the sleepwalkers of the time. Germany had no part in the arrangements of the Versailles Treaties and the arrangements following World War II. Guenther Grass, Nobel-Prize laureate, stated that his own father never gave up the hope of someday returning to Danzig and opening his cabinet shop. He waited and waited. "Er sass auf den Koffern bis er gestorben ist." He waited until he died.

Grass and his family were forced to leave in 1944 when he was seventeen years old. In his later years, he was elevated and honored as an honorary member of the city of Danzig.

Dr. Adenauer demanded that the Potsdam Agreement be revisited. It was not a binding agreement, because Germany had no input and no voice in the treaty whatsoever. It was pushed upon the Germans by brutal force, at gunpoint. In 1949, he wrote that the suffering and all the occurrences and mistreatment of the expellees were a contradiction to the Potsdam Agreement. Referring to the Potsdam Agreement, Konrad Adenauer held a strong opinion that the border was an open issue, until such a time that Germany would enjoy a true peace treaty, as a sovereign country. Germany is entitled to its historical border of 1937, which under international law and the present political climate might be peacefully achievable in the future. The danger exists that the war industry shall use it to justify another war.

The Germans in what was left of Germany, after the amputations, rose admirably to the challenges of accepting and making room for more than twelve million refugees, willingly sharing with them what little they had. They exemplified brotherly love, relief, and truth. FDR's insistence on unconditional surrender and the Morgenthau Plan contributed greatly to the destruction of Germany and the loss of millions of lives. The English blockade was designed to starve as many Germans, Austrians, and Hungarians as possible. It was the great humanitarian President Herbert Hoover, who put a stop to the starvation blockade and sent millions of tons of food to the starving people, saving perhaps eighty million lives.

Some accepted the refugees with open arms, and others considered them an unwanted intrusion. Within a few months, 7.9 million ended up in West Germany and 4.1 million in what was erroneously referred to as East Germany, which is

Middle or Central Germany. What was left of Germany, after all the territorial amputations, was a small portion of its actual historical former self.

All were in desperate need of help—the widows, the orphans, the invalids, the survivors of the fire-bombings, and the refugees. What made things worse was, for several years, Germany was not even allowed to clear its rivers and rebuild the country. The four occupational zones were governed by the respective military authorities. It was not until 1949 that the refugees were allowed to form a national organization, das Zentralverband der Vertriebenen Deutschen (ZVD). Four long years after the war, an organization for the East German refugees was organized, die Vereinigten Ostdeutschen Landsmannschaften (VOL). In 1950, a Charta der deutschen Heimatvertriebenen was formulated and published.

At the Yalta Conference, the Western Allies willingly caved in to Stalin's demands and agreed to reparation in kind, which was a euphemistic term for slave labor. That became a nightmare for millions of German men and women. America abolished slavery but was willing to agree to this inhumane brutality elsewhere, one of many flagrant contradictions. Those who still had able bodies were gathered and transported to the Soviet Union as slave labor. They were forced to work in fields, coal mines, factories, and anywhere the Bolsheviks ordered them to work. Many were forced to clear mine fields. Most of them never returned; they died of malnutrition, overwork, and lack of medical care. German life was cheap and expendable. More than a quarter of a million did not survive the transport to the Soviet Union and Siberia.

One of the deportees who survived, returned, and was able to talk about her ordeal was Eva-Marie S. She shared her hellish experiences with Freya Klier in a book entitled *Verschleppt bis ans Ende der Welt*. Eva-Marie recalls, "Als wir losfuhren, waren wir etwa 90 Menschen in einem Wagon … Die Fahrt ging durch Polen, wo oefter Steine gegen die Wagonwaende flogen. Ich kann mich nicht mehr an alle Einzelheiten des Transports erinnern, nur daran, dass bei uns im Wagon manche gestorben sind …"

She and other girls volunteered to remove the dead bodies and throw them into the coal bins. Every so often, some thirty frozen bodies were thrown out of the train. No one seemed to care enough to keep a record. They were nameless victims of a war that was officially over; for them, this war was far from being over. This was the depth of man's inhumanity to man.

Sixteen million Germans were expelled from their homes, the various German states and principalities, the Austro-Hungarian Empire, and various German-speaking regions, such as East Prussia, Pomerania, East Brandenburg, Silesia, Bohemia, Moravia, Slovenia, Croatia, Serbia, and Transylvania. They all called for help, but no one listened.

Many notable Germans called these regions their home. President Paul von Hindenburg, who served as president of Germany from 1925 until 1934 and was a field marshal during World War I, was born in Posen in 1841 when it was part of Prussia, and rocket and space scientist Dr. Werner von Braun, who took us to the moon and beyond, was also born in Posen in 1912. Ferdinand Porsche was born in the Sudetenland in 1885. He was commissioned to design and build the Volkswagen— the people's car. He too was ruthlessly expelled. He and his family settled in Stuttgart, where he died in 1951. Porsche also designed and built the premiere sports car that bears his name. The naturalist and Augustinian monk Gregory Mendel was born in Moravia in 1822. He discovered and formulated the laws of genetics.

Another German who contributed greatly to humankind is Nicolaus Copernicus, the great astronomer, whom the

382   Dr. Joe Wendel

Poles now also claim as their own. His works are the common property of Western civilization. Nicolaus Copernicus was born in 1493 in Thorn, a German city in West Prussia, which was founded in 1231 by Teutonic knights and remained part of the German Reich until the Peace of Thorn. Copernicus was born six years into the Polish occupation. His ancestors were all of German stock and hailed from Silesia. His family name goes back to the village of Koppernigk on the Neisse River. From 1772 to the end of World War I, Thorn remained part of the German Reich. His mother was Barbara Watzelrode from Thorn. Copernicus was trilingual; he spoke German, Italian, and Latin but not Polish. Melchior Adam, a contemporary of Copernicus, published a series of twelve books from 1615 to 1620, which included an autobiography from Copernicus called *Vita Germaniae Philosorum* (*The Life of German Scholars*) in which he referred to himself as being German.

The German poet Rainer Maria Rilke was born in Prague in 1875. The peace activist Bertha von Suttner was also born in Prague in 1843. Her most famous work is "Die Waffen Nieder" (Put Down Your Weapons). She was the first woman to receive the Nobel Prize. Franz Kafka was born in Prague in 1883, as was Franz Werfel. Sigmund Freud, father of psychoanalysis, was born in Moravia in 1856. The great romantic composer and conductor Gustav Mahler, who lived from 1860 to 1911, was born in Bohemia. The legendary conductor of the Leipzig Gewandhaus Orchestra and music director of the New York Philharmonic Kurt Masur was born in Silesia in 1919. Johnny Weismueller, Olympic champion and Hollywood's Tarzan, was born in Freidorf, Romania. Gerhard Hauptmann, who lived from 1862 to 1946, was born and worked in Silesia. The list of the many notable Germans who were born in "der verlorenen Heimat," their lost homeland, goes on. They all contributed greatly to our civilization and to our quality of life.

For centuries, the Germans lived and worked between the Bohemian Forest and the Urals and the Baltic and the Balkans, and many Europeans of various nationalities lived and worked in Germany, as they still do. The Czechs migrated to Bohemia in the Middle Ages. The ethnic Germans were generally indifferent to politics; they were apolitical. Bad politicians get into office because good citizens do not participate in the political process. They perpetuated their heritage and entrusted politics to someone else; that is a political sin of omission. They were farmers in East Prussia and the Romanian Banat and coal miners in Silesia; they all proudly contributed to and were proud of the success of their homeland.

With the exception of, the Greek-Turkish conflict from 1923 until 1926, the brutal expulsions of entire populations after a military conflict was something foreign and completely new to the civilized Europeans. Tragically, hate propaganda had its desired effect, and jungle law was applied. The redrawing of the European map and other parts of the world, the acute nationalism, the resettlement scheme, and the ethnic cleansing and expulsions were a direct result and outgrowth of World War I and the disastrous Versailles Treaties. For centuries, it was England's strategy to divide, conquer, and rule. All the atrocities of World War II and all the problems in the world today are a direct or indirect result of World War I and the justice that was denied to Germany and her allies.

By any other name, a war crime is a war crime and shall remain a war crime, regardless of who committed the crime; otherwise, the world makes a total mockery of any social and international legal order. Millions of ethnic Germans had their human rights severely violated. There is no legal, moral, or ethical justification for these brutal human rights violations against the Germans. What the twentieth century has taught the world is that it is not as important "to love thy neighbor as thyself" as it is not to hate him so much to be willing to terrorize and to murder him. The world needs to hinge itself from the love-hate equation to one of genuine tolerance and respect for others.

On February 11, 1918, President Wilson emphasized to the American Congress and to the world that "peoples and provinces are *not* to be bartered about from sovereignty to sovereignty ..." but that is exactly what happened. What Wilson demonstrated is that he could no longer be trusted; his actions turned him into a common politician. There was a concerted effort to destroy the German people. Self-determination and the perpetuation of cultural identity were intentionally and maliciously destroyed. This was done under the false pretense of giving the Slavs full self-determination, which also did not happen. The newly formed and expanded states, which were created at the territorial expense of Germany and Austro-Hungary, became puppet states of Stalin's Soviet Union.

The Versailles Treaty dictated that each Slavic state receive not only its own ethnics but also a number of other minority groups. This turned the expulsions of the ethnic Germans into nothing more than a brutal, revengeful hate campaign. It was an excuse justifying grand theft and murder. The Treaty of St. Germain amputated major industries and various resources in Silesia and the Sudetenland.

What was left of Austria was a greatly reduced state of barely seven million people. The multinational state of Czechoslovakia was established under false pretenses. It was comprised of 46 percent Czechs, not a majority; 13 percent Slovaks; 2 percent Poles; 3 percent Ruthenes; 8 percent Hungarians; and more than 3.5 million Germans, which is 28 percent. Germans were merely 18 percent less than the Czechs. All Austrian objections were summarily ignored, and the contested regions were not granted the benefit of a plebiscite, a choice of national sovereignty reflected by the direct ballot of the people's choice. The Allies spoke with a forked tongue. Self-determination by the German people and *justice* were *denied*. That was just so much more evidence for the hypocrisy of "making the world safe for democracy." The sacred principles upon which America was founded and defended also by German Americans were trampled upon in Europe.

The Harvard professor Archibald Coolidge asserted that the Germans might be "un-digestible." He stated that "to grant to the Czechoslovaks all the territory they demand would not only be an injustice to millions of people unwilling to come under Czech rule, but it also would be dangerous and perhaps fatal to the future of the new state." This was part of a ruthless scheme to reduce Germany in size and population. To add insult to injury, the northern border of Italy was pushed north, robbing Austria and giving Italy the historical Austrian region of South Tyrol. This was a promise to Italy in a secret meeting in London, bribing Italy to switch sides. Italy switched sides during both world wars. An honest politician is one who after he is bribed will stay bought. Due to English intrigue, Austria was forced to relinquish South Tyrol even though only 3 percent of the population was Italian and 97 percent were German. The fact that this farming region had throughout its history been a part of Austria, perpetuating its German heritage, had no bearing on the English or their allies. This is how rivalries for future military confrontations are arranged and the military industry profits.

Wilson's highly heralded principle of self-determination was firmly rejected, and it became an international farce. Ninety-three percent of the people of South Tyrol wanted to remain part of Austria; 90 percent of the people of Danzig voted to stay and remain part of Germany; and 60 percent of Upper Silesia voted to stay with Germany. The present Polish regions of Kattowitz and Koenigshuette voted 85 and 75 percent respectively to remain part of Germany. The ballot box and the people's self-determination were brutally ignored by the great democracies of the world. This is but another example that political talk is cheap.

The Polish provisional government and the Czech government in exile agreed to and promised the ethnic Germans a limited measure of cultural autonomy and legal parity. Both Poland and the newly created state of Czechoslovakia failed miserably to deliver on their pledges. After the governments gained some of their desired authority, they changed their reasoning, claiming that minority rights protection constituted an infringement of their national sovereignty. This faulty reasoning was not challenged by anyone, and the mistreatment of the Germans continued to be the rule and not the exception.

There existed a bright spot. The Germans in the Baltic States were treated considerably better than in Poland and the new Czechoslovakia. After World War I, some thirty thousand Germans lived in Lithuania, seventy thousand in Latvia, and twenty thousand in Estonia.

For a variety of reasons, the situation in Czechoslovakia gradually deteriorated, especially during the summer of 1938, when the Czechs were being inundated with viral anti-German hate propaganda. British Prime Minister Neville Chamberlain sent Viscount Walter Runciman to Prague and to the Sudetenland on a mission to maintain peace. Chamberlain sincerely believed in "Peace in our time." Furthermore, Chamberlain held that the 1919 Treaties of Versailles and St. Germain were extremely unjust. This is not what the war party in Britain wanted to hear. Pushing for their agenda, the war party took control in London, and Chamberlain was replaced with a known war hawk, the Honorable Sir Winston Churchill. He visualized himself as some kind of a Greek war god, destroying Germany.

As FDR said on occasion, things happen because they were planned to happen, in secret—of course.

Walter Runciman consulted with both sides and failed on both fronts, because Britain was sending mixed signals to Poland and the new Czechoslovakia. As a result, the Germans were severely mistreated. What escalated this even further is the fact that this brutality was being totally ignored, even encouraged, by England and its allies. The situation for the Germans became acutely hopeless. This brutality also helped Hitler unwittingly become a reality. This was also part of the plan of the big political world chess game. It is now a known fact that Hitler was supported by Wall Street and wealthy Americans and by Josef Stalin. In retrospect, World War I and the inhumane dictum of the Versailles Treaties created the problems that face the world today, including Europe, the Middle East, and elsewhere.

On September 15 and 16, 1938, Hitler reestablished the rights of the Sudeten Germans and granted them their self-determination. After years of terror, he permeated the Germans with a feeling of being treated fairly and with greater personal security. On March 31, 1938, two weeks after Hitler occupied and returned Bohemia and Moravia back to the Reich, England and France provided assurances to Poland, thereby, greatly escalating the confrontations. The paradox of these assurances is that England and France would have had to march through Hitler's Germany to deliver on these promises. England and France did not voice any objections to the Soviet Union occupying the eastern half of Poland; there was deadly silence.

The way the German civilians were treated in the Sudetenland, which was amputated from Germany and bestowed to the new Czechoslovakia. It was a dictated decree of the Versailles Treaty in 1919 and is one of the darkest chapters of European history. Pain and brutality were inflicted on the

German civilians before World War I and increased after the war. Had Hitler not liberated the Sudetenland in 1939, the German population was in serious danger of being wiped out by the fanatical Czechs and their policy of ethnic eradication. This ancestral German land had been inhabited by Germans for at least two thousand years. Centuries of hard work and diligence turned it into a virtual paradise. During the twentieth century, influenced by British propaganda, some of the Czechs terrorized the Germans, but many also remained pro-German.

Hitler found an ally in Josef Stalin. The Western allies had been negotiating with Stalin to encircle Germany again, like in World War I. Stalin made demands on the Baltic States, which London and Paris were unwilling to grant. Hitler, however, was willing to grant him the Baltic States. An agreement between Vyacheslav Molotov and Joachim von Rippentrop divided Poland between the Soviet Union and Germany. That could have been prevented. Hitler demanded Danzig and the German corridor, which were historically part of Germany. The Poles, misguided by English selfish interests, turned their back on Hitler and conducted themselves antagonistically toward their next-door neighbors.

Similar to J. Edgar Hoover's program, the Poles had lists drawn up of their ethnic Germans. To start with, some fifteen thousand Germans were evicted and deported to Eastern Poland. The swift German victories, however, created uncertainty and fear among the Poles, which greatly increased the tensions. The Poles murdered some five thousand German civilians during the first few days of the conflict. This brutality by the Poles was repaid with more brutality by the Germans. Sadly, both German and Polish civilians paid the ultimate price due to English intrigue.

At the time when the United States was not yet officially in the war, Churchill and FDR met aboard ship in the Argentia

Harbor off Placentia Bay, Newfoundland, in the middle of the Atlantic Ocean, clearly demonstrating that it was just a matter of time before FDR believed he would be able to drag America into the war. FDR's promise not to send our young men to war sounded rather shallow and unconvincing. Like Wilson's Fourteen Points, the Atlantic Charter, which was proclaimed on August 14, 1941, contained eight points. There was absolutely no mention of FDR's unconditional surrender, the total destruction of Germany, the fire-bombings of millions of German civilians, the deportations and expulsions of some sixteen million Germans, the extermination of millions, or anything about Eisenhower's Rhine death camps, where more than 1.25 million German POWs were mercilessly starved to death. Because of this starvation program, Germany lost more soldiers after the war was over than during the entire war.

There exists no evidence of a signed document; only a press release is known to exist. The first version was drawn up by Churchill and set out the defeat of Nazism. FDR understood the charter as an opportunity to put an end to colonial projects. He told Churchill, "I can't believe that we can fight a war against fascist slavery, and ... not work to free people all over the world from backward colonial policy ..." FDR added to Churchill's version and broadened its interpretation. He was pushing the British into granting independence to their colonies.

Four of the eight points of this Atlantic Charter proclaimed,

1. The Anglo-American alliance seeks no aggrandizement, territorial or otherwise.
2. The alliance desires to see no territorial changes that do not accord with the freely expressed wishes of the peoples concerned.
3. The Anglo-American alliance respects every nation's right of self-determination.

4. The alliance will endeavor … to further the enjoyment by
    all states, great and small, victor or vanquished, of access
    on equal terms, to the trade and to the raw materials
    of the world which are needed for their economic
    prosperity. It should be noted that this agreement was
    never acted upon, passed, sanctioned, or ratified by any
    governmental body.

In actuality, FDR and Churchill usurped dictatorial
authority. Twenty-six countries were persuaded to support the
Atlantic Charter and follow the Anglo-American lead in the
total destruction of Germany. They all were asked and agreed
not to enter into a separate peace agreement with Germany.

The question arose, to what extent was Benes being used
and manipulated. Benes's efforts were definitely not part of
any democratic process. Benes worked feverishly in securing
authority for the brutal expulsions of the ethnic Germans from
the newly formed Czechoslovakia. In addition, he requested
that the Munich Agreement be declared invalid, so that the
borders could be reestablished.

William Bullitt, US ambassador to France, wrote in a letter
on September 16, 1939, to FDR, "[France and England] could
see no basis for a Benes provisional government, except Benes's
desire to place himself at the head of something again … nearly
everyone in political life in both France and England considers
that Benes is an utterly selfish small person who, through his
cheap smartness in little things and his complete lack of wisdom
in large things, permitted the disintegration of his country."

The two governments in exile were recruited to
serve a purpose in the scheme of English intrigue and the
implementation of the reduction of the German population
and territory and in the elimination of Germany as an industrial
and commercial competitor. Additionally, FDR and Churchill

did not pressure Stalin to retreat to the borders preceding the Molotov-Rippentrop Pact of September 1939, to which they were morally and historically obligated.

What happened is no surprise. FDR pledged his support in a letter to Stanislaw Mikolajczyk, the prime minister of the Polish government in exile in London, stating, "If the Polish government and people desire in connection with the new frontiers of the Polish State to bring about the transfer to and from territory of Poland of national minorities, the United States Government will raise no objection, and as far as practical, will facilitate such transfers."

As usual, Churchill was far more unreserved and direct. On December 15, 1944, he stated to Parliament, "Expulsion is the method which, as far as we have been able to see, will be the most satisfactory and lasting. There will be no mixture of population to cause endless trouble ... A clean sweep will be made. I am not alarmed by these large transferences [expulsions and deportations], which are more possible in modern conditions than they were ever before." Was Churchill suggesting racial exclusivity? Furthermore, Churchill failed to reflect that after the brutal expulsions of the Germans, Poland and Czechoslovakia were still multiethnic states. He also failed to accept the fact that Britain was a multinational assemblage.

America outlawed slavery a long time ago, but at the Yalta Conference, both FDR and Churchill concurred with Stalin's demands for a slave labor program, in which millions of Germans would be deported to Siberia. To make this concept more palatable to the Western population, they coined the euphemistic phrase "reparation in kind." Although the greatest number of German slave labor was deported to the Soviet Union, there were also camps run by the Western allies. More than a million Germans were forced into slave labor in French coal mines and into British agricultural combines. There were also some five hundred thousand Germans in American-run labor camps in Germany itself. The details and existence of these camps did not make the evening news.

FDR died in office at the start of his fourth term; that undoubtedly was a blessing for Germans and German Americans. Their suffering may have been even more severe had he lived. Harry S. Truman became president. The Big Three met from July 17 until August 2, 1945, at the Cecilienhof in Potsdam, a beautiful suburb of Berlin. They passed judgment on the future of Germans and Germany. And the future looked very bleak.

FDR engaged in secret deals with Stalin, which were kept secret from the American people and even from his vice president, embarrassing Truman after FDR's death. This was an unholy destructive alliance with the worst dictator on earth, promoting the slogan that our GIs gave their lives fighting against tyranny and for democracy and liberty.

In 1939, Chamberlain rejected Stalin's request to march through Poland up to the German border and accept the occupation of the Baltic states for later annexation. FDR urged the Poles not to negotiate with Hitler regarding the Danzig corridor, which lead from Germany to her amputated city and German territory. Chamberlain urged the Poles to accept the German proposals thus partially correcting the terms of the preposterous Versailles Peace Treaties. However, Chamberlain was replaced by the Hon. Sir Winston Churchill.

President Truman was opposed to a Polish expansion to the Oder and the western Neisse Rivers. At most, Poland could gain territory up to the Oder River but no further. Truman pointed to the nine million Germans living in this territory. Stalin informed Truman gleefully that the Germans had either been killed or fled out of fear from the Red Army. He was insistent that not a single German was left, which was a lie. The American admiral William Leahy called over to the president, "Of course not, the Bolshies killed them all." Churchill disagreed with Truman and agreed with Stalin; with Churchill's support, Stalin got his demands, and the border was drawn at the western and not the eastern Neisse River.

More than five million German civilians fled, leaving everything behind. While they attempted to escape, they were told because the war was over they could return to their homes. More than a million actually tried to return. What awaited them, after their return, was that they were brutally mistreated, robbed, raped, and beaten, and many were murdered. Many ended up in Polish concentration camps. The partisans stole everything that they still had on their backs and threw them into starvation and labor camps. At the time, there were some five and a half million Germans living in the disputed territory. This was another merciless display of hatred, revenge, and severe brutality. Thousands were pushed into open cattle cars and shipped to the west without food and water. The humane part was that they survived the death camps but did not survive the trip back to Germany. Tragically, there is always a segment of any population that is more readily influenced by the rhetoric of hate propaganda and willing to act like wild animals toward fellow human beings.

A multitude of Germans stayed in their homes and did not leave. The conditions for them grew increasingly desperate. Thousands upon thousands were forced into Polish concentration camps. The Nazi camp at Lamsdorf became a concentration camp for Germans. Hitler's concentration camps were not dismantled but continued to be operated by their new masters, the Polish militia. At the Lamsdorf camp, 6,480 Germans died, including 623 innocent children. At the Polish Swientochlowice camp in Upper Silesia, prisoners were starved, brutally beaten to death, and forced to stand every night in ice-cold water up to their necks until their bodies gave out and they drowned. They called for help, but no one listened.

The Atlantic Charter and other agreements were full of contradictions. The charter spoke of *no* territorial changes that did not meet the freely, democratically expressed wishes of all the people affected. The East Prussians, the Silesians, and the Sudeten Germans voted to remain and be part of Germany; democratic procedure and their wishes were ignored. They were brutally thrown out of their homes, their earthly belongings were stolen, many were murdered, and thousands of German women were raped.

There was a mammoth amount of discussion about self-determination generated, but most was very discriminatory. Anthony Eden voiced his opinion in the House of Commons, stating, "We cannot admit that Germany can claim, as a matter of right on her part … that any part of the Charter applied to her part …" Churchill, as usual, could not resist adding his own venom: "Germany (should not be) enjoying any guarantees that she will not undergo territorial changes if it should seem that making such changes renders more secure and more lasting the peace in Europe." Churchill conveniently forgot who instigated both parts of this thirty-year war and who was determined to destroy whose industrial and commercial trade, turning its population into an agricultural society. What followed was the Cold War, the Iron Curtain, and perpetual war for perpetual peace.

Labor MP John Rhys Davies rendered a far more accurate and realistic account on March 1, 1945, before the House of Commons. He stated, "We started the war with great motives and high ideals. We published the Atlantic Charter and then spat on it, stomped on it, as we were at a stake, and now nothing is left of it."

Czechoslovakia was created as a direct result of the dictates of the Versailles Treaties. Tons of propaganda fueled emotions of hatred. Partisans in Czechoslovakia and Slovakia ordered their German victims to dig their own graves before they were murdered. This lawless brutality caused some of the German civilians to flee in August of 1944. Until then, most of the Germans did not fear for their lives and, therefore, did not feel they had to flee. Most of the Czech partisans were in Yugoslavia, raising havoc and murdering and raping the German women there, but in August, September, and October, they gradually returned to Czechoslovakia to terrorize and brutalize the Germans there. They were the worst of the worst, void of any moral conscience.

On May 5, 1945, a Czech rebellion broke out in Prague; Czech mobs engaged in acts of revenge against German civilians and soldiers. The Czech mob was able to take control of Radio Prague 2. They urged the Czechs to revolt and threatened death to the Germans, "Smrt Nemcum." The mob, as well as the revolt, quickly spiraled out of control, leading to unspeakable brutality. The Czech Communist National Guard tied German soldiers to stakes, doused them with gasoline, and set them on fire as living torches. Thousands of German civilians were brutalized and mercilessly murdered in town after town. The Czech National Guard gave the German residents at most two hours to pack their bags and leave their homes, all their possessions, and their homeland forever. Czechs justified their murderous acts by claiming, "You're German and deserve what you get!" Imagine the intensity of all this hatred to turn humans into savage animals. It is also a sad example of how human mobs can be manipulated.

Benes fueled anti-German sentiments by claiming to settle old accounts, nothing specific, just in generalities. These actions were the result of tons of anti-German propaganda. Benes turned judicial justice on its head by proclaiming that any crimes committed against Germans were not punishable by law; he legalized murder, if it was against Germans. He made a total mockery of jurisprudence, legalizing crime, which was condoned by the Allies and accepted as legal tender. Germans were also discriminated against by the local tax collectors, by being taxed at a higher level. In the Algauer region, even nuns were raped in churches, as were pregnant women. Even the church was helpless against this godless horde. The common folk were told that God is dead, so were morals and human compassion. These were the result of the Benes decrees.

On May 30, 1945, the *London Daily Mail* featured a story describing how some thirty thousand German residents of Brno (Bruenn), the capitol of Moravia, were ruthlessly driven out of their ancestral homes and hometowns. These were respected and upright members of the community. This is one of many examples of how the Benes decrees caused untold human rights violations and human suffering. This was but one of many examples of anti-German Czech acts of brutality. At about 8:45 p.m., Czech partisans marched through the streets ordering the Germans to stand at their front doors at 9:00 p.m. sharp, with only one piece of hand luggage and be ready to leave their homes and homeland forever. They were ordered to turn over all valuables, such as watches, jewelry, furs, and money to the partisans. They were allowed to keep only their wedding rings and the clothes they were wearing on their backs.

They were then forced to walk on foot some forty miles to the Austrian border and pushed across the border. However, the Austrian border guards refused to accept them, and the Czech Communist partisans did not allow them back. That created a huge human problem. They were pushed into a field, where they spent the night. The open field was turned into a concentration camp. The next day, a few Romanian soldiers arrived to guard them. No food or other provisions were provided. In a few days, typhus fever took its toll. One hundred people died a day. In all, two thousand people died. Among those who were forced to suffer by this out-of-control mob were an English lady, a seventy-year-old Austrian woman, and an eighty-six-year-old Italian woman. American medics ended up treating these unfortunate victims, who were also severely beaten by this mob. They could not resist demonstrating their version of brotherly love to their longtime neighbors.

In May 2015, the Brno city authority issued an apology for the suffering and deaths of this Brno Death March. The apology was welcomed by the Sudeten Germans as a big step toward reconciliation and building bridges based upon an honest dialogue and truthful treatment of all the facts and their mutual history. An honest and truthful dialogue about this and other mass murders against Germans is slowly unfolding.

For many centuries, Brno (Bruenn) has been a pillar and a showcase of German-Bohemian culture and harmonious coexistence. Throughout the centuries, there existed a cultural and racial cross-pollination. In Brno and in many other Czech towns and communities, there was a solid German element present. About 30 percent of the population of Vienna was Bohemian. They intermarried. They had their own schools, hotels, and businesses. While Vienna celebrated its ethnic diversity, Benes, on the other hand, used it to fuel and instill anti-German hate and hysteria among the Czechs.

Typhus fever is an acute infectious disease that is transmitted by fleas and lice, especially when people are forced to live in camps and close together. Infected people suffer from fever, nervous disorders, weakness, and red spots on their skin.

On July 31, 1945, there was a huge explosion in Aussig, a town on the Elbe River. Fanatical Czechs instantly jumped to the conclusion that it must have been an act of sabotage by the Germans. There was no credible investigation of the real causes of the explosion. Hate is like a fire, and it gets bigger when it gets fueled with propaganda. What followed could have been a scene straight out of the scariest horror movie Hollywood ever produced. Women and children were beaten, tortured, and thrown from the bridge into the river. This murderous scene went on for hours. Some 2,500 innocent victims were mercilessly brutalized and murdered. This was the law of the jungle. The Benes decrees, sanctioned by the Allies, authorized murder, without legal retribution. Elya Ehrenburg's propaganda demanded the murder of all Germans. No one was ever held accountable for any of these mass murders, because only Germans could be prosecuted for war crimes. Sadly, this is still the way it is, even after all these years. These war crimes were committed during peace time, because the war was officially over, but no one cared. After Vaclav Havel became president of Czechoslovakia, he personally placed an official plaque on the Usti Bridge in remembrance of all the German victims of this hateful, barbarous massacre, so that those who died so needlessly shall never be forgotten.

Czech partisans were encouraged to steal everything their hearts desired without fear of any repercussions. If Germans dared to file a complaint against the partisans for stealing everything out of their homes, they would then be visited by the local police officials, who would beat them and levy them a fine for leaving their residence without proper permission and not wearing the obligatory armband, even in their home, with the letter "N" on it. The letter "N" identified them as Germans and simultaneously as enemies of the state. People were beaten unconscious while being forced to stand on one leg, with arms raised high, screaming, "We thank our Fuhrer." Germans were not only forced to wear the letter "N," but they were also forbidden to use public transportation and visit local establishments or parks. They were forced to work on the streets as slave laborers. They were beaten until covered with blood or until they collapsed. They were threatened with punishment of death but all too often beaten to death. Sadly, being brutalized and beaten to death was not the exception but the norm. Should these criminals not be held accountable for their crimes?

Herta Ruthard shares her story.

> I myself am a surviving witness of this policy of extermination. Born in 1931, I had the worst possible start in life. Starvation from the cradle has a detrimental effect on one's health all the way to the grave. I was about three or four years old when I had to go to a Czech doctor in Reichenberg because of an intestinal problem. How well I remember those endless "sessions" on the potty, which produced nothing. Naturally, if nothing goes in, nothing can come out. The Czech doctor hated little children, maybe only German ones, especially if they screamed. I screamed. "Now, now, I'm not going to eat you up right away!" he roared at me.
>
> From my mother, I also know how German adult patients in Reichenberg were treated by another Czech doctor, Dr. Stransky; it was a little more than assisted suicide and degradation. The doctor told me: "The best thing for you is to throw yourself into the Neisse" (the river which passes through Reichenberg). Or: "Have you ever considered trying this?" He motioned to indicate hanging.

Germans were ordered to display appropriate respect to Russian and Czech officers, remove their hats or caps, and pass at an appropriate distance. Furthermore, Czech citizens were severely punished for aiding, abetting, or helping and showing human compassion to their German neighbors in any manner whatsoever.

The Benes decrees and FDR's unconditional surrender relegated the ethnic Germans to being homeless, having no legal rights whatsoever, and not being entitled to due process procedures. That was true for the German Americans, Latin German Americans, and Germans in Europe. Everything, including their human dignity, was taken from them. It should be noted that France never agreed to the expulsions or the deportations. Benes claimed that he worked feverishly on the expulsions of the Germans from the new Czechoslovakia since 1920.

The International Red Cross was not permitted to inspect the Polish concentration camps until July 17, 1947, after most of the Germans were either starved to death, brutally murdered, or able to flee. In Czechoslovakia, the Red Cross was allowed into the camps in the autumn of 1945, where they found the conditions deplorable. At the Svednik camp, the German prisoners were forced to clear mine fields.

Dr. de Zayas talks about H. G. Adler, a Czech Jew, who during the war was interned in the Theresienstadt concentration camp. He describes the concentration camps that now were housing German prisoners:

> But the majority, among them children and adolescents, were locked up simply because they were German. Just because they were German? That phrase is frighteningly familiar; one could easily substitute the word "Jew" for "German." The rags given to the Germans as clothes were smeared with swastikas. They were miserably undernourished, abused, and generally subjected to much of the same treatment one was used to

in the German-run camps ... The camps were
run by the Czechs, yet they did nothing to stop
the Russians from going in to rape the captive
women ...

On October 19, 1945, Bertrand Russell wrote in the *Times*:
"An apparently deliberate attempt is being made to exterminate
many millions of Germans, not by gas, but by depriving them
of their homes and of food, leaving them to die by slow and
agonizing starvation. This is not done as an act of war, but as a
part of a deliberate policy of peace." The German soldiers laid
down their weapons, and the war should have been over. Who
authorized and sanctioned all these atrocities after the war?

Trainloads of orphaned children arrived in Berlin. Most
of them were between the ages of two and fourteen. Half
of them were already dead when they arrived. The children
under two died before they could be put on a cattle train. This
horrific scenario repeated itself many times, unwanted German
orphans arriving from Poland and Czechoslovakia. Most of the
children who were still breathing were mere skeletons; their
bodies, bellies, knees, and feet swollen, well-known symptoms
of starvation. Justifying their sinister actions, Poles and Czechs
professed that these innocent orphans were paying for the sins
that their fathers may have committed. Most of these children
were already too weak to even feed themselves. Death was the
constant companion of these innocent orphans. Their parents
had already been killed and could no longer care for them.

The hatred in Poland was so acute and severe that they
even cleared their hospitals of all German patients, regardless
of their condition. Many were simply thrown out of the
second- or third-floor windows and their bodies carted into
mass, unmarked graves. Even German women and children
were mercilessly evicted from their hospital beds. Many women

were forced to witness their husbands being beaten to death. The anti-German hate was intense and inhumane, and no one listened or seemed to care.

On October 18, 1945, General Dwight D. Eisenhower failed to file a report to Washington that was sent to him. It stated, "In Silesia, Polish administration and methods are causing a mass exodus westward of German inhabitants. Germans are being ordered out of their homes and to evacuate New Poland … Death and disease rates in camps extremely high."

In 1945 and 1946, thousands of Germans were held prisoners in the Lamsdorf concentration camp, now Lambinovice. The Polish commander, Czeslaw Geborski, had women shot randomly. Children were starved to death; they died of malnutrition. One of the barracks happened to go up in flames, and guards forced German prisoners into the flames. Today, Lambinowice is a memorial site for both Polish and German victims of the war.

Because this was their ancestral home, which they loved, many Germans chose to stay. Some chose to stay because they were married to Poles, and some were needed because of their expertise. The Polish authority did everything they could to nationalize these Germans into becoming Poles; however, they failed. Life for the Germans who stayed was made as miserable as possible. The Germans were not allowed to speak German, not even in the privacy of their own homes. Well-maintained German cemeteries were leveled, and German monuments were defaced. The Polish authority did everything it could to extinguish all traces of its German minority, as if they never even existed. Kaufman's demand that *Germany must perish* was being ruthlessly implemented.

It would be extremely difficult, by any definition of the law, not to consider the murders, rapes, starvations, ethnic cleansings, and expulsions; Ike's Rhine death camps; and slave labor in Poland, Czechoslovakia, the Soviet Union, Hungary, Romania, and Yugoslavia as crimes against humanity. However, when will someone or some world organization bring charges against these perpetrators and when will justice be served? True justice does not have the liberty to pick and choose where and when to apply the rule of law. Justice must be blind, and the rule of law must be like the law of gravity—consistent, without exceptions, and void of all discrimination.

To attempt to argue that the ethnic cleansing, the tortures, the mass murders, the raping of millions of women, the mass starvations, the expulsions and evictions, and the slave labor camps were not war crimes because they were committed by the victorious powers would be a total mockery of any precept of justice and the rule of law in civilized societies. Justice that discriminates is no justice at all. In 1994, judgment was passed on two men who participated in the deportation of civilians to the Soviet slave labor camps. Justice has no borders, nor does it have any territorial limits. The criminal law that was applied in Jackson's Nuremberg Tribunal must also be applied to the crimes committed against Germans. To equate might with right would be reverting to the law of the jungle and turn such proceedings into an international legal farce.

US Commander Lucius D. Clay filed a complaint about Benes and the mistreatment of the Germans by the Czechs. He also remarked that the Czechs kept young and able workers and sent sick and starved old men, women, and children to the west. He stated that he was shocked by the sight of the victims, as they were barely able to get off the cattle cars. They were referred to as the walking dead. Most of the able bodies were gathered by the Soviets and transported to Siberia and beyond as slave labor.

Josef Stalin was a seminary student before he became the ruthless dictator and mass murderer. Elya Ehrenburg came from a Jewish family and wrote poems in Paris dedicated to the Virgin Mary before he became the merchant of hate and death. Stalin attempted to differentiate between the German people and its leader, stating, "History has demonstrated that Hitlers come and go, but the German people and the German state remain." He should have included himself among the leaders that come and go.

In taking East Prussia, the Soviet forces suffered the loss of half of its contingent; they lost 458,314 dead and wounded. Alexander Solschenizyn experienced the slaughter in East Prussia. He describes the experience in his poem "East Prussian Nights."

Most of the Soviet soldiers were men from poor farming families, who suffered hunger and terror in the forced Marxist collectivization program. They never strayed far from home. When they got to and saw German cities and villages, they experienced a culture shock, which far too often only intensified their dictated hatred toward the Germans. For the first time, they saw refrigerators, large radios, heavy carpets, and feather beds. They rode stolen bicycles and sat on comfortable couches, much too often totally intoxicated. Their government gave them permission to steal, rape, and murder, and they were encouraged to send their stolen loot back home.

The Soviets dropped tons of pamphlets filled with propaganda, filled with lies, of how good the Germans would have it with the Soviets. They attempted to reassure the Germans: don't fear the Soviet soldiers; they come as liberators. It was obvious these were nothing but bold-faced lies. The Red Army wreaked terror. On October 21, 1944, in a small East Prussian town, called Nemmersdorf, the Red Army left behind scores of dead old men, women, and children. They nailed women against the sides of barns after they were gang raped. These indescribable scenes of savage brutality created panic among the Germans from the Baltic to the Balkan. After the German Wehrmacht regained Nemmersdorf, they invited the International Red Cross to show the world what the Soviet forces had done to innocent civilians. FDR, Churchill, and the Allied media totally ignored the Red Cross report, erroneously blaming Hitler and the Nazis for these savage crimes, proving that truth is the first casualty of war. FDR and Churchill knew the truth.

In the fall of 1944, colonies of refugees were tracking westward, traveling from town to town. The author spoke to an elderly man who, as a young boy, walked with his family, including his grandpa, westward. His grandpa could not keep up and told the family that he was going to catch up with them as soon as he was able. Grandpa was never seen or heard of again; he was probably killed by the partisans for not walking fast enough. In addition to all the destruction, there were mountains of corpses along the road. These innocent civilian refugees were needlessly subjected to incomprehensible misery. Some of those that the Red Army passed returned to their homes, only to be subjected to more terror. All the furniture had been stolen and doors and windows torn out of their frames. The wind was hauling through the empty and open houses. Houses and people were riddled with bullets.

Thousands of children were roaming through the woods. These "Wolfskinder" somehow maneuvered from one structure to another. They were a stark reminder of all the devastation of the war. It is further proof that the Allied objective was not victory but total destruction of Germany. Millions of children and adults did not survive the flight to the west. They were buried in unmarked graves, or their bodies were left at the side of the road and picked up later and dumped into mass graves. Many were stabbed and then suffered from the agony of dying slowly from the unattended wounds.

H. Lehnsdorf wrote in his diary, "My brother was severely injured due to knife-stab wounds. My mother was able to bandage him up then the Russians came, asked who he was, then shot my brother and my mother. No one cared to know that my mother was incarcerated by the Gestapo." The deportations and expulsions of millions of people were a tragedy of unprecedented proportions. FDR and Churchill claimed that the Atlantic Charter did not apply to the Germans, because "we don't have a contract with our enemy." Actually, the Atlantic Charter was only a press release, and no charter was ever passed or accepted by any governmental body, but the media gave it a lot of coverage.

On November 4, 1944, the Polish National Liberation Committee ordered all Germans older than thirteen immediately to be put into concentration camps and subjected to forced labor. Others who could still move became part of caravans westward on horse-drawn wagons. Many pulled their belongings and the elderly in handcarts, and many carried suitcases. Many were much too weak to even step aside for an oncoming tank; they were exposed to the elements and to the nonexistent Soviet, Polish, and Czech human compassion and mercy.

German women from eight to eighty were gang raped in orgies that lasted from 8:00 p.m. until 9:00 a.m. Many were left behind motionless and dead; many women committed suicide. Now, decades later, many of these women have stepped forward and are talking about their ordeals publicly. Often, husbands were forced to watch their wives being gang raped. In the 1950s, more than forty thousand such cases were reported to the government of the Federal Republic of Germany. The brutality these German women were subjected to was so shocking that the Bonn Government for many years hesitated to publish their findings in fear of the public reaction and out cray.

Magdalene still has her diary that she kept when she was twelve years old and living in a refugee camp in Kiel, West

Germany. They lived in a one-room Quonset hut, made from corrugated sheet metal, for more than four long years. They planted a patch of corn alongside the barrack.

> The corn grew quickly and was tall enough to provide us some privacy. This patch felt like it was a heavenly place, a retreat, where I used to sit on the "Rasenbank" and compose poetry. On September 11, 1949, I wrote the following lines: 'The corn is swaying in the wind and it is so nice and cool. Briefly it felt like paradise.' Mother planted morning glories that climbed up on the side of the window frame. Below the window grew purple, rose and white asters. Even decades later, they still have a special place in my heart. They gave us a sense of beauty in our harsh surroundings, rows and rows of Quonset huts made from corrugated sheet metal. They served as temporary quarters for the overwhelming stream of refugees. It was home for almost five years.

She vividly remembers,

> In 1944, during the latter part of the war, the Germans in our region of Poland were evacuated to the Sudetenland. We lived with a Czech family in their home. We got along quite well; our relationship was congenial and rather harmonious. After the war, we were told to go home, to return to our homes.
> Chaos and oppression awaited us in our hometown of Nowy Dwor near Warsaw. Upon our arrival at the railroad station we were

escorted by the local police to the city jail. We were stripped of all our belongings. After we were cleared of any offenses against the Poles during the Nazi occupation, we were released. Our home was now occupied by a Polish family that was unwilling to allow us to use even one room for the night. We eventually found a place where other German families were staying, 23 of us in one room. There was no furniture, so we slept on the floor covered with straw. That is how our animals used to sleep. Bed bugs were in full force.

There wasn't any food available. My brothers Sieg and John went from house to house begging from people that used to be our neighbors. The Polish people did not have much, but a few kind souls took pity on us and offered a potato, a carrot or a piece of bread. It was appreciated. After a short while we all came down with typhoid fever. Then our heads were shaved. It really was a miracle that we did not all die.

Mother and my oldest brother found work on the army base. They peeled potatoes and prepared vegetables. There was no monetary pay, but they were given one meal at the end of their workday. Sieg managed to steal some potatoes for the rest of us. Brother John collected scraps of food in the mess hall from the soldiers' plates they left behind. A kind and compassionate soldier noticed him and offered to fill his little pail straight from the kitchen. We did not have to eat leftover scraps anymore.

One of my memories of this "Hungerzeit," starvation time, is when I was merely eight years old. I found cut off fish heads on a garbage pile. It was on the way to my mom's friend's house. Quickly I stashed them into my coat pockets. My mother's friends were sniffing their noses saying: something smells like fish here ... something smells like fish here. But I kept quiet knowing very well where that fishy smell came from. On the way back I showed mom my "precious find." That evening we enjoyed fish soup; it was one night we did not go to bed hungry.

One happy day we received a letter from my dad; it was a joyous day because we learned that dad was alive and where he was. Dad was a German POW on a Russian farm in Pomerania. He was an interpreter for the other German POWs, as he spoke Russian well. After dad found out about our miserable living conditions, he was able to arrange for us to join him on the farm. Mom helped in the kitchen and cleaned the quarters. It was such a relief not to have to scramble for scraps of food. However, the Russians were in the process of deporting the German POWs to Russia and so we stayed on the farm for only a few months.

With the help of a Polish friend we got away before dad was sent to Russia. During the late evening hours, as he was keeping the Russians busy drinking Vodka, we escaped to the next town on foot. We hid there in the attic of a friend's house for one week until it was safe enough to emerge. In Stettin, train transports heading for West Germany were being organized to depart weekly. However, only women and children could leave. Frau Behnke bribed the commandant with a cow to get her husband on the train to the West. Mom did not have a cow anymore, so she offered their wedding rings as a bribe and dad was signed up for the next train to the West. We were on our way to freedom, on a train to Kiel, West Germany.

Fifty years after the Jordan family was forced to leave their home and homeland forever, Baerbl took it upon herself to share those torturous days with her sister on her birthday. She writes,

Dear sister, it is your birthday ... on this day 50 years ago, on March 5, 1945, was the day we left our home in Schnatow to flee from the advancing Red Army. It was your fourth birthday, but your birthday cake never made it into the wagon that was to carry all our belongings that were gathered in haste. On the night of March 4, at around 11:00 p.m. a village official came around to warn us that we have to leave by 6:00 a.m., because our village will become the battle ground of the advancing Russian army and the retreating German eastern front.

All necessary items were hurriedly loaded into our horse-drawn carriage; most of our belongings had to be left behind, because they just didn't fit into the wagon. Our family dog, Bello, stayed behind; he knew something was wrong. It was already past the six o'clock deadline when we left. As we got to the Caminer Chausee, the road was clogged with all sorts of horse and oxen drawn wagons. All were packed high with their dearest belongings, coming from many neighboring villages. All were trying to reach the one bridge that was still open. Soldiers kept us from going to the Oder Bridge; it was already destroyed. The wagons moved at a snail's pace, all moving west.

The opposing lane was kept open for military reinforcement. I could hear the fear in the conversations of the adults not being able to flee the Red Army. They heard reports of Soviet brutality and how they treated the German women. This trek was comprised mostly of women and children and very old men; the younger men were off to war. As it became dark, fires could be seen. The people named the villages that were going up in flames. It was not long thereafter that we could hear artillery and see the projectiles shot from the tanks. We could see the opposing forces.

As the darkness increased, so did the fighting. There were the sounds of fighting in the distance and the fires on the horizon. Then there was an outcry, and then several more, and then shockwaves came across the group, because the Russians were driving their tanks and armored vehicles right over the wagons behind us. Before that message, with all the horror, could sink in, we heard rifle shots and saw dark figures in uniforms moving between the wagons. Horses shied and tried to flee, people were screaming and running for cover, horses were shot and people were shot. Mom quickly pulled us from the wagon on the side where the trees were and a deep ditch. Oma slipped and fell into the ditch; Aunt Gertrud tried to calm her. Mom put both of us behind a tree and told us to stay there and not to move. It could not have been a long time that we were behind the tree with mayhem all around us. These moments have been imprinted on my mind, with death and destruction all around us. The air was filled with frightened and hurt people, shots and rough yelling in a language we did not understand.

Mom took us by the hand and then climbed into the ditch; then with Oma and Aunt Gertrud climbed out again and walked out unto a freshly plowed field. The darkness provided cover that allowed us to move towards the wooded area beyond. The two of us children were told to keep quiet. After we reached the woods unscathed, the adults breathed a sigh of relief. It was so dark that we could not see the next tree in front of us. When we heard any sound, we all froze in our tracks and waited until it was quiet again. Oma tripped on a tree root and had fallen and lost the handbag she was carrying with all the documents in it. We could not find the handbags and our vital documents were lost. Our lives were in jeopardy, what worth are handbags.

We kept walking most of the night. At day break we came to a street where everything was quiet and seemed peaceful. Soon we came to a house where there was plenty of activity. The family was scurrying to pack up some of their belongings, as we had done the night before.

Mother begged for some bread for us and told them not to bother with the packing, just to get out, but they were not convinced. We moved on; we got to the bridge and were able to cross it. We kept on walking and got to Wollin, a city where Mom had worked for a superintendent and his family. They took us in with compassion, and gave us a warm meal and the guest room on the second floor. They tucked us in, and we fell asleep from exhaustion. And that is how we spent Erika's birthday fifty years ago.

The Nazis could have caused an evacuation and prevented much suffering. But how was anyone going to know the secret plans of the Allied powers and how the Germans were going to be treated, especially since this had been their home for centuries? They should have remembered Bismarck's premonition that in case of a German defeat, Germans would not be treated humanely by its victorious neighbors. In Breslau, some seven hundred thousand residents, refugees, and wounded were not evacuated even when the Soviets were at the gates of the city. Was this another of Hitler's insane treasonous acts? Gauleiter Karl Hanke left the city with the last plane and then left the people to fend for themselves. To flee, for everyone else, was verboten.

A thirty-nine-year-old E. O. from Elbing was with her two children, Horst, seven, and Christa, one, escaping westward when Soviet soldiers grabbed her and other women and locked them up into a room, which was set up as a brothel for the Soviet soldiers. These poor victims were gang raped for seven days. On the eighth day, they were sent on a death march totally naked and barefoot. Those women who still could get up and walk away did so under excruciating pain and suffering; the others died, and their bodies were unceremoniously disposed of in unmarked graves. Their lower bodies and thighs were covered with open soars. Many of the women had their genitals torn and ripped. Many of the women ended up committing suicide. They all agonized over their fate and wondered if all they were born for was to satisfy the sexual lusts of savages.

E. O. was one of very few out of more than six hundred women who survived this hellhole. She was able to locate her two children, and all three ultimately ended up in Germany.

E. O. had just enough strength to bring her children home, but their home was completely pillaged and looted. She fetched a hand-wagon and trekked with Horst and Christa westward. When they arrived at the little town of Weyer, she broke down and attempted to drown herself but, fortunately, was rescued and lived to tell her story to the rest of the world.

There is a small town in East Bohemia, which has feverishly been keeping its secrets about the Budinka Wiese, the Budinka Meadow. Even after all these years, everyone in town is tight-lipped about what happened during one dark night in May 1945. Perhaps this was their way of displaying remorse and shame. Sincere confessions are good for the soul. There was a masquerade dance at the local inn. A group of intoxicated men, upright members and pillars of the town, decided to go to the firehouse depot where fifteen Germans were being held to be deported. Armed with spades and clubs, they began to beat them and then drove them to an open area on the way to Nove Dwory. The Germans were forced to dig their own mass grave before they were beaten to death and buried. When farmers found limps hands, heads, and other human body parts sticking out of the ground, they attempted to quickly bury these human body parts again, but they kept appearing again and again as a permanent reminder of their deplorable crime. These criminals were never brought to justice, because, according to Benes and the Allies, only Germans could be tried for war crimes. When will the international court overrule the hideous Benes decrees and allow true *justice*, without discrimination, to prevail?

Because the German army did not retreat until the beginning of May 1945, almost the very end of the war, because of FDR's unconditional surrender, millions of Germans remained unprotected. In May 1945, radical communists organized demonstrations against the Germans. In April, the Czech National Front began its merciless ethnic cleansing of the Germans. The Czech units were comprised of partisans and members of the Sorboda Army, which fought alongside the Red Army. The Sudeten Germans were being "liberated" from their homes and their homeland and all their earthly possessions.

Robert Murphy, advisor to the military council, reported that the American army began to feel hatred toward the "liberated," newly created Czechoslovakia. Thousands of Bohemian Germans were put into Czech concentration camps and used as slave laborers. They were given pig's food but barely enough to stay alive.

A starving old man wanted to fetch an empty can from the garbage when a Czech guard noticed it. The German prisoners were ordered to line up. The old, hungry man had to undress down to his underwear. He was told to hold up his hands, stand on one leg, and holler at the top of his voice, "Wir danken unserem Fuehrer," while he was being whipped. The German prisoners were forced to watch this spectacle until he fell, covered in blood. This is one of many examples of Benes's decrees; he promised it would be written in blood. The world watched as the media ignored it.

German civilians in East Prussia and elsewhere were under no illusions about the fate that awaited them when the Red Army overran the territory. Millions of refugees were trekking in the direction of Schleswig-Holstein, Mecklenburg, and

Denmark across the ice-covered waters, hoping to find a ship that would carry them to safety. Of the millions who ventured this escape route, only some five hundred thousand reached safe harbor. The Soviets made safe retreat miserable and almost impossible; they dropped bombs to break the ice and caused millions to drown. Death was staring at them from all sides. Dead bodies and horses and wagons were frozen in the icy water. All the ships were filled to capacity; they faced the danger of Soviet U-boats, sinking German ships filled with refugees and wounded soldiers. More than nine thousand drowned on the *William Gustloff*, which was the greatest disaster in seafaring history. The loss of lives was ten times greater than that of the *Titanic*, and yet no one knows anything about the *William Gustloff* catastrophe.

Defenseless German ships were being sunk in the Baltic Sea while they were attempting to rescue refugees from the claws of the Red Army. Just between the SS *Cap Arcona* and the MV *William Gustloff*, more than seventeen thousand innocent people, mostly civilians, perished in the icy water. Many other ships were sunk by Soviet submarines and British Typhoon fighter bombers, such as the MV *Goya* and the *Thielbek* as they attempted to bring wounded soldiers, foreign citizens, and German civilians to safety. Compare this to Hitler's orders to allow the English to return safely to dear old England after the defeat of Dunkirk. Hoisting of the white flag proved useless; it was categorically ignored. The British fired relentlessly at these poor souls as they were trying to make their way to lifeboats. This was a gross violation of international law, but no one has held them accountable. More than 7,000 died on the *Goya* and 2,750 on the *Thielbek*.

For centuries, Danzig was one of the principal cities of the Hansa League. Prior to the war, 95 percent of its population was German. It became the wealthiest city in Poland. The

Polish king Kasimir IV gave the Germans special privileges and rights, including the right to coin their own money, in return for their continued support. Danzig was the most important harbor on the East Sea; 80 percent of Poland's exports were shipped through Danzig. For centuries, Germans and Poles lived harmoniously and peacefully together, mutually benefitting and contributing to the success of the city, the region, and the country.

The great majority of the city and the entire region were Germans. Sadly, the tranquility, harmony, and cooperation changed, because of all the venom that was being fueled against the Germans. Furthermore, the land and its people were amputated from Germany. The Allies used Poland and Czechoslovakia to weaken the shaky Weimar Republic.

All the murdering, the raping, the grand theft of properties and all the mistreatments can hardly be "a fight for democracy" and freedom. Until 1918, Wojciech Karfonty went by the name of Albert but then changed it. He became one of the main proponents leading the Polish anti-German activities. He promised a cow to every Pole after they got rid of all the hated Germans. That cow to every Pole never materialized, but most of the hatred still lingers on. For the Germans, the eastern border remains an open wound that needs to be addressed.

Stalin's forces totally destroyed Danzig and conducted themselves savagely. Helga Joachimiak remembers; she was eleven, hiding under a bed and shaking with fear, when her mother was gang raped by Soviet soldiers. Her father was a physician.

Not only the Nobel Prize laureate Guenther Grass but also Donald Tusk went to school in Danzig. The instructions were primarily in German. Disaster struck, and all things German were verboten; all things German and its German history became taboo, and speaking German was punished. This ancient German city had a new coat of communistic Polish paint applied to it. Years later, the Polish paint has been peeling, and the former German names and lettering are reappearing. The German history is gradually reemerging. Guenther Grass left as a seventeen-year-old. Later, he was named an honorary member of his hometown Danzig. Danzig and Poland are finding their new identity, gradually giving due credit and consideration to the indelible German layer of history.

The territorial demands of the Poles and the Czechs, following World War I, were encouraged by London and its allies. Most often, the Czech and Polish leaders met at Wilson's residence in London, so much for Wilson's neutrality. Their primary discussions were about how to parcel up Germany and reduce the German population. Poland's gains were to be Germany's losses. The Germans considered the loss of Danzig and the Polish Corridor, Posen, and West Prussia extremely unjust, which, unfortunately, also gave rise to Hitler. This is how the big political chess game is played and becomes a cause for a new war.

For decades, Poles were told that they now lived in regained German regions. The European map has never been redrawn so ruthlessly and drastically as in the twentieth century by Churchill and the victorious Allies. This is how the war industry plans the causes for future wars.

For decades, Poles and Czechs feared that the Germans would be coming back to reclaim their homes and property. This added significantly to the anxiety level of the people who have moved into and now live in a German home. Are property rights rewritten at the whim of the victors? The question begs to be answered. Are all those who were violently torn from their hereditary roots due to the destructive forces of hatred, greed, and vengeance entitled to anything, even an apology? Or do different rules of civil decorum apply to them, because they are

German? Many Poles and Czechs are rather sensitive about the forced expulsions and prefer to call them "voluntary emigration." The fact is that there was nothing voluntary about these brutal expulsions. This part of European history is being whitewashed in the media and in textbooks in Poland, Czechoslovakia, and even in Germany itself. Sadly, Germany may still have little to say about its own contemporary history, while the expulsions of some sixteen million Germans is marginalized and even killed with deafening silence. The textbooks and the media only talk about sole German guilt and German disgrace and say nothing about the brutality and suffering that the Germans were subjected to. A real historical balance is still unfolding. The world still continues to receive discriminatory information about what was done to the Germans and German Americans.

Some of the former East German authors demonstrated that the pen is mightier than the sword. While the East German Communist cronies ordered silence and obedient acceptance, several courageous authors stepped forward and discussed the many sensitive taboo issues. In 1950, Anna Seghers wrote *Gerda aus Ostpreussen*, describing her own experiences as a refugee as well as the suffering her family and relatives had to endure, during and after the expulsions, when they had not even a crumb of bread to eat. She talks about Franz, who not only lost his leg but also his Heimat. Christa Wolf caused considerable uproar with her 1976 novel *Kindheitsmuster*, in which she talks about her childhood and youth experiences.

Journalist and author Petra Reski is the daughter of an East Prussian father and a Silesian mother. She grew up in the Ruhr region in Germany and then lived and worked in Venedig. Her book *Ein Land so weit* appeared in 2000. It is the story of her own family. She also traveled to and found her ancestral roots in East Prussia, where she also found her relatives who did not run from the commies and the Poles. She found that the Poles had removed and attempted to eradicate even German cemeteries. The dead were not left to rest in peace.

When Petra visited her relatives, they had so much to talk about and catch up on. In the evening, while enjoying each other's company and reestablishing their family bonds, they sang the old familiar German folk songs. They concluded that "Was vorbei ist, ist nicht vorbei!" (What has past is not gone forever). She also observed that the anxiety level of the people living in her family's homestead rose noticeably. They were visibly concerned that she came back to reclaim her family's home. The question has been justly raised: Are all these victims entitled to any compensation for their stolen property, or will they continue to be treated differently? It is legally their property. Germany has paid billions in restitution; the time is long past due for others to display some moral and judicial justice.

Polish and Czech history is also German and Austrian history. Albrecht von Brandenburg-Ansbach created the first Protestant state, where persecuted Protestants could come for safety. Albrecht's uncle was the Polish king Zygmunt I. Emperor Karl IV ruled the Holy Roman Empire of the German Nation from 1355 until 1378. Silesia and Bohemia were part of his empire. In 1544, Zygmunt I founded the Protestant University in Koenigsberg. Under Friedrich the Great, 40 percent of the 8.7 million Prussian citizens were Poles. The Hansa League was a powerful commercial force; they were the merchants between the East and West. The first German university was founded by Otto the Great in Prague. The iron production in Silesia became the most modern in all of Germany; the steel production increased 500 percent between 1780 and 1800. Silesia became the center for weapons production for Prussia.

Given the cultural heritage of all the people who lived and dwelled here harmoniously, who cultivated and developed the land and culture, most certainly, they can accomplish that peaceful climate and the attitude of coexistence again, as they have done for centuries before, hopefully without foreign interference. Bridges of understanding and trust and mutual respect and tolerance are continuously being built. Not only are visitors reminded of the rich German history, but also museums are proudly displaying and documenting its colorful German history. Germans, Poles, and Czechs have been pushed so far apart by international propaganda and intrigue, the time has come for them to move closer together and display genuine tolerance and reciprocal respect. Tolerant people love truth and liberty and live together in a climate where truth, liberty, and justice for all flourish.

The 1939 Corridor Massacres, mountains of murdered Germans in Poland on the way to be identified.

The bodies of ten murdered and dismembered ethnic Germans were found at the exit of Thorner Street in Bromberg.

Eighteen bodies of murdered ethnic Germans were found at the Bromberger Canal; among them were two children. All, except one, had their hands tied behind them.

Here were eight murdered Germans at one location in Glinke near Bromberg. This was the result of all the hatred generated against Germans.

Foreign reporters were invited to show them the many Polish atrocities committed against ethnic Germans. To the left is Mr. Oechsener from the United Press.

Befehl.

Laut Anordnung der Regierung der Republik Polen hat die gesamte deutsche Bevölkerung das polnische Staatsgebiet zu verlassen. Vorgeschrieben ist das deutsche Gebiet über Görlitz an der Neiße. Der Weg geht über Frankenstein—Reichenbach—Schweidnitz—Striegau— Jauer—Goldberg—Löwenberg—Lauban—Görlitz. Bei Verlassen des polnischen Staatsgebietes dürfen nur 30 kg Gepäck mitgenommen werden.

Alle Personen, welche dieser Aufforderung nicht nachkommen, werden mit Gewalt entfernt.

Diejenigen Personen, die im Besitz einer Bescheinigung des Bevollmächtigten der polnischen Regierung sind, werden vom Verlassen des Gebietes befreit.

Bis zum 30. Juni 1945, mittags 12 Uhr muß der Befehl ausgeführt sein.

Glatz, den 29. Juni 1945.

Der Bevollmächtigte
der Polnischen Regierung
für den Bezirk XXIV
in Glatz

Die Kommandantur
des Polnischen Heeres
in Glatz

424

CHAPTER 11

Other Losses
The Eisenhower Rhine Death Camps

Other Losses is the title of a book written by James Bacque. It is a detailed and scholarly investigation into the mass deaths of German prisoners of war at the hands of the American and French after World War II. *Time* magazine called the book "Stunning" and the *Globe and Mail* called it "A hornet's nest." He discovered the material to this book while he was researching the life of a French resistance hero, Raoul Laporterie.

The first edition of *Other Losses* in 1989 caused an international scandal by revealing that more than a million German prisoners of war died of starvation in American and French death camps. Millions of German POW survivors applauded James Bacque for displaying the courage to publish his findings and turning the book into an international best seller. Furious academics, the American and French governments, as well as some journalists and Eisenhower's biographer, Stephen E. Ambrose, attacked Bacque for alleged exaggerations, but none was willing to provide an explanation of how many or why so many were murdered.

In 1992, Bacque flew to Moscow to visit the newly opened KGB archives, where he found further documentation of how more than a million Germans died in Western prison camps. The revised edition contains the additional information as well as the suppression of this material by academics, press, and governments, who might be somewhat embarrassed. Some of this material has also appeared in his book *Crimes and Mercies*, also on radio, as well as six hours of TV documentaries and news programs. Many survivors wrote to Bacque and thanked him for the book and for validating their brutal suffering and the deaths of their comrades.

Truth is the first casualty of war; truer words have never been spoken about Eisenhower's death camps. Anyone who even dared to whisper a word about Ike's death camps was threatened with court martial. George Bernard Shaw, in *The Devil's Disciple*, stated that "The worst sin towards our fellow creatures is not to hate them but to be indifferent to them; that's the essence of inhumanity."

Dwight D. Eisenhower wrote in a letter to his wife in September 1944, "God, I hate the Germans ..." Volumes could be written about the motives of this statement. Ike's mass murders would likely have remained a secret forever had it not been for a Canadian, James Bacque, who published his findings in a book *Other Losses*, which was the title of a box in which he found the documentation in the archives at the Pentagon. Because of the explosive contents, the book *Other Losses* has not been readily available in the United States. It has, however, enjoyed much success in Europe, Canada, and the rest of the world.

Many good and upright people in America found the facts so shocking and disturbing that they wept as they read these accounts of mass murder. Many knelt in prayer, asking God to forgive Ike and the soldiers who obeyed his orders for this mass murder. Many vowed to dedicate their lives for a just cause so that this sort of treachery will never happen again among civilized nations. Many have asked, "What has happened to our nation?"

Because of Ike's murderous treachery, Germany lost more soldiers after the war was over than during the entire war. The war was "officially" over, but not for the German soldiers. The German soldiers surrendered, believing they would be treated humanely and according to the Geneva Convention rules. Many surrendered to the Western allies, to the American forces, believing they would be treated more humanely by the Americans than by the Russians.

Soldiers do not have the luxury of choosing where, when, and if they are going to fight. They are conditioned to strict obedience, to follow orders. The retreating German soldiers found their fatherland totally demolished, the cities in total ruins, and many of their family members either missing or killed. This happened to be the coldest winter in a century; their army rations were not all that great, but they managed to survive. Their boots were tattered and their uniforms falling apart, and there was confusion all around them.

The Americans had some two hundred POW camps scattered throughout Germany, mostly along the Rhine River. They came to be known as Rheinwiesenlagern, or Ike's Rhine death camps. Upon surrendering, the German soldiers were pushed onto large meadows, makeshift corrals surrounded by barbed-wire fences and guarded by soldiers with machine guns in watchtowers. Large meadows became prison camps; sanitary facilities, like latrines, were nowhere to be found. Thousands upon thousands of German prisoners, as far as the eye could see, were pushed unto these pens and then kept without food or water for days. These German soldiers were exhausted, hungry, thirsty, and dirty. A US Army order on April 7, 1945, read "Cover is not essential," thus condemning hundreds of thousands of German prisoners to remain in the fields without any shelter for months. Their food rations, once they were given to the prisoners, were below the survival rate.

Thousands more were pushed into these corrals; all looking for a latrine or restroom facility, but none was to be found. At the end of the day, they were jammed together so tightly that there was no room to squat or sit down and rest one's tired legs. None of the prisoners had any food for that day and many not for the last two or three days, nor did they receive any from the Americans that any surviving prisoner could testify to. Without food and water, it was just a matter of time before they would die an agonizing death by starvation.

The German prisoners were wondering why the Geneva Convention rules weren't being followed. Surely, this must be an oversight or some kind of mistake. American soldiers are good and honorable men. This was contrary to the rules of the Geneva Convention; they couldn't treat them worse than animals, but they did. Somehow, they kept on hoping through the first night, but the slightest hope for any humane treatment evaporated quickly. Without shelter protecting them from the elements and with their uniforms sopping wet, they became weaker and weaker. Brave, grown men wept as they watched buddy after buddy die from lack of food, water, sleep, and shelter. They were in total despair as more and more soldiers died face-down in the mud, mixed with the waste of those who had died before. This was General Eisenhower implementing the Morgenthau Plan and FDR's unconditional surrender.

Dead and cold bodies were picked up and taken to a special tent where their clothing was stripped off of their dead bodies, so that the identity of these brave men would be forever forgotten. Their dog tags were snipped in half, and their dead bodies were covered with chemicals for rapid decomposition and buried in unmarked mass graves. This was the implementation of a policy of extermination by starvation, exposure, and disease under the direct orders of Dwight D. Eisenhower.

A month prior to the end of the war, Ike issued special orders regarding the treatment of German POWs. Included in these orders was the directive that "prison enclosures are to provide *no* shelter or other comforts." According to his personal correspondence, he stated that he hated the German people as a race. Why this hatred? His ancestors migrated to America from Germany and about a third of the soldiers and far more than seven hundred of the officers in the US Armed Forces and under his command were German Americans. Bacque's research of the mass deaths of German POWs is substantiated by numerous witnesses, survivors, and official documents. General Eisenhower accomplished this by switching the status of the German POWs to disarmed enemy forces (DEF), depriving them of visiting rights, use of mail, inspections by the International Red Cross, and protection of the Geneva rules. The German Red Cross had already been banned in the American Zone. The army-imposed censorship on the DEF prison camps was stricter than during the war. These death camps became shrouded in secrecy; Ike was determined to keep it a secret forever, but he fortunately failed.

According to international law, Ike's mistreatment of German POWs was illegal as hell. It appears that Ike's objective was to kill as many Germans as possible, and one way was to starve German POWs to death. On March 10, 1945, he issued the order reclassifying German POWs as "disarmed enemy forces." This was mind-boggling, since the war was over and these soldiers were not taken prisoner during any military conflict but surrendered and laid down their arms. Ike seems to have had the full support of the political power elite in Washington. Ike concluded and ruled that, as a consequence thereof, these German POWs did not fall under or would not enjoy the protection of the Geneva rules. No one dared to point out the fallacy and criminal objectives in this policy. The POWs were not to be fed, given any water, or receive any medical care, since their destiny was death.

Tragically, because of the secrecy, the media kept silent about these crimes. Had the American public been told about this mass starvation program, there would have been an uproar against these misrepresentations of American and international military legal conduct. Because of this reclassification of POWs, Eisenhower behaved as if he was immune from international military law. The International and the Swiss Red Cross were not allowed to visit or inspect the camps. Eisenhower ruled that the Red Cross had no authority or justification to visit or inspect his Rhine camps. His orders amounted to mass murder. Ike has the blood of over a million German POWs on his hands.

Months after the war was officially over and Germany had surrendered, Eisenhower's DEF Rhine starvation camps were still in operation. The German prisoners were dying daily by the thousands, and no one was allowed to raise a voice or allowed to help. Good Samaritans were not welcome. By remaining silent, the media became a partner in crime.

There is some good and some evil in all of us; the world is checkered with good and evil. The beast, the devil, may be conquered but never destroyed. Truthfulness is the cornerstone of an honorable character. An upright and honorable character is established by vigorous and persistent resistance to evil tendencies. Judas, by accepting thirty silver coins, became void of any redeeming qualities. Everyone is the architect of his or her own persona and character. The one who acts wickedly in private life should not be expected to act nobly in public, because only the place has changed, not the person.

The two men, General George Patton and Ike, could not have been more different. At the end of the war, General Patton turned his prisoners loose and allowed them to go home as best they could. The war was over but not for Ike; he was infuriated over Patton's humane and proper treatment of his prisoners and ordered Patton to turn over all of his prisoners to Ike's DEF death camps. It is believed that Patton largely ignored Ike's orders. It would have been contrary to his persona to treat prisoners in such a manner, and besides, the war was over. It has been alleged that Patton's untimely and curious death may well be the result of what Patton knew about Ike's starvation camps. Ike may well have feared that Patton would have berated him for his starvation program and spoiled Ike's chances for the presidency.

What turns this into such a sad tragedy, an abyss of inhumane behavior, is the realization that the Allies had sufficient stockpiles of food, clean water, and medicine to take care of these German soldiers. What made this even worse is that many prisoners also died because of gangrene, caused by frostbite. Ike's orders were those of a monstrous *unmensch*.

General Patton was the only commander in the European Theater who released significant numbers of German POWs. Others tried to do the same thing, such as Omar Bradley and General J. C. H. Lee, commander of Com 2, but were stopped. A SHAEF order on May 15, 1945, signed by Eisenhower, countermanded them.

It is true that thousands of German POWs brought to the United States were treated humanely, because that was in our own backyard. However, once the war was over and the Germans were released, the American POW policy changed. Some 371,683 German prisoners were sent back to join their starving comrades in Ike's Rhine death camps. George C. Marshall, army chief of staff, observed on January 5, 1945, that "our soldiers in German hands" were treated as governed by the Geneva Convention. On April 27, 1945, Judge Advocate N.

I. Marguerite stated in St. Louis, "The Germans even in their greatest moment of despair, obeyed the Geneva Convention in most respects." Furthermore, the American Red Cross reported in 1945 that "99% of the American POWs in Germany have survived and are on their way home." That was not so for all the unfortunate German POWs. General Eisenhower destined them to a slow death by starvation. When will he be held accountable?

Other Losses by James Bacque ripped the ordered silence of Ike's death camps wide open. The Canadian news reporter, Peter Worthington of the *Ottawa Sun* read *Other Losses* and then also did some of his own research and detective work. He reported in his column on September 12, 1989, the following: "It is hard to escape the conclusion that Dwight Eisenhower was a war criminal of epic proportions. His policy killed more Germans in peace than were killed in the European Theatre ... For years we have blamed the 1.7 million missing German POWs on the Russians. Until now, no one dug too deeply ... Witnesses and survivors have been interviewed by the author; one Allied officer compared the American camps to Buchenwald."

A survivor of these death camps shared his experiences. After several weeks and after almost half the prisoners had died, a woman somehow found out that her husband was in the camp. She came to the camp with a suitcase filled with food for her husband and his buddies. When she was at the gate to the camp, the GI in the watchtower ordered her to get lost. She did not understand the GI, since she did not speak American. She believed she was doing something good and decent; then the GI opened fire with his machine gun and cut her body into two pieces and scattered the food for her husband and friends all over the entrance. Her dead body was left lying there for several days as a reminder for others not to come to feed these unfortunate prisoners. This was murder of a civilian during peace time. Ike prohibited the locals from feeding the prisoners, or they would be shot. In America, Eisenhower has been celebrated as an American hero, but there are millions who hold him to be a callous mass murderer.

The US Mint in Philadelphia, Pennsylvania, issued a special Eisenhower centennial silver dollar in 1990. Four million of them were issued and promoted with the slogan, "Remember the Man ... Remember the Times." They were promoted especially to our veterans. Some veterans, however, refused to purchase the Eisenhower silver dollar. Col. James Mason and Col. Charles Beasley served in the US Army Medical Corps. In 1950, they published a paper about Ike's Rhine death camps. In part, they stated, "Huddled close together for warmth, behind the barbed wire was a most awesome sight ... nearly 100,000 haggard, apathetic, dirty, gaunt, blank-staring men clad in dirty gray uniforms, and standing ankle-deep in mud ... water was a major problem, yet only 200 yards away the Rhine River was running bankful."

Martin Brech of Mahopac, New York, was an eighteen-year-old private first class in Company C of the Fourteenth Infantry. He was assigned guard duty and as an interpreter at Eisenhower's death camp in Andernach, along the Rhine River. He shared his experiences. "My protests [regarding the treatment of the German DEFs] were met with hostility or indifference, and when I threw our ample rations to them over the barbed wire, I was threatened, making it clear that it was our deliberate policy not to adequately feed them ... One Captain told me that he would shoot me if he saw me again tossing food to the Germans ..."

Unfortunately, this has remained the unknown Eisenhower holocaust for much too long. If we want to see a death camp, where the survivors would not survive the incarceration, a closer look at Ike's Rhine death camps is long overdue. Under the orders of the Supreme Allied Commander, Dwight D. Eisenhower, disarmed German soldiers and civilians were systematically exterminated. This criminal genocide was one of the worst committed during the twentieth century. One question remains: Was Ike acting on his own accord, or was he following orders?

Following World War I, during the Hague Peace Conference, the civilized nations of the world agreed to submit to international law, which was aimed at eliminating ruthless brutality. On January 26, 1919, the United States and others signed "The Hague Regulations." What the United States and others agreed to was that "they [POWs] should be treated humanely ... After the peace treaties have been signed the immediate release of the POWs has to be secured." Ike found loopholes to circumvent the Geneva agreement.

On July 27, 1929, the Protective Regulations of the Geneva Convention for wounded soldiers were formulated to include POWs. The regulations stated, "All accommodations should be equal to the standard of their troops. The Red Cross supervises. After the end of the hostilities the POWs should be released immediately." All the Allies, including the United States, signed this document. Ike decided to ignore international agreements and mistreat the German POWs by reclassifying them as DEFs and engage in mass murder.

On March 10, 1945, Eisenhower issued orders not to release German prisoners captured on German soil but to keep them in captivity as DEFs. These orders were issued seven weeks before the official end of military hostilities. There is a huge legal problem with Ike's orders. These POWS were not captured but surrendered and laid down their arms; the war was over. Eisenhower's actions and the way the German prisoners were treated made it amply clear that they became part of a mass starvation plot. Ike implemented their death sentence, the

Morgenthau/Kaufman Plan for the deliberate starvation of the German people. A document was drafted, the JCS (Joint Chiefs of Staff) Directive 1067 in which the US military government of the occupation of Germany was ordered to "to take no steps in looking toward an economic rehabilitation of Germany!" Furthermore, it mandated that starvation, disease, and civil unrest should be kept at levels where it would not pose a danger to the troops of occupation.

Henry Morgenthau published *Germany Is Our Problem—A Plan for Germany*, which was influenced heavily by Theodor N. Kaufman, who published a book in 1941, *Germany Must Perish*. There is a photo in the FDR Library in the Morgenthau folder with the following handwritten note from FDR: "For Henry from one of two of a kind," which displays Morgenthau's influence rather succinctly. Much of this material ended up in JCS 1067 and the Potsdam Agreement and was implemented by Eisenhower. Until July 1947, JCS 1067 provided the primary instructions for the Allied forces in how to deal with Germany and Germans.

After crossing the Rhine River in March of 1945, Eisenhower ordered the creation of death enclosures for the German POWs. Vast areas were confiscated and fenced in with barbed wire. These outdoor pens were set up after the German soldiers laid down their weapons and surrendered. The war was officially over; however, every day, more POWs were herded into these pens. Among the prisoners were amputees, women, children, and older folks.

These Rheinwiesenlagern, prisoner-of-war temporary enclosures, also known as Ike's Rhine death camps, were set up near the following towns: Andernach, Bad Kreuznach, Bickelsheim, Dietersheim, Bretzenheim, Buederich, Budersheim, Hechterheim, Heidesheim, Ingelheim, Koblenz, Cuetzel, Ludwigshafen, Ludwigshafen-Rheingoenheim, Mainz,

Mainz-Kassel, Mainz-Zahlbach, Mannheim, Mannhein-Kaefertal, Mannheim-Sandhofen, Mannheim-Schoenau, Mannheim-Waldorf, Miegenheim, Plaidt, Remagen, Rheinberg, Rheinheim, Schwarzenborn, Siershan, Sinzig, Trier, Urmitz, Wickrathberg, and Winzenheim.

On May 8, 1945, the war was over but not for German POWs, nor the Germans. They were subjected to ruthless brutality—murder, rape, starvation, slave labor, expulsions, and exploitations. The German soldiers surrendered at different fronts of the war. Those who could escape from the Soviet force believed they would be treated humanely by the Western Allies. They were imprisoned, cramped into cattle wagons, and pushed onto open fields surrounded by barbed-wire fences. Many of the prisoners were already dead when they arrived. As the American forces advanced further east, they established more camps on German soil. After a while, these camps were closed, and the prisoners were relocated to the camps along the Rhine. Somewhere between five and six million prisoners were cramped into Ike's Rhine death camps; over a million did not survive Ike's starvation program.

Conditions were extremely horrible and alarming. Spring was exceptionally chilly and wet. In spite of the snow, sleet, and icy rain, prisoners were forced to be without shelters and had to sleep on the bare, cold, and wet ground, which after a while turned into a bottomless quagmire. POWs were not allowed to build shelters. They did not receive any tents, even though both the German and the American army depots were full of them. They dug holes in the ground to protect themselves from the cold.

When the camps first opened, the prisoners did not receive any food or water, even though German and American army depots were well stocked. The German depots were then plundered. Thereafter the prisoners received minute portions of egg powder, milk powder, cookies, chocolate bars, and coffee powder but no water. The prisoners suffered from acute hunger and severe intestinal diseases. Death by starvation is extremely painful.

The prisoners were intentionally shut off from the outside world; there was absolutely no incoming or outgoing mail. These brave soldiers were intentionally meant to feel lonely and worthless in their dying agony. The media still portrays the German soldiers as criminals and Allied soldiers as heroes. Most served honorably and followed orders. The public was threatened with death if they, in any way, attempted to give these dying prisoners a piece of bread. The seriously ill or dying received little or no medical care; these were starvation camps, not goodwill medical centers. The Red Cross was not permitted to enter the camps; they were not even allowed to come into Germany. Swiss Red Cross trains, loaded with much needed food and supplies, were rudely ordered by Eisenhower himself to return to where they came from. This caused Eisenhower some concern, because the word got out about Ike's Rhine death camps. It was no longer a total secret to the world. Why did it remain a secret to our media? Humanitarian aid for dying German POWs was callously refused by the supreme commander, Dwight D. Eisenhower. Whose orders was he following?

James Bacque, in his book *Other Losses*, shares the story of one American. On page 51, we read,

> April 30 was a stormy day, rain and snow and a bone-chilling wind blowing from the north across the flats of the Rhine Valley. The prisoners were huddled together for warmth—hundreds of thousands of emaciated, dirty, gaunt men, with hollow eyes, wearing dirty battle fatigues and ankle deep in mud ...

Here and there you could see dirty-white
spots. When looking closer you could notice men
wrapped their heads or arms with bandages or
men wearing merely their shirts. The German
division commander said they did not eat for at
least two days and getting water caused a major
problem even though the Rhine River was only
200 meters away.

Millions of German soldiers, some five to six million, were
forced into Ike's death camps. Among them were sick people,
people straight out of hospitals, women from the military
support services, and civilians who were captured and driven,
like cattle, into Ike's Rhine death camps. One prisoner in the
Rheinsberg camp was eighty years old, another only nine.
Hunger, thirst, and disease were their constant companions.
Every day, they were increasingly more malnourished, sicker,
and a little closer to death. Not knowing anything about Ike's
death camps, the media remained silent. German Americans
overwhelmingly voted for Ike for president, not knowing
anything about his death camps. They were deceived, believing
Ike was their German-American hero, such was and is the
power of the mass media.

Bacque writes on page 52, "A cruel sky poured down,
week-long, torrential rains. Amputees were sliding through
the quagmire, sopping wet and shivering. Day in, day out,
night after night, without shelter, they camped hopelessly
on the bare ground." These conditions were created by the
Americans to handle the huge number of prisoners who should
have been released to go home but couldn't as the direct result
of Eisenhower's orders.

Dr. Ernst F. Fisher, a US Army colonel, wrote,

Eisenhower's hate, tolerated by his submissive military bureaucracy, caused the horrors of the death camps, unique in the annals of American military history. When the occupation zones were formed, in July 1945, some of the lagers [camps] were handed over to the British or French, depending on the geography. The British, to their credit, tried to improve the food supply for the prisoners. The French did nothing of the sort but transported the still physically able as forced labor to France. Only a few of these slaves ever returned. (My friend Waldemar Pollock, a pilot, was one.)

The English were not totally blameless; they sent some of their POWs to Italy to be starved to death there.

Right from the start, the conditions in the camps were deplorable; Ike's orders were to make life in their final days as painful and miserable as possible. This was nothing less than hateful revenge. It has been observed that men have provided for the survival of humans against all enemies except his fellow men. If animals could speak, they would state a case against man that would stagger humanity. The army doctors at the camps witnessed a terrible increase in the death rate—some eighty times higher than they had ever experienced. The doctors registered very consciously and efficiently the causes of death. Their reports document that they died from diarrhea, dysentery, typhoid fever, tetanus, and blood poisoning at rates not heard of since the Middle Ages. The most exact medical terminology could not begin to describe the catastrophe that the doctors were witnessing.

Every morning, the cold, dead bodies were collected, hauled away, and dumped into unmarked mass graves after their rags were removed from their bodies and the dead bodies were covered with chemicals for faster decomposition. The corpses of all who died of starvation and other causes were transported on military trucks out of the camps and dumped into deep pits, five layers deep. Many more bodies were submerged in the quagmires and the latrines, never to be recovered. The magnitude of the death rates can better be comprehended if we consider the fact that at the Buederich camp alone, it was estimated that some 230 corpses were buried each night. None of the deaths were properly registered; these human beings were treated as if they never existed. It was hoped that these murders would be shoved under the carpet and would never see the light of day. Ike was very concerned that these murders would be reported by the media.

Following are some personal accounts of German prisoners at the Bretzenheim camp who survived to talk and write about it.

> I was born 1924 and as a member of the 3rd Parachute Division captured by Americans on April 20, 1945, some three weeks before the German surrender, in the Harz Mountains near Quedlinburg, after a hasty retreat from France. A few days later we were transported in Belgian coal freight cars to Bretzenheim near Bad Kreuznach. Sixty men in a car, standing shoulder to shoulder—no food, no water, or toilets. After 24 hours we were unloaded in an open field. Hardly anyone could walk. The camp was a bare field fenced in with barbwire - not a tent, no buildings …
>
> We bivouacked body on body on the muddy ground, one wool blanket for three men. The latrine consisted of a room-sized pit with a rough

edge and no seating facilities. If you fell into the pit, you drowned in the muck. Cleaning water was not available. Every morning first aid guards walked along the rows of prone men and kicked them to see if they were dead. The first night about 180 dead were counted.

After a few days, we received the first drinking water and food, one slice of wheat bread, a spoonful of coffee powder, milk powder, egg powder and sugar for 50 persons. At that camp, I stayed until June 12, 1945 when I was officially released.

Another prisoner filed this report: "Emaciated to a skeleton, you stared with burning eyes at the sky and tried to figure out when you will join your dead comrades who were collected every morning, then lined up at the edge of the road to be dumped." Another prisoner wrote, "From April until July 1945, the people of Bretzenheim could have seen every morning piles of up to 180 corpses at the gate and watched the loading of the deceased on lorries, then speeding away to the Galgenberg Kreuznach and the Stromberg. That means that at Bretzheim camp at least 15,000 men died. The number who suffocated in the mud or fell into the latrines is not known and should be added to the death total."

Alex Perry is a World War II combat veteran, and thus a member of the greatest generation. He stated the following,

Instead of praise, Ike should be remembered for the mass murder of millions of hapless German prisoners after World War II ... The appalling story is told by reporters willing to brave the unspoken journalistic taboo of silence when it comes to Ike's crimes. One of these reporters is the Canadian James Bacque. Bacque has told the chilling story of Ike's mass murder of over a million disarmed, surrendered German soldiers in 1945 in his book *Other Losses*. Published in 1989 in Canada, the book received so much notoriety because it accused Gen. Dwight D. Eisenhower, as head of the American occupation of Germany in 1945, of deliberately starving to death German prisoners of war in staggering numbers.

In 324 pages, Bacque describes the conditions in which the German prisoners were kept.

"Unconditional surrender" demands by FDR and Secretary of the Treasury Henry Morgenthau's plan were orders to systematically ruin the German nation and starve them to death, which significantly increased the resolve of the remaining Germans, caused the German resistance to stiffen. They fought with all they had in desperation, knowing they were sentenced to die one way or another. General Patton told General LeRoy Lutes, after Eisenhower's and Morgenthau's murderous plans became known to the Germans, that "some fanatical young Germans attack and die to the last man, refusing to surrender."

Thus, FDR and Ike were totally and singularly responsible for all the American deaths before, during, and after the Normandy invasion. Patrick J. Buchanan accurately described World War II as the unnecessary war. Eisenhower's invasion was merely to bring further destruction and devastation to Germany, which was already totally destroyed. Furthermore, since Eisenhower was not invited or provoked to come to France, the Normandy invasion could be called an international trespassing. Hitler, and more so his generals, made multiple overtures to the Allies for peace, including sending Rudolf Hess with a personal offer of peace to Scotland, which became a blunder of the highest order.

Many have asked, "Why would Ike, whose ancestors are buried in German soil and the Eisenhauer family who came from Germany and who have expressed pride in their German roots, anglicized the spelling of their name to Eisenhower, demonstrated such hatred toward Germans and be willing to implement the Morgenthau/FDR Plan on such a huge scale?" Someone else might explore this topic in scholarly research or a dissertation. One possible explanation might be the preparation exercises and execution of the D-Day invasion. The loss of lives, on both sides, was totally superfluous, since for more than a year, the Germans made repeated overtures for peace but were ignored. It is readily visible that FDR's, Morgenthau's, and Kaufman's primary objective was not victory but the total destruction of Germany and the reduction of the German population.

Slapton Sands, in southern England, is were half as many American soldiers were killed on the English side of the English Channel during the practice and preparation exercises for the Normandy invasion as were killed during the actual invasion on June 6, 1944. The preparation for the Normandy invasion began in January 1944. A seventy-year blackout was placed on the release of any and all information regarding the invasion practice disasters. Allegedly this was done to protect Ike's military reputation, and, more importantly, so that this would not interfere with FDR's fourth-term bid for the presidency.

Eisenhower was a known womanizer. Kay Summersby, General Eisenhower's mistress in Europe, stated that Eisenhower witnessed the drowning of several hundred American soldiers in April 1944 during an amphibious landing exercise on beaches near Dartmouth. She stated, "These [beaches] were built up to carbon-copy actual landings expected in France. The reviewing stand was a seaborne infantry landing craft. But the maneuver went sour; bombers, Navy vessels, airplanes and special units fouled up from timing to orders. One or two landing craft were sunk, with casualties numbering several hundred." Each landing craft carried about four hundred soldiers.

There were additional foul-ups. There were sentries guarding the radar site who were not informed of a commando-style night landing exercise that was to take place. When the sentries spotted an incoming flotilla of dinghies, they automatically assumed they were part of a German invasion and detonated the drums. The next morning, the beach was covered with charred corpses.

These practice disasters were caused by compounding several mistakes. Live shells from the supporting warships landed among the troops acting as German defenders on the higher ground, and some of these shells also hit the landing crafts. The practice invasion was made far too realistic. The reasoning went that it might not have served its purpose, thus causing thousands of casualties. American soldiers, acting as German defenders, were issued live ammunition. One of the convoys was attacked by make-believe German torpedo boats. This caused confusion, and they began firing on each other with real bullets.

General Montgomery gave Eisenhower the idea of supporting the land forces with air power. Ike ordered the bombing of German lines, but the bombers missed their target. Due to poor visibility, on June 24, 1944, they hit the American lines. The bombing was called off but not until after a great many bombers were in the air and over the wrong target. The next day, when better flying weather had been predicted, Ike ordered another bombing attack. Again, the bombers missed their target and hit the American lines. Thousands of American soldiers lost their lives because of Ike's military incompetence. This was not his only blunder.

Kay Summersby relates Ike's consternation as a result of the misdirection of American falling bombs, stating, "He [Eisenhower] ... sank into depths of despair when the Air Force messed up a coordinated assault by dropping its bombs 'short,' killing some of our own troops, including Lt. Gen. L. J. McNair, a high War Department observer who had been wounded in Tunisia." Because of Eisenhower's incompetence, Americans suffered some seventy-seven thousand casualties. General George Marshall told Eisenhower, "You are much too weak to fill the position you are now occupying." From then on, General Marshall ran the war by remote control from the Pentagon.

Ike did not have a reputation as a military planner or strategist. Tom Brokaw stated in his book *The Greatest Generation*, "He [Ike] had no major combat command experience." General Sir Alan Brooke, England's chief of the Imperial General Staff, expressed his opinion that he thought that Ike was a general who knew nothing of strategy. He stated,

> It must be remembered that Eisenhower had never even commanded a battalion in action when he found himself commanding a group of armies in North Africa. No wonder he was at a loss to what to do and allowed himself to be absorbed in the political situation at the expense of the tactical. I had little confidence in his having the ability to handle the military situation confronting him, and caused me great anxiety ... Tactics, strategy and command were never his strong points.

Perhaps Dwight D. Eisenhower was ready to redeem himself by demonstrating his ruthlessness regarding the German prisoners and his willingness to implement the

Morgenthau Plan. At the end of World War II, a handbook was being prepared for the postwar government of Germany. This document became available in August 1944. It advocated a quick restoration of Germany and the German people to normalcy and the reconstruction of a devastated Germany to become a vibrant member in the European community. Henry Morgenthau Jr. took it to FDR with the sole purpose of belittling and criticizing it. As a result, FDR rejected the document, as Morgenthau requested.

After FDR's rejection of this plan, a new document was drafted, the JCS (Joint Chiefs of Staff) Directive 1067. Henry Morgenthau wielded considerable power over the JCS and over the occupying forces. JCS 1067 became the rule and guide for the American and Allied military occupation forces. The Morgenthau Plan was designed to reduce and degrade German living standards. Germany was not permitted to engage in any capital improvements nor to clear their rivers from the remnants of the destruction of the war; thus, the rivers would not become navigable for some time. JCS 1067 was the primary instructions for the Allied forces until July 1947.

The Morgenthau Plan dictated "not to react to the ongoing ethnic cleansing" on the continent. The Allied forces were also instructed "to hold back from being involved in any economic care to Germany … (nor) have any plan to uphold or strengthen German institution or its population in any form."

Michael R. Beschloss, in *The Conquerors: Roosevelt, Truman and the Destruction of Hitler's Germany, 1941–1945*, relates a conversation in which FDR was told that JCS 1067 was not realistic and that it would let the Germans "stew in their own juice" to which FDR replied "Let them have soup kitchens! Let their economy sink!" When he was further asked if he wanted the Germans to starve to death, he replied, "Why not?"

The situation became more deplorable with each passing

day. The conditions were worse in 1947 than in 1945. The US Senate Judiciary Committee declared that "the first two years of the Allied occupation the (Morgenthau Program) of industrial dismantlement was self-evident; that because of its vigorous pursuit by American and its Allied officials JCS 1067 was a success!" US High Commissioner in Germany, General Lucius D. Clay, shared his opinion, disagreeing, "It seemed obvious to us that Germany would starve unless it could start generating goods for itself and export. Steps will have to be taken quickly to revive its industrial productivity." Chief adviser to General Clay, Lewis Douglas was extremely critical of JCS 1067, he stated, "This thing was assembled by economic idiots (or malefactors), it makes no sense to forbid the most skilled workers in Europe from producing as much as they can in a continent that is desperately short of everything."

If something is likely not to go according to plan, even Morgenthau's Plan, it most likely will. Sometimes that turns into a blessing. Several things happened. First, the SWNCC (State War Navy Coordinating Committee) approved a plan that had been mercifully purged of the most insidious elements of the Morgenthau Plan. President Harry S. Truman expressed his reservations about many of FDR's administrative personnel, including Morgenthau. He singled Morgenthau out, stating "that he would not appoint someone like Morgenthau as dog catcher." Morgenthau demanded that Truman give him a public statement of confidence; when Truman refused, Morgenthau resigned.

This was not the end of the Morgenthau era. Morgenthau passed on his legacy on postwar Germany and the rest of Europe through the OMGUS (Office of Military Government United States), commonly referred to as the "Morgenthau boys." These treasury officials were acting as advisers to Eisenhower. It was their assumed duty to interpret the guidelines of JCS 1067 and

Kaufman's book *Germany Must Perish* as strictly as possible. When Morgenthau resigned, Colonel Bernard Bernstein took over as chief adviser to Eisenhower.

The Morgenthau boys resigned when JCS 1779 was approved but not before they totally destroyed the old German banking system by demolishing the internal relationships of German banks, cutting off the flow of credit between the banks, and seriously limiting the German industry to short-term funding, thereby preventing any real recovery of German industrial and commercial productivity. The Morgenthau Plan was a road map for the deliberate deindustrialization, starvation, and destruction of Germany.

With the increase of distrust between the old allies and the Cold War on the horizon, General Clay and the Joint Chiefs of Staff in Germany became increasingly concerned about the Communist threat to Europe and the rest of the world and warned Washington of the serious danger of continuing to pursue JCS 1067. With the changing times and political conditions, Secretary of State George Marshall convinced President Truman to replace JCS 1067 with JCS 1779. What also followed was the Marshall Plan, assisting Europe to rebuild. Thus, in a way, the Cold War became kind of a blessing to Germany.

In 1943, Wendell Willkie published a book *One World*, in which he relates his visit to Moscow in the autumn of 1942. FDR sent him to negotiate with Stalin seven objectives of the war about Germany. On page 85, he relates the first objective: "Abolition of racial exclusiveness." It dictated that the Allies have the authority to bring into Germany illegal aliens, under whatever excuse, and Germany would have no recourse to defend itself against being overrun by illegal aliens. This has turned into a continuation of the destruction of Germany by other means. Presently, one in five residents in Germany is an illegal alien. Germany has been providing the aliens with significant governmental subsidies, and the Germans themselves have no legal recourse to object, other than to demonstrate. This has been referred to as a forced and intentional destruction of Germany. Many see this as a continuation of FDR's unconditional surrender and the Morgenthau/Kaufman Plan of the destruction of Germany, just with other means. Germany is rapidly approaching the limits of its possibilities. Many believe it has long ago surpassed it. The asylum law has no upper ceiling. Tensions among the population are increasing rapidly and concerns are growing. The very continuation of Germany is at stake.

According to records, only 2 percent of the new arrivals are true asylum seekers; 98 percent have been smuggled in by unscrupulous profiteers. The German government seems powerless or unwilling to send the 98 percent back to where they came from. The guilt feeling that Germans have been brainwashed and saddled with appears to be the cause of their inability to defend their borders. The percentage of Germans in Germany is continually decreasing. The German government needs to formulate new programs; otherwise, the Germans will become a minority in their own country.

Wendell Lewis Willkie was born on February 18, 1892, in Elwood, Indiana, and died of a heart attack on October 8, 1944, in New York City. Like Eisenhower, he was of German stock. He climbed the political ladder rather quickly. His entire life he was an active member of the Democratic Party, but somehow in 1940, he was nominated as the presidential candidate, the dark horse, on the Republican ticket, running against the incumbent Franklin D. Roosevelt. FDR was reelected with 55 percent of the votes. There was little difference between Willkie's and FDR's platforms. Willkie supported FDR's New Deal, was for military support for England, for greater preparation for entering the war, and for going to war against Germany. Willkie did much to pave the way for America to enter the war against Germany.

There is currently a $120 million memorial being contemplated in Washington, DC, to honor President Dwight D. Eisenhower. To millions, on both sides of the bond, this represents insult to injury. Eisenhower's record should be scrutinized a little closer. Thousands of GIs died needlessly invading Normandy and during the practice for the invasion, and thousands of Frenchmen, our allies, were killed by the invaders. Also, thousands of German and other Europeans died defending French soil. Many question the invasion as a strategic move.

Unlike most of his fellow West Point graduates, Ike never saw action in World War I. Actually, he never faced a day of combat in his entire life. In 1929, he was appointed executive officer to General George Moseley, then secretary of war. In 1933, he was appointed chief military aide to General Douglas MacArthur, who then accompanied him to the Philippines.

In 1939, he returned from the Philippines. In June 1941, Eisenhower, now a colonel, was appointed to the War Department General Staff in Washington, a position holding the rank of brigadier general. In 1943, FDR appointed Ike to become the supreme commander in Europe, and he advanced him to the rank of a four-star general. The record shows that Ike was a protégé of Bernard Baruch, who was the adviser to presidents Wilson, FDR, and Truman. It was a case of not what you knew but whom you knew.

The announcement of Ike's promotion sent shock waves through the American and Allied forces, as he was promoted over the heads of at least fifty far better qualified and seasoned military leaders. In 1944, Ike was confirmed as a five-star general and chief of the army. In spite of the American military superiority, Ike' D-Day invasion nearly failed.

General George Patton was seriously injured in a suspicious road accident near Mannheim, Germany. A few days thereafter, Patton died—some say he was murdered—in a hospital. On the day following the accident, Patton was to fly back to Washington and meet with President Truman to brief him about Eisenhower's incompetence. To counter the claims and rumor mills, Ike allegedly authorized the leak of stories damaging to Patton, including the claim that Patton was mentally unstable and a Nazi sympathizer. Add to all that, Ike's direct orders in Operation Keelhaul forced "repatriation" of two million former Russian prisoners of war and defectors of Josef Stalin.

There are millions who strongly oppose a memorial to Ike; they see Ike as a five-star mass murderer. Ike perpetrated the crimes by reclassifying the prisoners and naming them DEFs and by completely ignoring the Geneva Convention rules. German prisoners were starved to death and died of exposure to the elements. They died because they were denied shelter in one of the coldest winters in Europe in a century. Millions are doing everything in their power to stop a monument to Ike. Perhaps the planners should consider a new design of a one-hundred-foot pencil with the names of his victims inscribed on its shaft.

In October 2011, there was a presentation of a formal letter of apology from a former US Army officer to the German people for the mistreatment of German prisoners at the end and after World War II and on the twenty-second anniversary of the publication of Bacque's book *Other Losses*.

US Army Major Merrit Drucker has apologized to the German army for the mass deaths of German prisoners in US army camps at the end and following World War II. After extensive private investigations in the United States and Germany, Merrit P. Drucker sent an email to Lt. Colonel Max Klaar, head of the Verband deutscher Soldaten (German Veteran's Association) regretting the lethal conditions in the

US camps, where more than 750,000 Germans died while they were being denied available food and shelter. German civilians were forbidden to bring any food to the starving soldiers, with threats of being shot to death, as some of them were. Drucker formed a committee of six people in Germany, the United Kingdom, Canada, and the United States to pursue further investigations and make amends by way of apologies to the families of the dead and veterans' institutions.

Colonel Dr. Ernest F. Fisher, formerly a senior historian of the US Army Center for Military History wrote an eloquent foreword to *Other Losses*. Dr. Fisher wrote, "Starting in April 1945, the United States army and the French army casually annihilated about one million men, most of them in American camps." *Other Losses* is a worldwide best seller, which has been published in thirteen countries and has been suppressed in the United States for some twenty years. Lt. Colonel Klaar observed that "Germany is a country of wounded souls."

JCS 1067 was a catastrophe to Germany, Europe, and the United States. With a change in policy, the Marshall Plan, and the currency reform in 1948, Germany eventually made a miraculous recovery only to have it described "as unintentional consequences." In time, it was accepted as Germany's Wirschaftswunder (economic miracle), which it was and still is.

Karl Siegler, the editor of Talonbooks of Vancouver, is the son of a former prisoner and survivor of US Army camps. When his father told him what had happened to him in the US camp, Karl said, "I don't believe you." He became a believer after reading *Other Losses*, so will you!

Open-air prisoner of war camp for German POWs in Sinzig, Germany, May 12, 1945.

Rheinberg, one of eighteen of Ike's Rhine death camps, where more than one million German soldiers were intentionally starved to death. Ike was ruthlessly implementing the Morgenthau Plan.

German soldiers were driven onto open fields, surrounded by barbed wire, and left to die by starvation, one of the many secrets of World War II. Retired US Army Major Merrit Drucker has publicly apologized to the German people for this inhumane brutality.

CHAPTER 12

Recovery and Revelation

Germans talk about the year 1945 as year *zero*. That is the year Germans faced FDR's unconditional surrender, destruction, total humiliation, grand theft, and rebirth, the end and the beginning—alpha and omega, das Ende und der Anfang. After Germany surrendered, Germany's holocaust continued in earnest. Because of Eisenhower implementing the Morgenthau Plan, Germany lost more soldiers after the war was over than during the entire war. Germany lay in ruins and millions of ethnic Germans were driven like cattle into what was left of Germany, after huge regions had been amputated. Germany had been treated as a totally defeated country and the Germans as the worst criminals. However, a few years thereafter, Germany was courted by the victorious occupying Western powers to join the North Atlantic Treaty Organization (NATO) to form a common defense against the Soviet Union and the spread of Communism.

The reality for Germany and for the German people was total despair, but simultaneously, there also existed a flicker of hope, ever so distant and small. There is nothing more powerful than hope. The only thing more tempestuous inflicted upon the German people continues to be the deafening silence by the media establishment, the textbook industry, and religious and civic leaders who should be voicing their concerns about the atrocities committed against the German people. Germans have truly been baptized by fire.

FDR declared his fight against the dictatorships of Germany, Japan and Italy, but not against the Soviet Union. Stalin's brutality was known to be by far the worst, but FDR claimed he could do business with Josef Stalin which caused a climate of self-defense against Communism in Germany. FDR erroneously claimed that Stalin and Communism were a harmless agricultural nation and a democracy in coming. As one of his many violations of the US Neutrality Acts and the Constitution, FDR began to supply the Soviet Union with war material already in 1939.

Not only Germany but also Berlin, which ended up in what was referred to as East Germany, was divided into four occupational zones. When Moscow attempted to force the Americans out of Berlin, the Truman administration responded with the now legendary "Luftbruecke"—the air bridge—keeping the West Berliners alive and free. America's rearmament was ignited after North Korea invaded South Korea. The ensuing Cold War and the threat of Communism became a kind of blessing for Germany, because Germany was now needed to defend European and American interests. In 1954, Germany joined the NATO; the reasoning was that an economically strong Germany was essential in preserving the interests of Europe and the West. Let us not forget that the only thing of permanence is perpetual and continual change.

As World War II slowly ground to its Wagnerian finale, a prophetic expression circulated, "Enjoy the war while you can; the peace will be horrendous." The peace that Germany was handed was no peace at all. Tragically, from 1945 to 1950, all the victorious occupying powers—the Americans, the English, the French, and the Russians—continued implementing the Kaufman, Morgenthau, FDR, and Ehrenberg Plan, namely "Germany Must Perish." This firmly demonstrates that the war was against the German people and not against Hitler or the Nazis. It was England's determination to destroy Germany's industrial and commercial success; it was against Germany's industrial strength.

Following the war, the Ruhr region resembled a giant heap of rubble. The English took machinery that was still intact as war reparations to dear old England, since Germany was to become an agricultural state anyhow and since it would not need any industrial machinery. The Soviets shipped trainloads of looted material to Mother Russia. The Soviets were transporting all the German scientists they could get their hands on to Russia. The Americans brought Dr. Werner von Braun and his team of some 260 space scientists from Penemuende and others to America in an operation referred to as Paperclip. The United States placed and trusted Dr. Werner von Braun as chief of its immense aerospace project; the German space scientists took us to the moon and beyond. German scientific achievements have and will continue to transform the world. Dr. von Braun traveled the country and lectured at many universities throughout the country, inspiring and motivating young scholars in space science and research.

Whenever they could, American GIs helped themselves to "souvenirs." The Soviet Union confiscated the scientific papers of the Kaiser Wilhelm Institute of Physics in Berlin. The German scientists who were contracted by Soviet officials and taken to the Soviet Union were Manfred von Ardenna, Gernot Zippe, Peter Thiesen, Max Steenbeck, Werner Schuetze, Heinz Barwich, and Gustav Hertz. They continued their research under Gen. Avram Zavenyagin. Their research and the work of Dr. Werner von Braun and his team of scientists have become legendary; their respective rockets greeted each other in outer space—in German, of course.

Under the terms of FDR's unconditional surrender, Germany had no rights whatsoever; she was forbidden to write any part of her own history. The victors made up rules and wrote the laws, das Grundgesetz. Germans were brainwashed and deemed guilty on all accounts. They were the only ones guilty, all others were immune from any wrong. Fearful of being incarcerated or shot, no one dared to disagree with the dictated, politically correct version of the occupying forces; there was no freedom of speech or expression. Furthermore, the portrayals of the Germans, even in the German media, were anything but flattering.

The victorious Allies, both east and west, were looting everything of value, such as rocket and aircraft designs, advanced military hardware, industrial machinery, scientific advancements, and thousands of patents, furniture, refrigerators, and radios. They were dismantling entire factories and communication facilities and rounding up German scientists, engineers, and technicians to show them how to operate the equipment.

The German scientific and technical achievements were highly sought after by all the victorious occupying powers. As evidence of the value attached to the German achievements, the Americans, the English, the French, and the Russians were scrambling to kidnap or recruit all the leading German scientists they could get their hands on, looting German industrial secrets, confiscating patents and trademarks, and stealing everything that was not nailed down.

The English interned ten of the top scientists at Farm Hall, England, for six months and placed highly sensitive microphones into their cells, eavesdropping on their conversations. Among these scientists were Paul Harbeck, Werner Heisenberg, Otto Hahn, Kurt Diebner, von Weizaecker, Max von Laune, Erich

Bagge, Walter Garlach, Horst Korsching, and Karl Wirtz. All the Allies knew that the scientific future of the world lay in these German laboratories. Dr. Werner von Braun and his team of scientists chose to surrender to the American forces already months before the war was officially over. They knew the war was over long before May 8th.

After Germany's defeat and the kidnaping of German scientists, researchers have gathered sufficient evidence to present the argument that the material captured from the German submarine U-234 while it was en route to Japan was used in the American bombs. The U-boat, U-234, was carrying 560 kilograms (1,232 pounds) of uranium oxide and highly advanced fuses. Major John F. Vance interrogated Dr. Schlicke and General Kessler. Ironically, even though the U-234 did not arrive in Japan as planned, its cargo eventually arrived there via two atomic bombs.

Then came the Nuremberg mock trials; they kept the media busy and occupied, reporting sensationalized horror stories of German atrocities. The media was saturated with what the Germans did but were completely silent when it came to the atrocities committed against the Germans. The Nuremberg Trials reeked of hypocrisy and double standards. The chief Soviet jurist was Andrej Vyshinsky, who was the chief prosecutor at Stalin's 1930 show trials. These show trials horrified the world even before the dictator became FDR's "good friend and uncle Joe." Victims of Stalin's 1930 show trials included English engineers who were recruited to work in Russia and later were abandoned as "imperialist spies." Stalin's show trials served as a prototype of the Nuremberg mock trials.

At the trials, Germans were accused and found guilty of crimes they definitely did not commit. Due process, cross-examinations and any meaningful defence were strictly verboten. Rear Admiral Dan V. Gallery (USN) said,

> This kangaroo court at Nuremberg was officially
> known as the International Military Tribunal.
> This name is a libel on the military profession.
> The tribunal was not a military one in any sense.
> The only military men among the judges were
> the Russians … At Nuremberg, mankind and
> our present civilization were on trial, with men
> whose own hands were bloody sitting on the
> judges seats. One of the judges came from the
> country which committed the Katyn Forest
> massacres and produced an array of witnesses
> who swore at Nuremberg that the Germans had
> done it.

Tragically, no one objected to these lies, fabrications, and perjury, knowing them to be such. Germans were found guilty of crimes others committed.

The Nuremberg Trials were a crude example of a barbaric display of the concept "the winner is always right and the hell with justice—might is right." This was a total mockery of justice. It was an implementation of the Morgenthau Plan. The Dresden holocaust and the indiscriminate firebombing of civilians, which were initiated by Great Britain and the United States, and the dropping of both atomic bombs were excluded from consideration as war crimes. Selective justice is no justice at all.

The trials did not allow any kind of defense or cross-examination, which is standard in any court procedure and guaranteed by the American constitution. The victims were guilty as charged, and they had no legal recourse. It was the Wild West at its worst. The court relied heavily on evidence that was extracted through torture; furthermore, the courts made up laws and rules as they went along. The wickedness of these mock trials haunted the British chief prosecutor, Sir Hartley Shawcross, for the rest of his life. He was often heard saying that the war with Germany was unnecessary and a terrible mistake leading to Britain's downfall.

The Nuremberg Trials were described as being at best nothing more than media hype, feeding the public actual and fabricated Nazi atrocities. The media flexed its muscles. The accusers acted as prosecutors, judges, jury, and executioners. Real justice was denied and made a total farce of. The US Senator Robert Thaft had this to say about the trials: "About this whole judgement there is a spirit of vengeance, and vengeance is seldom justice. The hanging of eleven men convicted will be a blot on the American record which we shall long regret."

Admiral of the Fleet Lord Chatfield, PC, GCB, had this to say: "I consider it wrong to try admirals, generals and air marshals for carrying out definite orders from the highest authority ... The Allies are far from guiltless and should have taken that into fuller consideration." He further stated, "The most brutal act of the war was the dropping of the atom bomb on Japan."

T. S. Elliot stated, "The trials are only of the crimes committed by the vanquished and the fact that the Katyn Massacre of Polish officers was never properly investigated cast doubt on the conduct of such trials."

These mock trials were a diabolical process of humiliation, torture, and death. After the officers were captured; they were shackled and under constant armed guards. They were stripped of their uniforms even in freezing conditions. Their decorations and insignia were torn from them, and they were placed in unheated cells. Bright lights burned all night, and they were kept awake as a form of torture. Beatings were commonplace, and they were being starved to break them down for interrogation. Confessions were forced out of them. These proceedings would not pass the lowest threshold of legal proceedings in any civilized society, but it was the norm at the Nuremberg Trials.

Dr. M. M. Rost van Tonningen, former high commissioner for the League of Nations in Vienna and president of the Bank of the Netherlands, was transferred to the Scheveningen prison. He was told that he would never leave the prison alive before he was beaten to death with poles. Brutality prevailed; the public was told that these prisoners who were murdered committed suicide. These trials represent a very low point in Allied and American jurisprudence; we allowed it to happen, and, therefore, have a responsibility to rectify it.

Just a few of the victorious countries were responsible for the Nuremberg mock trials; neutral countries were excluded. Even the US Supreme Court washed its hands of any responsibility for these proceedings. At the Dachau US Military Tribunals, interrogators posed as priests to extract false confessions. The faces of the prisoners revealed overwhelming evidence of torture and deprivation of sleep. Since they were going to be killed anyhow, they were denied proper defense. Some of the prisoners had been executed in secret, and the final resting places have been kept secret. Postmortem examinations could prove very embarrassing.

These court proceedings had been described as one-part American political kangaroo court, another part Communist show trial, and still another part English theater. Admiral Husband E. Kimmel said, "The war crimes trials were a reversion to the ancient practice of the savage extermination of the defeated enemy and particularly its leaders."

"Collective guilt" and "sole guilt" are examples of the absence of any judicial balance and credibility. There is something contradictory in the claim that Germans alone are guilty of all war crimes; there are always two sides to every story. In any conflict, no one is purely innocent and walks away with totally innocent, clean hands. The only one pure and totally innocent was crucified on the cross.

The Nuremberg tribunals have been described by thousands of jurists, ecclesiastics, military leaders, politicians, diplomats, historians, and writers throughout the world as kangaroo proceedings. These courts were given a judicial veneer to add legitimacy to the wholesale slaughter of a defeated nation's military personnel. The public in its judicial ignorance could not recognize it as a comic opera. Some of the finest statesmen and jurists of the century have condemned the Nuremberg mock trials as the worst kangaroo court. They even compared them to the mock trials of Jesus Christ that sentenced him to torture and crucifixion. The Germans who were later proven not guilty were executed, a violation of the ex post facto principles of the US Constitution. These trials have been described as a fraud, a farce, and a travesty against justice. If these miscarriages of justice were carried out against German generals, what will keep them from being carried out against generals of other nations in the future?

US Supreme Court Justice William O. Douglas said this about the Nuremberg Trials: "No matter how many books are written or briefs filed, no matter how finely the lawyers analyzed it, the crimes for which the Nazis were tried had never been formalized as a crime with the definiteness required by our legal standards, nor outlawed with a death penalty by the international community ... Their guilt did not justify us in substituting power for principle."

The following is an example of Ehrenberg's, Stalin's hate demon's, propaganda:

> The Germans are not human beings. From now on the word "German" is for us the worst imaginable curse ... we shall kill. If you have not

killed at least one German a day, you have wasted that day … If you cannot kill your German with a bullet, kill him with your bayonet … If there is calm on your part of the front, kill a German in the meantime … If you kill one German, kill another—for us there is nothing more joyful than a heap of German corpses. Our historic mission is a simple and honorable one: to reduce the German population. We shall make an end of Germany; the country must be eradicated.

Tragically, the rhetoric of Ehrenberg, Kaufman, and Morgenthau are not dissimilar by accident but by design. Elya Ehrenberg urged the Red Army to destroy German racial pride by killing the men and raping the women. Churchill stated that Germany was to be reduced to a desert of dust and ashes and removed from the surface of the earth along with its people for all times. After serving Stalin and the Bolsheviks and producing tons of anti-German hate propaganda, Ehrenberg retired in Israel.

Following World War I, the compassionate British elite blockaded the German ports to starve the Germans and others to death. Following World War II, the German population was put on a starvation diet of about 1,000 to 1,400 calories a day. This was just enough for a slow death by starvation. The Red Cross and the UN Relief and Rehabilitation Administration were denied the opportunity to feed the starving population. During the first two years following the war, food parcels from charitable organizations were not permitted to be delivered. The care packages from American relatives were not delivered at first. The Allied Command did everything they could to keep the Germans down and starving. Still today, Germans refer to 1947 as "das Hungerjahr." The starving people went to the country to beg for food for their families. In smaller towns, the unemployed offered their services to the local farmers just for the bare necessities of life. After the potato harvest, they went through the fields to find whatever was left. Although there was plenty of food to feed the hungry, the German people were starving and freezing because of Allied policy.

Over a million German POWs were starved in Ike's Rhine death camps and buried in unmarked mass graves, covered with lime for quicker decomposition. It would be morally right and historically just to uncover the mass graves of lime-covered German POWs from Ike's Rhine death camps and have the findings made public. Is Washington pressuring Berlin to turn a blind eye toward Allied crimes? German men and women were rounded up and deported to the Soviet Union and elsewhere as slave labor. German women from eight to eighty were raped, some in the open for additional humiliation. German properties were confiscated; industrial, cultural, and private holdings were looted and members of the Volkssturm (young boys and old men) were declared bandits and shot at will when captured. The Volkssturm was another of Hitler's insane and treasonous acts.

Field Marshall Montgomery described the behavior of the Red Army in his memoirs; he wrote,

> From their behavior, it soon became clear that the Russians were in fact barbarous Asiatics ... Their treatment of women was abhorrent to us ... Out of the impact of the Asiatics on the European culture, a new Europe was born. In some areas in the Russian sector hardly any Germans remain."

US General Keating compared the actions of the Red Army in the Battle of Berlin to those of the barbaric hordes of Ghengis Kahn. Ambassador George F. Kennan describes the scene on German soil thus:

The disaster that befell this area with the entry of the Soviet forces has no parallel in modern European experience. There were considerable sections of it where scarcely a man, woman or child of the indigenous population was left alive after the initial passage of Soviet forces; and one cannot believe that they all succeeded in fleeing to the West. The Russians swept the native population clean in a manner that had no parallel since the days of the Asiatic hordes.

With millions of displaced people wandering aimlessly across Central and Eastern Europe, nature also took its toll. People were starving and dying of typhoid, which further reduced the German population. Furthermore, all means of survival were blocked assisting nature to take its fatal course. Corpses littered the roads, byways, and highways of towns and cities of ethnic Germans. What Stalin brought earlier to the Ukraine, he now brought to Central Europe; his actions were tacitly supported by Churchill and FDR. Churchill explained, "Six million Germans have lost their lives in the war. We can expect that by the end of the war many more will be killed, and then there will be room (in what will be left of Germany) for those expelled."

All the schools, from kindergarten to the university level, as well as the entire media, were placed under the direct control of and managed by the occupational military forces. They spoon-fed the Germans about their guilt and responsibilities in regard to the war, giving the Germans indigestion compounded by an inferiority complex. Germans were being reeducated on a grand scale. To some extent, this scenario still survives in the mass media, sensationalizing Germans with negative characteristics. They were forced to accept an open-ended occupation; the presence of American forces, which Germany still pays for, is still part of that policy. All the military forces of the other occupational powers have been removed from German soil. America is still dragging its feet on removing its forces and offering Germany a genuine peace treaty. Washington has a moral responsibility to initiate a peace treaty as it also has in passing the Wartime Treatment Study Act.

Noteworthy is the fact that Winston Churchill and the English government made a proposal to accept the government of Admiral Doenitz as the legitimate postwar interim government of Germany. This proposal was met with great opposition from Washington, and the concept of a Doenitz government was dropped. This move would have partially negated the Morgenthau Plan. Supreme Commander Eisenhower, operating under JCS 1067, ordered the immediate arrest of Admiral Doenitz and his ministers and charged and treated them as common war criminals.

The victorious Allies—America, England, France, and Russia—passed a decree that Germany would never again become a major economic, industrial, or military power. Dear old England would never again need to be concerned about Germany's industrial and commercial competition. Thus, it was resolved at the Teheran, Yalta, and Potsdam Conferences that Germany would be divided into four occupational zones, and each zone would be governed by each respective occupational military power. Germany would be torn apart. The zones of the three Western allies became West Germany, and the zone of the Soviet Union became East Germany. All occupational powers, except the United States, have left German soil as a result of the Four Plus Two Agreement, which is not a peace treaty at all. It merely brought western and central Germany together; eastern Germany is still under Polish administration.

The stated objectives of the victorious powers were dismemberment, dividing up what was left of the country;

denazification, reeducating the public, which was perceived as brainwashing, and the elimination of all personal and national pride; deindustrialization, the dismantling of Germany's industry, since it was decreed that Germany was to become an agricultural state and the Germans were to become farmers and herdsmen, greatly reduced in size; and demilitarization. Germany was never again going to have a standing army, German personal and national pride were to be eradicated, and Germany was going to be held liable for endless reparations. Any nation that is not allowed by the victors to display any national pride and interest, cannot long remain a nation. Germany has and is paying billions of dollars. At present, however, some three thousand German troops are fighting alongside the United States and English troops in the Middle East, and some one thousand German troops are patrolling the Hindu Kush, a former English colony.

A comparison of how France was treated by Germany after the war of 1870–1871 is relevant and revealing. France declared war on Prussia and lost. As part of the peace treaty, which was signed in Frankfurt on May 10, 1871, France agreed to return Alsace and Lorraine and pay five billion French francs in reparations. So far, Germany has paid far more than 150 billion dollars in restitution alone, and there seems to be no end in sight. France was not occupied by German forces; the French were treated humanely and with respect. The French had input during the negotiations, which the Germans were denied by the victorious powers. The demands on France were a trifle and a reasonable sum, especially when compared to the astronomical, endless demands placed upon Germany at the Versailles Treaty and following World War II, which were intended to totally bankrupt and destroy Germany. The French occupied the Ruhr region and the Rhineland; they took all the coal that was mined in that region, while the people of Germany were freezing and starving.

Allied media and mainstream historians continue to depict Poland as the innocent victim of Nazi aggression. It is their unquestioned paradigm of the spark that was the cause of World War II, placing the full responsibility, the sole guilt clause, on Hitler and the German people. According to this reasoning, he hated the Poles and wanted to destroy them as the first step on the road to world conquest. However, this is more propaganda than fact; almost a century later, it is time to disclose all the facts and provide some factual balance. Germany entered into a nonaggression pact with Poland in 1934. The relations between the two countries had been strained long before the National Socialists gained power. Innocent lives on both sides of the disputed territories, as a result of the Versailles Treaty, were lost.

The Polish-German nonaggression pact brought some relief into the volatile climate, in large part a credit to Josef Klemens Pilsudski, the Polish chief of state, who was an anti-Communist and who built up his military force with modern weapons. He was planning to break up the Soviet Union, but he died of liver cancer, along with his plans. Working toward closer relations and a possible eventual alliance against the Soviet Union, Hitler entered into a very generous trade agreement with Poland in June. Since Germany was the most important export market for Poland, this agreement was extremely important to Poland. This gave Poland a most-favored-nation status, as it also cleared up several economic issues between the two countries. They cooperated militarily; the Polish air force and the German Luftwaffe flew military combat missions on the same side of the Spanish Civil War for Franko's Nationalists from 1936 to 1939.

Following the capitulation in October 1939, Hitler called for an independent Polish state, which was opposed by Stalin, whose forces occupied about half of Poland. The media and textbooks mention very little about Russia invading Poland; the focus has been on Hitler's invasion, reclaiming German

territory. The reception of German diplomats in Poland changed
dramatically; the amiable Polish-German relations vanished, as
a direct result of FDR's personal operative in Europe, William
Christian Bullitt Jr. He urged Polish leaders to stop dealing
with Germany and to provoke Hitler into a war over the Free
City of Danzig. Bullitt told them that if war came, England and
France, lavishly supplied by the United States, would invade
Germany. He also promised them eastern Germany as far as
Berlin. Blinded by greed, arrogance, and ignorance, the Polish
leadership abandoned their previous peaceful position with
Germany for the nonbinding promises of a foreign diplomat.

Unaware of Bullitt's and FDR's agitations, the Germans were,
to say the least, perplexed. The leading Polish newspaper *Kurier
Polski* increased its anti-German hostilities with headlines like
"Germany must be destroyed!" The commander of the Polish
armed forces, Edward Rydz, stated publicly, "Poland wants war
with Germany, and Germany will not be able to avoid it, even if
she wants to." This agitation had an adverse influence on how
the ethnic German minority was treated in Poland.

The Germans were mistreated and terrorized. All the
complaints by the Germans were ignored, claiming they were
no more than atrocity propaganda used to justify Hitler's
actions. Medical and legal observers from the United States, the
International Red Cross, and forensic pathologists verified the
complaints as truthful, but they were ignored. Dr. Alfred-Maurice
de Zayas describes the atrocities suffered by the German minority
in his book *The Wehrmacht War Crimes Bureau, 1939–1945*.

In Hans Schadewalt's book *Polish Acts of Atrocity against
the German Minority in Poland*, we read,

> Up to November 1939, the closing day for the
> documentary evidence contained in the first
> edition of this book, 5,437 murders, committed

by members of the Polish armed forces and by Polish civilians on men, women and children of the German minority had already been irrefutably proven ... The actual number of murders far exceeded this figure, and by February 1, 1940, the total number of identified bodies of the German minority had increased to 12,857 ... there must be added more than 45,000 missing, all of whom must be counted dead since no trace of them can be found ... These murders were intentional, and for the greater part, committed by Polish soldiers, police and gendarmes, but also by armed civilians, schoolboys and apprentices and vigilante partisans. Protestant churches and parish halls were destroyed and burnt in Bromberg-Schwedehoehe, in Hopfengarten near Bromberg, in Gr. Leistenau near Graudenz, in Kl. Katz in Gotenhafen ...

Altars were defiled and altar lights destroyed. Bibles and altar coverings were torn to rags. The oldest man murdered was the eighty-six-year-old Peter Rieriast of Ciechoreinek, and the youngest victim was the two-and-a-half-month-old infant Gisela Rosenau of Lochowo, who died on the breast of her murdered mother. Death notices in many city newspapers, such as in the *Deutsche Rundschau* in Bromberg as well as in the *Posen Tagesblatt*, portray an appalling picture of how German men, women, old men, cripples, invalids, and children were murdered and how most of them were mutilated in a ghastly way and robbed. All too often, Germans were merely herded together, driven off, and massacred in isolated spots, so the eyes of the world would never see their remains. The numbers of the murdered ranged from 39 to 104 at a time. A mass grave of

40 Germans from Thorn and its neighborhood was discovered close to Alexandrowo; their bodies were so mutilated that only three could be identified. Their eyes were gouged out, teeth smashed, brains oozing out of the skulls, tongues torn out, abdomens slit open, arms and legs broken, fingers hacked off, and feet and lower portions of the legs chopped off. According to documented reports, this is how these unfortunate victims took their last breaths.

We must be fair and understand that the great majority of Poles were exceedingly appalled by the animal-like behaviors by some of their countrymen. Every country has a radical element, villains, not just the Poles. Many Poles, risking their own lives and being accused of being pro-German, intervened and took actions to prevent these murders. Many Polish civilians and officers saved many Germans from the claws of the bloodthirsty partisans. Many Poles acted courageously, protecting the German minority at the risk of their own lives.

The more courteous Polish-German relations were replaced with a display of covert behavior as a result of FDR's personal operative in Europe, William Christian Bullitt, Jr. Misguided by Bullitt's promises, Beck and the Polish government cut off direct talks with the Reich, only escalating the confrontations. Hitler invited a Polish emissary with full power to Berlin. Beck responded by flying to London, meeting the British foreign secretary, Lord Halifax, and signing a Mutual Assistance Pact, while at the same time Poland's armed forces were being mobilized.

Ultimately, Poland was attacked to rescue the German minority from terror and mass murder. These facts are usually not mentioned in the media, nor are they taught in our schools. A balanced account of that part of history has a long road ahead, as do the causes of the hostilities between the two countries. If that would happen, that would invalidate the official claim that

Poland was merely the victim of Hitler's lust for world conquest, as it would also diminish the claim of an Allied moral high ground. We take solace in Shakespeare's promise that "Foul deeds will rise, though all the Earth o'erwhelm them, to men's eyes" (*Hamlet*, Act 1 Scene 2).

The authors of the *Marshall Cavendish Illustrated Encyclopedia of World War II* stated, "The German invasion of Poland was launched after the Polish ambassador in Berlin refused to discuss Hitler's proposal for a peaceful solution to the problem of Danzig and the Corridor." Unfortunately, Beck and the Polish leadership were being used or abused as justification for aggression against Germany. It should be pointed out, President George W. Bush ordered the attack on Iraq on March 20, 2003. This did not start World War III, because no one wanted to expand it into a world war.

In 1948, the international political climate changed drastically; Germany received permission to clean up its rivers and the rubble and begin rebuilding its economy. The Cold War and the threat of Communism became a kind of a blessing for Germany. Germany was needed to defend European and Western interests. The American, English, and French zones became West Germany, the Federal Republic of Germany, and the Soviet zone became East Germany, the German Democratic Republic. There was little federal in West Germany and even less democratic in East Germany.

In just ten short years, like the phoenix of classical mythology, Germany rose again from the ashes of the funeral pyre prepared by her enemies and was once again on the road to recovery and becoming a major economic and industrial power. Germany rose from its ashes and rubble into the shining, caring, and compassionate community of people that they have always been—the land of Luther, Goethe, Schiller, Beethoven, Mozart, Hegel, Nietzsche, Kant, Plank, Einstein, and von

Braun and millions of other wonderful people. As explained in a previous chapter, in the National Socialist state, workers and employers worked harmoniously together for the common good of all. The younger Germans remembered the advice of their elders and constructed the most up-to-date production machinery.

Over a million deaths in Ike's Rhine death camps were listed in the American archives as simply "Other Losses." The English newspaper the *Independent on Sunday* described Ike's death camps as "one of the most successful cover-ups in history." Eisenhower told the American journalist J. Kingsley Smith, "Our primary purpose is the destruction of as many Germans as possible. I expect to destroy every German west of the Rhine and in that area in which we are attacking."

Kaufman stated in his book on page 88 that there is "A final solution: Let Germany be policed forever ..." Almost a century later, America is still policing Germany with American forces on German soil. Germany has been paying for and supporting American forces in Germany for all these years, with apparently no end in sight. Germany and Japan paid the lion's share, some 80 percent, for Desert Storm.

Germany surrendered on May 8, 1945. The last Wehrmacht report read in part,

> The weapons have now been silent on all fronts since midnight ... the Wehrmacht has now stopped fighting a battle that has become hopeless. And so, a struggle that has been fought heroically for six years has now come to an end. It has brought us great victories, but heavy losses as well ... The home front has supported our forces to the end with all possible effort and at great sacrifice. This unique display of loyalty on the

part of both soldiers and the home front will at some later day receive its just recognition in the annals of history ...

The achievements and sacrifices of German forces on land, in the air, and at sea will not have escaped the notice of our enemies. Every soldier can therefore proudly lay down his weapon and bravely and resolutely undertake in these most difficult days in our history the work required so that our nation can survive. At this hour, the Wehrmacht remembers the many comrades who have fallen before the enemy. The dead demand from us the living unconditional devotion, discipline and order in staunching the countless wounds in our bleeding fatherland.

May all who perished so needlessly rest in eternal peace.

True miracles are rare, especially national economic miracles. Germany's recovery after the destruction and devastation is a shining testament to the persistence, patience, and unwavering determination of the German people. The Marshall Plan provided some assistance, the Cold War became a kind of a blessing, but the diligence and the resilience of the German people themselves supplied the main vital spark to what is generally referred to as the "German Economic Miracle" or "das Wirtschaftswunder." The Marshall Plan was genuinely appreciated, but it was a loan, not a gift. The Marshall Plan was not even enough to pay Germany's reparation payments. The Marshall Plan was a loan that had to be paid back with interest, and the money had to be spent in America. The last installment was paid off in 1971.

The Marshall Plan, 1948–1952, provided a total of $12 billion in loans to the European countries. England received the largest amount, $3.2 billion. Italy received $1.5 billion, and West Germany received the smallest amount of $1.4 billion. Germany and Finland are the only two countries who paid back the loan and the interest; the payments from the other countries are still outstanding. Perhaps Washington intends to chalk it off as a loss or as a gift. Perhaps the American tax payer will pay the bill. Germany has always paid and never received financial gifts like other countries. Furthermore, Germany is paying for the American troops stationed in Kaiserslautern, Baumholder, and Ramstein. In comparison, all the equipment and stuff taken or looted after the war from Germany has been estimated in excess of ten billion (1950) dollars.

In the United States, the Marshall Plan is all too often credited for Germany's miraculous economic recovery. That is only part of the story. The $1.4 billion loaned to Germany, the smallest amount to all the European countries, was not even enough to offset the $2.5 billion Germany was obligated to pay annually to cover the cost for the occupational forces. In addition, Germany was obliged to pay endless reparations and restitutions, which they are still paying almost a century after the war. There seems to be no end in sight.

In 1949, the Allies "supervised" the creation of the German basic law, das Grundgesetz. Several Morgenthau Plan demands found their way into the Grundgesetz, such as the "abolition of racial exclusivity." Because Germany still has no genuine peace treaty, this provisional legal framework is still in place and unaltered. Germany was obligated to admit all "asylum seekers" that come to her borders. If the present influx of migrants continues, Germans will soon become a minority in their own country. With all its economic power, Germany lacks complete sovereignty over its internal and external affairs. At present, German politicians do not appear to have the fortitude to defend their borders or demand their rightful place in the sun.

At that critical historical juncture, following the war, Germany was blessed with exceptionally competent leaders. Dr. Konrad Adenauer was at first appointed chancellor and then reelected. For some sixteen years, he provided Germany with very skillful and reassuring leadership during this very difficult period. In 1955, he negotiated the release of the remaining German POWs from the Soviet Union, those who were still alive. Under his guidance, the German Civil Service remained basically intact with low- and mid-level former Nazi officials filling their former duties; most senior Nazi officials, however, were removed.

Replacing JCS 1067, the Morgenthau Plan, with JCS 1779 was drastic and a life-saver for Germany and ultimately for all of Europe and the world. JCS 1779 stressed that an orderly and prosperous Europe necessitated the economic contributions of a stable and productive Germany. That began the economic ascent to Germany's Wirtschaftswunder—economic recovery. The most significant factor in rebuilding Germany was the *Truemmerfrauen*, the rubble women in all the cities. Since the men were being held as POWs and being starved to death, it was up to the German women to clean up Germany. They did a herculean job.

Equally important for Germany's recovery and reconstruction was the appointment of Professor Ludwig Erhard as economic minister. He was part of the school of economic thinking that is referred to as "Soziale Marktwirtschaft," social free market economy. They tested the political climate and verified the promise that they actually were allowed a free hand and could practice and manage their own economy. Erhard and Adenauer negotiated the Petersburg Agreement and were able to end all further dismantling of the German industry, and they were able to open commercial routes for international trade.

Ludwig Erhard introduced the free interplay of market forces of supply and demand. The policy encouraged fair competition and private initiative for profit. Erhard's motto was "as little state as possible and as much state as necessary." To stimulate competition, the Kartellgesetz forbade large-scale mergers in industry. The government cut tax rates and provided tax incentives to drive the industrial machine. The most punitive military controls were lifted, and the Germans were able to run and manage their own economic affairs.

In late 1948, the government passed the *Waehrungsreform*, the currency reform. Two policies contributed greatly to building trust and establishing ownership in Germany's recovery. The West German D-mark became one of the strongest and most solid currencies. The *Mitbestimmungsrecht*, codetermination policy, and the *Betriebsratsgesetz*, the factory committee law, were key factors in establishing trust and a climate of cooperation, all pulling in the same direction. In all workplaces, labor would sit at the table with management to resolve issues amicably, eliminating the need for strikes or production slowdowns. As a result of this cooperative climate, creating stability and mutual trust, the German economy grew to one of the strongest in the world. Germans took great pride in their superior products stamped "Made in Germany," and the Germans gradually began to enjoy a better standard of life.

Germany saw itself faced with a huge housing problem. The survivors of the fire-bombings, the total destruction of Germany, and the millions of homeless ethnic Germans who were expelled from their homes and homelands, all were in dire need of somewhere to live. Adequate housing was in very short supply. The government put top priority on the immediate existential and survival needs, food and shelter. Laws were passed to minimize some of the problems. The Germans have proven to be very resilient, persevering, compassionate, reliable, and industrious, with exceptional work ethics. The German people rose admirably to their challenges. They displayed a collective discipline. Germany is perhaps the only country where someone may ask a person crossing the street on a red light if he or she is colorblind. They display the motto "If all follow the rules, all benefit." They take ownership in the affairs of their community and society. They still need to increase their involvement in politics.

The government required all West Germans with available space to share it with and allow refugees and the homeless to move in with them, which most did cheerfully. In 1950, there were ten million, and in 1961, there already existed sixteen million housing units for the fifty million plus people. Some five hundred thousand new dwellings were being added each year. Simultaneously, the German economy increased as well. Nine million new jobs had been created by 1960, and the unemployment rate fell to a mere 1.3 percent. In a short time, West Germany became the third strongest economy in the world. By 1963, West Germany was, with the exception of the Soviet Union, the strongest economy in Europe.

Had the Kaufman/Morgenthau/FDR Plan been fully implemented, continental Europe would have most likely fallen to Communism, which is what Moscow was scheming for. The creator of the Morgenthau Plan was allegedly Harry Dexter White, who was accused of being a Soviet agent working closely with Kaufman and Morgenthau.

Charles de Gaulle reflected in his memoirs about Germany, writing, "It swept aside all the armies of France in six weeks," and in 2005, it exported $1 trillion in goods. Finally, rather than military confrontations, Europeans gradually embraced a policy of mutual support, cooperation, and tolerance. Gradually building upon reciprocal trust, they began to celebrate each other's and their own beautiful and colorful European common heritage. The European Union was born, and all have benefitted. After some false starts in the past, the sons and daughters of millions of Europeans united. In spite of themselves and some minor differences, they formed the most powerful economic, social, intellectual, and political consortium on planet earth. Instead of killing, they began to help and support each other.

Throughout the centuries, most bloody European military conflicts were carried out on German soil. Germans have historically not identified at the national but at the regional level. For centuries, that characteristic flaw has been exploited very skillfully by its vigilant neighbors. Imagine American pride and interests being placed at the state rather the national level. That may mark the beginning of the end of a meaningful and strong union.

Article 5 of the German Grundgesetz, basic law, a temporary measure, guarantees that everyone is free to express his or her opinion with some alarming exceptions, such as the politically correct version of World War II, the National Socialists, and any open discussion of the Holocaust. Any deviation from the official, politically correct version will end one up in jail. Included in these demands are the allegations that the freedom-loving democracies had to defend themselves against Hitler's plans to conquer the world—with no mention of England's determination to destroy the industrial and commercial success of Germany. Freedom of speech with limitations is no freedom of speech at all. Americans treasure their freedom of speech; they must be also willing to grant it to the Germans and others as well. Otherwise, we speak with a forked tongue. Paragraph 130 was ordered into the German Grundgesetz, which limits freedom of the press and speech and prevents any scholarly, substantive controversial debates. Germans are still told what to say and write, because Big Brother is watching! This is still the law in Germany, even almost a century after the war. Our government has accused Hitler's and Stalin's and other regimes of curtailing freedom of speech and the press. We are curtailing it in Germany, partially because Germany still does not have a peace treaty and does not enjoy full sovereignty. Why is Washington afraid of granting Germany absolute freedom of speech and sovereignty? Are we concerned that the archives might contain information that might be embarrassing? If so, are Americans and the people of the world not entitled to know all the facts? Who is afraid of revealing the whole *truth*? An honest discussion concerning all the issues is long overdue. Procrastination will not change the facts. Friedrich Schiller stated, "Die Gedanken sind frei!" Thoughts are free and are not limited to Article 5 of the German Grundgesetz. What are the reasons why we maintain double standards?

The atom bombs that were dropped on Hiroshima and Nagasaki on August 6 and 9, 1945, not only destroyed the cities and killed and crippled their inhabitants but also destroyed any political significance of international diplomacy. Wars are no longer "extensions of politics by other means," as von Clausewitz stated, but the savage ends that justifies the means. Might has become right. The old form of warfare has become outdated. Partisan warfare has taken on biblical dimensions of brutality with no limits to the destruction caused. Children have become assassins in designer civilian clothing.

The fall of the Berlin Wall has changed the political power equation from the Washington-Moscow Cold War confrontations and saber raddling into a multipolarity. The United States, Russia, China, and Israel have emerged as nuclear powers, and India and North Korea are waiting in the wings. The world is now faced with the threat of nuclear war; that threat will not disappear from the international world stage. Peace on earth and good will to all men is now more elusive than at any time in history. We are now able to destroy ourselves. Churchill admitted that there was no real peace after the war, and the dangers in the world after the war were actually greater than prior to the war. This was an honest admission of failure. Tragically, the war destroyed much of the colorful European heritage and Western culture. What has the world gained by Britain's thirty-year war?

Realizing that all wars have been and are economic conflicts, the European Union was born. A solid economic union would bring about a political unity and ensure peace for Europe, which it has so far accomplished. Furthermore, the world has been moving ever closer together as powerful industrial complexes are gradually gaining ever greater political clout. Germany has developed into a European industrial and commercial superpower, and yet, Germany has not been able to secure its sovereignty and a real peace treaty. The victorious Allies "fighting for democracy" refuse to accept the concept that democracy and national sovereignty are essential to national statehood. Democracy, by definition, is collective self-determination of a nation, which includes Germany. The reeducation and brainwashing of Germany has been attempting to diminish national self-esteem and national pride. Fortunately, the Germans are rediscovering their rightful personal and national pride in Europe and the world.

If after almost a century no reconciliation has occurred, in regard to a real peace treaty, then there most likely may never be one; it will likely remain an open-ended issue, just like the unending reparation payments. The most destructive catastrophe of the centuries, destruction, mass murder and rape, and unconditional surrender were unleashed by Churchill, Hitler, Stalin, and Roosevelt. Without World War I and the Versailles Treaty, World War II would have never become a reality. What did the wars accomplish? Centuries from now, historians will be able to ascertain if there was a worldwide conspiracy against the German people. Instead of a long period of peace, the world has been faced with unending wars and rumors of wars. A long period of peace has been just another empty political promise.

The pagans of centuries past conducted themselves under the concept that might is right. They professed that God was always on their side, hence the gods would bless them with being victorious. When the Greeks won, the Trojans had no rights. The men were killed, the women were raped, and the children became slaves. After the Romans were victorious, the Carthaginians had no rights. All the men were killed, and all the women and children were raped and enslaved. According to the standards of modern society, the behavior of these pagans was abominable. Has the Morgenthau Plan reverted humankind to such savage paganism?

If an American soldier rapes an American woman on American soil or even in a foreign country, will he not be held accountable for his actions? Should not the same standards apply to foreign women, especially after the war was over? For various reasons, Germany was not granted a peace treaty. Would not every self-respecting court rule these rapes as crimes? Might can never be legally equal to right; otherwise, the criminal with a gun would always be right, at least until he is disarmed. This is what perpetuates a continuous war mentality. For justice to be true justice, it must be as solid as a rock and predictable as gravity. It is now a known fact that raping and looting, especially by Russian soldiers across all of Germany, far exceeded any barbarity the Germans were accused of at the Nuremberg mock trials. For example, the colonial French troops under Eisenhower's command entered Stuttgart, herded local women into the subways, and raped them. French Negro soldiers from Senegal, wearing American lend-lease uniforms raped more than four thousand German women of all ages, engaging in a raping orgy that lasted three days. Where these unfortunate German women being "liberated" by Eisenhower's forces?

According to an AP dispatch (Frankfurt, June 25, 1946), "Three American paratroopers stabbed and beat a German father and mother when they refused the Americans a midnight rendezvous with their daughter." This German father and mother firmly believed they had a legal right and a moral obligation to protect their daughter even against these savage victors. Perhaps these soldiers had a daughter of their own back in the States. As in so many other cases, these criminals were never held accountable for their criminal behavior. Crimes against Germans have never been prosecuted and, most likely, never will be. Justice continues to be denied. What is Washington's relationship with Berlin? We have acted steadfastly in not granting Germany its sovereignty and a peace treaty. Are we legally still at war with Germany? Why have we not removed our troops from Germany?

Cardinal Bernard Griffen of England visited Central Europe; he described what he witnessed,

> Such raping and looting is the story of Berlin, Danzig, Budapest and even pro-Russian Czechoslovakia. The Red Army troops acted like rustic louts that had come out of the woods into civilization for the first time. The looting of homes, the violation of women, the deportation and often murder of the non-Communists and clergymen, and the Bolshevizing of property are crimes our government connives at every time it cooperates with Russia by double-crossing any other nation. Some of these crimes are irreparable. A woman violated is violated forever. A few months of Russian occupation and the damage is done—dead men stay dead, starved children are destroyed, and violated women, even if they live, have suffered a fate worse than death.

Might or physical strength never gives any man, even a soldier, the right to rape or physically overpower a woman. Tragically, FDR's unconditional surrender stripped Germans of all rights, and no German girl or woman had any rights or recourse to refuse the lustful, animal demands of an American, English, French, or Russian soldier. Just as the victor may not carry off a girl's honor, so may he also not walk off with her wristwatch, her mother's silverware, or her father's livestock and rob them of their ancestral homes and land. The Germans put saboteurs and political opponents into concentration camps, but they were under strict orders not to rape or loot. When will FDR's unconditional surrender and the Morgenthau Plan be condemned for what they truly are, crimes against Germany and the German people?

The German leadership has repeatedly expressed remorse for the pain and suffering that Germany inflicted. The leadership even expressed their and Germany's gratitude to the victorious powers for the liberation of Germany. Many have waited for an explanation of the term *liberation*. Where the hundreds of thousands of raped German women being "liberated"? Was all the looting of German property part of this "liberation," and were the millions murdered being liberated from their pain and torture? All the dead and all who were violated hold the respective governments and the world's conscience accountable.

A principal responsibility of the government of every country is to secure and protect its borders, just as private citizens protect their homes. The "abolition of racial exclusivity" clause in the Grundgesetz denies Germany that right. The present mass invasion of illegal aliens is the continuation of the destruction of Germany by other means. Germany's industrial and commercial success has attracted millions of refugees. Many profess to be "asylum seekers," looking for a safer life for themselves and their families. For millions, Germany has become an immigration destination. Chancellor Merkel's policy of accepting all undocumented migrants in Germany has created the European Union's greatest crisis since its foundation, because Mama Merkel has failed to protect her borders and the safety and well-being of her citizens, which is every government's primary obligation and duty.

Merkel's generous pledge, which traveled via social media around the world in minutes, opened the floodgates to a situation that Berlin and the EU may be ill equipped to handle, considering all the economic, cultural, and divergent religious schisms and the EU security, as well as all the educational and political issues. No one has an accurate picture of how many undocumented migrants there are, what viruses they brought with them, or how many criminals there are among them and at what cost to the taxpayer. Merkel's inability to refuse unlimited asylum seekers is based on No. 16a of the German Grundgesetz, Germany's temporary basic law. This became part of the German basic law as a result of Washington's insistence on the "abolition of racial exclusivity" and part of the Morgenthau Plan. However, this law does not apply to *Wirtschaftsfluechtlinge*, those who seek economic opportunities and whose lives are not in danger. They can be denied entry and deported. Time will tell how Berlin will act; it is under pressure to act resolutely in Germany's and Europe's best interest. Time is of the essence. Merkel, whose ratings have dropped and who is up for reelection to her fourth term, has changed her rhetoric to accelerating the return of the aliens.

The German media, ever so obedient, has been asserting that any German who is opposed to accepting all these refugees must be some kind of a radical Nazi or a racist. For Germans, these are very sensitive issues. The German media has been known to lecture all too often, telling Germans what is expected of them, when they should be reporting just the facts.

Because Germans are generous and caring people by nature, at the beginning, thousands of Germans were seen welcoming thousands of refugees, showering them with food and gifts. That enthusiasm ceased swiftly, because there was no end in sight and due to a lack of gratitude of the migrants themselves.

There are a few genuine asylum seekers, but the great majority of them are economic opportunists, seeking better prospects in Europe. Promoting this massive migration are unscrupulous smugglers promising millions of migrants a new house, a new car, and lots of money in Germany. The smugglers are criminals making false promises, for which they charge the naïve migrants large sums of money. Once inside the EU, the damage is done, because the migrants can now travel freely to whichever country appears most welcoming within the Schwengen area. As a result, several countries in the EU have imposed border controls to stem the tide of the migrants. Mama Merkel has persisted in her failed policy. The Germans have demonstrated, "Nein, das schafft Deutschland NIE."

Some one-and half million refugees have arrived in Germany just the last year. During the past few years, Germany has accepted some seven million illegal aliens. The actual number is not known, because most are undocumented. Some of them will return to their homeland willingly; many will not. England and other European countries have expressed their concern that these refugees will find their way into England and other European countries. A growing number of Germans and Europeans understandably want Berlin and Europe to demonstrate more resolve and send them back. Last New Year's Eve in several German cities, gangs of Arab and North African men robbed and raped thousands of German women. For days, these crimes were not reported because the government feared an outcry against Merkel's open border policy.

Many individuals are genuinely concerned about these

refugees, because they all seem to have one destination—
Germany. Germany did not really create it, nor is she solely
responsible for this crisis. This is a man-made crisis, due to failed
foreign intervention policy.

Among the many examples of invaders are more than ten
thousand migrants who came out of the forest within a two-
week period and overran a small town called Breitenberg. They
were guided by smugglers through Austria and brought to the
German border in buses. The smugglers even posted signs in
the forest in the colors of the German flag and arrows pointing
them in the direction of Germany. Why were the smugglers not
arrested and prosecuted for their crimes?

The migrants, who are seen by many as invaders, have been
involved in physical altercations with governmental personnel
and civilians and have demanded better accommodations and
food more to their liking. Many displayed a complete lack of
appreciation of German generosity. They demand freedom of
choice, where they want to settle, how they want to live, and
how they want to be served by their German hosts. Germany
has showered them with more than 10,000 euros per person
per year. That includes 670 euros free spending money per
month, additional child support, free housing, free medical
care, free education for all from kindergarten to the university
level, and German-language instruction for all who need it.
Why has Mama Merkel and the German government been so
extremely generous? The German taxpayers are forced to pick
up the tab. In comparison, Denmark gives them 450 euros
and Lithuania 10 euros. No wonder, their favorite destination
continues to be Germany. Chancellor Angela Merkel has
proclaimed: "Das schaffen wir!" For the smugglers, the
millions of migrants mean big business and huge profits, but
for Germany and the EU, they have become a major migraine
headache. Germany pays more to the unwanted refugees than

it pays unemployment compensation to its own workers who have paid into the system.

The German historian Hans Ulrich Wehler is not the only one who has a strong opinion regarding the integration of millions of Muslim refugees. He holds that it is impossible to integrate Muslims into the German and Central European culture. At present, there are over three million Turks and an equal or greater number of Syrians and other Muslims in Germany. He asserts that Germany does not have a problem with foreigners, but it does have a Muslim problem. The Muslims have made outrageous demands on the German government and the German people; they have demanded that the German government build them an additional two thousand new Muslim Mosques, at government expense, and they demand special treatment. Many fear that if the Muslims are not returned to their native country, they will become a major political, cultural and religious problem.

There is a limit to how many refugees Germany, or any country, can absorb without becoming the minority in their own country. This influx of Muslims is seen as an explosive element, the continuation of the destruction of Germany, but by other means. All immigration countries eventually pull the emergency brakes. Germany and other European countries have seen a serious increase in crimes. All the arguments for closing the borders and returning the invaders have already been made by many respected German and European politicians, who are strongly opposed to Merkel's open-border policies.

Among the thousands of migrants are many terrorists who already have inflicted much pain and terror on their German and European hosts. The crisis in Germany and Europe has generated much discussion around the globe. Among those who have voiced their concerns about Germany being there for the Germans is the religious leader, the great Dalai Lama.

He stated that Germany is rightfully the land for the Germans and may not be changed into an Islamic / Muslim state. He has observed that this massive migration has not produced greater diversity, tolerance, and openness but will continue to destroy centuries-old Western culture and civilization. The time has arrived when Chancellor Merkel and the migrants realize they're only temporary guests and need to return home again, sooner rather than later.

Berlin has argued that they welcomed thousands of refugees in the past to fill their need for its growing workforce. The migrants are only a temporary solution. The problems that have been created far outweigh any solution. It might be conceivable that the German economy could stagnate and then the economic burdens to the German taxpayers will become a great burden. If Germany remains economically strong and continues to be generous to its neighbors in the EU and uses that economic strength prudently, it will continue to be a blessing for and greatly contribute to a bright and peaceful future for all of Europe. Germany does not need to accept false asylum seekers to fill its labor demands, because there are many ready and willing workers within the European Union itself. Accepting more migrants will not negate but greatly add to the present European crisis.

An overarching issue is the fact that the Germans did not have enough children of their own; the pill and the ease of obtaining an abortion are the biggest culprits. Too many Germans view children as costly and a distracting factor of their lifestyle. That attitude needs to change dramatically. Politicians have totally failed in this regard. The government needs to be more child-friendly. Merkel herself has no children and could hardly serve as an example of the bliss of motherhood. German women's career ambitions come at the expense of children and the future of Germany. The attitude of German men plays an equally important role. All children need their fathers to provide for them and guide them in a well-functioning family environment.

The question has been raised: Are the Germans slowly dying out? Germany will not die out; it will continue to thrive and prosper and be a pillar in the European and world community. The present situation is merely a minor bump in the road. Children are Germany's and every country's greatest wealth and its future. The German government must become more actively involved in Germany's attitude to children and incorporate policies that are child friendly. Many German women have demonstrated that they can combine and enjoy the bliss of motherhood and a great career at the same time.

If the German industry needs more workers, it can easily hire workers from EU member countries, who will return to their native countries after their tenure. The workers from neighboring EU countries are not migrants or illegal aliens and require no German governmental assistance. They are fellow Europeans. This is a no-brainer and a win-win situation for both Germany and the EU. Since the citizens of the EU member countries have a legal right to come to Germany anyway, they will not become a burden to the German taxpayer. One of the fringe benefits of EU membership is that its citizens can travel freely within the EU and be gainfully employed within the EU. Furthermore, Europe will not be infiltrated with an Islam/Muslim religion and culture that for centuries has proven to be unfriendly and confrontational to a European Judeo-Christian culture. The recent terror attacks in Europe and America have brought the issues of the increased level of crimes and terror to the surface.

Another possible solution to Germany's need for its workforce is to open and operate production facilities in neighboring EU countries, which Germany has already done. So far

Germany has relocated and is operating facilities in neighboring Poland, Spain, and Portugal, simultaneously mitigating the unemployment issue in those countries. Such relations will solidify the European Union and promote harmonious and friendly European human and economic relations.

For generations now, the German youth have been indoctrinated with that toxic "collective guilt" virus, brainwashing them that they are guilty by association of all crimes. They are being accused of crimes they did not commit. The German youth are indoctrinated with what the Germans did, but know little or nothing about the suffering and what was done to the Germans. The only thing that these accusations serve is the unending payments of reparations, and the perpetuation of the guilt feeling, which Professor Finkelstein calls "the Holocaust industry." This must stop because it has no validity and possesses no credibility. Just like the Jews of today cannot be accused of being guilty nor held accountable of Christ's crucifixion by association. All that is just so much misguided poisonous propaganda, and the world is already saturated with poisonous propaganda. Hate must be replaced with tolerance and truth. The world has a choice: we either continue killing each other, or we tolerate each other and live in peace. The choice seems simple enough.

The concept of a chain of guilt that is attached endlessly, mercilessly, through innocent generations is rooted in the Old Testament practices and teachings. There never was a collective guilt of the Germans or any other nation. There is no such thing as a predetermined casualty. It would be wrong to punish a whole class of students for the misbehavior of one individual. Germans have been told, "You have been deemed to be collectively guilty and therefore, have a historical responsibility and a duty to behave and obey as ordered, even if it is wrong and contrary to your personal or national interests." There are no good or evil nations, only good or evil individuals; they exist in all nations. Senator George Voinovich stated so eloquently, "Show me a person who is proud of his ethnic heritage, and I'll show you a good American."

One can only wonder why Hitler acted as he did and turned his back on the Ukrainians and the Russians who offered to fight on his side. Had Hitler accepted the alignments from the Ukrainians, the Belarussians, the Tartars, the Georgians, and others, he could have, at that time, given Stalin the final blow, gaining victory over Stalin. Entire Cossack regiments put down their weapons and waited for the Germans. These "Ersatz-Germans" were prepared to tell Hitler that his forces were not fighting them, only the Soviet system, but, tragically, Hitler was not listening. He committed another treasonous, fatal military error. Bolshevism was saved as a result of Hitler's direct orders. Tolstoy describes in his book *The Minister and the Massacre* how tens of thousands of Cossacks were handed over to Stalin after the war, knowing they would be executed. He also discusses how over a hundred thousand Slovenes, Croats, and Serbs were lied to, told they were being transported to safety in Italy, and then handed over to Tito's executioners, who tortured and murdered them.

The German people and many others paid dearly for Hitler's arrogant, treasonous mistakes. Thereafter, Stalin ordered increased partisan activities behind German supply lines, terrorizing the pro-German local population. One can begin to understand the frustration and disappointment with Hitler and his regime. The only logical explanation is that he was receiving and following orders. The German forces could no longer protect the pro-German local population because of personnel shortages. Hitler made too many treasonous military mistakes to be victorious. The only thing victorious was all that bombast verbiage coming out of his mouth; he and the others

494 Dr. Joe Wendel

on the world stage were great orators. This action was a gift from Hitler to Stalin, at a mammoth cost of human lives and destruction.

By now, Stalin's brutality and butchery have been well documented. On May 11, 1943, Stalin ordered all female partisans who became pregnant by their comrades to be killed because they became a burden to partisan operations.

History is a chain of events, connected together by endless moments in time. Corrections of recorded history are continually unfolding as historians scrape off the layers of poisonous, self-serving propaganda and are getting closer to the unbiased and balanced truth. Individuals as well as nations are checkered with good and evil. Let all aspire to make all men better.

We are social and active members of society. God created man independent of all other creatures, for protection and security, as dependence is one of our strongest bonds. This dependence provides man opportunities for human reciprocal love and friendship. Man is the noblest part of the work of God; men need to act accordingly in a way that is acceptable to our Creator.

As we travel on this level of time, we may encounter a fork in the road. In a tree, at that intersection, we may encounter a Cheshire cat. We asked the cat for directions. Should we take the well-traveled road to the right or the less-traveled road to the left? "Why," replied the cat, "this depends totally on where you want to go and where you want to be at the end of your journey." Are we continuing on the well-traveled road to benefit the few at the expense of the many, the road of profit and greed for the select few, or are we going to travel the road to benefit the multitude, of social equality and tolerance? Whichever road chosen, there will continue to be challenges and obstacles.

We all need to contribute to the elimination of the vast ocean of ignorance of the past and to add to the common stock of knowledge and understanding, being more educated and informed, thus less likely manipulated about current events. Our constant mission should be to bring history into accord with the facts.

History is old news, and news is new history. History is far too important to be left to special interest groups, regardless of how noble their intentions might be. Orwell told the world that whoever controls the past controls the future. History has been described as prophecy in action. History is knowledge, and knowledge is power. It is a great source of pride and a record of accomplishments, as it also is an indictment of the evildoers. History is a great teacher, ever eager to impart her wisdom. We need to keep an open mind and remain intellectually curious. Our mind is like a parachute; it only works when it is open.

It is a sign of wisdom to periodically pause and reflect and recalibrate our compass to true north. The conflicts caused by the various special interest groups caused imbalance and destroyed equilibrium. Man vainly credits his misfortunes and fortunes to obscure and mysterious causes, when the causes are within his own bosom. Man, like the world around him, is governed by natural laws, regular in their course, uniform in their effects, and predictable in their cause and effect. The common denominator of good and evil are within these laws of nature, of which man is a pivotal part. Men inherently know to differentiate between the forces of good and the forces of evil; he has been given a free will to decide which road he shall travel. Each decision carries with it predictable consequences. The great German philosopher Immanuel Kant called this knowledge the categorical imperative. There exists a regular order of causes and effects, of principles and consequences, which under an appearance of chance, governs the universe and everything in it. There is regularity to physical and moral order. Man has been made the framer of his own destiny. He has been the cause of his successes and of his failures; his actions have caused both catastrophes and blessings.

In the first verse of Genesis, we read that God created the heaven and the earth. In the last verse of that chapter, we are told that God saw everything that He had made, and it was very good. God created a perfect world. He also gave man a free will. The snake continues to betray man's ego with thoughts of greed, power, and all kinds of selfish motives. Man has been recreating this perfect world in man's image, void of peace, happiness, and plenty for all. Why is it in our world of plenty that we allow people to go to bed hungry? There are power-blinded individuals who manage the flow of the food supply and waste tons of food, while erecting blockades to intentionally starve millions of people.

The prophecies in the Scriptures refer to a time when man shall possess the earth, a time when tears and sorrow shall be unknown, peace and plenty shall be everywhere. The earth is filled with treasures as yet undiscovered. How else did the prophets of old foretell, thousands of years ago, the airplane, the cannon, and the radio? How else can their descriptions of artillery in the Apocalypse be explained or that the gospel would be uttered from the housetops?

The same wind propels ships in every direction; their direction depends not on the direction the wind is blowing but on how their sails are set. The critical issue is not so much what happens to us but how we react to the challenges. The strong man rose up against the weaker and took from him the fruits of his labor. The weaker man involved another weaker man to repel the stronger man; the strong align for oppression and the weaker for resistance. Profit should not continue to be the guideline of human conduct. This same wind of self-perpetuation, moderate and prudent, fulfills the principles that lead to happiness, but also when blind, selfish and disordered was transformed into a corrupting societal poison and out of ignorance becomes the cause of evil and destruction. Ignorance, greed, ego, and lust are the sources of man's torments, injurious to his existence, while violating his own morality.

History is filled with man's brutality and inhumanity to his fellow human beings. Our media has been bending to the forces of special interests, supported with huge sums of money. Man's unchecked greed seems to have no limit. The media has not always fulfilled its obligation and been an honest broker between competing interests; far too often, it acted as judge of what is and what is not newsworthy. Money has been able to influence the media. Perhaps a legal and moral shield needs to surround the media to protect it from undue financial influence.

The First Amendment of our Constitution states that "Congress shall make no law respecting an establishment of religion, or prohibiting the free exercise thereof; or abridging the freedom of speech, or the press."

Great importance was placed upon the freedom of the press so that future generations of our republic were to survive long and in reasonable harmony by placing it among the first important amendments. It obligated the press to serve as a watchdog on powerful politicians, corrupt institutions, greedy businesses, out-of-control government agencies, and presidents usurping excessive power. The press must display courage to report all opposing opinions to remain free and place itself above being financially bribed.

Justice is that standard or boundary of right that enables us to render to every man just due without distinction. This virtue is not only consistent with divine and human laws but is the very cement and support of civil society. It should be the invariable practice of every individual and every nation. We must aspire to always act prudently. Prudence teaches us to regulate our lives and actions according to the dictates of reason, and it is that behavior by which we wisely judge and prudently determine all things relative to our present as well as our future happiness. We all travel on this level of time to that undisclosed place from whence no traveler returns. Always practice charity, because charity extends beyond the grave through the boundless realms of eternity.

It is out of ignorance and arrogance, which is a form of ignorance, that man armed himself against other men, families rose against families, and nations against nations, turning our earth into a theater of blood and destruction. Secret wars have been fermented, turning societies into oppressors and the oppressed, into masters and slaves. Solomon told us thousands of years ago that all is vanity. Every attempt must be made to resolve conflicts by negotiations and arbitrations rather than by military force. War will disappear when it is no longer profitable. What one steals today, another will take tomorrow. All need to respect the labor of others in order to secure their own. We, the people, need to be vigilant not to have a tyrant disposed of only to have tyranny continue.

Reason provides the person we injure and harm the right to injure and harm us in return. By attacking our neighbors, we awaken their sentiments of revenge and, thereby, endanger our own safety because of the effects of reciprocity. Thus, the perpetual cycle of evil and destruction continues, benefitting the very elite. Conversely, by acting and being good to others, there is an inherent truth in the expectation of an equivalent good in return. That is why the Golden Rule has such universal appeal. That is the foundation of social virtue, namely, "Do unto others as you would have others do unto you! Do not inflict unto others the harm you do not want inflicted upon yourself."

Education is the key to equivalence. Teach the poor to know their rights, and permit no one to transgress them. The poor must resist seduction and the rich the allurement of avarice.

Christ's only commandment, "Love thy neighbor as thyself," could be rephrased to "Bestow upon your neighbor all the good you wish to receive in return from your neighbor." That is the tacit law of moral reciprocity, the natural law of cause and effect. We have been told to forgive and to forget. There are those who believe that the wise forgive but do not forget. Pay your debts; otherwise, your debts become a point of irritation and contention and ultimately a cause for confrontation. It is a sign of wisdom to treat your enemy as if he might become your friend and your friend as if he might become your enemy. Always, be and act justly, because justice alone incorporates all virtues of society.

Provide the light and the truth, and people will find the way. Insist on transparency and education, and man shall not be so easily tempted by the biblical snake. Education and truth are the only sure pillars for the preservation of liberty. Benjamin Franklin warned that those who would trade liberty for security deserve neither and eventually will lose both. We pray, may justice delayed never become *justice denied*!

Lager Professor Peters Platz in Kiel, Germany
This was home from 1946 until 1950. In front are remnants of a junkyard—burned-out cars and trucks and so on. This territory served as our playground. One day, we found an upholstered double seat in one of the burned-out cars. We were happy to

take it to our barrack, and we took turns sitting on it, because it was so wonderfully soft.

This refugee camp was erected temporarily in Kiel, West Germany, to accommodate the thousands of refugees from the East. We lived there from 1946 to 1950, four and a half years in one room with no toilet and no bath. These Quonset huts were bitter cold in the winter and extremely hot in the summer. In 1951, we finally got an apartment with a bath in a building, erected by the Marshal Plan. We were very happy.

—Magdalene Link Wendel

Auf dem Professor Peters Platz in Kiel
Ottilie Link, 1948
Auf dem Professor Peters Platz in Kiel
Da war unser deutsches Landen
In Nissenhuetten eingefercht
Da gingen wir fast zu schanden
Die Not und der Hunger drueckten uns sehr
Der Frost und die Kaelte noch viel mehr.

Kein Menschenherz war in Kiel zu finden
Das uns half unser Elend zu lindern
Deutsche, Schweden, Amerikaner, Kommisionen
Schauten unser Elend an
Sprachen auch von einer Hilfe
Doch die Hilfe kam nicht an.

Bitter schwer getraenkt mit Traenen
Ist der Flecken Erde hier
Wo ich so oft mit Sehnen
Gebetet hab' zu Gott.
Ich muss es ertragen und nicht versagen
Und gebe die Hoffnung nicht auf.

BIBLIOGRAPHY

Adenauer, Konrad. *Memoirs 1945–53*. Chicago: Henry Regnery Company, Die Vereinigung Deutschlands im Jahre 1990, Eine Dokumentation, Bonn: 1991.

Allen, Martin. *The Hitler / Hess Deception*. Harper Collins Publications, 2003.

Andelman, David A. *A Shattered Peace: Versailles 1919 and the Price We Pay Today*. Hoboken, NJ: John T. Wiley & Sons, 2008.

Bailey, Thomas A. *Woodrow Wilson and the Lost Peace*. New York: Macmillan, 1944.

Barber, Noel. *Seven Days of Freedom: The Hungarian Uprising 1956*. New York: Stein and Day, 1974.

Barnett, Correlli. *The Collapse of British Power*. New York: William Morrow, 1972.

Bethel, Nicholas. *The War Hitler Won: The Fall of Poland, September 1939*. New York: Holt Rinehart Winston, 1973.

Bittinger, Lucy Forney. *The Germans in Colonial Times*. First published in 1901. New York: Russell & Russell, 1968.

Brody, J. Kenneth. *The Avoidable War: Lord Cecil & the Policy of Principle: 1933–35*. New Brunswick, NJ: Transaction, 1999.

Buchanan, Patrick J. *Churchill, Hitler, and the Unnecessary War*. New York: Crown Publishers, 2008.

Burt, Alfred Leroy. *The Evolution of the British Empire and Commonwealth from the American Revolution.* Boston: D. C. Heath, 1956.

Cameron, Norman, and R. H. Stevens. *Hitler Table Talk: 1941–1944: His Private Conversations.* New York: Enigma, 2000.

Churchill, Winston S. *Triumph and Tragedy.* Boston: Houghton Mifflin, 1953.

Churchill, Winston S. *The World Crisis: 1911–1918.* New York: Free Press, 2005.

Clarke, Peter. *Hope and Glory: Britain 1900–1990.* London: Allen Lane, Penguin Press, 1996.

Cole, Wayne. *Roosevelt & The Isolationists: 1932–45.* Lincoln, NE: University of Nebraska Press, 1983.

Collier, Richard. Duce!: A Biography of Benito Mussolini. New York: Viking Press, 1971.

Collier, Robert. *The Secret of the Ages.* Terrytown, NY: Robert Cillier Publications, Inc., 1948.

Cunz, Dieter. *They Came from Germany.* New York: Dodd, Mead & Co., 1966.

Dallas, Gregor. *1945: The War That Never Ended.* New Haven and London: Yale University Press, 2005.

de Zayas, Alfred-Marice. *A Terrible Revenge, the Ethnic Cleansing of the East European Germans, 1944–1950.* New York: St. Martin's Press, 1994.

de Zayas, Alfed. *50 Theses on the Expulsions of the Germans from Central and Eastern Europe 1944–1948.* Inspiration Unlimited, 2008.

de Zayas, Alfred-Maurice. *Anmerkungen zur Vertreibung der Deutschen aus dem Osten.* Stuttgart, Berlin, Koeln, Mainz: Verlag W. Kohlhammer, 1946.

de Zayas, Alfred-Maurice. *The German Expellees: Victims in War and Peace.* New York: St. Martin's Press, 1993.

de Zayas, Alfred-M. *Nemesis at Potsdam: The Expulsion of the Germans from the East.* 3rd Edition. Lincoln, NE: University of Nebraska Press, 1989.

de Zayas, Alfred M. *The Wehrmacht War Crimes Bureau, 1939–1945.* Lincoln: University of Nebraska Press, 1984.

Donald, Heidi Gurcke. *We Were Not the Enemy. Remembering the United States' Latin-American Civilian Internment Program of World War II.* 2008.

Douglas, R. M. *Orderly and Humane.* New Haven & London: Yale University Press, 2012.

Epstein, Julius. *Operation Keelhaul: The Story of Forced Repatriation from 1944 to the Present.* Old Greenwich, CT: Devin-Adair, 1973.

Faust, Albert Bernhardt. *The German Element in the United States with Special Reference to Its Political, Moral, Social, and Educational Influences.* 2 Vols. Boston and New York: Houghton Mifflin Co., 1969.

Finkenstein, Norman G. *The Holocaust Industry.* Varso. London. New York. 2000.

Ford, Brian. *German Secret Weapons: Blueprint for Mars.* Ballantine Books, Inc., 1970.

Friedman, F. Louis, and Ira Peck. *Between Two Wars.* Vol. 3. New York, Toronto, London, Sydney, Auckland, Tokyo: Scholastic Book Services, 1970.

Freeman, Marsha. *How We Got to the Moon.* 21st Century Science Associates. Washington, DC, 1993.

Fromkin, David. *Europe's Last Summer: Who Started the Great War?* New York: Alfred A. Knopf, 2004.

Grenfell, Captain Russell, RN. *Unconditional Hatred: German War Guild and the Future of Europe.* New York: Devin-Adair, 1953.

Griffin, G. Edward. *The Creature from Jekyll Island: A Second Look at the Federal Reserve.* 3rd Edition. American Media, 2000.

Gollancz, Victor. *Leaving Them to Their Fate*. London: Gollance, 1946.

Hightower, Jim. Thieves in High Places: They've Stolen Our Country and Its Time to Take It Back. Viking, Penquin Group, 2003.

Hillgruber, Andreas. *Germany and the Two World Wars*. Translated by William S. Kirby. Cambridge, MA: Harvard University Press, 1981.

Hoover, Herbert. *Freedom Betrayed: Secret History of the Second World War*. Hoover Institution Press, Stanford, CA. 2011.

Hughes, Emrys. *Winston Churchill, British Bulldog: His Career in War and Peace*. New York: Exposition Press, 1955.

Irving, David. *Apocalypse 1945: The Destruction of Dresden*. London: Focal Point Publications, 1995.

Jaksch, Wenzel. *Europe's Road to Potsdam*. New York: Frederick A. Praeger, 1963.

Jacobs, Arthur. *A Prison Called Hohenasperg: An American Boy Betrayed by his Government during World War II*. Universal Publishers, USA, 1999.

James, Lawrence. *The Rise and Fall of the British Empire*. New York: St. Martin's Griffin, 1994.

Kaufman, Theodore N. *Germany Must Perish*. Argyle Press, New York, NJ. 1941.

Keegan, John. *The First World War*. New York: Vintage, 2000.

Keynes, John Maynard. *Economic Consequences of Peace*. MacMillan & Co. Ltd, London, 1919.

Kissinger, Henry. *Diplomacy*. New York: Simon & Schuster, 1994.

Krauter, Anneliese "Lee." *From the Heart's Closet*. The Schatzi Press, Hawthorne Publishing, 2005.

Liddell Hart, B. H. *History of the Second World War*. New York: G. P. Putnam's Sons, 1970.

Lukacs, John. *June 1941: Hitler and Stalin*. New Haven and London: Yale University Press, 2006.

Mahl, Tom E. *Desperate Deception: British Covert Operations in the United States, 1939–44*. Washington, DC: Brassy's, Inc., 2003.

McDonogh, Giles. *The Last Kaiser: The Life of William II*. New York: St. Martin's Press, 2000.

Manchester, William. *The Last Lion, Winston Spencer Churchill: Alone, 1932–1940*. Boston: Little, Brown, 1988.

Mee, Charles L., Jr. *The End of Order: Versailles 1919*. New York: E. P. Dutton, 1980.

Millis, Walter. *Road to War: America 1914–1917*. Boston and New York: Houghton Mifflin, 1935.

Morgenthau, Henry. "Germany Is Our Problem."

Neilson, Francis. *The Makers of War*. Appleton, WI: C. C. Nelson, 1950.

O'Conner, Richard. *The German-Americans*. Boston: Little, Brown & Co., 1968.

Pakenham, Thomas. *The Boer War*. New York: Random House, 1979.

Palmer, John M. *General von Steuben*. Port Washington, NY: Kennikat Press Inc., 1937.

Ponsonby, Arthur. *Falsehood in Wartime. Propaganda Lies of the First World War*. Institute for Historical Review, 1928.

Pochmann, Henry A., and Arthur R. Schultz. *Bibliography of German Culture in America to 1940*. Madison, WI: University of Wisconsin Press, 1953.

Powell, Jim. *Wilson's War: How Woodrow Wilson's Great Blunder Led to Hitler, Lenin, Stalin & World War II*. New York: Crown Forum, 2005.

Rau, Jes. *It's All the Bank's Fault*. Staats: XLibris Corporation, 2012.

Richthofen, Bolko Frhr. V. *Kriegsschuld 1939–1941.* Der Schuld anteil der anderen (2. Teil). Arndt Verlag-Vaterstetten. Munchen, 1970.

Russert, Bruce M. *No Clear and Present Danger: A Skeptical View of the United States Entry into World War II.* Boulder, CO: Westview Press, 1997.

Rubinstein, W.D. *The Left, the Right and the Jews.* New York: Universe Books, 1982.

Shirer, William L. *The Rise and Fall of the Third Reich: A History of Nazi Germany.* New York: Simon and Schuster, 1960.

Smith, Gene. *The Dark Summer: An Intimate History of the Events That Led to World War II.* New York: MacMillan, 1987.

Solzhenitsyn, Aleksandr. *The Gulag Archipelago 1918–1956: An Experiment in Literary Investigation II.* Translated from the Russian by Thomas P. Whitney. New York: Harper & Row, 1974.

Speer, Albert. *Inside the Third Reich.* New York: Macmillan, 1970.

Steininger, Rolf. *South Tyrol: A Minority Conflict of the Twentieth Century.* New Brunswick, NJ: Transaction, 2003.

Stinnett, Robert B. *Day of Deceit: The Truth about FDR and Pearl Harbor.* New York, London, Toronto, Sydney, Singapore: Touchstone, Simon Schuster, 2001.

Tansill, Charles Callan. *Back Door to War: The Roosevelt Foreign Policy 1933–41.* Chicago: Henry Regnery, 1952.

Taylor, A.J.P. *From Sarajevo to Potsdam.* New York: Harcourt, Brace & World, 1967.

Taylor, A.J.P. *The Origin of the Second World War.* 2nd Edition with Reply to Critics. Greenwich, CT: Fawcett, 1961.

Tenz, Maria Horwath. *The Innocent Must Pay. Tito's Death Camps 1944–1948.* Munchen / Bavaria: Eugen Verlag, 1991; Bismarck, ND: University of Mary Press, 1989.

Tolstoy, Nicolai. *The Minister and the Massacres*. London: Century Hutchinson, 1986.

Tolzmann, Don Heinrich. *The German American Experience*. Humanity Books, 2000.

Tolzmann, Don Heinrich. *German-American Selected Essays*. Little Miami Publishing, 2009.

Toye, Richard. *Lloyd George and Churchill: Rivals for Greatness*. London: Macmillan, 2007.

Veale, F.J.P. *Advance to Barbarism: How the Reversion to Barbarism in Warfare and War-Trials Menaces Our Future*. Appleton, WI: C.C. Nelson, 1953.

Vincent, C. Paul. *The Politics of Hunger: The Allied Blockade of Germany, 1915–1919*. Athens, OH: Ohio University Press, 1985.

Von Hagen, Victor W. *Der Ruf der Neuen Welt*. Muenchen and Zuerich: Droemer Knaur, 1970.

Vonnegut, Kurt. *Slaughterhouse-Five or The Children's Crusade: A Duty Dance with Death*. New York: The Dial Press, 1969.

Wandel, Joseph. *The German Dimension of American History*. Chicago: Nelson-Hall, 1979.

Wassermann, Charles. *Unter Polnischer Verwaltung*. Tagebuch, 1957. Bluechert Verlag Hamburg, 1958.

Watt, Donald Cameron. *How War Came: The Immediate Origins of the Second World War, 1938–1939*. New York: Pantheon, 1989.

Wedemeyer, Albert C. *Wedemeyer Reports: An Objective, Dispassionate Examination of World War II, Postwar Policies, and Grand Strategy*. New York: Henry Holt & Company, 1959.

Wheeler-Bennett, John W., and Anthony Nicholls. *The Semblance of Peace: The Political Settlement after the Second World War*. London: MacMillan, 1972.

Wlossak, Traudie Mueller. *Die Peitsche des Tito-Kommissars*. Passau: Passavia Druckerei, 1987.

Wilbert, Friedrich von. *Das Oder-Neisse Problem. Eine Europaische Aufgabe.* Ostfriesland: Verlag Gerhard Rautenberg-Leer, 1968.

Wilson, A. N. *After the Victorians: The Decline of Britain in the World.* New York: Farrar, Strauss and Giroux, 2005.

Wittke, Carl. *We Who Built America.* New York: Prentice-Hall Inc., 1939.

Articles, Speeches, Internet Articles, and Documents

Buchanan, Patrick J. "Fake News and War Party Lies." New Yorker Staatszeitung, No. 50, 11. December 10, 2016.

Butler, Maj. Gen. Smetley. *War Is a Racket.* Title of two works, a speech and a 1935 short book.

Churchill, Winston S. "Zionism Versus Bolshevism: A Struggle for the Soul of the Jewish People." *Illustrated Sunday Herald.* February 8, 1920.

Davies, Norman. "How We Didn't Win the War … But the Russians Did." November 11, 2006. http://www.timesonline.co.uk.

Fenton, Ben. "Churchill Wanted to Use Gas on Enemies." *Daily Telegraph,* January 3, 1997.

Glancy, Jonathan. "Gas, Chemicals, Bombs: Britain Has Used Them All Before in Iraq." *Guardian,* April 9, 2003.

Lind, Michael. "Churchill for Dummies." *Spectator,* April 24, 2004.

Mayer, Steven. "Carcass of Dead Policies: The Irrelevance of NATO." *Parameters.* Winter 2003–2004, 83–97.

"Prime Minister's Personal Minute to General Ismay for COS Committee. Winston Churchill's Secret Poison Gas Memo." Center for Research on Globalization, www.globalresearch.ca.

Rosie, George. "UK Planned to Wipe Out Germany with Anthrax." *Glasgow Herald,* September 14, 2001.

OHIO SENATE

HONORING JOE WENDEL
FOR SUPERB ATTAINMENT

On behalf of the members of the Senate of the 131st General Assembly of Ohio, we are pleased to applaud Joe Wendel on being honored at the 2016 American Nationalities Movement Luncheon.

Your selection for this prestigious accolade is a fitting tribute to you for the numerous contributions you have made to the community and to the world around you. The host of the German radio program on FM 89.3, you have been commended for your heritage and service, and through your tremendous work, you have set an example of responsible citizenship worthy of emulation.

In all of your endeavors, you have expended countless hours and seemingly inexhaustible energy in strengthening cultural pride, and it is no surprise that you have won a host of admirers. It is through the unsurpassed efforts and consistent support of conscientious citizens such as you that the State of Ohio has grown and prospered and has promoted the heritage and diversity of its residents.

Thus, it is with genuine pride that we extend special recognition to you on your outstanding achievement and salute you as a fine Ohioan.

Senator Keith Faber
President of the Ohio Senate

Senator Thomas F. Patton
Majority Floor Leader

509

HOUSE OF REPRESENTATIVES

UNDER THE SPONSORSHIP OF

REPRESENTATIVE MARLENE ANIELSKI
HOUSE DISTRICT 6

REPRESENTATIVE TIM GINTER
HOUSE DISTRICT 5

On behalf of the members of the House of Representatives of the 131st General Assembly of Ohio, we are pleased to congratulate

DR. JOE WENDEL

on receiving a 2016 Freedom Award from the American Nationalities Movement.

You are a remarkable individual, combining civic concern and dedication with selfless initiative to become a dynamic leader in the area. A retired teacher, soccer coach, and school administrator, you have performed with your German American band, the Joe Wendel Orchestra, throughout Greater Cleveland, the United States, Canada, and Caribbean, and you have served in the broadcasting field since 1961, commencing your career on WXEN-FM. Through your unfaltering devotion to service and achievement, you have distinguished yourself as a conscientious and hard-working Ohioan.

Willingly giving of your time, energy, and abilities, you have striven to better the world around you, and through your generous contributions, you have earned the respect and esteem of the entire community. We are certain that in the years to come, you will continue to demonstrate the same unwavering commitment to excellence for which you have become known, and you are truly deserving of high praise.

Thus, with sincere pleasure, we commend you on your recent accolade and salute you as one of Ohio's finest citizens.

Representative Marlene Anielski
House District 6

CLIFFORD A. ROSENBERGER
SPEAKER
OHIO HOUSE OF REPRESENTATIVES

Representative Tim Ginter
House District 5

510

THE COUNCIL OF THE CITY OF CLEVELAND

extends its heartiest congratulations to

Dr. Joseph Wendel

on the special occasion of

being honored with the "Freedom Award" by the American Nationalities

Movement, Inc. for his commitment, dedication and passion in representing

and promoting the German Community of Greater Cleveland at the

organization's Captive Nations Commemoration Program on Thursday,

July 14, 2016. This Council applauds Joe's significant achievements,

patriotism and contributions and extends best wishes to him for much

continued success and happiness in the future.

The Council has been apprised of this occasion which is most noteworthy and deserving of special recognition.

THEREFORE, THE CITY COUNCIL extends its warmest congratulations and offers its best wishes for continued success and happiness in the years ahead.

Michael D. Polensek
Councilmember – Ward **8**

President of Council

IN WITNESS WHEREOF, I have hereunto subscribed my hand and affixed the official seal of the COUNCIL OF THE CITY OF CLEVELAND.

City Clerk, Clerk of Council

511

In the name and by the Authority of

THE STATE OF OHIO

THE OFFICE OF THE
OHIO ATTORNEY GENERAL
A Proclamation Recognizing Joe Wendel
As a 2016 American Nationalities Movement Honoree

WHEREAS, Dr. Joe Wendel began his musical career in 1955 and his German-American band performed in prestigious venues around greater Cleveland and at many festivals throughout North America; and

WHEREAS, Dr. Wendel's band entertained in Las Vegas at the Taj Majal and were the featured band at the Ameriflora Expo where they played for some five million visitors from around the world; and

WHEREAS, Dr. Wendel was invited by Joe Bauer in April of 1961 to join the staff of the former ethnic station WXEN-FM, has since produced thousands of hours of programming on various stations, and for two years was the sportscaster of Cleveland's professional soccer team, the Stokers; and

WHEREAS, Dr. Wendel recently completed writing Justice Denied, a book about German American history, and is currently a personality of WCPN-90.3 FM;

THEREFORE, as Attorney General of the State of Ohio, it is my privilege to recognize Dr. Joe Wendel as a 2016 American Nationalities Movement Honoree.

July 14, 2016
Date

Mike DeWine, Ohio Attorney General

ROB PORTMAN
OHIO

United States Senate

WASHINGTON, DC 20510

COMMITTEES:
BUDGET
ENERGY AND
NATURAL RESOURCES
FINANCE
HOMELAND SECURITY
AND GOVERNMENTAL AFFAIRS

July 14, 2016

Mr. Joseph Wendel
1788 East 228th Street
Euclid, Ohio 44117

Dear Mr. Wendel,

Congratulations on being recognized by the American Nationalities Movement in Cleveland, Ohio. I applaud your outstanding dedication to promoting your German heritage and culture in the community.

Please accept my best wishes for continued success, and keep in touch.

Sincerely,

Rob Portman
United States Senator

448 RUSSELL SENATE OFFICE BUILDING
WASHINGTON, DC 20510
PHONE: (202) 224-3353

312 WALNUT STREET
SUITE 3075
CINCINNATI, OH 45202
PHONE: (513) 684-3265

1240 EAST 9TH STREET
SUITE 3061
CLEVELAND, OH 44199
PHONE: (216) 522-7095

37 WEST BROAD STREET
SUITE 300
COLUMBUS, OH 43215
PHONE: (614) 469-6774

420 MADISON AVENUE
SUITE 1210
TOLEDO, OH 43604
PHONE: (419) 259-3895

www.portman.senate.gov

Presented by the Corporation for National and Community Service to

Josef Wendel

In recognition and appreciation of your commitment to strengthening our
Nation and for making a difference through volunteer service.

1962

Corporation for
NATIONAL &
COMMUNITY
SERVICE ★★★

ABOUT THE AUTHOR

Dr. Joe Wendel is a retired educator. As a teacher, soccer coach, and school administrator, his goal was to inspire his students to attain their potential and realize their loftiest dreams. His former students and players continue to express their gratitude for his guidance and motivation.

His avocation includes being a musician and band leader. He and his band have entertained at many of the finest establishments, and they were the featured band at the Ameri-Flora Expo, where some five million guests from around the world enjoyed their music. The universal language of music gives expression to the deepest and noblest sentiments of the heart and soul.

Dr. Wendel began producing and hosting radio programs in 1961. He has aired thousands of hours of programs on various stations and interviewed many dignitaries. For two years, he enjoyed being the sportscaster for the Cleveland Stokers, the outdoor professional soccer team. He was in the press box at the Cleveland Stadium, while the great international soccer star Pele displayed his athletic skills. Dr. Wendel was honored with the Freedom Award by the American Nationalities Movement and is the recipient of the prestigious Presidential Lifetime Service Award for his significant contributions and patriotism.

Americans are aware that our entire Japanese population was uprooted and incarcerated during World War II. What most Americans seem to be unaware of is the fact that these cruel injustices were perpetrated also against tens of thousands of German Americans as well as Italians, Hungarians, Bulgarians, Latin American Germans, German Jews, and Jehovah's Witnesses. Prior to being released, the internees and their guards were forced to sign an oath never to speak or write about their experiences in the camps, with threats of being reincarcerated.

Justice Denied familiarizes the reader with historical facts that have, all too often, been ignored, falsified, or killed with deafening silence. This book provides more light regarding the many human rights violations in the American internment program and the brutality against Germans in Europe at the end of and following the war.

The reader will enjoy four hundred years of German-American history and their monumental contributions to this great nation. The book presents a comprehensive picture of the twentieth century. May justice postponed not become *justice denied*.